Microprocessors, Manpower and Society

A Comparative, Cross-national Approach

Edited by
Malcolm Warner
Professor and Research
Coordinator, The
Management College,
Henley; and
Brunel University,
United Kingdom

St. Martin's Press   New York

Library of Congress Cataloging in Publication Data

Main entry under title:

Microprocessors, manpower and society.

    Includes index.
    1 Machinery in industry–Addresses, essays, lectures.
2 Automation–Addresses, essays, lectures. 3 Microelectronics–Social aspects–Addresses, essays, lectures.
4 Industrial relations–Addresses, essays, lectures.
I Warner, Malcolm.
HD6331.M5 1984   338.4'54   83-40148

ISBN 0-312-53187-7

Contents

Contributors

Colin A. Carnall is Director of the MBA Programme, Joint Graduate Programme, The Management College, Henley and Brunel University, United Kingdom.

Rowena Cowan is a Research Assistant at the Department of Social and Economic Studies, Imperial College of Science and Technology, London SW7, United Kingdom.

Annette Davies is now a Lecturer in The Department of Management Studies, University of Wales Institute of Science and Technology, Cardiff, Wales, United Kingdom.

John E. Ettlie is Associate Professor, Department of Management, DePaul University, Chicago, Illinois, USA.

Joel Fadem is Senior Fellow, Institute of Industrial Relations, UCLA, Los Angeles, California, USA.

Bill Ford is Associate Professor in Organizational Behaviour at the University of New South Wales, Kensington, NSW, Australia.

Arthur Francis is Senior Lecturer, Department of Social and Economic Studies, Imperial College of Science and Technology, London SW7, United Kingdom.

Donald Gerwin is Professor of Management, Department of Business Administration, University of Wisconsin, Milwaukee, Wisconsin, USA.

David Guest is Senior Lecturer, The Department of Industrial Relations, London School of Economics, London WC2, United Kingdom.

Gert Hartmann was until recently a Research Fellow at the International Institute of Management, Science Centre, Berlin West, Federal Republic of Germany.

Anders J. Hingel has been researching at the Copenhagen School of Economics, Copenhagen, Denmark.

Akihiro Ishikawa is Professor of Sociology, Faculty of Letter, at Chuo University, Tokyo, Japan.

Richard J. Long is Professor of Organizational Behaviour and Industrial Relations, University of Saskatchewan, Saskatoon, Canada: he is currently a Visiting Research Fellow at the Management College, Henley.

Roderick Martin is a Fellow and Tutor of Trinity College, Oxford, United Kingdom.

Anthony J. Medland is a Lecturer in the Department of Special Engineering and Management Systems, Brunel University, United Kingdom.

Ian J. Nicholas is a management consultant and until recently was Assistant Director of Research, Ashridge Management College, Berkhamstead, Herts, United Kingdom.

Riccardo Peccei is a Research Fellow at the Tavistock Institute, London NW3, United Kingdom.

Sheila G. Rothwell is Director of the Centre for Employment Policy Studies, The Management College, Henley, United Kingdom.

Howard Rush is Prinicpal Lecturer in Business Studies, Brighton Polytechnic, Brighton, United Kingdom.

Robert J. Schlesinger is a Research Associate, Joint Graduate Programme, The Management College, Henley; and Brunel University, United Kingdom.

Peter Senker is Senior Research Fellow, Science Policy Research Unit, University of Sussex, Brighton, United Kingdom.

Mandy Snell has been researching at the Department of Social and Economic Studies, Imperial College of Science and Technology, London SW7, United Kingdom.

Arndt Sorge is a Research Fellow at the International Institute of Management, Science Centre, Berlin West, Federal Republic of Germany.

C.P. Thakur is Professor of Management Studies, Shanti Prasad Jain Advanced Management Research Centre, University of Delhi, India.

Vivien Walsh is Lecturer in Innovation, University of Manchester, Institute of Science and Technology, Manchester, United Kingdom.

Malcolm Warner is Professor and Research Coordinator, Joint Graduate Programme, The Management College, Henley; and Brunel University, United Kingdom.

Robin Williams is Research Fellow, Technology Policy Unit, University of Aston, Birmingham, United Kingdom.

Paul Willman lectures in the School of Management at Cranfield Institute of Technology, Cranfield, Bedfordshire, United Kingdom.

Graham Winch is a Research Assistant at the Department of Social and Economic Studies, Imperial College of Science and Technology, London SW7, United Kingdom.

Preface

This volume attempts to deal with a major problem facing advanced economies, namely the challenge of the 'chip'. It is designed to parallel a publication of which I am a co-author (Arndt Sorge, Gert Hartmann, Malcolm Warner and Ian Nicholas *Microelectronics and Manpower in Manufacturing*, Gower, 1983) dealing with the specific impact of Computer Numerical Control (CNC) of machine-tools on workplace relations, based on a research study financed by the Anglo-German Foundation for the Study of Industrial Society.

This collection of papers by an interdisciplinary, international group of contributors deals with a wider canvas, but ties the problems of new technology, manpower and society down to specific research contexts covering Industrial Robots (IR), Flexible Manufacturing Systems (FMS), Computer-Aided Design (CAD), as well as a range of other applications.

I should like to thank all those who made the endeavour possible, especially John Irwin and Sue McNaughton of Gower Ltd., Jill Ford whose administrative and secretarial assistance has been invaluable, and the many colleagues at Henley who have been supportive, particularly Colin Carnall, Annette Davies, Sheila Rothwell and Bob Schlesinger who have contributed papers to the volume.

Malcolm Warner
Spring 1984

Introduction

Malcolm Warner

Is a second 'industrial revolution' upon us? Many have surveyed this theme with expressions ranging from the 'collapse of work' at one extreme, (Jenkins and Sherman, 1979) to the super-abundant 'post-industrial society' at the other (Bell, 1974). In this collection of papers, we hope to look at some of the concerns triggered off by 'the new technology' and explore their manpower and other wider implications.

Underlying this 'technological revolution' is a miniature data-processing 'machine' so tiny, it fits easily onto a finger nail, its complex circuits etched onto a chip of silicon (see Evans, 1979). Yet the micro-computer can fit into a washing-machine at home or a typewriter in the office, and is getting smaller month by month. It cuts costs, requires little space, and will be increasingly widespread in its applications.

Factory automation has, of course, fascinated media audiences for some time since Charlie Chaplin's *Modern Times*. Studies on this important topic have recently received a boost from the prospect of 'chips' guiding the assembly-lines, and the onset of industrial robots. A new thrust has been given to the 'automation' debate of the 1960s (see Warner, 1981). The onset of the information society has been vividly described by Forester (1980), who surveys the impact of new technology on office and factory, as well as the consequences for employment and industrial relations. Offices are 'ripe for the techno-logical revolution' (p.xv) according to Forester. But the author notes: 'The potential for labour shedding is enormous: as Victor A. Vyssotsky, an executive director at Bell Laboratories, recently pointed out, a two

1

per cent per annum reduction in office staffs in America would displace twenty-five million workers by the year 2000 . . . there seems little doubt that the pace of labour-substitution will increase substantially in the near future with the rapid reduction in costs and the growing sophistication of products that only microelectronics can provide' (p.xv). Furthermore, 'Rather than creating new products or completely displacing old ones, the introduction of microelectronic technology will mean that it will take less time to produce existing products. This is partly because production lines can be automated or speeded up, but mainly because the number of components in a product – and thus the time taken to assemble it – can be greatly reduced by the incorporation of chips. A colour TV once contained 1200 components. Now, with chips, it contains only 450' (p.xv). The new technology thus raises a wide range of problems, human as well as technical. The implications for the workforce and their representatives in the trade unions are extensive, and will constitute the main focus of the contributions to follow.

This volume is divided into three parts. The first deals with the ways in which microprocessor technology has been introduced into the workplace; the second, with the manpower consequences of the new technology; and the third, with experiences across a range of countries and societies.

The implications of industrial robots for manufacturing, work and society are set out by Schlesinger. He suggests a growth between 1975–1990 of 30% per year and that such automation on a large-scale will reduce employment. Confidence will increase amongst the user-community over time as the robot technology becomes more accepted. Japan's lead will continue: and Western factories will have to automate to compete. We might ultimately be able to produce all our needs, concludes the author, with perhaps 10% of the present workforce.

Evolving an implementation strategy is the main theme of chapter 2 by Ettlie. This chapter explores the theory and practice of implementation of discrete parts manufacturing technologies in organisations. He argues that implementation success is a function of a number of key variables including the nature of the process innovation itself, (e.g. its cost and sophistication), the availability and allocation of slack resources to the project, and, especially, the implementation strategy used to incorporate the new technology into the workflow of the organisation. Contextual variables are also thought to influence implementation success, including economic conditions, vendor participation in the implementation process, and history of the firm – in particular the nature of the adoption process that leads to the procurement decisions.

Is computer-aided design necessarily going to enhance managerial control-systems? Carnall and Medland deal with the application of this new computer-aided development and its human and organisational implications. They try to provide the designer with rapid access to data, rather than to achieve greater control of those in charge via subdivision of tasks and deskilling of operators.

Innovation, microelectronics and manufacturing technology are the main themes of the chapter by Gerwin. He critically examines European and American firms which have purchased microelectronics manufacturing systems. Propositions on evaluation, initiation, implementation and routinisation are used to help identify significant patterns in the data. At the same time, the data are employed to suggest where revisions are needed in the theories, such as those by Hage. Within this framework, Gerwin argues that the most critical role is played by a factory's infrastructure as the main factor needed to support the innovation.

Peccei and Guest argue the case for the evaluation of change, and outline the criteria used in this process. They develop the case for the use of 'process' measures and present a methodology for evaluation in the case-study of the introduction of word-processors in British Rail. This case highlights some contrasts between process and content criteria and between subjective and objective criteria. At the same time it illustrates the importance of the context, in this example a highly bureaucratised organisation, in attempting to make judgements about success or failure of the introduction of technological change.

How does new technology affect company employment policies? Rothwell's chapter deals with new technology in both manufacturing and service sectors. The concept of 'company employment policy' is operationalised in terms of its relationship to business strategy, long-term future planning orientation, significant role for the personnel function, employee-centred philosophy and a consistent range of personnel policies and procedures. Findings drawn from research based on 23 cases of applications of information technology in manufacturing and service industries are drawn on to test the forms of change and innovation (if any) which were found on each of these dimensions. Conclusions suggest that while there has been a measure of change, particularly in the structuring of internal labour markets, the lack of change has been more striking, that technology is not the major determinant, and that a more plausible hypothesis would suggest that the direction of causality is reversed: that employment policies are more likely to determine the manner of implementation of new technology.

What are the implications of automation for training? Senker's chapter looks at attitudes to training in Britain as contrasted with attitudes in Japan. It is concluded that successful training policies need to include measures to stimulate industry's demand for skills. Economic theory is based on assumptions that firms demand the skills

3

they need to maximise short-term profits. Analysis based on such assumptions results in bad policies when competitive success depends on firms' strategic behaviour. Japanese success results partly from firms' strategies involving investment in training as the basis for future competitiveness. Other governments could encourage industry to improve its strategic planning, and this could lead to increased demand for the skills necessary to use automation effectively.

How do trade unions react to technological change? Davies, in her chapter, argues that a reactive defensive strategy can only have a limited impact when faced with well-formulated management plans. Trade unionists also lack information upon which to develop alternative strategies. Union officials are overloaded and do not have the time to develop broad-based, rather than localised, responses. They need to spread their wings further into the area of design and manufacture.

Consultation and change in the electronics industry are themes of the chapter by Rush and Williams. They argue that there are many firms which recognise the merits of consultation and disclosure of information in assisting the change-process, whilst others remain unconvinced. Technology Agreements have become an emotional issue. Trade union representatives expected more out of such accords than managers. The authors argue that there is considerable scope for improvement.

How does new technology affect industrial relations in the auto-mobile industry? Winch and colleagues examine the British Leyland 'Metro' line and the trade union involvement in the investment in high technology needed to make the company commercially viable in world markets. This was a case of 'bargained acceptance' by the workplace organisation: the unions were unable to resist the imposition of new working practices. The new technology proved to be a lever for changes on the shop floor, but the overall developments in the industrial relations system, argue the authors, proved to be more a decisive influence.

The effect of new technology on the Post Office and its manpower requirements and labour relations is the theme of the chapter by Walsh. Faced with competition from electronic mail services by British Telecom and by private firms, the Post Office has had to diversify its services. The trade unions are only cooperating with this plan on a limited basis, and call for a reduction in hours worked.

What will be the impact of banking services on their manpower requirements? Willman and Cowan in their chapter, describe the effect of 'autotellers' on bank staff numbers, using a case-study approach. They argue that the changes may affect job content and career prospects for employees, but on a fairly long time-scale. Personnel policies, argue the authors, need to focus on skill development as well as cost-containment.

The chapter by Martin deals with new technology and industrial relations in Fleet Street. He asks whether the new technology will make it possible 'for managers to manage' and whether in the long-run managerial control will be increased.

Turning now to cross-national studies, the effect of new technology on industrial relations across a range of Western European countries is considered by Hingel. The trade union movements in Europe, he argues, encountered the introduction of new technologies in the seventies without any clear and consistent strategies by which to contain them. Indeed, owing to the complexity and speed of technological development, he concludes, the latter will constitute an unprecedented challenge which could lead to noteworthy changes in union structures, relations between unions, between unions and research (and researchers), unions and employers, unions and the State as well as between unions on a cross-national level.

A Canadian perspective is offered by Long, who examines the implications of the new technology on the quality of working life broadly defined, covering such issues as job and organisation design, health and safety, and security of employment. He believes implementation will be both slower and more limited than believed by both pessimists and optimists. He argues that the education system must recognise changing needs within society to develop general skills of analysis for 'knowledge-workers'. He concludes a reduction of the working week may be necessary.

Fadem's chapter explores issues associated with the nature of automated production systems and their impacts on the work environment. Selected North American experiences of the design and management of computer-based manufacturing technology are reviewed, *vis-à-vis* varying degrees of responsiveness to the 'human aspect'. These range from negligible to substantial in terms of their impact on 'the quality of working life' (QWL). The relationship between technology and the processes by which work systems are designed is explored, specifically to show that there are alternatives to the dominant view of scientific management of new technology in the workplace.

How do British and German firms apply computer-numerically controlled technology in manufacturing, and do the consequences for skills differ in the two national contexts? Hartmann *et al* argue that great caution must be called for in looking at the effects of new technology. They conclude that the degree to which skills are affected depends on the socio-technical tradition of the respective national work-culture, and that the manpower consequences must be seen in their societal context.

Are the manpower consequences of computers different in a third-world, labour-surplus context such as is the case in India? Thakur, in his analysis argues that despite the macro-economic constraints, the new technology is finding its entry into the Indian economy, computerisation in banks being a prominent example. Office automation has received considerable opposition given the threat to employment, but trade union protests have been token in nature in this sector. Thakur concludes that the incidence of unemployment and the rate of additional job-creation will determine future diffusion of the new technology.

The subject of technology, women and employment is the theme explored by Ford. He discusses the recent changes affecting employment in Australia and looks at the policy-options available comparing them with changes in Western European countries.

Ishikawa's chapter surveys research results provided by institutions and organisations in Japan concerned with microelectronics and their socio-economic effects, and looks into the situation of spread of microelectronic technology *vis-à-vis* Japanese industrial realtions. Regarding workers' attitudes to microelectronic technology, most workers he argues seem willingly to accept it, and their formerly acquired skills seem largely relative to it on the spot. Most of the establishments which introduced microelectronics have retrained the existing workforces to keep them in the same workplace, while in cases of workforce surplus, transfer takes place within the establishment. Unions are likely to positively approve the introduction of new technology in order to allow the enterprise to survive, in his opinion.

Given the foregoing examples, we may well ask if the present technological 'revolution' is unprecedented? It might be argued that the rate of change is no faster than, say, at the end of the nineteenth century, or in earlier periods. On the other hand, given the impact of technological changes we are facing, the effects may be greater than we expect; we must now review the evidence.

Malcolm Warner

References

Bell, D., *The Coming of the Post-Industrial Society*, Heinemann, London, 1974.
Evans, C., *The Mighty Micro*, Gollanz, London, 1979.
Forester, T., *The Micro-electronics Revolution: The Complete Guide to the New Technology and its Impact on Society*, Basil Blackwell, Oxford, 1980.

Jenkins, C. and Sherman, B., *The Collapse of Work*, Eyre Methuen, London, 1979.

Warner, M., 'Organization, Technology and Society', *British Book News*, May 1981, pp.261—4.

PART ONE

**INTRODUCING MICROPROCESSOR TECHNOLOGY
INTO THE WORKPLACE**

1 Industrial robots, work and industry: past, present and future

Robert J. Schlesinger

Introduction

This chapter will present an overview of the emerging field of robotics with emphasis on the industrial robot (IR). This 'steel collar' worker does not fit the historical stereotype of the science-fiction android that lumbers about doing its master's bidding and, on occasion, displaying a degree of intelligence equal to that of a dog or even a moron. The truth is that modern day IRs are generally not mobile at all and have neither the sensory perception nor the intelligence of the most primitive living creatures.

How then can a device that is deaf, dumb, blind, generally has only one arm, and is 'chained' for life to a bench or wall, have a major impact on employment, society and, perhaps, the wealth of nations? The answer lies in the rate of change taking place in the field of robotics. Each year, the size of the robot population and range of applications increase significantly. And robots are getting 'smarter' fast!

History: from RUR to IR

The 'history' of the modern day industrial robot (IR) properly begins with the introduction of the class of hardware that today qualifies as an industrial robot according to definitions currently accepted by engineering societies around the world. Since such hardware first appeared in the late 1950s and early 1960s, the historical period of interest is perhaps 25 years at most.

Approximately 40 years before the first industrial robot, a Czechoslovakian by the name of Karl Capek wrote a play entitled 'R.U.R.' (Rossom's Universal Robot). The play is about a scientist who develops android workers to increase the world's production capacity. A number of science fiction-type problems develop with a rather classical outcome, but 'R.U.R.' does provide some interesting reading. The lasting contribution of the play, however, is its use of the Czechoslovakian word 'robota' that means work or worker; the translation of the play in 1922 is generally conceded to be responsible for the introduction of the word robot into the English language.

Twenty years later, in 1942, science-fiction writer Isaac Asimov suggested that robots would indeed be developed and therefore proposed the following Laws of Robotics as a guide for the safe development and use of robots:

1   A robot may not injure a human being or, through inaction, allow a human being to come to harm.
2   A robot must obey the orders given it by human beings except where such orders would conflict with the First Law.
3   A robot must protect its own existence as long as such protection does not conflict with the First or Second Law.

While these laws are well publicised and repeated somewhere in the opening address of just about every robot conference held in recent years, all three may well have already been violated.

It should be noted that the First Law was violated in Japan in 1982 when a worker attending a robot was killed by it. Anyone who has ever programmed a computer has experienced occasional performance contrary to the programmer's intention. Since robots are computer driven, Law Two could well be in question. The Third Law has been violated by this very writer, who openly admits to having programmed a robot incorrectly which then proceeded to 'injure' itself. Taken as a whole, Asimov's three laws do give some insight into problems that society may face as robot technology advances and applications grow.

As for the actual development of hardware, building a robot was a far cry from merely providing the name. From an engineering point of view there were many technical contributions along the way, not all of which can be covered here. However, two concepts should be mentioned. One is feedback; the technique of sampling information from the output of a device and comparing this signal with a reference signal. The difference between the two, called an error signal, can be used to control the device, correcting the output to the desired point. One can appreciate the importance of this technique in the context of controlling the position of a robot's arm. The second important concept concerns the stored program computer. This gives the robot the flexibility that sets it apart from early automated machinery. To be sure, the robot was not the first machine to be coupled with a computer. But the robot's articulated arm gave it a work volume that could be varied over much greater dimensions than traditional computer numerical control (CNC) machines could handle. The articulated arm or manipulator, while not a fundamental engineering concept in the same sense as feedback theory or stored program computers, is indeed critical to the uniqueness of the robot.

There has been a good deal of discussion as to just which devices can and cannot be classified as robots. By the mid-1970s Japan appeared to have a considerable lead in the number of robots being used in its factories. To be sure, there were more robots in place in Japan than in any other country, but the exact number was questionable depending on how one defined a robot. A robot manufacturer trade association, The Robot Institute of America (RIA), put forth the following definition:

> A robot is a reprogrammable multifunctional manipulator designed to move material, parts, tools, or specialised devices through variable programmed motions for the performance of a variety of tasks. (Hunt, 1983)

This definition accomplished two things. First it defined more specifically than had heretofore been done, just what a robot was supposed to consist of. Secondly, by virtue of the trade association's definition, Japan wasn't that far ahead of the USA in the use of robots after all. This made a lot of people feel better.

One can see from the definition that an industrial robot must meet certain requirements. It should be programmable; have a manipulator; and since it must move throughout its work space, a power system capable of moving the arm is an implied necessity. The industrial robot has evolved to consist of three basic components:

1 A programmable control system
2 A manipulator with an 'end effector' (either a gripper or a tool)
3 A power system to move the arm, end effector, and load (tool or part). Power systems are generally either pneumatic, hydraulic or electrically driven.

The first patents filed for a device that would qualify as an IR were filed by George C. Devol Jr. in 1954 (US patent *no.* 2988237). This work resulted in the eventual formation of Unimation Inc. which subsequently made the first installations in the 1961−1962 time-frame.

For any innovative activity there is a long road from the first application to the creation of a viable industry. This topic is considered in detail later in the chapter. From a historic point of view it is simply worth noting that the population growth of robots from 1962 to 1972 was relatively slow. It was during this time that the cost of computing capacity decreased sharply (Mackintosh, 1978); a necessary requirement if robot applications were to become cost effective. In the 1970s, the growth curve of robots in just about every industrialised nation in the world started sharply upward (see Figure 1.1).

State of the art

It has already been pointed out that the family-tree of industrial robots is short, extending back only 20 years or so. The very early devices, those used in Japan that did not quite meet the Robot Institute of America's definition, might be thought of as Neanderthal robots. They were closer to hard tooling than they were to robots. Whatever flexibility they could muster for varying their performance required a physical change in mechanical configuration. This was frequently the repositioning of mechanical stops, or the adjustment of cams. Whether these changes are considered 'programming' or not is a moot point. At any rate these devices were considered outside of the current definition and will be excluded.

Up to now, robot genealogy has included only two generations; the first and second. The first generation comprises the vast majority of robots used in industry today. This first generation robot (IR-1) meets the conditions of a programmable manipulator. It has found a wide range of applications in industry, and its sphere of influence is still growing. However, IR-1 is blind and very dumb. It does not rely on sophisticated sensors nor does it make use of the computer power associated with artificial intelligence programming. Such capabilities will be found in second generation industrial robots (IR-2), which will also require that fifth generation computer power be available. Although IR-2s are in various stages of development in university laboratories, it will be well into the 1980s before they make major inroads in industry. The all-important sensor capability consists of two types; vision and tactile. Both types are available today for use with robots. However, they are costly, have limited response, require advanced programming skills; and in the case of vision, operate slowly and need a relatively large computer memory. The important attribute that these sensors bring to robotics is the ability to interact with the external environment. This will allow the robot to adapt to changes in its 'world' just as a human uses eyes and fingers to modify his/her

14

Figure 1.1   Robot populations by year

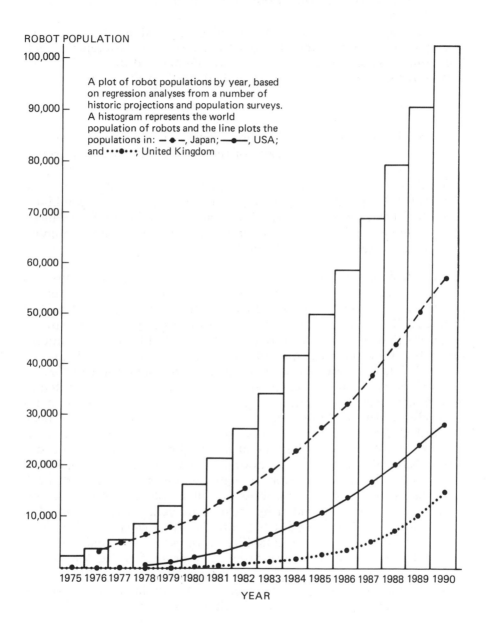

ROBOT POPULATION

A plot of robot populations by year, based on regression analyses from a number of historic projections and population surveys. A histogram represents the world population of robots and the line plots the populations in: — ◆ —, Japan; —●—, USA; and •••●•••, United Kingdom

YEAR

15

actions. The IR-2 will therefore make decisions and react to unplanned stimuli in its workplace that would cause an interruption in the operation of an IR-1.

A new industry typically has trouble establishing standards for specifying its product, and the robot industry is no different; in fact, the more technical the product the more complicated the problem. For a robot the specifications can be roughly divided into four categories:

1　Physical characteristics. Examples might include weight, floor-space required, and cost.
2　Static characteristics. Examples might include control system type, power system type, reach of the arm (X,Y,Z axis), and degrees of freedom.
3　Dynamic characteristics. Examples might include linear and angular velocity, lifting capacity, position accuracy, and repeatability.
4　'IQ' characteristics. Examples might include computer memory size, number of I/O lines, number of programming methods, number of sensors useable, and word length.

As the data required by a prospective user progresses from physical characteristics to 'IQ'-type information, it becomes more sparse. Robot industry directories published by such groups as the Japanese Industrial Robot Association (JIRA) and the Society of Manufacturing Engineers (SME) use various formats to present technical specifications. Invariably these provide quantitative data for categories 1 and 2, minimal data for category 3, and little or no data for category 4. When information is offered in this latter category it is presented as text rather than as quantitative data in a uniform format. Orderly methods of data measurement and presentation have not yet been established for the advanced or second generation robots. As might be expected, it is exactly the type of information identified in category 4 that distinguishes second generation robots from their first generation predecessors. There is, however, enough data on parameters and specifications of first generation robots to fill a volume the size of this book. Some are now provided by most manufacturers on a reasonably consistent basis. This includes the robot's lifting capacity, maximum linear velocity possible, repeatability with which the end effector can return to a desired work location, and degrees of freedom of the robot's arm (the human arm has six degrees of freedom). An analysis of over 600 robots (Schlesinger (a), 1983) manufactured worldwide yields the following average values for these basic parameters:

Lifting capacity	102kg
Linear velocity	1044mm/s
Repeatability	0.73mm

Degrees of Freedom (DOF):

DOF	Frequency of Occurrence (%)
2	4
3	10
4	16
5	29
6	32
7	8
8	1
	100%

Why use a robot?

The decision to use a robot in an industrial application is not easily made, for three conditions must be satisfied. The task in question must be one that the robot can handle, the economics must be viable and the labour/management climate must be favourably disposed to robotics. A series of developments originating in the early days of the industrial revolution has enhanced the economic feasibility of current robot use. Just after the turn of the century the concept of the production line was inaugurated by automobile manufacturer Henry Ford. Shortly thereafter the F.W. Taylor concept of scientific management gained widespread support, with its suggestion that jobs be broken down into the simplest, most basic steps to increase productivity (Benson and Lloyd, 1983). Implicit in Taylorism is the replacement of skilled workers by the semi-skilled or unskilled as jobs are reduced to a series of elementary, repetitive tasks; and correspondingly low wage scales for performing these tasks.

As the industrial sector expanded, so did the total number of low-paid factory workers. This led to the second important trend; the growth of strong unions. With strong unions in place, what heretofore had been cheap labour for simple tasks started to cost more. This trend toward increasing wage scales has continued throughout the current decade.

The third important activity, unnoticed by either the scientific management fraternity or the unions until recently, was research into robot automation. The marriage of the computer and the articulated arm driven by advanced control systems created a very unskilled but dutiful 'steel collar' worker.

The climate was now perfect for this new type of worker to seek employment, since:

1 Many tasks had been made idiot-simple.
2 Mr Robot was exempt from the union wage-scale.
3 Technology had become sufficiently advanced for robots to compete with humans in selected jobs — both economically and in terms of performance.

(See Figure 1.2, based on data from the US Department of Labor Statistics and experience factors associated with the amortisation of typical robot costs).

Other factors may also influence the adoption of robots. In the 1970s the Occupational Safety and Health Act (OSHA) was passed in the United States. The intent of the act is implicit in the name. Certain factory operations such as loading and unloading of hazardous materials (asbestos for example), paint spray work, and tasks in environments that did not meet OSHA standards were no longer acceptable for workers. Factories were faced with one of several options: modify the operation to meet OSHA standards, cease operations or be heavily fined, or discover another way to accomplish the job. The latter option in many cases led to the use of a robot, particularly when it seemed to be the least expensive solution to the problem.

When Japan in the late 1960s and during the 1970s enjoyed a production boom, labour was in short supply for many tasks (Ikehata *et al.*, 1982). The Japanese Ministry of Labour noted in 1980 that there was a nationwide shortage of 34,000 welders and 21,600 painters. These are both tasks that are cost effective applications for the IR. Faced with the unattractive option of paying competitively higher wages to attract workers, some Japanese firms chose instead to try robots.

There are several ways to determine the economic viability of a capital investment such as a robot (Engelberger, 1980; and Heginbotham, 1973). A simple approach is to ask how long it will take to recover your investment. If the calculated payback time is substantially less than the normal accounting amortisation period, then the investment would appear reasonable. Consider the following example using one of the simplest approaches.

$$R = \frac{C}{L + OC}$$

where

R = Recovery time of investment in years
C = Cost of robot in pounds

18

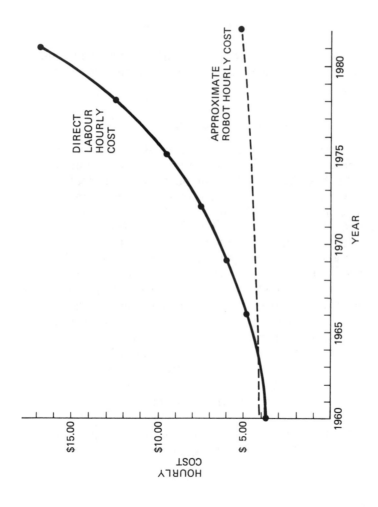

Figure 1.2   Typical cost comparison between labour and robot costs

19

L = Labour cost replaced in pounds per year
OC = Operating cost of robot per year

The current average cost of a robot system installed is close to £50,000. Given that a single shift work year has 2000 hours, a wage of £5 per hour replaced by the robot yields a labour cost replaced per year of £10,000. The maintenance and operating cost of the robot per year is dependent on the total number of robots used by the firm. Since some specialised skills are required to maintain the robot system, the cost should be pro-rated among the number of robots. For the moment allow that 25% of a skilled worker's time will be devoted to maintaining the robot at a yearly cost of £3,000. Putting this data into the equation yields:

$$R = \frac{50,000}{10,000 + 3,000} = 3.84 \text{ years}$$

If the robot is used over a two-shift period, replacing a second worker and incurring twice the operating cost, then the capital recovery time is:

$$R = \frac{50,000}{20,000 + 6,000} = 1.92 \text{ years}$$

Since companies generally amortise capital equipment over a five to eight year period, both of the above analyses look encouraging.

Robots fit best in a production operation that makes neither too few nor too many of a single product. Clearly, then, robots cannot be 'all things to all manufacturers', and people are still more flexible than robots. Manufacturing that involves very small production runs with frequent changes can be more effective with a few willing workers than with a reprogrammable robot. However, as the volume of a product increases, the cost of human labour will increase linearly. As shown above in the single and double shift example, the added shift production using the robot actually brings the effective cost per unit down. The robot, however, does have a speed limitation as discussed previously. As the volume continues to grow, if the same part is to be made in quantities of millions continuously over several years, then high speed, special purpose automation will prove to be the most cost effective. Such situations exist in the manufacturing of parts that are used in automobile transmissions for many models over several years. This trend is shown in Figure 1.3. The regions where optimum productivity occurs are shown for each method. Region II represents the proper place to consider robots.

20

Figure 1.3   Comparison among production techniques for cost/unit
              produced -*vs*- production volume

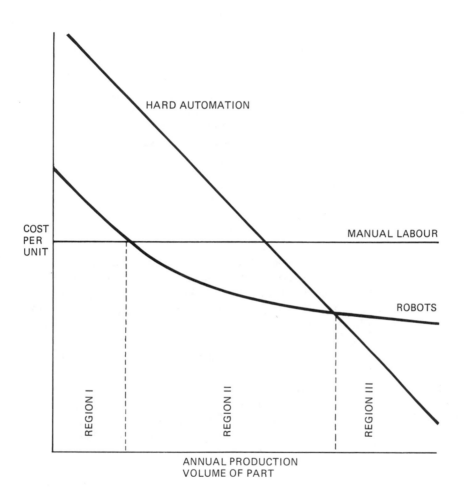

HARD AUTOMATION

COST
PER
UNIT

MANUAL LABOUR

ROBOTS

REGION I

REGION II

REGION III

ANNUAL PRODUCTION
VOLUME OF PART

21

Applications

Of all the applications that robots can be used for, the most important one for a particular company to consider is the first one! If the first one works as expected, the management problems of 'risk avoidance' will be overcome, and future installations will be openly considered. For the first application to be deemed successful not only do technical problems need to be resolved in a timely fashion, but the apprehensions of the workforce need to be allayed. The general rule is to select the most straightforward task that can be identified for the first robot application. By choosing the simplest job, the manager increases the likelihood that the installation will proceed on schedule and work as planned. This also gives the engineering staff the opportunity to gain experience and confidence in the new technical area.

Major applications fall into five broad categories:

I   Material movement
II   Tool movement
III Process control
IV   Assembly operations
V   Educational and R&D activities

In the most common application the robot is called upon to move a part. This can be more complex than it appears; for example, in palletising parts. Here the robot has to keep track of number and location of parts until the pallet is filled, and then signal for another empty pallet. If parts are to be taken from the loaded pallet automatically to feed another machine, then the robot must be quite accurate about the orientation and location when placing the part on the pallet.

Tool movement includes drilling, riveting, spot welding, buffing, polishing and the like. Process control includes two of the most successful applications of robots, spray painting and arc welding (Schlesinger, (b) 1983). In the case of spray painting the task can cause injury to the painter's health. Since the robot does not breathe, the problem is eliminated. In the case of arc welding, considered a process since a bead of metal from the welding rod is deposited on the work-piece, robotics has been very cost effective. The reason is that the robot can apply the welding gun more steadily than a human can, averaging almost a 100% production increase over a manual welder.

Assembly is a form of material movement in a gross sense. However, here one generally thinks in terms of bringing two or more pieces together in a prescribed way. The accuracies required may be very high and the entire procedure a complex operation. Robots have so far been successfully used to assemble typewriters and electric motors.

The potential for assembly robots is very great since it is estimated that as much as 40% of manufacturing labour is devoted to assembly operations. To make major inroads in this area the second generation robot with advanced sensory technology and software is required.

A list of most of the typical operations currently carried out in the industrial workplace by robots and the general category to which the task might be assigned is given in Table 1.1. (For those desiring a detailed description of these operations, see Engelberger, 1980.)

Table 1.1
Robot applications

No.	Task	Category
1	Spot welding	II
2	Arc welding	III
3	Spray painting	III
4	Machine loading/unloading	I
5	Palletising	I
6	Pick & Place	I
7	Investment casting	I
8	Forging	I
9	Press tending	I
10	Plastic moulding	I
11	Foundry fettling	I & II
12	Inspection	I & II
13	Assembly	IV
14	Glass (boule) control	III
15	Gluing	III
16	Buffing & polishing	II

In an industrial environment the robot must work in conjunction with other machines. One of the major impediments to increasing the range of applications is the lack of common interface standards, data base, and programming language between CNC, CAD/CAM and FMS installations. For the robot to reach its full potential this interface problem must be solved so that the factory can be integrated effectively.

Technology diffusion and the industrial robot

New product diffusion is a socioeconomic function as well as a technological one; frequently, market acceptance lags well behind technological innovation. The time scale for the process from invention, through innovation, to the point when a product or technique is readily available to a large percentage of the society through the accepted channels of distribution, is more protracted than is generally appreciated by inventors, innovators and in many cases corporate management.

A great deal has been written on the process of technology diffusion in general (Mansfield, 1968; Kingston, 1977) and robots specifically (Zermeno-Gonzalez, 1980; Conigliaro, 1983). Both Mansfield and Kingston point out that for approximately 85% of the population to adopt a new technology may take an average of 20 years. This population would cover the groups from the innovators through what Kingston calls the 'late majority'. Mathematically stated it covers the population under a normal distribution curve from minus infinity to approximately plus one sigma. Beyond this 85% is a group that might eventually use the technology (it will by then no longer be called a 'new technology') comprising another 13% of the population. Finally, there is 2% of the population that may be called the 'nevers'; that is, they will never adopt the new technology. For example, there are people who will never use a computer-based word processor because they 'like the feel' of the manual typewriter. There are dozens of such examples.

It is generally assumed that the growth scenario for a new technology such as robotics develops in the form of the traditional 'S' curve (Bright, 1970). Bright observes that this type of analysis rests on the assumption that technical application generally advances in a relatively orderly manner over time and exhibits an orderly behaviour pattern: the S curve pattern undergoes three distinct growth phases.

Region I depicts the beginning of the process in the robotics field – a long, slow growth phase. Kingston refers to this as the innovation phase. It is during this period that the adventurers or innovators attempt to use the first robots for a variety of applications. In this early phase there is little or no established market and accordingly, the robot industry is characterised by a limited number of small pioneering companies.

As the technology becomes more accepted and additional applications are found, confidence grows within the user community. This increases the size of the manufacturing sector willing to try this new technology of robots. This is the beginning of the upturn after the long tail of the 'S'. As the market grows to encompass 'early users' as well as 'innovators', the new market shares are not generally split evenly among competitors; some of the companies grow stronger while others fall by the wayside. In the terminology of the financial community, this is a shake-out period.

Somewhere in this time phase the fledgling robot-fraternity starts to take on the image of a bona-fide industry. Now, successful companies address national and international markets as well as regional ones. As the advertising budgets grow, so does the awareness of robots, both in and out of the industrial sector. Press coverage of the major robot conferences increases, and the whole process begins to show signs of geometric growth. Suddenly, old-line, established companies that five or ten years earlier would not have seriously backed a 'crazy robot engineer' are prepared to plunk down considerable amounts of cash to acquire a start-up robot company. In many instances this can prove a life-saver for the small, sinking, under-capitalised robotics firm. This is the beginning of the Phase II exponential growth.

Some attribute this 'band wagon' behaviour of old-line companies to a lack of imagination early on. There is, however, an important argument in defence of this Johnny-come-lately strategy: The larger a company, the later in the industry development cycle it is still able to 'buy in'. In the spring of 1983 Westinghouse acquired Unimation; the latter was a 20-year-old robot manufacturing company and an industry leader in the robotics field. The point is that Westinghouse had the resources to enter the field when it felt certain about the potential of the robot industry. On the other hand, if a group of individuals or a small company wants to participate in a new technology, it must join the fray relatively early in an industry's development. The reason is clear; small, start-up organisations do not have the resources available to pay the 'ticket of admission' price too late in the cycle. This concept might well be called the 'moving window' theory. It suggests that timing is critical when entering a new technological field, or 'going through the window'. Furthermore, the window is effectively a different size for different-sized companies, making the timing factor somewhat less critical for the larger firm. Finally, there is a point in time when the window closes for all potential players.

If a small company enters the robot field early in the innovation cycle, the market is shown to be small due to minimal penetration of the new technology. This requires that the small company have a good deal of staying power — a euphemism for substantial financial resources. On the other hand, if entry is delayed until the upswing is well advanced the cost of admission is too great for the small company. The ideal point of entry is just prior to the upturn. At this point the cost of entry is acceptable, staying power likely to be within the resources available and there are prospects for an early growing market.

One reason for the large company shunning early entry into a new technology is the dearth of good management talent that frequently plagues established corporations. What talent is available must therefore be allocated to those tasks most likely to yield speedy returns, rather than activities demanding a slow start-up phase of ten or more years.

Furthermore, it is generally perceived that large companies are not very good at handling entrepreneurs who, almost by definition, tend not to be 'company men', and finally, the executive who backs an early innovation needs a lot of 'guts' and vision. Since the probability of failure in the world of inventions and innovation is a lot greater than of success, the executive who champions an innovation places a lot on the line from a career point of view. With its greater resources the larger the company, the more it can invest to enter a market. If one accepts that the later the entry, the more costly it is, then presumably all companies eventually reach a point in time when entry is not feasible. For instance, it is very difficult today for a company of any size to enter the personal computer market. The days of an Apple or a Sinclair are over (stated without proof and I would like to be proven wrong). The window of opportunity has passed for most practical purposes. However, it is interesting to note that as late as 1982 IBM did indeed enter the PC market. IBM could afford the entry price, and of course had a substantial position in other segments of the computer industry. But even with IBM's resources the window for entry into some areas, such as automobile manufacturing, is evidently closed to all comers; consider the long trail of failed attempts at entry over the last forty years.

Time-scale for diffusion of robots

Unfortunately, the title for this section raises false hopes. It is not currently within the ability of practitioners in the field of technology forecasting to offer closed form solutions for the future. Most of us have 20/20 hindsight; few, if any of us have 20/20 foresight. It is equally difficult to determine where the industry is on the diffusion curve at any given point in time. The difficulty arises in trying to assess the total size of the market for robot automation.

Between now and the year 2000, the population of the developed nations of the world will grow to about 859 million people between 15 and 64 years of age; the prime work-years (Barney, 1982). What percentage of these people will be employed in industry and specifically the manufacturing sector of industry, is a very difficult question to answer. Countries such as Japan and for a while France actually increased their percentage in the manufacturing sector during the 1970s. However, most of the other countries of the industrialised world (USA, UK, Germany, Canada and Sweden) have been decreasing their percentage (Marsh, 1982). On average the percentage is expected to decrease worldwide.

Currently, the world robot population is about 28,000. Out of approximately 771 million people now in the workforce in the developed nations, perhaps 35% are involved in the manufacturing sector. Based on this data, there are about 10,000 workers for every industrial robot in use. By 1990, if trends continue as they have for the last ten years, the robot population may reach slightly over 100,000. During this same period the total workforce is expected to reach 847 million, but only 30% (and perhaps less) will be gainfully employed in manufacturing. The result of these developments will be a robot-to-worker ratio of 1 to 2500 by the 1990s.

Implicit in this projection is a set of conditions that has held for the last ten years of robot development. With all due caution relative to projecting the future based on history, this includes the assumption that trade union problems will be resolved to the mutual satisfaction of all. Equally important is that the technical capability of robots keep pace with the requirements specified by new applications. This continued technical growth will assure that industry saturation does not occur within the time frame considered. Among a host of conceivable social and technical problems, the social barriers may be the most difficult to resolve. The engineer and scientist seem to effect technical change at a faster rate than society can adapt its mores and norms. When second generation robots controlled by fifth or sixth generation computers move into the factory, will managers as well as workers be ready for them?

Conclusions

From 1975 to 1982 the growth-rate for the installation of robots on a worldwide basis was close to 45% per year. It is estimated that the growth between 1982 and 1990 will be about 18% per year. The overall rate of growth for the period from 1975–1990 will therefore be 30% per year.

Obviously, robots do not operate by themselves. An increase in their use implies an increase in manufacturing technology in general. This is not really a new development, but rather the continuation of a trend that has been going on for close to 200 years. It is one thing for a historian to have perspective on the mechanisation of agriculture and industry, given the vantage point of two centuries. It is quite different to address the problem in 'real-time'.

Japan is perhaps further ahead with the automated factory than any other country. Not far from Tokyo, Fujitsu Fanuc has built a plant that employs about 100 people. This plant is just about as close as one can get to the 'factory of the future' in 'real time'. The plant produces some 500 machine tools per month and about half as many new robots. This factory is not as automated as will be possible when a full complement of second generation robots comes on line. However, it is estimated that a conventional plant (pre-1960 technology) would employ 500 people instead of 100. The plant is able to operate three shifts a day; the third shift with only two or three workers to watch the robots. Traditionally, Japanese industry has had little or no resistance from unions as a result of introducing robots (McGill, 1983). Recently, however, the unions are beginning to see robots increasing in factories at a faster rate than union membership. The loss of membership and member dues has created concern among union leaders. In one instance factory management offered to pay a union contribution for each robot 'employed'. Does this make a robot a union member?

For a Western factory to remain competitive in the world market it will be necessary either to exploit a very cheap source of labour or to automate. Going offshore for cheap labour has been used extensively by the semiconductor and electronics industry in the United States during the last decade. Now to create an option, automation on a large-scale is necessary.

There is every reason to suppose that increased automation on a large scale will reduce employment. The experience in Japan seems to point that way. Data based on experience with microprocessors also shows reductions in the labour force (Weston and Roberts, 1982). These reductions follow the traditional pattern; that is, they hit at the least skilled. For example, one study indicated that typists in companies that installed word-processors were reduced by 3% to 73% while work output increased from 10% to 300%. The 80% reduction in the Japanese workforce cited previously consisted mainly of employees who were replaced by 'pick and place' robots. Hardly highly skilled labour.

Given that the identification of this trend is correct, it is important for decision makers to separate the two parts of the problem: first, getting factory production profitable and second, addressing unemployment. The use of robot automation may produce unemployment but at the same time should create a viable company which then has resources available to address the problem. The option: no automation, no profits, no employment, no company. While the sequence of events might not be as clear cut as suggested here, there is considerable evidence to show that technical obsolescence is a factor in the demise of companies (Bursk and Chapman, 1963).

One final observation: In the late 1800s something like 40% of the people in the United States worked on farms to feed the rest of the country (Ginzberg, 1982). Today that number has fallen to about 4%, while vastly increased agricultural productivity enables American farmers to feed people in the rest of the world as well as in the USA. The workers displaced by automation of agriculture migrated to the city. The same industrial revolution that impacted farm life also created the need for factory labour. If automation displaces workers from factories, what is on the horizon to take up the slack in the Western world this time? The service sector can perhaps offer some options. If food can be produced with 4% of the workforce and automation can produce the desired material goods with perhaps 10% of the workforce (maybe less), does this not suggest rethinking the concept of work?

References

Barney, G.O. (ed.), *The Global 2000 Report to the President*, Penguin Books: New York 1982, Part 1, Sec.2, p.16.

Benson, I. and Lloyd, J., *New Technology and Industrial Change*, Kogan Page: London 1983, p.64.

Bright, J.R., *Practical Technology Forecasting*, Industrial Management Center, Inc., Austin, Texas: USA 1970, p.70.

Bursk, E.C. and Chapman, J.F., *New Decision-Making Tools for Managers*, New American Library, Mentor Series: New York 1963, p.318.

Conigliaro, L., 'Trends in the Robot Industry: Where Are We Now?', in *Proceedings of 13th International Symposium on Industrial Robots and Robots VII, 17–21 April, Chicago, Ill*, Society of Manufacturing Engineers: Dearborn, Mich., USA, Vol.I, p.1.

Engelberger, J.F., *Robots in Practice*, Kogan Page: London 1980, p.100.

Ginzberg, E., 'The Mechanization of Work', in *Scientific American*, September 1982, p.38.

Heginbotham, W.B., 'Factors Influencing Economic Exploitation of Industrial Robots', in Brock, T.E. (ed.), *Proceedings of First Conference on Industrial Robot Technology*, 27–29 March, University of Nottingham, International Fluidic Services Ltd: Bedford 1973, p.197.

Hunt, D.V., *Industrial Robotics Handbook*, Industrial Press, Inc.: New York 1983, p.7.

Ikehata, K. et al., *Industrial Robots: Their Increasing Use and Impact*, Foreign Press Center: Japan 1982, pp.4ff.

Kingston, W., *Innovation*, John Calder: London 1977, pp.68ff.

McGill, P., 'Unions Meet the Robots', *The Observer*, 13 March 1983.

Mackintosh, I.M., 'Micros: The Coming World War', in Forester, T. (ed.),

The Microelectronics Revolution, Basil Blackwell: Oxford 1978, pp.83ff.

Mansfield, E., *Technological Change*, W.W. Norton & Co., Inc.: New York 1968, p.73.

Marsh, P., *The Robot Age*, Abacus: London 1982, p.161.

Schlesinger, R.J., *The International Robotics Yearbook 1983*, Aleksander, I., (ed.), Kogan Page: London 1983(a).

Schlesinger, R.J., 'Robots Join Hands', in *Dec User*, Computer Publications Ltd.: London, April 1983(b).

Weston, P. and Robert, M., *Computers: Applications and Implications*, Harrap Ltd.: London 1982, pp.105ff.

Zermeno-Gonzalez, R., *The Development and Diffusion of Industrial Robots*, PhD Thesis, University of Aston, Birmingham, 1980.

2 Implementation strategy for manufacturing innovations

John E. Ettlie

Introduction

Problems of productivity growth in advanced economies have become a major concern. Among the many proposed solutions to this problem is the upgrading of process technology in manufacturing sectors of the economy (OTA, 1981). However, most firms experience at least some problems implementing process innovation. In particular, we are not effectively utilising discrete parts manufacturing innovations, like computer-aided-design and computer-aided manufacturing (CAD/CAM) systems, even when they are installed. Most firms do not get the full productivity benefits of discrete parts manufacturing technology (Stecke, 1981). Even when firms do apparently achieve acceptable levels of performance with new systems, it often takes longer and uses more resources than most managers anticipated (Gerwin, 1981). One estimate suggests that CAD/CAM systems have the potential to enhance productivity by 5 to 20 times, but seldom is this potential realised (Donlan, 1980).

As Gunn (1982, p.115) argued, 'the opportunities for mechanisation in the factory are widely misunderstood . . . direct labour accounts for only 10 to 25 per cent of the cost of manufacturing'. The challenge now is in the 'organising, scheduling, and managing the total manufacturing enterprise'. The great appeal of this line of research on the implementation of discrete parts manufacturing innovations is the enormous potential of new process technology to enhance organisational effectiveness in manufacturing. Among the next generation of discrete parts manufacturing technology, integrated computer-aided manufacturing (ICAM), is currently being used in the aero-space and electronics industry. 'A robot driller cart uses templates transferred to its memory from a design computer as guides to drilling bolt holes for the 240 floor panels in Boeing 747 jumbo jets . . . [saving] Boeing about $500,000 annually over the old manual drilling system . . .' (Kinnucan, 1982, p.54). A group technology system containing information on 400,000 parts at John Deere was recently reported to have saved the company $6 million in 18 months (Kinnucan, 1982). Adding group technology concepts to these systems can save up to 80% of new part redesign requirements (Gunn, 1982, p.121).

These ICAM systems are moving manufacturing control one step closer to the automated factory that would ultimately incorporate material requirements planning (MRP) and even suppliers and customers via computer terminal into system planning and control. But these systems have hidden costs and benefits that have been difficult to measure, especially during the pre-adoption stages of process change. For example, computerised MRP systems can potentially optimise throughput in a manufacturing system but scheduling a prototype product innovation on this type of system is virtually impossible. In the food equipment industry, prototypes are often assigned as a project to a seasoned shop veteran and much of the machining and assembly is done on conventional equipment out of the main work flow. One respondent recently told this investigator that they attempted to schedule six parts and the computerised MRP system continually rejected the order. Eventually, the parts had to be contracted out to a vendor.

Even more important but difficult to document is the tendency for most installations of CAM to be under-utilised or to encounter severe problems in long start up periods that were not anticipated by management (Stecke, 1981; Gerwin, 1982; Adams, 1980). A recent survey conducted by the Numerical Control Society (Jenkins, et al., 1981) and reviewed in the *American Machinist* (October, 1981) found that 50% of the 100 responding firms did not measure performance of their contentional or numerical control machine tools, although 20% of this group did take measurements but not in the format of the survey. It seems reasonable that more sophisticated CAD/CAM systems would require integrated planning of the whole system, but even the largest companies rarely approach the problem in this way. It is much more of a trial and error process (Gerwin, 1981, 1982; Kinnucan, 1982, p.56). There is a disturbing tendency in much of the dialogue and writing on computer mediated manufacturing systems that suggests every installation is unique and that there is no 'transfer' of knowledge gained from the experience from one case to the next (Gold, 1981).

32

The overall objective of this paper is to explore theoretical and practical answers to the general question of why some firms that adopt new production technology are more successful in utilising these innovations than other firms. In spite of the importance of this issue, no general theory of implementation exists (Anderson and Hoffman, 1978; Eveland, 1981; Meredith, 1981; Schultz and Slevin, 1975). This type of research should eventually contribute to the fund of knowledge on implementation as well as provide summary recommendations to practitioners faced with implementation planning and problems for discrete parts production technology in both the supplier and user organisations. What are the problems encountered during implementation? What are the best strategies for implementation? How do these strategies vary by situation? These are the types of questions guiding this inquiry.

Propositions

It is proposed that the factors which influence implementation success can be divided into three categories. First, the technology incorporated into the innovation can be characterised by attributes (e.g., cost, sophistication, etc.).

The second broad category of variables that will influence implementation success is the nature of the organisation attempting to install process change. Examples of variables in this category are implementation strategy and availability and allocation of slack resources.

The third category of variables is the context of the organisation. Examples of variables in this category are original equipment manufacturer (OEM) behaviour supporting implementation of customers, adoption history and economic conditions.

It is assumed that the implementation period begins when the decision to adopt has been made and the organisation actively plans for installation. Further, it is assumed that the implementation period can be broken down into two general phases: (1) early implementation, which includes planning, installation and testing; and (2) integration, or the assimilation of the technology into the general workflow and routine of the organisation.

The propositions are presented next in the three categories introduced above: attributes of the technology, organisation, and context.

Attributes of technology

Radical versus incremental innovation   A number of authors have advanced a convincing argument that incremental and radical innovation change ought to be distinguished when we study the innovation process in organisations, because the causal model for the two general types of innovation is different. Probably the most comprehensive presentation of this view is given in Hage (1980). In this treatment, radical innovation can be defined in many ways. Radical change involves more risk, often because of the large magnitude of the proposed innovation, the lack of certainty of outcomes when using the innovation, and the degree to which the change is discontinuous with past experience. On occasion, a radical change has been specified by whether or not it was new to the industry or the set or organisations generally used for comparison with the adopting unit, for example, the school district (Daft and Becker, 1978).

There is considerable variety in the type of automated equipment now available in manufacturing — not only in type of machine by purpose (e.g., turning, boring, drilling or multifunction) but also in sophistication and cost. Numerical control (NC) machines have optical readers of mylar tape. Computer numerical control (CNC) use microcomputers for control, and more sophisticated computer-aided-design and computer-aided-manufacturing systems (CAD/CAM) are very widespread in use including about 15 very sophisticated flexible manufacturing systems (FMS) that use multiple machines and centralised control. In an earlier study (Ettlie, 1973) the complexity of the numerical controlled machine tool was controlled in three categories. Four firms installing 4-axis machining centres were included by design in the study. It is important not to exclude samples from the less sophisticated installations in studies of this type. Approximately 90% of all manufacturing companies employ 250 or fewer employees. The average cost of the CAD system alone has risen from $85,000 in 1975 (*Manufacturing and Information Systems*, 1975, pp.14, 15) to about $150,000 today, which may make many CAD systems too expensive for a small firm. Only about 2% of all machine tools are in the general category of NC. This amounts to about 52,900 pieces of equipment (of a total 2,630,700 units in use) according to the *National Machine Tool Builders Economic Handbook*, (1981). Aircraft and parts have the most NC (5.3% of all NC in use) by industry category. A recent survey by the *American Machinist* (December 1978) confirms these statistics, and adds that 14% fewer machine tools are in use since 1973 but they produce more. Since the installation of NC machines is doubling every five years, the potential of widespread productivity gains is evident. Yet the same article cites statistics that show that the US is lowest among seven countries in age of machine tools 10 years or under with 31% of all machines in this category. Japan has 60% and Canada 47% of both cutting and forming tools in this new category.

One of the overriding differences between the incremental and the radical change process is the relative importance of people. Because radical change is truly a rare occurrence in the life-cycle of an organisation, there is something very special about it. It is often difficult to justify radical change (Gerwin, 1981; Gold, 1981). It stands out as a real difference in the normal day-to-day, year-to-year routine of patterns of behaviour. It often fails because it is evaluated too soon (Hage, 1980). It has been hypothesised that because the skills necessary to accomplish radical change are rare, some manpower flows will be a necessary condition for radical change to go forward (Ettlie, 1980). In a recent study of food equipment and packaging supply firms, a president of one of these firms told this investigator that their general experience had been that incremental innovations fail for economic reasons. That is, either the cost is too great or the demand was less than expected, and the return on the innovation was not sufficient for it to be modified further and attain a successful status. He also said that radical innovations fail for lack of appropriate and sufficient human resources. That is, not enough qualified professionals are available or could afford the time to spend on the implementation problem in the host organisation. Keeping in mind that implementation success or failure is an over-simplified dichotomy, the following proposition is offered.

Proposition 1
Incremental process innovations fail for economic reasons, e.g., costs become too high, or demand is insufficient at the selling price. Radical process innovations fail primarily because of insufficient human resources, especially during implementation.

Other attributes Whenever one focuses on a particular type or example of an innovation, the general characteristics of that technology become quite important for adoption and implementation (Hage, 1980, p.174). Writers have gone to great lengths to list out and define all the possible attributes of any technology (Rogers and Shoemaker, 1971; Zaltman, et al., 1973), but there are problems with this approach. Attribute concepts overlap, a long list doe not further theoretical development and does not help managers decide which innovation is appropriate for their organisation. Downs and Mohr (1976) do little more than allocate these lists into two categories — primary, or adoptor independent, and secondary, or adoptor dependent.

A more promising approach is represented by two recent treatments of the attribute question. First, Tornatzky and Klein (1982) conducted a meta-analysis of 75 attribute studies and found that among the ten most studied technology attributes, only two, *compatibility* and *perceived relative advantage*, consistently promoted the adoption of innovations. They also note that only one of these studies attempted to track implementation as well as adoption of the innovation. Second, Hage (1980, p.190) makes a strong theoretical case that *cost* and *divisibility* are the two key attributes to be studied. Cost is important because it decreases or increases the need for slack resources and accounts for the reason why most organisations do not react to crisis with radical innovation. Divisibility is important because of the tendency of the dominant coalition to minimise risk and favour incremental over radical change. A divisible innovation can be adopted a little at a time. Gerwin (1982) recommends that firms implementing CAD/CAM systems do so in stages or gradually in phases.

One approach to this issue has been to attempt to build a reliable index of technology-organisation congruence using several of the most important attributes that cluster empirically. We have had some initial success with this approach. In one study, using mail survey data of food processing firms, a scale containing the attributes of (lack of) complexity, trialability, and compatability was constructed with a resulting Cronbach alpha of .71. Three other attributes, risk, relative advantage and profitability estimates did not cluster on a scale (Ettlie, et al., 1982). It is assumed that these attitudes can moderate the success of the implementation strategy used by a firm.

The following proposition is offered for testing:

> Proposition 2
> The congruence, or degree of fit, between an organisation and a specific process innovation will predict the rate and degree of successful implementation of that technology. Congruence is a scaled combination or index of any of several important attributes of the technology as perceived by key organisation members.

Organisation variables

Implementation strategy   The most important predictor of utilisation success is likely to be the strategy formulated and implemented that firms use to integrate new manufacturing equipment into their organisations. In one study of the implementation of ten NC machine tools, Ettlie (1973) found management's commitment to the philosophy of the new approach to manufacturing to be the second most significant correlate of utilisation rate (e.g., tape time) of the equipment. The correlation between commitment and utilisation was Kendall tau = $\cdot72$ (p < $\cdot01$) for nine of the ten firms with sufficient data. The largest correlation was found for the degree of workflow integration achieved with utilisation (Kendall tau = $\cdot94$, p < $\cdot01$). Gerwin (1982) strongly suggests that a firm has to have a strategic commitment to CAM systems in order for integration to be possible.

Hage (1980) discusses three ways to overcome resistance to change in organisations that amount to types of implementation strategies. The first two are extremes on a continuum of evolutionary vs. revolutionary change. Evolutionary strategy includes no discussion with those affected by the change, no participation, relatively fast change of pace, de-emphasis on cost, a conception of a permanent change, relatively high levels of conflict during implementation, and a variable amount of change actually implemented. Revolutionary strategy includes the opposite on all these dimensions with the exception of the last, where low levels of implemented change are expected by Hage. The third strategy which Hage believes is most effective for implementing radical change is the creation of a new organisational unit like a pilot plant or set-apart implementation team. This approach was taken by an implementing firm in a case study documented by the author, Ettlie (1971). Perhaps one of the most distinguishing features of this implementation case was the physical separation of the installation site that was attempted by management in order to isolate it from the rest of the shop during the early stages of implementation. The foundation for the new machine was poured near the door to one of the main locker rooms in the plant. (There were three doors in total.) Once the machine arrived, a second door was closed off, and the remaining door that was not in proximity to the machine was next to a foreman's office with glass walls, and anyone entering or exiting the locker room was clearly visible to first-line management. The area around the new machine was sealed off with 8 foot high plywood walls. Entering and exiting the new machine installation area was accomplished by using the door to the locker room near the foreman's office and then the door near the machine. It appears obvious that management in this case went to great lengths to separate the installation of the new machine from the rest of the organisation, in terms of physical isolation of the implementation site, but based on the reported dissatisfaction with performance of the system, and the other observations of the case that indicate that no implementation team was likewise separated, management failed to follow through completely on a separate organisation implementation strategy as suggested by Hage (1980) and Gerwin (1982).

One of the reasons that organisations do not fully realise the timely benefits of these CAD/CAM systems is that the production department and its managers rarely have a strong voice in the strategy formulation process (Miller and Graham, 1980). Firms rarely appreciate the variety of centralised CAD/CAM vs. decentralised microprocessor controlled NC options that are available to them, and have difficulty matching the newly found process technology alternative with an appropriate structure. Key personnel like the programmer are not selected systematically. In the typical large industrial firm, manufacturing, distribution and accounting procedures are much better integrated than the procedures between manufacturing and marketing or engineering (Miller, 1982, p.32). But in fairness to the firms that have gone ahead with especially the more sophisticated ICAM systems, sometimes in the face of opposition or competition among functional groups in the organisation, the documented gains that have been reported have been significant. We can learn much from these installations but without some organising framework for comparison, it will be difficult to generalise this experience because the average organisation is not ready for ICAM, nor will the reasons for relative success or failure be understood.

What are the range of implementation strategies that are possible? What determines (causes) implementation strategy? These are two of the primary research questions to consider. Firms can set goals, can choose structures and key people — that is, have human resource policies — that would be part of implementation. But foremost in an implementation strategy is likely to be the place that *technology policy* has in the firm's overall strategy and the nature of this technology policy. There are a number of recent reports of the importance of technology strategy in predicting innovation and success of organisations (Hayes and Abernathy, 1980; Foster, 1982, Maidique and Patch, 1978; Cooper and Schendel, 1976; Cooper, 1978). There are also a few empirical studies that substantiate the connection between the firm's environment, technology policy, and innovation. Innovation is much more likely to occur in firms that have an aggressive, forward-looking technology policy (Ettlie and Bridges, 1982; Ettlie, 1983).

The following propositions are offered for testing:

Proposition 3a
Organisations that have an explicit, long-term commitment to a new manufacturing process — a commitment that is promulgated and understood by key organisation members as the implementation strategy of the firm — will be more successful implementing the new technological process.

Proposition 3b
The greater the participation of production personnel in implementation strategy formulation, the more successful the installation of manufacturing process innovation.

Proposition 4
Organisations that have an aggressive technology policy are more likely to adopt and formulate a successful implementation strategy for sophisticated production process innovations.

Proposition 5
The more sophisticated the new production innovation, the more important technology and implementation strategy will be in determining successful integration of the innovation.

Proposition 6
An organisation's implementation strategy and structure are matched or congruent in the most successful cases. The implementation strategy that results from a very aggressive technology policy for radical innovation will produce flexible structural arrangements, with a special implementation team usually physically separated from the normal workflow. Less ambitious implementation strategies will use existing structural arrangements.

Organisation structure Organisation structure is the configuration of roles and duties among members. Structure is thought to have various dimensions, but the three dimensions that emerge most often in the literature are complexity, formalisation and centralisation. Although there are alternative methods of measuring these dimensions (cf., Sathe, 1978), their definitions are rather straightforward. Complex organisations have more professionalised occupational specialities. Formal organisations write more things down like rules, policies and communications. Centralised organisations concentrate more on decision-making authority than decentralised organisations. Zaltman, et al., (1973) hypothesise that the influence of organisation structure on the innovation process is very much dependent on the stage of the process. Certain types of organisations, that is, organisations structured in a certain way, will be more likely to adopt an innovation but not necessarily ready to implement that same innovation. It is hypothesised that complex organisations are more likely to initiate innovation adoption but will encounter more problems implementing innovation. Formalised organisations are less likely to initiate change but will be more successful at implementation once change has been adopted. Finally, the pattern for centralisation follows that of formalisation: centralised organisations are less likely to initiate innovation but are better implementing.

The rationale for these propositions is also quite simple. Complex organisations have more occupational specialities scanning the environment, and specialists, primarily professionals, are encouraged to use expertise to solve problems and bring more problems to the organisation's attention. Therefore, more innovations are considered to solve these problems and more are consequently adopted. But a complex organisation does not necessarily do a good job of implementing an innovation where many diverse groups may have to pull together as as a team. Occupational divergence now works against innovation, because change is in the implementation stage. It follows that firms that are more formalised and centralised will be less likely to entertain innovative solutions to problems because these organisations are more rigid, maintaining the status quo. But once a change is initiated, these same organisations are more capable of implementing innovation.

The empirical evidence concerning these propositions is sparse indeed. Probably the most frequently tested proposition, and the one consistently supported, is that complex organisations are more likely to adopt innovations (Hage, 1980). Hage (1980, p.193) also offers a caveat concerning the centralisation hypothesis. When the dominant coalition of decision-makers in an organisation has a very strong set of prochange values, centralisation is more likely to promote change, especially radical innovation. There is some evidence available for the implementation stage and formalisation. Marino (1979, p.246) found that formalisation was significantly correlated with compliance to affirmative action regulation, controlling for the effects of the other structure dimensions. He failed to support the centralisation hypothesis and suggests, as have others, that formalisation and central-isation are alternative methods for achieving control in organisations but may not work equally well in all circumstances as substitutes. He also found that professionalism, often considered to be part of complexity, was not related to compliance which raises questions about the proposition that complexity and implementation are inversely related. Marino found that the relationship between differ-entiation (number of job titles) and compliance was direct; partial $r = \cdot 31$ ($p = \cdot 13$). The zero-order correlation between differentiation and compliance was $r = \cdot 39$ (significant at the $\cdot 05$ level).

It is often the case that groups responsible for initiating change in an organisation are not the same groups responsible for implementa-tion. Organisation structure measures may not be as sensitive to these conditions as would be desirable in an empirical study. Centralisation, in particular, does not seem to promote radical process installation when a special project team would be required (Hage, 1980). Although Marino's (1979) results were for compliance to a regulatory mandate in the human resources area which might limit the generalisability of the findings. Adaptation to governmental-caused environmental conditions often appears to follow quite a different pattern than coping with other environmental factors (Ettlie and Bridges, 1982). Also, it is often the relationship between the supplier of technological innovation and the host firm that accounts for much of the variance in successful implementation (Ettlie, 1973; Ettlie and Rubenstein, 1980). This latter, contextual variable is discussed below in the next section.

There are usually some special structural arrangements that may be used by organisations as part of their implementation strategy. Implementation project coordination and member positions might be created (Mehra and Reid, 1982; Gerwin, 1982). The site of the implementation may be physically isolated from the rest of the organisation workflow and then the installation of the new system is reintegrated into the organisation after the initial startup period is over (Ettlie, 1971). Hage (1980) suggests that the latter is a necessary requirement for implementation of radical innovation. An exploration of the implementation strategies pursued by organisations and how successful these strategies are is a major objective of this study. It is generally proposed that structure follows from strategy (Chandler, 1962).

The following three propositions are offered for testing:

Proposition 7
Organisations that have more complex structures are more likely to initiate and adopt innovation but are likely to encounter problems in implementation, regardless of innovation type.

Proposition 8
Organisations that are more formalised and more centralised are less likely to adopt incremental innovations but are more successful at implementing incremental process innovations when they do attempt change. The opposite is true for radical innovation, less formalised and centralised firms adopt.

Proposition 9
Organisations that use special structural arrangements like implementation teams for radical process introduction, and organisations that use existing structural roles and relationships with expanded duties for incremental process introduction, will be most successful.

Slack resources Changing an organisation requires a variety of resource requirements. As stated above, human resources will be one necessary resource. But other resources will also be needed including money, facilities and time — especially managerial time. If the organisation is unable to allocate sufficient resources to technological change, it may not even consider innovation as an alternative to closing a performance gap. Once begun, an innovation project may fail for lack of sufficient resources. Premature evaluation of an implementation project may cause its failure (Hage, 1980). Again, the more radical the technology is, chances are the more slack resources will be required for change-over and integration of the innovation into normal organisational routine (Gerwin, 1982).

The following proposition is offered for testing:

41

Proposition 10

Sufficient slack resources consisting of people, money, facilities, support systems, and time will be allocated in successful innovation implementation cases. One of the most important causes of failure of innovation in the implementation stage will be lack of sufficient resources, especially when the technology is a radical departure from existing practice in an industry.

Contextual variables

Economic conditions   The machine tool industry and related manufacturing industries are very sensitive to economic conditions. Capital investment can fall drastically in a short period of time if even brief economic recessions are forecasted. The impact of an economic recession on implementation is to decrease the urgency of implementation success, to make financial resources scarce, but to provide time for experimentation with process innovation (Abernathy, 1978). With less work being scheduled on machines, utilisation rates drop. The long-range impact may be beneficial, however costly, by providing more experimentation time with the new process.

Proposition 11

In the short-run, economic recession will decrease utilisation success with new process technology. In the long-run, for stable firms, economic recession will increase the probability of success in implementing especially radical process innovation.

Suppliers of innovation   Most manufacturing innovations are produced by suppliers of machine tools and related equipment and subsequently adopted by user organisations in some manufacturing industry (see Figure 2.1). Therefore, the relationship between suppliers or original equipment manufacturers and their customers or users of the new technology will be an important determinant of implementation success. Suppliers of new manufacturing technology are not likely to sell new technology, especially radically new, complex innovations, to customers that are doomed or likely to fail. It is obviously in the original equipment manufacturer's (OEM) interest to selectively approach some customers they think have the characteristics that will promote success with the new technology and enter into a type of joint venture with them. Initial acceptance of a new manufacturing technology will be a key to continued modification for improvement and eventual success of the new line. Another way of looking at this issue is to say that the host organisation or user of the new technology has only partial control over the success of the implementation of an innovation. The supplier of the technology will also have an important influence on the outcomes of the implementation process, especially during the early phases of installation and for the first year of trial operation (Ettlie, 1973). The OEM service policy and other policies covering customer relations will be an important factor not only in implementation but in the initial adoption decision by the user. If the supplier is unable or unwilling to allocate sufficient slack resources, including personnel, to the installation of especially radically new technology, installation success is jeopardised.

Proposition 12
Suppliers of new technology that allocate sufficient slack resources and sustain a support customer service policy for implementation of especially radically new technologies are likely to substantially promote successful installations of innovations.

It has been suggested (personal communication to the author from Professor Donald Gerwin) that the involvement and support of the vendor in implementation might have a curvilinear relationship with utilisation. For too little or too much support, lower levels of utilisation obtain. For moderate levels, the greatest utilisation occurs. Again this might be moderated by the degree to which technology is radical.

History   Although it is probably a general truism that the firm's history will influence the utilisation rate that results from its implementation efforts, what aspects of its history are paramount? The focus here is on the immediate adoption history that precedes implementation of the specific manufacturing innovation. In a recent study of the food sector it was found that two of the most important variables in the innovation decision-making process are technology policy and organisation slack. Both of these variables have been included in earlier propositions. Further, organisations that develop accurate expectations about implementation experience higher utilisation rates with discrete parts innovations (Ettlie, 1973). These firms are more likely to forecast implementation problems, plan for implementation and more quickly utilise the innovation. Experience with related types of technology is expected to be correlated with the accuracy of these expectations, as well as the degree to which the innovation incorporates incremental vs. radical technology (radical technology is more difficult to predict). In those organisations where manufacturing process simulations are used for justification, the greater the agreement between OEM and implementing firm simulations, the more accurate these expectations will be.

Proposition 13
Firms that develop accurate implementation expectations during the adoption process are better prepared to more fully utilise new process technology.

At what point in the adoption process is it appropriate to introduce implementation issues? Which issues should be raised? What residue of the adoption process has a significant impact on implementation? These questions will be explored as part of the investigation of this proposition.

A final contextual variable, workflow technology, (Dewar and Hage, 1978) could be included here as a control parameter or moderating variable because it has been shown to influence work group and task design organisation (Morgan and Jackson, 1982; Gerwin, 1979).

Conceptual framework summary

Implementation success with manufacturing technology is proposed to be a function of three types of variables: (1) attributes of the technology (e.g., cost, sophistication); (2) organisation variables, like strategy and structure; and (3) contextual variables, e.g., original equipment manufacturer behaviour. The candidate variables and propositions within these categories are considered to be the starting point, not the ultimate end of the study of the implementation process. Some considerable effort should be expended in evaluation of these variables through field case study testing, both in supplier and user organisations. The recommended methodology is the longitudinal panel study (Ettlie, 1977; Miller and Friesen, 1982). A summary of the propositions in general model form is presented in Figure 2.1.

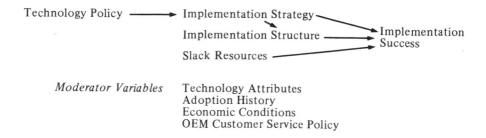

Figure 2.1 Conceptual model

Conclusions

There appears to be some measure of optimism that a general theory of implementation may evolve over a long period of research into this most interesting phase of the technological innovation process. It has been suggested that one of the key factors to be considered in any implementation, regardless of its unique technological or administrative characteristics is the implementation strategy selected by management. Although several other variables will affect implementation success, once management is committed to a particular course of action that has long-range implications for the manufacturing process technology in a plant, whether by default or by conscious plan, many other predictions can be made, including the level at which utilisation of manufacturing innovation is likely to stabilise.

References

Abernathy, W.J., *The Productivity Dilemma: Roadblocks to Innovation in the Automobile Industry*, John Hopkins University Press: Baltimore 1978.

Adams, R.L., 'Some Early Problems in Introducing Computer-Aided Manufacturing Systems', paper presented at the ORSA/TIMS Joint National Meeting, Colorado Springs, Co., 1980.

Anderson, J.C. and Hoffman, T.R., 'A Perspective on the Implementation of Management Science', *Academy of Management Review*, 3: 1978, pp.563–71.

'CAD/CAM: Where Is the Leader?', *Manufacturing and Information Systems*, 5: 1975, pp.14–15.

Chandler, A.D., *Strategy and Structure*, MIT Press: Cambridge, 1962.

Cooper, A.C. and Schendel, D., 'Strategic Responses to Technological Threats', *Business Horizons*, 2: 1976, pp.61–9.

Cooper, R., 'Strategic Planning for Successful Technological Innovation', *The Business Quarterly*, 43: 1978, pp.46–54.

Daft, R.L. and Becker, S.W., *Innovation in Organizations*, Elsever: New York, 1978.

Dewar, R. and Hage, J., 'Size, Technology, and Structural Differentiation: Toward a Theoretical Synthesis', *Administrative Science Quarterly*, 23: 1978.

Donlan, T.G., 'A CAD/CAM World?', *Barons*, 22 December 1980.

Downs, W.W. and Mohr, L.B., 'Toward a Theory of Innovation', *Administrative Science Quarterly*, 21: 1976, pp.700–14.

Ettlie, J.E., 'A Real-Time Case Study of Organization and Innovation', working paper, 71/22, Program of Research on the Management of Research and Development, Department of Industrial Engineering and Management Sciences, Northwestern University, 1971.

Ettlie, J.E., 'Technology Transfer from Innovators to Users', *Industrial Engineering*, 5: 1973, pp.16–23.

Ettlie, J.E., 'Validation of an Unobtrusive Measure of Technological Utilization', *Psychological Reports*, 40: 1977, pp.123–8.

Ettlie, J.E., 'Real-Time Studies in Organizational Research', *Academy of Management Review*, 2: 1977, pp.298–303.

Ettlie, J.E., 'Manpower Flows and the Innovation Process', *Management Science*, 26: 1980, pp.1086–95.

Ettlie, J.E., 'Organizational Policy and Innovation Among Suppliers to the Food Processing Sector', *Academy of Management Journal*, 26: 1983, pp.27–44.

Ettlie, J.E., Bridges, W.P. and O'Keefe, R.D., 'The Adoption of Radical Innovation by Organizations', working paper, 1982.

Ettlie, J.E. and Rubenstein, A.H., 'Social Learning Theory and the Implementation of Production Innovation', *Decision Sciences*, 11: 1980, pp.648–68.

Eveland, J.D., 'Innovation as Specification: Issues and Implications', working paper, 1981.

'Fewer, More Productive Machines', *American Machinist*, 12th Inventory of Metal Working Equipment, 1978, pp.133–48.

Foster, R.N., 'A Call for Vision in Managing Technology', *Business Week*, 5: 1982, pp.24–33.

Gerwin, D., 'Relationships Between Structure and Technology at the Organizational and Job Levels', *Journal of Management Studies*, 2: 1979, pp.70–9.

Gerwin, D., 'Control and Evaluation in the Innovation Process: The Case of Flexible Manufacturing Systems', *IEEE Transactions on Engineering Management*, EM-28: 1981, pp.62–70.

Gerwin, D., 'Do's and Don'ts of Computerized Manufacturing', *Harvard Business Review*, 60: 1982, pp.107–16.

Gold, B., 'Improving Managerial Evaluations of Computer-Aided Manufacturing', Report to the Air Force Supreme Command by the Committee on Computer-Aided Manufacturing, National Research Council, National Academy Press, 1981.

Gunn, T.G., 'The Mechanization of Design and Manufacturing', *Scientific American*, 247: 1982, pp.115–30.

Halal, W.E. and Brown, B.S., 'Participative Management: Myth and Reality', *California Management Review*, XXXII: 1981, pp.20–32.

Hage, J., *Theories of Organization*, Wiley: New York, 1980.

Hays, R.H. and Abernathy, W.S., 'Managing Our Way to Economic Decline', *Harvard Business Review*, 1980, pp.67–77.

Jackson, J.H. and Morgan, C.P., *Organization Theory*, Prentice-Hall: Englewood Cliffs, N.J., 1982.

Jasinski, F.J., 'Adopting Organization to New Technology', *Harvard Business Review*, 1959.

Jenkins, L.J., Gay, J.M., Muldoon, T.F., Smith, D., Hunt, R.C. and Harrington, J., 'Getting More Out of NC', *American Machinist*, 10: 1981, pp.185—92.

Kinnucan, P., 'Computer-Aided Manufacturing Aims for Integration', *High Technology*, 2: 1982, pp.49—56.

Maidique, M.A. and Patch, P., 'Corporate Strategy and Technology Policy', Copyright by the President and Fellows of Harvard College, 1978.

Marino, K.E., 'Organization Structure and Environmental Adaptation: A Case of Regulatory Compliance', *Proceedings* of the American Institute for Decision Sciences, 1979, pp.244—6.

Mehra, S. and Reid, M.J., 'MRP Implementation Using an Action Plan', *Interfaces*, 12: 1982, pp.69—73.

Meredith, J.P., 'The Importance of Impediments to Implementation', *Interfaces*, 11: 1981, pp.71—4.

Miller, J. and Friesen, P.H., 'The Longitudinal Analysis of Organizations: A Methodological Perspective', *Management Science*, 28: 1982, pp.1013—34.

Miller, J.G., 'The Manufacturing Futures Project, Summary of Survey Responses', School of Management, Boston University, Boston, MA, 1982.

Miller, J.G. and Graham, M.B.W., 'Production/Operations Management: Agenda for the 80's', *Decision Sciences*, 12: 1981, 47—571.

Mulder, M., 'Power Equalization Through Participation', *Administrative Science Quarterly*, 16: 1971, pp.31—9.

National Machine Tool Builders' Association, *Economic Handbook of the Machine Tool Industry*, McLean, VA, 1981.

Office of Technology Assessment, *U.S. Industrial Competitiveness — Summary*, ORA-ISC-136, Washington, D.C., 1981.

Rogers, E.M. and Shoemaker, F.F., *Communication of Innovations*, Free Press: New York, 1971.

Rubenstein, A.H., 'A Real-Time Study of Information Requirements for Project Selection in Research and Development', *Proceedings* of the Fourth International Research, 1966, pp.947—59.

Sathe, V., 'Institutional Versus Questionnaire Measures of Organizational Structure', *Academy of Management Journal*, 21: 1978, pp.227—38.

Schultz, R.L. and Slevin, D.P., (eds), *Implementing Operations Research/Management Science*, Elsevier: New York, 1975.

Stecke, K.E., 'Linearized Nonlinear MIP Formulations for Loading a Flexible Manufacturing System', working paper No. 278, Division of Research, Graduate School of Business Administration, University of Michigan, Ann Arbor, MI, 1981.

Tornatzky, L.G. and Klein, K.J., 'Innovation Characteristics and Innovation Adoption-Implementation: A Meta Analysis of Existing Findings', *IEE Transactions on Engineering Management*, EM-29: 1982, pp.28–45.

Zaltman, G., Duncan, R. and Holbek, J., *Innovations and Organizations*, Wiley: New York, 1973.

3 Computer-aided design: social and technical choices for development

Colin A. Carnall and Anthony J. Medland

Introduction

The application of computers in engineering, and the human and organisational implications which flow therefrom, are of major current concern. Some would argue that we stand at a technological 'crossroads' in respect of computer-aided design (CAD) and computer-aided manufacture (CAM). For example, Rosenbrock (1979) argues that technological choices being made now in the development of CAD technology will have major implications for the work of engineers and the organisation of engineering. In this chapter we intend to examine important aspects of the choices available to us for the development of CAD concentrating upon these implications. The argument in the chapter is grounded upon a survey of CAD applications in the United Kingdom conducted by the authors with colleagues and upon research underway at Henley and at Brunel University.

Computer-aided design

Computer-aided design refers to the use of the power of computers in the design and analysis of engineering structures, components and products based upon a data-base utilising component part descriptions. In outline terms various alternative approaches to CAD exist, namely the purchase of complete CAD systems (often referred to as 'turnkey' systems), the purchase of general purpose software packages, which must then be implemented on a computer system, and the purchase of general purpose modules which can be integrated within a specially devised set of software, designed to meet the requirements in the particular application.

Typically applications include the production of detail and general arrangement drawings, engineering design analysis, production engineering (including the production of manufacturing specifications, numerical control tapes etc.), the provision of estimates and quotations and as a means of improving the standardisation of drawings and designs. The most commonly discussed criteria for establishing the feasibility of CAD in practice is the 'productivity ratio'. The productivity ratio may be defined as the ratio of the time taken to complete a task using CAD to the time taken using manual methods. A survey commissioned by the DofI (1979) reports that the productivity ratio obtained from a survey of applications in the main applications areas varied from less than 1:1 for some detail drawings to 200:1 in some engineering analysis applications (see below for more detail).

The impact of CAD

There now exists a rapidly developing literature in this field. As we would expect in such a changing field many and diverse approaches are contained therein. For many CAD and CAM provide important opportunities. Others recognise these opportunities but also identify engineering, human and organisational problems which require solution before these can be exploited. For some these developments have profound ideological and political implications; an important choice is available to us, as to whether we utilise this technology in a 'human-centred and enhancing' way.

CAD as an 'opportunity'

It is not difficult to identify detailed areas in which computers can contribute to design analysis. Areas such as the dynamics of mechanisms, stress analysis and component design are obvious examples. Thus far CAD has been seen as a means of generating and presenting geometric data which could be used for automatic drafting and NC manufacturing and involves the use of a computer based system to assist in translating a concept into an engineering design, utilising a data-base, followed by the production of information. This technology is now increasingly widely applied. Computer-aided manufacture involves the use of computer based information to control manufacturing plants, inspection and test equipment.

Another concept to consider is the 'linked business system' in which CAD/CAM systems are coupled to marketing, buying, production planning and control, and financial systems. Such a system would include a data-base of customer requirements, product design information, manufacturing plant availability and so on. The six main potential applications of CAD/CAM are as follows:

1 Production of detail and arrangement drawings
2 Engineering design analysis
3 Production engineering tasks
4 Engineering support, including project engineering
5 Estimating
6 Quality control/inspection

In general, the simple applications, such as detail drawing, are widely used, although design analysis is increasingly common. An example in the motor industry is the design of body shapes both for aerodynamic characteristics and for safety. The use of turnkey systems (i.e., stand alone systems) has grown rapidly over the last year, a recent survey estimated well over 500 systems installed in Britain (*Engineering Today*, 22 March 1982). Networking (having a central computer at one location and intelligent terminals at other, remote, sites, linked to the centre via the telephone system and a modem) is a major development area. Motor car companies in the UK are moving toward the networking of presently installed and new systems.

The motor industry was one of the earliest users of CAD. We have already noted body design applications. Mechanical analysis to allow weight reduction is also an important application. CAD also allows for a reduction of lead times in the design/introduction of new models. Vehicle and component companies are becoming increasingly interdependent, with joint engine developments becoming possible. Networking will become important here.

Application areas

Applications are expected to be concentrated in the following areas:

1 repetitive detail drawing with a high proportion of standard elements;
2 engineering analysis where there is 3-dimensional complex geometry input requiring long and difficult, interdependent, calculations;

3 production engineering, particularly where errors in design can be eliminated by 3-dimensional graphical simulation (e.g. production of NC tapes).

There is evidence to suggest that the most frequently used justification of CAD expenditure is productivity. A recent survey (by Coopers and Lybrand and Ingersoll Engineers) discusses the *productivity ratio* (defined as the time required to complete a task using CAD compared to manual methods, noting that productivity ratios in the various applications areas vary from less than 1:1 to up to 200:1). They note that detail draughting was the most common application with a productivity ratio of 4:1 often claimed. However, they also note that such claims are rarely supported by good evidence. *We would argue that benefits from CAD are too complex and interdependent to make justifications based on 'productivity ratios'.*

Another survey reported by Lipchin (1982) claimed the following productivity ratios:

Integrated circuits	18.4
Engineering analysis	6.0
N/C application	5.6
Schematics	4.2
Plant layouts	3.4
Printed circuits	3.3
Civil	3.0
Mechanical assemblies	2.7
Mechanical details	2.4

In addition, account must be taken of the following potential benefits:

1 reduction in product lead times;
2 improved quality of drawings;
3 improved designs following the application of computing power to complex engineering analyses;
4 better use of standards

and also the following potential problem areas:

1 impact on overhead costs;
2 engineering management control;
3 the high sensitivity of CAD projects to reduction in productivity ratios or reduced capacity utilisation.

Coopers and Lybrand and Ingersoll Engineers conclude that:

'. . . a four terminal system in the UK . . . operating on *two shifts* at a productivity ratio of 4:1 should pay for the capital outlay in 2·2 years . . . at present it is difficult to operate a CAD/CAM system economically in the UK on a *single shift* basis or on a productivity ratio of less than 3 : 1.'

CAD as an innovation

Arnold and Senker (1982) report on a recent survey of the application of CAD in the United Kingdom engineering industry. They note that applications outside of engineering include military applications, architecture, and in the garment and the shoe industries. Within engineering,

'. . . firms using CAD are frequently in sectors where draughts people form a greater than average proportion of employment . . . Thus established users are found among electronic capital goods firms ranging from computers through radar to scientific instruments, among aerospace firms and process plant designers. Engine makers are also becoming increasingly involved'.

They go on to suggest that the technology is now beginning to penetrate sectors such as machine tool, mechanical handling and machinery, particularly manufacturers of pumps and valves. They note also that two CAD user sectors fall outside this pattern of using a high proportion of draughtspeople: micro-electronics and motor vehicles. Micro-circuit makers reported that complexity and the need for precision had made CAD an essential feature of design. The motor industry was one of the earliest users, partly in body-design and partly to reduce weight by detailed analysis of existing components. Reductions in weight lead to reductions in production cost and improvements in fuel consumption. CAD has also helped the reduction of design lead times and allowed for more detailed design investigations, particularly in the field of crash simulation.

But what benefits do firms gain from the use of CAD? Arnold and Senker (1982) report four main areas of benefit as follows:

1 increased productivity within the design and drawing function;
2 improved design quality;
3 improved links between design and manufacture;
4 indirect benefits flowing from the process of introducing computers in design, leading to a review of design systems, improvements in access to data and so on.

Crucially, for our purpose, however, they conclude,

'Most CAD systems we saw are primarily used as draughting systems and were cost-justified on the basis of saving draughting labour. There is no evidence that this is the most productive use of CAD. Draughting productivity is, however, the easiest benefit to quantify particularly for the benefit of non-technical management. In some cases, the need this imposes to save draughting labour inhibits the reaping of other potential benefits.'

For them the question of how CAD is used is a question of managerial competence, not of the technology. We agree but believe that there is much more to be said on that subject.

The political implications of new technology: the case of CAD

Arnold and Senker (1982) identify but then do not pursue what appears to be the fundamental contradiction within CAD as currently being developed. CAD systems are used as draughting systems, in the main, because draughting productivity (the productivity ratio referred to above) is the easiest benefit to quantify. Thus the full potential of CAD is not being utilised. This case has been put in most eloquent fashion by Cooley (1980) and the practical potential of interactive CAD has found early demonstration in the work of Rosenbrock (1974, 1977, 1979). Both Cooley and Rosenbrock argue that present approaches to the development of CAD fail to exploit the opportunity provided by interactive computing. The computer and the human mind have different but complementary abilities. The computer excels in analysis and computation. The human mind excels in pattern recognition, the assessment of complex situations and the intuitive leap to new and creative solutions. Rosenbrock argues that developing CAD '. . . to subdivide and codify the design process, incorporating the knowledge of existing designers so that it is reduced to a sequence of simple choices' would lead to a de-skilling of design. An alternative approach is based upon accepting the skill and knowledge of the designer providing an interactive computing facility to support that facility by providing the designer with the analytical computational power. Cooley argues that CAD has been applied in ways which appear to be subject to five criteria, as follows:

1 Subordination of the designer to the requirements of the machine, which includes the introduction of shift working;
2 Emphasis on a machine-centred system;
3 Use of standardised routines;
4 Dominance of routine over human choice, intervention, creativity and so on;
5 The subdivision and codification of the design process to reduce it to a series of simple and constrained choices in a logic of intensification of work.

54

Thus in developing and using CAD we are faced presently with an important choice. For Cooley the choice lies in whether we use the technology in a human centred and enhancing way. In this paper we will describe an approach to the use of the technology based upon an understanding of the design process; an approach which we argue is human centred in that it puts the computational power of the computer at the command of the designer. We view the design process as an iterative choice process starting from a statement of the functional requirements the design must fulfil which leads to an overall concept, and leading on to complex hierarchies of possible means of achieving the original concept and beyond. Designers do not necessarily work through the hierarchies from apex to base. In most designs this would be a complex and time-consuming business. Rather designers establish 'rules of thumb' which enable them to short-circuit much of the original design process (i.e. they do not attempt to 're-invent the wheel' every time). Moreover, production, cost and other constraints will often limit the design choices which are, or appear to be, feasible. CAD can support the creative capacity of designers by enabling them to quickly examine the available options, leading to a wider-ranging and a more detailed analysis.

The system to be described in this chapter developed on the assumption that everyone working on design is capable of creative work in some degree and that the computer can enhance those capacities in two ways:

1   As already discussed by providing the designer with greater computational power to allow the consideration of a wider range of options and to consider options in greater analytical detail.

2   By organising the data-base to provide for cross-checking procedures. We have already argued that a primary part of the Chief Designer role lies in the question of control. Beyond that, information, communication and discussion between designers provides a means by which colleagues 'cross-check' to ensure compatibility. On a rather personal note anyone who has spent any time in a design office will have observed designers talking together often on rather general, even not work-related matters. This is crucial to good design in that it provides a   means of communication and cross-checking as designs are being generated. Moving around a design office means that the designers see the work of others and can see how his work relates to that; giving opportunities for people to observe and resolve any incompatibility. CAD applications subject to Cooley's criteria will evidently reduce this informal interaction. The approach we offer allows for such interaction

because the designer is not tied to the work station and enhances the ability for cross-checking, as described above.

CAD and the design process

The development of CAD techniques has been rather piece-meal to date following the specific needs of particular applications or companies. This process of devising solutions for particular problems is an entirely understandable one, indeed most students of innovation would predict just such a course of events (see Kingston, 1977 for a recent and interesting study of innovation). In this section we will identify some general principles of design as a prelude to discussing an approach to the development of CAD for the future.

The design process

Classically described as the method whereby the conceptual solution of an engineering problem is turned into reality we must recognise that the activities involved and the relative importance of these activities will vary from situation to situation. In general, however, design proceeds through a series of stages from specification, problem formulation, through to analysis and choice of solution, to the detailing.

The design process can be considered theoretically as a simple linear system containing three elements, concept, analysis and detail. In practice it takes on a far more complex format. Rarely is one phase completed before another started. Usually differing aspects of the design develop at differing speeds. Some areas of the design are hardened down immediately (perhaps there is a desire to use an existing component or format) whilst others are allowed to float until a very late stage in the complete development of the product ('Last Minute' decisions). The non-uniform advance across all the elements can also create confusion in the process as pictured due to the interdependence of many of these elements. Some aspects even after final detailing may be forced to return to the analysis (or even the concept) phase in order that they can be made compatible or function with all other elements. The process being iterative in nature is thus seen to take on the characteristics of both oscillating and cycling systems rather than that of a simple linear one. It then becomes confusing to talk simply about the 'concept', 'analysis' and 'detailing' phases as these terms tend to suggest the single once-only operation rather than the possible large number of iterations. It seems incongruous to talk about a concept or analysis activity for a particular element when the major activities have reached the detailing stage. It then becomes more appropriate to call them the primary, secondary and tertiary phases of design, (as shown in Figure 3.1).

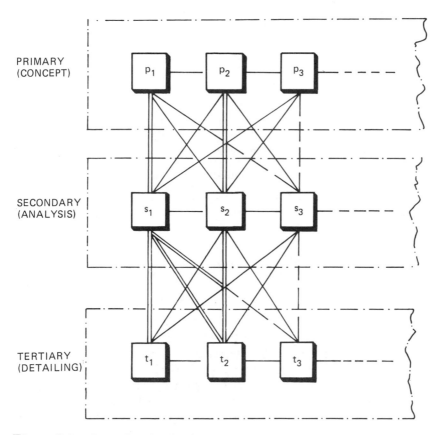

PRIMARY (CONCEPT)

SECONDARY (ANALYSIS)

TERTIARY (DETAILING)

Figure 3.1   Iterative design process

If then the existing techniques (or available programs) are categorised under these three headings their role within the overall design process becomes apparent. It also helps to clarify those areas of design which have been successfully computerised and those areas which have been neglected. This grouping of techniques within 'CAD/CAM' allow the potential user to choose or assemble a system, from all that is available, which will best fit his needs. No longer is it necessary for us to all use the same words to mean completely different things. The table in Figure 3.2 gives the broad outline of the classification for electrical, mechanical engineering and architecture.

Topic \ Class	Primary Design CAD 1 (Conceptual)	Secondary Design CAD 2 (Analysis)	Tertiary Design CAD 3 (Manufacturing information)
Electrical Engineering		Circuit Analysis	LSI & PLB Layout
		Component Selection	
Mechanical Engineering		Stress (F.E.M.)	Drafting
		Kinematic/ Mechanism	
		Vibrations/ Dynamics	NC Tape Production
		Pipe runs	
Architecture		Structural Analysis	Cartography
		Purpose/ Layout Analysis	Plans

Figure 3.2   Categorisation of CAD programs

Tertiary design

When such a classification is employed it becomes obvious that the majority of work has been directed towards the tertiary activities. The main aim of the normal turnkey CAD/CAM system is to operate in this region. This approach is not surprising as whilst the inputs (in terms of component requirements) are varied and numerous the output format is very well defined. These fall into two well documented categories of either man-readable instructions or machine-readable instructions. Two types of data are prepared; drawings or schedules. The drawings contain both pictorial and symbolic representations. Many levels of pictorial description are available from the simple two-dimensional representation of the drawing sheet through to the full three-dimensional solid body of complex shape. The correct level of representation can then be chosen to fit the needs of the particular work in hand. The type of drawing (or 'language') used again depends upon the particular application. The rules of presentation and representation change depending whether the output is an electrical diagram, engineering drawing or site plan. The techniques employed for the geometric representation of three-dimensional bodies varies as does the methods storing and retrieving the data. These again must be chosen to match the needs. (The construction of solids for interference analysis imposes quite different geometric constraints to those for the construction of isometric (or perspective) pictorials.

Whilst the production of numerically controlled tapes for production is usually separated off as 'CAM' it is really the machine-readable part of the tertiary design phase. The decision to instruct a machine to automatically produce an item rather than produce a pictorial representation takes the designer down the 'CAM' route.

Secondary design

The word 'design' when used in common English tends to imply that some creative activity is taking place. Our expectation of what is deemed to be 'creative' is equally vague. Anything that is simple and obvious is not creative and hence not design. There is thus a tendency for some engineers to say that drafting (and hence tertiary design) is not really design. The mundane activities necessary to produce an artefact are not really design, solely production engineering. Design really takes place only from the conception of an idea until it can be seen to be a fully developed and workable solution. Thus when many people talk (or think) about CAD they are referring to the secondary design activity wherein the seed of the idea is fully investigated and developed.

Within this secondary category are grouped all the engineering analysis activities normally performed using computers. Many such programs have been developed over the years to exploit the computer's ability to retrieve and/or manipulate large quantities of data. Complex matrix and iterative processes can be employed to resolve or optimise a large number of variables in a complicated interactive model. It is thus not surprising that to these people design means the application of high level analysis programs such as finite element structural analysis and automatic circuit analysis programs. Whilst these are perhaps the most complex pieces of analysis that need to be performed they are not at present really interactive design programs; simply the analysis of a specified configuration. However, much analysis and design work can be performed on the existing turnkey computer system by making use of its large graphics capabilities with a limited amount of numerical manipulation. Much design at present is performed against codes of practice and standards. Programs can be provided or written which interpret the component design in accordance with these rules. The program output can be in the form of specified data or given as nomograms which can be interpreted by the designer. Many companies have developed a range of these programs to satisfy their own needs and requirements. They thus tend to be very company dependent and remain unpublished as their content is only of interest to their direct competitors. It is thus in the area of secondary design that the software houses are most active. Packages are developed in accordance with customer requirements or by recognising that a common need exists within a particular field.

Primary design

Little or no work has been published on this conceptual activity. Whilst the desired output and constraints can be specified in both the secondary and tertiary activities it is extremely difficult at times to specify the form of the output required in the primary stage and more difficult to attempt to quantify it. When asked, many designers are either unaware that they are performing any creative activity or are unable to rationally describe it. ('It just comes' or 'It's obvious'.) Without an understanding of the logic, weighting and constraints of their design situation, it is impossible to provide the supportive design aids. This is the area where the greatest benefit could occur but the effort necessary to develop the techniques may be enormous.

The development of a CAD system for mechanical design

In 1979 the authors became involved in a research programme investigating the application of CAD in the UK engineering industry, collaborating with a number of large companies engaged in the manufacture of precision machinery and in aerospace. Greater, technical detail may be found in Medland (1982a, 1982b). It soon became apparent that an ability to check upon the effects of any proposed design activity would be of great benefit. Demands for changes brought about by constant development and pressures of the market place can lead to a pattern of iterative re-works as the equipment under consideration is never maintained in a known state for long. These changes create problems in two main areas: that of geometric interference and functional interference. It is relatively easy to establish a new part or mechanism to perform a new function. Its performance can be checked mathematically or experimentally and the form of the parts established (to give the necessary strength, stiffness, inertia etc). The most difficult aspects of this type of development is to establish whether the parts will fit onto (or in) the existing machine without at some stage interfering with the rest of the assembled mechanism and structure. It is also difficult to ensure that the performance of that mechanism and/or the rest of the machine is not corrupted by the interactions generated between the parts of the new assembly. As the functional problems in most mechanical engineering problems are seen to arise out of (or at least be related to) the geometrical arrangement of parts it was decided to commence by constructing a process which would handle and control the geometric parameters. This would be later extended to include the functional performance of individual components and the complete machine.

Design data relationships

It was decided to investigate a procedure in which a matrix relationship was established by each part being maintained in separate job (or model) files (i.e. the columns of the matrix) with certain aspects or details being assembled into different layers (i.e. the matrix rows). This allowed all the details of a particular piecepart to be found by a 'vertical' search and any combination of known attributes found by a 'horizontal' search. It was realised very early on that a prerequisite for successful implementation of this type of system would be that the 'filtering' of the data, into its separate layers, should be performed automatically. It was thus decided that all these operations, no matter how complex, would be called simply from a series of tablet keys on the graphics terminal. Some keys thus call many lines of instruction including various computer graphics programmes.

Drawing file structure

The vertical structuring of the drawing file was chosen to give four basic sub-files with their own internal formats. These are working space, a spatial file, an engineering and a technical file.

Working space   All geometric constructions and pictorial inputs are performed initially in the working space. This is effectively a sketch pad area where ideas can be tried out and refined. Multiple drawings can be inserted in order that alternative arrangements can be considered and compared. If the workspace is being used by the designer it can be used together with the technical file in order to convey, by written instructions, the necessary constraints and design parameters. Once these sketches are completed the working space and technical file areas are saved.

Spatial file   This section of the drawing file is used to store the three-dimensional co-ordinate relationships which define the body within the machine space. These relationships are held in a hierarchical fashion such that greater definition is achieved as lower levels are displayed. The highest level contains only a single location point for each occurrence of the item in the assembly. This may be considered as a node or tooling point which can be used to position and align the object within the machine space (shown in the following examples as a triangled 3-axis cross with a directional arrow through it). The next level contains information on the maximum and minimum excursion of the object in all three co-ordinate directions. This data is then used to define the enveloping box which just contains the part. Lower levels are used to retain successively the primary silhouettes, specific sectional silhouettes, surfaces and internal details. By displaying all these lower levels together a wire-frame representation of that object can be constructed in three dimensions.

Engineering file   Up until this point in the design, the manufacturing constraints have been of secondary importance. The main aim has been to design a spatial arrangement which will provide the required performance or function. Details indicating how this is to be made must now be entered into the engineering file. As the spatial file contains all the geometric relationship necessary to specify the body, this can be used to generate any pictorial view. It is thus not necessary to produce an engineering drawing specifically for the purpose of showing everyone what it looks like. The engineering file should thus contain only the instructions necessary for the complete manufacture of the item. The file can thus be used to store detailed engineering drawings (operations related drawings, assemblies etc.), NC instructions and schedules. If, for example, the part is to be produced by a completely automated process no formal engineering drawing would be necessary. The file may only contain NC details and a set of checking instructions. The engineering files are thus seen to be data stores containing both man-readable and machine-readable instructions for the manufacture of the specified articles.

Technical file   The final section contains the technical design data. With this arrangement it is possible (and desirable) to keep the manufacturing details and the technical considerations together on the same complete file. Corruption of the design is then less likely as 'flags' can be set to refer the draughtsman to relevant sections in this file. It is envisaged that this section will contain text files (instructions from the designer, component purchasing details, etc.), equations for calculating features and relationships as well as pictorial data. The graphics capability can also be exploited to the full by constructing design nomograms in this space which can then be accessed by the drawing office staff.

Design and checking procedures

When this system is in use it is intended that all members of the design team will be allowed to view and manipulate some of the filed data, but not necessarily all of it. Whilst all can be accessed via the keyboard, it is planned to provide each member with an individual menu containing all the functions necessary to carry out his/her prescribed set of activities.

Whilst everyone will be allowed to view the original design sketch, only the 'designer' menu will allow modifications to be made to that level of data. The draughtsman's menu will contain keys which carry out the automatic 'filtering' of geometric details down from the working space, through the spatial file, into the engineering file. His menu will also contain functions providing the activities and constraints necessary to comply with the company codes of practice or 'house-style'.

In order to check the relationships that exist between individual pieceparts and the original design, an assembly procedure is provided. This can also be used in an 'inspection' role. By searching a data file containing all the piecepart 'boxes' the simple relationship between parts can be established. The boxes can be shown to be remote, adjacent, interfering and one-inside-the-other. A draughtsman or inspector can thus search the local area around a given piece (by digitising or constructing a search box) and have the system automatically insert all the parts lying in that space into his working drawing. Assemblies can thus be performed and interference checks made. The position of each piece in space can be disturbed slightly or grossly to give respectively either positional tolerance checking or exploded views.

Function analysis

The ability to reposition the individual components within the machine space can be used to advantage in any kinematic analysis. Mechanism parts can be repositioned to give a sequential picture of the complete system throughout its complete cycle. Various positional and angular values can be retrieved and employed in the construction of elemental and system function diagrams. These can be converted, using a time base, to give velocity and hence acceleration profiles.

Conclusions

At the time of writing this chapter both authors happened to be participating in a workshop on CAD. Discussing means of justifying CAD with engineering managers involved in this field the issue of productivity ratios arose. We were struck by the general acceptance that it was impossible to 'justify' CAD in terms of productivity. All claimed that their own installations were not achieving the productivity ratios often claimed to be necessary arguing that this was too restricted an approach in any event. Participants were much less clear about how best to apply CAD to achieve the benefits they sought!

In this chapter we have summarised the literature on this emerging field in order to elaborate what appears to be a crucial choice to be made. Much of the choice seems to lie in the data structures and data-base design field. We have briefly described a data-base design which facilitates and supports the creative work of draughtsmen whilst allowing for the control processes operated in the manual situation, *but no more than that*. Thus our approach is not concerned to achieve greater control through sub-division and de-skilling but rather to provide the designer with rapid access to data and to the analysis/ computational power of the computer. Our purpose has been to elaborate the choice we have before us in the development of CAD *through example*. Thus we have shown that it is possible to construct a computer based procedure which contains the features and controls inherent in the traditional design process. In this roles of designer, draughtsmen and inspector (or checker) are retained in order that the development of the individual pieceparts can be controlled. The development of the system was directed towards providing a method of establishing the positional relationships between part within the machine space. This allows tolerances, assemblies and movement of parts to be investigated. A development programme has now been established with the objective of turning these 'prototype' techniques into practical design office tools.

References

Arnold, E. and Senker, P., 'Computer-Aided Design in the UK Engineering Industry'. *Paper presented to CAD 82, 5th International Conference on Computers in Design Engineering*, Brighton, England, March 1982.

Cooley, M., *Architect or Bee? The Human/Technology Relationship*, Langley Technical Services, Slough, 1980.

Cooley, M., 'Computerization — Taylor's Latest Disguise', *Economic and Industrial Democracy*, vol. 1, 1980, pp.523–39.

Department of Industry, *Report on CAD* Coopers & Lyband Associates Ltd and Ingersoll Manufacturing Consultants International SA, 1979.

Kingston, W., *Innovation: The Creative Impulse in Human Progress*, John Calder: London, 1977.

Lipchin, L., 'CAD/CAM' *Paper presented to CAD 82, 5th International Conference on Computers in Design Engineering*, Brighton, England, March 1982.

Medland, A.J., 'The Impact of CAD on the Design of Mechanical Elements for Machines', *Department of Engineering and Management Systems*, Brunel University, England, 1982a.

Medland, A.J., 'The Development of a CAD-system Based Upon the Mechanical Engineering Design Process' *Paper presented to CAD 82, 5th International Conference on Computers in Design Engineering*, Brighton, England, March 1982b.

Rosenbrock, H.H., *Computer Aided Control System Design*, Academic Press: London, 1974.

Rosenbrock, H.H., 'Interactive Computing: A New Opportunity', *Control Systems Centre Report* no. 388, UMIST, England, 1977.

Rosenbrock, H.H., 'The Re-direction of Technology', *IFAC Symposium* Bari, Italy, 1979.

4 Innovation, microelectronics and manufacturing technology

Donald Gerwin

Introduction

Recently, Hage (1980) developed a theory of innovation which represents an important step forward in our understanding of the adoption and implementation of new technologies. The theory concentrates on radical innovations, those high risk changes which are major departures from the existing situation in an industry or a society. These have been rarely studied, mainly from a case viewpoint, but are significant because of their potential for widespread impacts. The theory is also characterised by a process-oriented view rather than a structural perspective. In so doing it goes well beyond the mere identification of stages in the innovation process. For each stage hypotheses are specified in causal chains which trace the impact of critical variables upon one another. The result is a sound foundation for further theory development and for policy guidelines in sufficient detail to be of interest to decision-makers.

This contribution, however, is based primarily on studies of new products and services as opposed to throughput processes. As he pointed out, there has not been much research combining new methods for converting inputs into outputs. Nowhere is this lack of knowledge more critical than in manufacturing. The microelectronics revolution has created a new generation of sophisticated equipment which has great potential for stimulating productivity growth. Yet study after study indicate that lack of understanding of the technology and its impacts is a significant barrier to diffusion (Gerwin, 1982, Gold et al., 1980; Putnam, 1978).

This chapter attempts to match Hage's theory with evidence recently compiled from case studies of companies which have committed themselves to radical microelectronics manufacturing innovations. The chapter examines the generality of his propositions and suggests ways of revising them. It also helps to organise our knowledge concerning the way in which an important type of innovation is adopted and implemented.

Nature of the technology

A microelectronics manufacturing system (MMS) consists of several machine tools, each usually under CNC control, and a central computer which transmits operating instructions to the machines and receives operating information from them. When material handling between machines is manual the system is known as direct numerical control (DNC). When there exists automated material handling under the guidance of a computer we have a flexible manufacturing system (FMS). Because MMSs are highly customised the number, type and configuration of machine tools, computers and material handling systems varies from one application to another.

MMS's have their greatest impact in mid-volume batch manufacturing of discrete parts as exemplified by aircraft, trucks, tractor and automobile service parts. Until recently, these manufacturers had to choose between dedicated transfer lines best suited for mass production or general purpose machine tools designed for small batch production. An MMS provides more flexibility than transfer lines and lower unit costs than general purpose machine tools. It can manufacture a mix of parts at any one time, add new parts to the mix over time, reroute a given part if a machine breaks down, and implement engineering design changes. FMSs also allow random processing. Parts capable of being machined by the system can be run in any sequence at any time without costly setups.

In 1979 and 1980 case studies were conducted to uncover the difficulties firms experience when adopting and implementing MMSs. In order to obtain the broadest possible insights and due to access problems, size, task and stage of MMS development varied among the companies. The international interest in MMS technology prompted the selection of firms in different countries. Data were collected from one firm in the United States, three in Great Britain, two in West Germany, and one in France. Due to ease of access more information was collected from the American company.

In the first three countries semi-structured interviews were held with managers and engineers in various levels and functions. Access problems dictated that the people interviewed were not in the same positions in every company. Respondents were asked predetermined questions such as, 'Explain your role in the decision to have an MMS', 'What major changes have occurred in your job and department?' and 'What changes would you like to see occur?' These probes stimulated discussion which led to additional *ad hoc* questions. In France my colleague Jean-Claude Tarondeau obtained written responses to the predetermined questions. Available supporting documents supplemented the interview information.

In virtually every case the innovation fit Hage's definition of radical as a significant departure from existing conditions in the industry or society. The American firm purchased that nation's second FMS for its tractor division. The British manufacturer of industrial bearings was one of two firms in the country with a rudimentary DNC system. The British producer of medium and large size motors was one of the first there to be installing a fully-fledged DNC system. The large engineering oriented British company was engaged in designing the first locally produced FMS. One German company, a producer of transmission systems, was designing the country's first FMS for rotary parts. The other, an aircraft manufacturer, was one of the first German firms to install an FMS. The French transportation vehicle manufacturer was designing its nation's first FMS for a plant producing gear boxes.

Four stages of innovation

Hage divides the innovation process into four stages. During *evaluation* an organisation assesses its performance to identify failures and searches for means of correcting them. These means which may include a radical innovation then need to be assessed to find which one is more likely to correct existing problems. *Initiation* involves a search for the human, physical and financial resources needed to support a radical innovation. In the *implementation* stage the organisation tries out the innovation for the first time and encounters resistance and conflict. Finally, *integration* refers to deciding whether to retain the innovation based on an evaluation of its performance and the subsequent incorporation of the innovation into the organisation.

Evaluation

In such a theory an organisation assesses its performance through the identification of performance gaps. A performance gap is the positive difference between aspirations and performance on some relevant dimension. The main theme is that usually there is not enough information to easily measure gaps. As the ease of measurement, the frequency of measurement, and the number of dimensions analysed decrease, the frequency of detection of performance gaps will decrease. As frequency of detection in turn decreases, the size of any detected gap will increase. The size of the gap also depends upon the ease of measurement, the level of aspiration, and the length of the time horizon used in assessment. As the size of a gap increases and the time horizon lengthens the number of affected dimensions will increase as poor performance on any one spreads to others. An organisational crisis ensues reflected in the existence of many large size gaps. The stage has been set for adoption of a radical innovation.

The role of crisis as the motivation for radical innovation is exemplified by the American company in the microelectronics sample. Basic changes in the nature of farming were creating a demand for large sophisticated customised tractors. However, the division was still producing small and medium sized vehicles with antiquated manufacturing processes. Declining sales and profits necessitated that the corporation either sell the tractor business or regenerate the division. The division's proposal for a new product line and new manufacturing equipment were developed in a crisis atmosphere in which survival was at stake.

However, most of the other companies were reacting to opportunities in their environments at least as much as crises. The French, British and German firms which were designing FMSs took advantage of their respective governments' desires to stimulate the development of microelectronics manufacturing systems through partial funding of the projects. Once more, all three companies had ambitions beyond merely installing the new technology in their own factories. They saw an opportunity to become leading vendors in what was believed to be a profitable new market. The German aircraft enterprise purchased an FMS in conjunction with being awarded a large military contract that almost doubled the capacity of its main plant.

Hage is mostly silent on the second aspect of evaluation, a search for and assessment of alternative solutions to the performance problems. This provides a chance to expand upon his ideas. Identification of a possible need for radical innovation leads next to a decision on what Pelz and Munson (1982) have called originality level. The organisation must decide whether to develop its own solution (invention), modify features of an outside source's solution (adaption), or essentially copy another source's ready-made solution (borrowing). For a large complex innovation such as an MMS it is possible that some components may be invented, others adapted and the rest borrowed.

What factors determine originality level? The data show that four of the seven firms invented substantial parts of their MMSs. Since invention is the most expensive and risky option firms which have no other choice will adopt it. Given that three of the companies were considering becoming vendors innovation was their only alternative. The fourth required highly customised equipment which could not be obtained in the market. Invention will also be employed when the substantial costs and risks can be reduced. The three prospective vendors had partial financial support from their governments. They also could install their initial MMS in one of their plants to demonstrate viability to prospective customers. It was not necessary to run the risk of trying to sell it in order to show it was successful.

Whether an organisation decides to invent, adopt or borrow, it must assess alternative designs. The data indicate that Hage's main points concerning performance gap analysis also apply here. There is typically not enough information to easily measure the expected performance of alternative designs. It is very difficult to predict net financial returns for an MSS, particularly when a new product is being considered simultaneously. As in the public sector benefits tend to be long run and intangible while costs are short run and concrete.

An MMS's major advantage of flexibility to change over time the mix of parts being manufactured cannot be quantified because of lack of information. A conventional transfer line will machine a few specified parts at the lowest possible cost. An MMS will machine the same parts at higher cost but at some unknown times in the future can machine other unspecified parts. Similarly, it is difficult to measure the gains from having the computer provide a central source of operating information versus the necessity to search for the same data at several different locations in the shop. Consequently, sophisticated financial analyses are not typically made for MMS adoption decisions. In the American firm the decision to have an FMS was made by the head of manufacturing engineering and the head of the task force appointed to select manufacturing equipment for the new product line. Formal analysis was confined to an evaluation sheet which rated four machining systems on each of twenty-six dimensions including capital cost, labour requirements, flexibility to add parts, time to deliver and install, and estimated amount of running time per week. The FMS came out far ahead of its closest competitor. In part the evaluation served to help crystallise the decision-makers' thinking. However, the fact that their minds were already partially made up probably had some effect on the evaluation's outcome. There was not much formal analysis in the British motor producer or the German aircraft manufacturer. A determination could not be made for the others.

Ease in measuring expected performance is likely to be affected by the length of the time horizon adopted, a relationship not discussed by Hage. Managements with a long term outlook will find it relatively difficult to measure relevant aspects of expected performance such as meaningful but intangible benefits. Decisions among alternative designs will be based more on judgement than on financial analysis. Radical innovations such as MMS will be in a favourable position for adoption. Where management has a short term horizon it is easier to measure expected performance since long run intangible considerations will be disregarded. Radical innovations such as MMS will be at a disadvantage. Decisions will be based on financial analysis techniques using return on investment and payback period. Costs, which are relatively simple to quantify, will be the dominating factors. The innovating task force in the American firm used acquisition cost as one of its major criteria. The FMS had a relatively small acquisition cost which counteracted the discounting of its long run benefits.

Where management has a short term outlook the task force may employ various tactics for increasing the chances of winning approval for an MMS. It can take advantage of opportunities to reduce the visibility of its proposal. In at least two enterprises recommendations for an MMS were incorporated into extensive capital improvement programmes involving many different kinds of equipment. The sheer number of machines combined with their technical complexity tended to hinder an exhaustive analysis by management. The task force may also quantify intangible benefits as was admitted by an accountant in one of the firms. However, such biasing of information must be tempered by the realisation that managements which lose confidence in task force recommendations are likely to reject them. Finally, a task force which appears to be sure about its proposals is likely to inspire the confidence of management. In one company sales forecasts for a new product line to be machined by an MMS were changed so frequently that management lost faith in them.

Initiation

During initiation the infrastructure needed to support a radical innovation is located and assembled. Hage's only hypothesis states that the more radical the innovation the greater the need for new personnel, funds and technologies. To this list should be added systems and procedures. While initiation is the least developed portion of the theory it is extremely crucial for advanced production technology. Evidence compiled by Gerwin (1982) and Skinner (1978) indicates that MMSs and similar equipment require a sophisticated factory infrastructure if they are to function effectively. The first proposition of Ettlie's chapter in this volume states that radical process innovations fail primarily because of insufficient human resources. Yet many companies for one reason or another fail to put together the necessary ingredients.

The microelectronics data identify some critical infrastructure elements stemming from technological requirements. People are required to develop new kinds of skills mainly due to an MMS's technical complexity and large acquisition cost. First line supervisors must have extensive technical knowledge and experience in order to know when to call a repairman and what kind of repairman is needed. They must also retain interpersonal skills to motivate direct workers in their inspection and loading activities, and to solicit cooperation from process engineers, parts programmers, maintenance workers, and quality control people. Skilled operators are needed to monitor machine operations. Only they can sense when a problem has occurred and can handle the situation until a maintenance worker arrives (Sorge et al., 1983). However, they dislike not being able to control the cutting of metal and the routine nature of monitoring activities. Skilled electronic maintenance workers are needed to deal with frequent breakdowns which are difficult to diagnose, but their specialisation in terms of functions and type of machine reduces the flexibility of maintenance resources.

MMS characteristics force the development of revised systems and procedures. The continuous nature of operations in an FMS reduces the opportunities to make inspections by eliminating most of the natural pauses in the work flow. When quality checks are performed at the end of lengthy machining sequences discovery of a defect may occur too late to prevent other parts or the machine tools from being damaged. Automated continuous monitoring is still too limited in scope to substitute for manual inspection (Senker et al., 1981). Cost accounting can no longer be based on direct labour hours which is the most widely used approach. Due to the automated nature of operations labour hours cannot be attributed to the machining of a particular part. A company which must switch to the less common machining hours basis may find there are still tricky accounting problems left to be solved and that the investment in retraining accountants and factory managers is not negligible. Conventional pay incentive schemes which reward workers for the amount of production no longer apply when output levels are largely machine controlled. New kinds of plans based on rewards for planning, coordinating and learning new skills have to be developed.

In general the companies studied had not yet devised satisfactory solutions to these and other infrastructure problems. Why don't firms have support systems capable of facilitating MMS operations? Exploring this question would be useful for developing badly needed theory for the initiation stage. Between Hage and the microelectronic data six possible reasons can be identified. Hage stressed that finding capable people who were willing to accept risks is a barrier. In some of the MMS companies a single individual absorbed most of the risk by assuming responsibility for the success or failure of the project either voluntarily as in the American firm or by appointment as in the British motor manufacturer. It then became his duty to gather the necessary resources. This task is facilitated by higher level commitment as reflected in the individual's being relieved of operating responsibilities or being able to survey manufacturing facilities elsewhere. Once infrastructure resources are assembled, however, it may not be easy to retain them due to their marketability. At least three firms reported losing key managerial, operating or staff personnel, in some instances after they had been trained.

Some companies simply do not realise the necessity for developing infrastructures. They assume that the introduction of new manufacturing technology will automatically lead to productivity increases; the more sophisticated the technology the greater the increase. Support systems need not be considered or can be dealt with in an *ad hoc* manner during implementation. They do not understand that the latest technology in an unprepared setting will not function as effectively as unsophisticated equipment in a compatible environment (Schumacher, 1973; Trist, 1981). In one firm the project leader perceived only technical engineering problems. He believed that placing the MMS in a plant with a good record of union-management relations would handle the infrastructure issues.

Where management has a short term horizon there is pressure for immediate returns on investment, particularly when the size of the investment is large. Once an MMS has been installed on the factory floor management will want it incorporated into daily production. Staff and service people are consequently prevented from learning about the capabilities and limitations of the system. Foremen and workers are not adequately trained in how to operate it. Two of the firms noted this problem.

Faced with considerable complexity and uncertainty a company may choose to rely heavily upon the vendor for support functions such as training and maintenance. The extreme is a turnkey project in which the vendor assumes responsibility for the effective functioning of the system at least initially. As Ettlie states in this volume, vendors are motivated to assume responsibility by their desire to ensure that the innovation is successful. However, there are negative consequences for the user in this policy. First, dependence upon the vendor reduces the motivation to develop the internal resources which will be eventually needed. Consequently, key infrastructure elements are beyond the customer's control. Second, even vendors have not amassed a great deal of knowledge concerning MMSs. In part the systems are too new. They may also be too large and complex to temporarily set up in the vendor's test facility. Third, vendors may tend to oversell the labour-saving features of MMSs, particularly to firms not willing to accept their intangible benefits. These companies may be led to believe that a sophisticated infrastructure is not required.

A capable infrastructure is the product of considerable prior exposure to advanced manufacturing technology. The more experience a company has had with NC and CNC machine tools the better equipped it is to cope with the demands of an integrated system. Generalised problem solving methods are available to aid in dealing with new ones. Coping mechanisms have been developed to augment tolerance of further changes (Hage, 1980). Confidence in being able to handle the future has been accumulated. The enterprises studied varied extensively in their NC and CNC experience and therefore in their infrastructure development. The British motor producer had virtually no such exposure at the site chosen for its DNC system. It had to forge from scratch a comprehensive development plan to accompany implementation. The German aircraft manufacturer had considerable NC experience so fewer adjustments were needed. However, the research also suggests that there is a qualitative leap in complexity from individual machines to an integrated system. No amount of NC and CNC experience can completely handle the problems.

Ettlie argues in this volume that organisations which develop accurate implementation expectations during adoption will increase the chances of success for the innovation. Waiting until implementation may mean that problems can be handled only after a considerable time lag. It takes time to train someone, develop a new procedure, or purchase additional equipment. However, infrastructure development prior to implementation of a radical innovation is impeded by a lack of information on the consequences for people, systems and procedures, and technologies. It will not be possible to identify during initiation all the resources which will be needed to support an MMS. Consider, for example, the American FMS which needed high quality raw castings with narrow tolerance limits. Only when it became clear that external suppliers were not meeting this need could a decision be made to have the division's foundry produce the castings. A great deal of time and financial resources had to be invested to modernise the facility. The implication for Hage's theory is that there can be no neat separation of initiation and implementation for a radical innovation. His assertion that the four stages of the innovation process occur in the stipulated order without back and forth movement must be called into question.

Implementation

A radical innovation introduces new personnel, occupational specialties, and technologies into an organisation. It also leads to considerable job autonomy for the innovators. These variables have the following

74

structural impacts. They force changes in the behaviour required from organisational positions which creates role conflict. They force changes in the amount of power and status associated with certain positions which leads to power and status conflict. However, when a consensus exists between the innovators and other personnel as to the extent of the performance gap all three types of conflict will be decreased. The existence of the three types of conflict leads management to recentralise decision making which reduces the innovators' job autonomy. Consequently, the innovators will diminish their attempts to change behaviour. Conflict will be lessened but the innovation will become less radical.

The microelectronics data provide numerous examples of conflict processes in action. Consider role conflict. During the design of the American FMS the innovators consisting of the vendor's and customer's engineers believed that it would be possible to have the finished parts adhere to rather close tolerances. Their high expectations imposed tough behavioural requirements on operating personnel who had to attain the tolerances and on quality control people who had to measure them. The ensuring role conflict was only resolved after exhaustive tests revealed the tight tolerances were beyond the capability of the manufacturing system. The theoretical specifications were adjusted to more realistic levels which reduced the need to change behaviour and the radicalism of the innovation.

Power conflict occurred in the American firm as lower level manufacturing managers on the shop floor became more dependent upon staff and service departments such as accounting and maintenance. These managers had always used informal procedures based on direct labour hours for controlling operations as they made their rounds of the shop. The procedures were of little use in controlling FMS operations because of the diminished relationship between how much people worked and the amount of production. In addition, manufacturing managers could not readily interpret the meaning and significance of the new cost accounting concepts based on machining hours. Due to the FMS's technical complexity supervisors could no longer contribute to the repair of machines. They had to rely upon electronic and electrical maintenance people without having much control over the timing and quality of their work. Survey data collected in the company dramatically demonstrate the loss of control of the FMS's first line supervisors (Blumberg and Gerwin, in press). On autonomy, the degree to which their jobs provide freedom in determining procedures, they scored below a normative sample and below three of the four kinds of FMS workers.

The British bearing manufacturer furnished an instance of status conflict. The process planning department, which had the task of choosing the machines, operations and tools for each order, was also assigned the task of preparing parts programmes. In order to encourage people to take on the new challenge a new higher top level was added to the pay scale. It could be attained by excelling in at least one of the two tasks. The older men in the department, however, were unwilling to learn programming while two younger men became proficient in both tasks. Once more, the older men who had been on top of the original pay scale found themselves below the younger men on the new scale. The resulting status incongruence has been the cause of a great deal of friction in the department.

Due to an MMSs' technical characteristics even those people associated with the innovation can suffer similar types of problems. In the British bearing producer two skilled operators of conventional machines were selected to run the new machines during testing and development. Later they were joined by additional less skilled operators. Then a joint union-management task force rated the skill level and pay rate of the jobs on the new machines as lower than the skilled operators' previous level and rate. In the American firm those operators of conventional equipment who are in lower pay grades than FMS operators receive more take-home pay because of an individual incentive programme. A feasible incentive plan for the FMS has not yet been devised. In both companies dissatisfaction and conflict have resulted.

Strategies for implementing change

Ettlie in this volume calls implementation strategy the most likely predictor of a successful innovation. What strategies are available? Hage identified three: revolutionary, evolutionary and creating a new permanent organisational unit with new people. A revolutionary strategy involves the dominant coalition utilising its powers to implement the entire innovation in a brief amount of time. Usually so much dissatisfaction and conflict ensues that the actual amount of change is low. However, when there is a crisis and a centralised structure radical innovation may occur. The evolutionary strategy allows participation of the affected interests in planning and implementation. Dissatisfaction and conflict are minimised as change occurs slowly in increments. However, the radicalism of the innovation is diminished through consultation.

Hage believes that creating a new unit is the best alternative for radical change provided the unit has its own source of resources, and enough time to handle implementation issues. A new unit permits the recruiting of human resources who are committed to the innovation. Problems can be solved without having to make concessions to the existing staff. There are no vested interests with which bargaining must be undertaken. However, other than mention the necessity for a great deal of financial resources Hage does not sufficiently explore the limitations of the third alternative.

Building a factory on a greenfield site involves much more than bricks, mortar and equipment. The other essential ingredient is an infrastructure to conduct and support operations. Skilled people, systems and procedures are required for production scheduling, materials supply, inventory control, process planning, accounting, training and supervision, performance evaluation, maintenance, safety, wage determination, organisational structure, information systems, union relations, and community relations among others (Skinner, 1978). Where is the infrastructure to come from? Specialists in all the necessary occupations capable of dealing with a microelectronics manufacturing system will be different to recruit. As John Kenneth Galbraith (1978) noted, 'To create a technostructure for a new task is a difficult, costly, and uncertain undertaking'. Once more, radical innovation will introduce considerable uncertainty in the form of unexpected problems with no readily available solutions. To handle them it will be necessary to look for similarities with previous problems and solutions and then to modify the old. The advantage will be with the existing infrastructure who have already worked together in a similar factory situation. Consequently, where implementation of a radical innovation requires a large, sophisticated infrastructure with many different occupational specialties, and where the required infrastructure already exists, the tendency will be to use an existing unit.

The German aircraft manufacturer considered building a new plant because it was almost doubling its capacity, but ultimately ruled it out precisely because the existing factory already had a well developed support system. This was a sound choice because the support system was instrumental in reducing the trauma of implementation. For example, the process planning department in selecting machines, operations and tooling for specific parts to be run on the FMS assumed there would be some similarities with the decisions that had been made on parts run on the shop's NC equipment.

The revolutionary and evolutionary strategies are undoubtedly more frequent alternatives for radical process innovations than creating a new unit because of the financial resource and infrastructure problems. The latter's use is limited mainly to the situation in which major resistance is likely in existing operations. Bessant, Braun and Moseley (1981) found that creating a new unit was not used as much as the evolutionary strategy for microelectronic manufacturing innovations. It tended to be employed where labour relations were poor on the assumption that an isolated operation would be less threatening to the workforce. Originally, the British bearing producer desired an autonomous unit set up in a separate location in its factory with new operators and infrastructure components. It wanted to avoid conflict with existing employees who are dedicated to hand skills. The plan was never realised because the necessary funding was withdrawn during an economic recession.

All seven of the companies interviewed had installed or planned to install their MMSs in existing plants. As far as could be told the implementation strategy was much more evolutionary than revolutionary due to the divisibility property of MMSs. Most firms were ableto install one machine at a time which limited the problems faced at any one point and contributed to the development of the infrastructure's experience. CNC capabilities on individual machines allowed autonomous operation until all were ready to be hooked up into an integrated system.

Routinisation

During routinisation a decision is made on whether or not to incorporate the innovation into the organisation permanently. The decision process involves some of the concepts from the first stage. According to Hage the larger the sunk costs and the greater the consensus about the performance gap the longer will be management's time horizon. The longer the horizon and the greater the ease of measurement the larger will be the innovation's perceived benefits. However, the greater the sunk costs, the ease of measurement, and the extent of conflict the larger the perceived costs. The larger the benefits and the smaller the costs the greater the likelihood of institutionalising the innovation.

The microelectronics data focus on ease of measurement as the critical variable. The technology's characteristics and other factors create uncertainties in the reference points against which increased benefits and/or decreased costs are measured. Costs and benefits therefore contain arbitrary elements which limit their utility for decision making. Surprisingly, the problem exists whether one considers routine operating efficiency or indirect impacts on the rest of the shop. Supporting data are from the American company (Gerwin, 1981).

The division's evaluation of operating performance occurs through a standard cost accounting system which compares planned costs at planned production levels to actual costs at actual production levels on an overall and component basis. Variances are computed between planned and actual elements which indicate where costs are out of control. Variance analysis requires a set of standard cost parameters which reflect what per unit costs should be under normal conditions. They provide the underlying basis for establishing the accounting system's planned cost reference points.

From where was reliable data for calculating the values of standard cost parameters to come? Originally, there was no relevant information in the factory because the FMS was radically different from other machines and because the new product line could not be manufactured elsewhere in the shop. Data could not be obtained from other facilities because only one other system of its kind was in operation. Consequently, standards had to be based on problematical intuitive estimates. By the time the interviews were conducted a completely reliable basis for computing standards had still not been found. Although data were available for seven years of FMS operations they included starting up conditions and a period of abnormally high demand. Once more only about eight other systems had been installed in the United States and they were highly customised. Overall planned costs are a fairly reliable benchmark. The planned values of important cost components are still uncertain making it difficult to learn whether actual costs are within acceptable limits of control. The accounting department is forced to attend to those items such as rework and maintenance which represent large fractions of the budget and over which some control can be exerted.

Machine utilisation is one of the key variables that manufacturing management tries to control in its efforts to lower costs. This quantity represents the number of hours a facility is actually used divided by the number of hours it could have been used in a given time period. Typically, the denominator reflects an adjustment for time lost due to normal machine breakdowns. If an FMS machine breaks down parts can be rerouted to other machines in the system which take longer to perform the same functions. Since it is far too complex for the accounting department to calculate the necessary adjustment the FMS's values of machine utilisation tend to be understated by some unknown amount. The FMS appears to be less efficient than it really is.

There is no reference point for determining to what extent the assumed benefits of the FMS such as reduced lead times, in-process inventories, and material handling have occurred. Values for these variables after the FMSs adoption are available. No relevant data exists on these variables for the situation prior to adoption because the product line is new. Respondents sometimes made vague comparisons against a hypothetical collection of conventional equipment that would have been needed without the FMS. However, the precise configuration of equipment and its cost and benefit consequences have never been made explicit.

The indirect costs and benefits of MMS operations are even more difficult to ascertain. Consider the following list of impacts from the companies interviewed. In the American firm the foundry had to be modernised which upgraded the quality of the castings provided to the rest of the division. The British motor manufacturer found production scheduling had become more difficult. Products designed for machining on the new equipment could not easily be run on the shop's conventional equipment. In the British bearing producer machining activities had been organised according to type of operation performed. The new equipment had to be organised in a single unit because each machine performs a number of different operations. The German aircraft manufacturer found that in order to keep pace with the FMSs need for material inputs pre-machining activities had to quicken the pace of their production. This created a quality control problem.

Conclusions

In general, Hage's theory is a good starting point for study of radical manufacturing innovations including microelectronics technology. However, revisions are in order especially in regard to emphasising the role of the infrastructure throughout the process. A support system is needed to search for and evaluate alternative designs during Stage One. Its composition must be augmented in Stage Two. It smoothes implementation problems during Stage Three and conducts evaluations of the innovation in Stage Four. Let us consider each step in detail.

With respect to evaluation Hage's contention that crisis is the primary motivation for radical innovation is not supported. A crisis explains the behaviour of the American firm. A majority of the companies, however, were more influenced by environmental opportunities such as the chance to lead in marketing MMSs in their countries.

Hage dwelled on the first aspect of evaluation, the measurement of performance gaps. The second aspect, the identification of alternative designs, is critically important for manufacturing innovations. This includes a decision on originality level. Surprisingly, a majority of the firms chose the expensive and risky alternative of invention. They were either constrained to invent by their situations, as the British company which required highly specialised equipment, or found a way to reduce the associated costs and uncertainties. In the European countries the latter approach was facilitated by the availability of governmental funds, a policy which is currently being hotly debated in the United States. Hage believes that the most critical factor in the evaluation of performance gaps is ease of measurement. My evidence indicates that it is also crucial in the assessment of alternative designs. Not enough information exists to measure the expected financial performance of radical technology even in the manufacturing area of business firms. Measuring the benefits of flexibility is an example.

The data also indicate a relationship between ease of measurement and management's time horizon. The shorter the horizon the easier it is to measure expected performance since long run intangible factors will not be considered. Hence, the chances of selecting radical manufacturing innovations will be reduced. This is exactly one of the problems which has made American industry so susceptible to foreign competition. To counteract top management's tendency to think in the short run task forces which request radical technology may reduce the visibility of their proposal, bias financial analyses, and appear to be more confident than they are about their choices. However, these strategies are limited by the need to retain credibility.

Initiation, the least developed section of the theory, turns out to be very significant for manufacturing innovations. A new technology will function effectively only if it is interfaced with a compatible infrastructure. Yet the data indicate that skills and attitudes, systems and procedures, and ancillary technologies are often not adequate to support MMSs. In my opinion this is an example of a growing imbalance in degree of sophistication between computerised manufacturing technology and the support systems of companies. Too much attention is being paid to technical innovation and not enough to developing infrastructures. The inevitable result is implementation problems that are likely to worsen as single-minded pursuit of the automated factory continues.

Several factors account for the observed incongruities between the factories' hard and soft components. Management may not see the necessary interconnections between machines and support systems especially when it desires to substitute capital for labour. Managements with a short term orientation will concentrate on meeting daily production quotas rather than gradually building up technical expertise. There may be not enough prior exposure to new manufacturing concepts or there may be too much dependence upon vendors for support functions. Finally, it is not possible before implementation to completely identify the composition of needed infrastructure components. Contrary to Hage's assertion, initiation and implementation will partially overlap for radical manufacturing innovations.

The propositions on implementation as a confrontation over changes in behaviour, power and status were substantiated. However, they do not make provision for the ability of an experienced support system to reduce conflict by limiting the need for behavioural change. Second, conflict is not strictly between those associated with the innovation and those who are not. It can appear among supporters when some discover that the innovation's characteristics have reduced their status and power. A case in point concerns workers who voluntarily choose to operate MMSs only to discover their wages have been lowered.

The need for a sophisticated infrastructure will influence the choice of implementation strategy at least for radical manufacturing innovations. Although Hage favours creation of a permanent unit with new personnel he did not consider that the necessity for an experienced support system mitigates the viability of this alternative. It is difficult to develop a new infrastructure from scratch while the existing one can make use of its experience in problem solving and working together. Consequently, a radical manufacturing technology is likely to be installed in existing facilities unless major resistance is expected. An evolutionary strategy is likely to be employed when the technology has the divisibility characteristic. Due to the significant problems with all three implementation strategies one must sympathise with Hage's pessimistic view of the chances for successfully implementing radical innovations.

Hage did not identify a critical variable during routinisation but the evidence indicates that ease of measurement should have this role. Lack of information is prevalent whether assessing routine operating efficiency or indirect impacts. It is especially difficult to establish reference points against which to measure changes in benefits and costs. Coupling new equipment with new products aggravates the situation. Four of the seven companies linked their MMSs to new products. Consequently, the decision on whether or not to institutionalise a radical innovation cannot be made on rational grounds even in the private sector.

Finally, it appears that the theme of uncertainty may serve as an organising framework within which more refined theories of radical manufacturing innovation can be developed. The tension between the technical core's need for certainty and new manufacturing equipment's generation of uncertainty is likely to account for a good deal of human behaviour during innovation. We have seen that there is not enough data to measure performance gaps and assess alternative equipment designs. A sophisticated infrastructure is required to cope with the technical and financial uncertainties created by the innovation. Yet its composition cannot be completely known during initiation. The risks in developing an infrastructure from scratch make it impractical to create a new unit. Measurement difficulties contribute to the institutionalisation decision being an uncertain one. Research currently underway is exploring the fruitfulness of this approach.

References

Bessant, J., Braun, E. and Moseley, R., 'Microelectronics in Manufacturing Industry: The Rate of Diffusion' in T. Forester (ed.) *The Microelectronics Revolution*, The M.I.T. Press: Cambridge, Mass., 1981, pp.198–218.

Blumberg, M. and Gerwin, D., 'Coping with Advanced Manufacturing Technology', *Journal of Occupational Behaviour*, in press.

Galbraith, J.K., *The New Industrial State* (3rd edn.), The New American Library: New York, 1978.

Gerwin, D., 'Do's and Don'ts of Computerised Manufacturing', *Harvard Business Review*, 60: 1982, pp.107–16.

Gerwin, D., 'Control and Evaluation in the Innovation Process: The Case of Flexible Manufacturing Systems', *IEEE Transactions on Engineering Management* EM-28: 1981, pp.62–70.

Gold, B., Rosegger, G. and Boylan, M.G., *Evaluating Technological Innovations*, Lexington Books: Lexington, Mass., 1980.

Hage, J., *Theories of Organizations*, John Wiley: New York, 1980.

Pelz, D.C. and Munson, F.C., 'Originality Level and the Innovating Process in Organizations', *Human Systems Management* 3: 1982, pp.173–87.

Putnam, G.P., 'Why more NC isn't being used', *Machine and Tool Blue Book*, 1978, pp.98–107.

Schumacher, E.F., *Small is Beautiful*, Blond and Briggs: London, 1973.

Senker, P., Swords-Isherwood, N., Brady, T. and Huggett, C., 'Maintenance Skills in the Engineering Industry: The Influence of Technological Change', *Engineering Industry Training Board*, occasional paper 8, Watford, England, 1981.

Skinner, W., *Manufacturing in the Corporate Strategy*, John Wiley: New York, 1978.

Sorge, A., Hartmann, G., Warner, M. and Nicholas, I., *Microelectronics and Manpower in Manufacturing: Applications of Computer Numerical Control in Great Britain and West Germany*, Gower Press: Farnborough, 1983.

Trist, E., 'The Evolution of Socio-Technical Systems', *Ontario Quality of Working Life Centre*, occasional paper 2, 1981, Toronto, 1981.

5 Evaluating the introduction of new technology: the case of word-processors in British Rail *

Riccardo Peccei and David Guest

Introduction

For organisations to survive and prosper they must be able to adapt and change. Most recognise this and seek opportunities to improve their performance. One path to such improvement has traditionally been the introduction of new technology. More recently the rate and range of technological innovation, and perhaps most dramatically the widespread application of microprocessor technology, has been such as to set new challenges to the ability of organisations to manage change.

The challenge of new technology is unlikely to diminish; therefore there is much to be learnt from studying cases of success or failure and absorbing the lessons for the future. Yet all too often the introduction of new technology is so difficult that when it is finally implemented, those involved want to forget the whole painful process of change and get on with operating the system. The central purpose of this chapter is to argue the case for the evaluation of change and for the importance of learning from previous experience.

Four major reasons can be identified to justify an increased concern for the evaluation of technological change. The first, and in a sense the most obvious, is that evaluation of past changes can provide useful feedback to aid decisions about future practice. If a particular scheme is judged to be a success or failure, then it is essential to understand the reasons for this, to know why it did or did not succeed. An analysis of this type can help to improve decisions on choice of technology,

* The research reported in this paper was funded by British Rail. However the views expressed are those of the authors and should not be interpreted as those of British Rail.

on the level of performance targets it is reasonable to expect and on the appropriate methods of introducing the new technology into the organisation.

A second reason for evaluation is to provide feedback while the introduction of new technology is actually in progress. It often becomes clear, during what may be quite a lengthy programme of change, that progress is falling behind schedule or that unforeseen problems, such as technical difficulties, opposition from employees or lack of support from top management, are occurring. Evaluation implies that regular reviews of progress are held. For this to be useful, it is essential that data are available on which to base judgements about reasons for any problems and that there is sufficient flexibility to allow for adjustments to be made within the overall change programme.

The third reason for conducting *systematic* evaluation of the introduction of new technology is the need for information to influence or complement the subjective judgements which people will inevitably make about whether the change is a success or failure and why. Subjective judgements are open to error and can cause conflict. For example the use of potentially competing criteria such as speed of introduction and quality of operation may lead to directly contradictory conclusions about the success of the introduction of new technology. At the same time, however, organisations are political systems and the importance of subjective judgements must be recognised. Evaluation should utilise these, but complement them with a range of more systematic data, so that decision-makers may be better informed and have the opportunity to avoid the mistakes which can result from a lack of such data.

The final reason for emphasising the need to concentrate on the evaluation of technological change is that it is a topic which has been relatively neglected and less than adequately treated in the writing on change in organisations (see Goodman and Kurke, 1982). However the subject has not been totally ignored. For example, there has been some interesting work on failures in organisation development (Mirvis and Berg, 1977). There is also a more general literature on evaluation, although very little has dealt specifically with technological change. Typically it has focussed on topics such as training, supervisory development or improvements in the quality of working life. However most of the work reflects a general approach to evaluation which can therefore be applied to the evaluation of technical change. Four main approaches to the evaluation of change in organisations can be identified.

The first approach is primarily concerned with organisational effectiveness (see, for example, Goodman and Pennings, 1977) which has traditionally been defined in terms of goal achievement. This can be readily adapted to the evaluation of technological change by defining the effectiveness of the change as the extent to which the new technology does in fact produce the results and benefits it was expected or intended to achieve. There are three main problems with this approach. The first problem arises from the need to establish which goal or goals are the most important and most valid. In practice goals are often vague, ambiguous or 'unrealistic' and consequently do not always provide a sound basis for assessing success. The second problem is that both the nature of the goals and the level of goal attainment may have limited validity if judged in isolation from the organisational circumstances. The same goal may be unrealistically high for one organisation and unrealistically low for another. This has encouraged the development of a variety of systems models of effectiveness which seek to take these differing circumstances into account (see Goodman and Pennings, 1977). The third problem with the goal achievement approach is that it has tended to focus too exclusively on the goals of those directly involved in decisions about the introduction of technological change to the exclusion of those affected by the changes who therefore have a very direct interest in the outcome. The priority goals may differ across the various interest groups associated with the change.

The second approach accepts that power, conflict and subjectivity are inevitable ingredients of any organisation and builds evaluation of change around this. Hesseling (1966) has developed a general framework for the evaluation of change which uses as its starting point two key questions – evaluation by whom and evaluation for whom. Only when these two questions have been answered is it possible to identify what should be evaluated and how. People undertaking evaluation of the same change in an organisation will often have different purposes, use different methods and focus on different criteria. For anyone concerned there are many choices of approach centering around whether to evaluate, for whom, what to evaluate and how. Hesseling therefore sees evaluation strategy as the central issue, with evaluation becoming an integral and positive part of a continuing process of change.

The third approach, most fully developed by Thurley and Wirdenius (1973), argues that it is necessary to evaluate the whole change process, focusing on four issues; these are the case for intervention, the choice of direction, the choice of strategy and the cost-benefit analysis of the various possible change strategies. This emphatically shifts the emphasis from evaluation of outcomes to evaluation of the change process. It helps to widen the scope for evaluation and therefore makes it less difficult to explain success or failure.

The final approach is primarily concerned with the technology of organisational assessment and evaluation, rather than conceptual analaysis of the nature and role of evaluation of change. In this respect it can be distinguished from the three previous approaches (see Lawler, Nadler and Cammann, 1980 and Seashore et al., 1982). This work has progressed on a number of fronts including the development of instruments to assess changes in attitudes, organisation structure, job characteristics and performance outcomes, improvements in model building and research design and improvements in the statistical techniques of evaluation.

The need for a new framework

Each of the main approaches to evaluation has important strengths. At the same time they are limited as a result of their focus on a particular aspect of evaluation. Indeed setting the four approaches alongside each other illustrates the range of issues that must be encompassed within any comprehensive evaluation of change. It will not always be necessary to evaluate every dimension of change — Hesseling's emphasis on choice in developing a strategy of evaluation highlights this — but we do need a framework which can embrace the key dimensions and make explicit some of the conceptual distinctions about what to evaluate. This becomes particularly important where organisations have to assess pay-offs between, for example, the costs of change, the time investment and the quality of the end result.

Following this introduction, the chapter presents a framework and outlines a method of evaluating the introduction of new technology. The next section examines the specific case of the introduction of word processors in British Rail, and the final brief section highlights some of the key general issues emerging from the case study.

A suggested framework of the evaluation of technological change

The development and implementation of a new technological project or scheme is a complex task commonly involving and requiring the making of a large number of both major and minor, routine and non-routine decisions by different individuals and groups within an organisation. For analytical purposes, therefore, a technological change initiative can usefully be thought of as a complex process of decision-making involving a series of discrete but related decisions, with the particular scheme which is eventually introduced representing the output of the process. Viewed in these terms then, the problem of evaluation is essentially a matter of analysing and assessing the complex process of decision-making associated with the development and implementation of an initiative.

Evaluation exercises, however, can take different forms depending on their particular focus, that is depending on whether it is the output, nature or efficiency of the decision-making process which is the object of assessment. On this basis, three main types of evaluation exercise can be distinguished. In the first·case, the main focus of attention is the substantive content and aims of technological change, to seek to identify its actual and potential impact and consequences as a basis for assessing what might be termed the effectiveness or success of the initiative. In the second case, by contrast, the main interest is in analysing the nature of the decision-making process associated with the development and implementation of a scheme, in terms, for example, of its rationality and participativeness, with a view to assessing the 'quality' or 'appropriateness' of the process of change *per se*. The third type of analysis examines what, in broad terms, might be thought of as the ratio of inputs to outputs in the decision-making process, as a basis for evaluating the actual efficiency of the change process. This, for instance, can be judged in terms of the time, money, manpower and energy spent to develop and implement a scheme, and by looking at such factors as budget and target date over-runs. For ease of reference these three forms of evaluation will henceforth be referred to as output, process and efficiency evaluations.

These three types of evaluation exercise will now be examined in greater detail by looking more closely at the different kinds of evaluation criteria and methodologies for assessment used in each instance. It is important to keep in mind, however, that these three forms of evaluation are not mutually exclusive. Rather, they are complementary to each other. One of the main arguments of the present paper, in fact, is that evaluation exercises which focus exclusively either on outputs, process or efficiency are, by their very nature, bound to be partial and incomplete. The evaluation of technological change initiatives requires an analysis of all three elements of a change process. This is an issue, however, that we will return to again later.

Output evaluation

Output evaluation, as we have seen, focuses on the substantive content of a technological change initiative rather than on the process whereby the technology was introduced, and is essentially concerned with assessing the effectiveness or success of the change programme as such. As the introductory section indicated, the traditional approach to output evaluation has been to examine goal achievement. Three major difficulties with this were identified, namely the difficulty of specifying a set of explicit and widely accepted goals, the difficulty of assessing goal achievement without taking account of the organisational circumstances and the neglect of the goals of interest groups affected by technological change but not directly involved in decisions about its implementation. To overcome these difficulties it seems essential to take account of the focus of Goodman and Pennings on inputs and constraints and to integrate Hesseling's concern about for whom and by whom evaluation might be conducted.

This approach should therefore start by identifying the main groups within an organisation which may have a stake in a change programme, in the sense of being either directly or indirectly affected by the introduction of the new technology. The next step is to discover the specific advantages and disadvantages of the change as perceived by each group. The aim, in other words, is to draw up what may be thought of as a balance sheet of costs and benefits for each group as a basis for arriving at a more informed and comprehensive assessment of the change. The specific groups which might be included in the analysis would vary depending on the situation. Minimally, however, the list might include policy makers among senior management, users/operators, the representatives of user/operators (i.e. trade union officials and shopstewards), managers of user/operators, and systems and personnel/industrial relations specialists. The specific factors which might be included in the group cost-benefit analysis will also tend to vary from one exercise to the next. It is therefore not possible to specify the criteria of effectiveness in advance, although the 'researcher' may have a potential checklist of criteria of his own. The analysis aims to look not only at possible short and long term economic and financial costs and benefits but also at a variety of social, physiological, psychological and industrial relations factors and criteria. The evaluation of outcomes, from the perspective of each interest group is therefore likely to be complex, multi-dimensional and non-additive. It is also likely to be dynamic and fluid and the timing of the evaluation, or sequence of evaluation, therefore becomes crucial.

Process evaluation

The reasons why a change initiative takes the form it does and why, therefore, it may be more or less successful, cannot be properly understood unless one looks at the nature and quality of the decision-making process associated with the development and implementation of the scheme itself. Process evaluation focuses on the analysis of such complex processes of decision-making.

Decision-making processes can be described, and therefore, evaluated, in terms of a number of variables or criteria. Hage (1980), for instance, identifies thirteen major variables in terms of which it is possible to describe and analyse a decision-making process, ranging from the degree of routinisation and delegation of decision-making to the amount of information search, conflict and deliberate delay there is in the process. This list could easily be extended. Our aim here, however, is not to provide an exhaustive list of process variables, but rather, to look briefly at a few of the main criteria in terms of which it is possible to analyse and evaluate the nature and quality of a process of decision-making.

The main variables we will concentrate upon here are the rationality, bureaucratisation, centralisation, participativeness and degree of conflict of the decision-making process. The reason for focusing on these variables is that, as we will have occasion to see more fully below when we look at the development of the word-processor initiative in BR, there tend to be close links between these features of a decision-making process and the actual output and efficiency of the process itself. The tendency noted in the literature for more participative processes of decision-making to be slower and more time consuming but to produce better quality decisions and greater commitment to change, is but one example of the possible links there can be between the nature, output and efficiency of a decision-making process (Jacobs et al., 1977; DIO, 1979). By looking at the above set of variables therefore, one is likely to be in a better position to understand and explain not only why a process of change may be more or less efficient, but also why schemes take the form they do and are more or less successful.

As noted by Simon (1957), decision-making in organisations is characterised by bounded rationality with decision-makers normally engaging in 'satisficing' rather than 'optimising' behaviour. Decision-makers usually neither can nor do carry out exhaustive information searches before making a decision. Nor do they carefully examine and evaluate all possible alternative solutions and courses of action. Instead they tend to operate with simplified models of reality and look only at a few alternatives, choosing the one which appears to be the most satisfying at the time. The amount of information search which takes place, the number of alternative solutions which are examined and the care with which these various alternatives are evaluated varies, however, from one decision-making process to the next. As such, some processes can be said to exhibit a greater degree of rationality than others. More specifically, the rationality of a decision-making process can be said to vary depending on the extent of information search and the extent to which systematic attempts are made to consider and evaluate alternative solutions, as evidenced, for example, by the emphasis which is placed on systematic data collection about decision issues, and by the use which is made of sophisticated analytical techniques as aids to decision-making. This implies a greater investment of time, money and effort into the process but can, in turn, be expected to have a positive impact on decision quality since it decreases the likelihood that potentially important questions or facts relating to an issue will be overlooked or ignored when a decision is being made.

90

As noted above the development and implementation of a techno-logical change initiative commonly involves the making of a large number of both major and minor decisions. In principle, therefore, when looking at the question of the rationality of the decision-making process, one could examine how each of these various decisions was arrived at. This, however, is not likely to prove either feasible or fruitful. A preferable strategy is to focus on an analysis and evaluation of a few key decisions. The specific decisions that are analysed will vary from one exercise to the next. Minimally, however, one would need to look at the three key issues in a process of change identified by Thurley and Wirdenius (1973) — the case for intervention, the choice of direction and the choice of strategy. This essentially involves looking at three main decisions — the original decision to go for new technology, the decision about what particular type of technology to introduce, and the decision on how to go about introducing the new technology — and then analysing and evaluating how each of these major decisions was made.

Turning briefly to the other process variables identified above, bureaucratisation refers to the degree of formalisation and routinisa-tion of a decision-making process. It can be measured by the extent to which there are set practices, procedures and routines governing the process and specifying what steps should be followed when a decision is to be made, who should be involved, and when. The use of set decision routines and practices introduces an element of order and stability into the process which may be conducive to greater rationality and have a positive effect on the quality of decision-making. Bureaucratisation however also introduces an element of rigidity into the process which may stifle innovativeness and creativity and make it more difficult to deal effectively with non-routine decisions (see, for example, Perrow, 1972; and Burns and Stalker, 1961). As we will see from the BR case study though, bureaucratisation is important mainly for the impact it has on the efficiency of the decision-making process; the adoption of elaborate decision-making practices and routines, such as complex formal mechanisms for vetting and clearing decisions, can make the process unduly slow and cumbersome at times.

Efficiency is likely to suffer most when bureaucratisation is coupled with centralisation. Centralisation refers to the extent to which decision-making tends to be concentrated at higher levels in the management hierarchy, as evidenced, for instance, by the degree of involvement of senior management in the decision process, and by the extent to which decisions normally have to be approved and authorised at higher levels in the hierarchy. The practice whereby decision options and recommendations are elaborated at lower levels and then passed up the hierarchy for formal consideration and approval by a variety of individuals and/or committees, is likely seriously to delay and retard the decision-making process (Mintzberg et al., 1976).

The inclusion of non-managerial interest groups in the decision-making process, seen here as an element of participation, is likely to have a similar effect. More specifically, the degree of participativeness of a decision-making process refers to the extent to which workers and/or their representatives are involved in the process, as evidenced, for example, by the amount of say or influence they have over the final decision outcome (IDE, 1981; Wilson et al., 1982). As such, participation and centralisation are separate dimensions. Thus, for instance, one can have both centralised/participative and decentralised/non-participative processes. In the latter case decision responsibility rests mainly with managers at lower levels in the hierarchy, but workers and their representatives are excluded from the process. In the former case decision responsibility on the management side rests mainly with senior managers but shop stewards or trade union officials are also directly involved in the process and have a major say in the decision. Such participation by non-managerial groups can, as we have seen, have an important impact on both the output and efficiency of the decision-making process. Participation may also increase the amount of conflict in the decision-making process, measured in terms of the extent or severity of disagreement to be found among individuals and groups involved in the process, and this, in turn, may slow down progress on a scheme. Delays due to conflict, however, can also occur when non-managerial groups are excluded from the process, as when, for example, there are serious disagreements on technical matters between specialist departments involved in developing a scheme, or staff-line conflicts on how to go about introducing the new technology or on the timescale of implementation (Pettigrew, 1973).

Efficiency evaluation

Efficiency is commonly defined as the ratio of inputs to outputs. In these terms a change process could be said to be more or less efficient depending on the level of output obtained for a given level of input. The level of output might, for instance, be measured in terms of the benefits, financial or otherwise, resulting from the implementation of a scheme. The greater the benefits obtained for the amount of time, money and effort spent in developing and implementing a scheme, therefore, the more efficient the process may be said to be. As we have seen, however, different interest groups may incur and derive different costs and benefits from change. The evaluation of outcomes or benefits, therefore, is likely to be multi-dimensional and non-additive. Consequently, it may not be either meaningful or feasible to assess efficiency by reference to outcomes and benefits.

Given these problems it is preferable to abandon the notion of benefits when trying to evaluate efficiency and adopt, instead, a simpler approach. This approach, which involves using relatively simple criteria of project success as a basis for evaluating efficiency, focuses attention on four main questions concerning the inputs and outputs of a process of change. The first two questions relate to outputs and are designed to establish what the process of change has or has not produced, as a basis for arriving at a judgement about the relative success of the change initiative. The second set of questions relate to inputs. More specifically, they refer to the timescale and cost of implementation, and when taken in conjunction with the first two questions, provide a rough indication of the efficiency of a process of change.

There are two simple criteria in terms of which it is possible to assess the relative success of a technological change initiative. The first criterion is whether a scheme has actually been introduced and, if so, whether it has been implemented in full. For a variety of reasons, projects are often discontinued or abandoned (Mirvis and Berg, 1977). In such cases one can legitimately speak of an initiative as having failed. Often, however, schemes are introduced but not in full (see, for example, Mumford, 1967). In assessing the success of a change process, therefore, it is important to consider not only whether or not a scheme has actually been introduced, but also the extent of its implementation. The second criterion refers to how well the new technology works once it is introduced. The fewer the teething troubles, the more reliable the technology and the better the new system performs once it is in place, the more successful the change initiative can be said to be.

On the input side, there are, at the very least, two main questions which need to be considered. Firstly, how long did it take an organisation to develop and implement the scheme, and secondly, what were the costs involved, in terms of money and manpower. Each of these questions can be approached in two ways: either in terms of goal achievement, by looking at the extent to which there are overruns in costs and target dates for implementation; or in comparative terms, by looking at how much it cost and how long it took for a scheme to be developed and implemented in an organisation, as compared to similar projects in other organisations. There are, however, problems with both these approaches. Frequently, for example, no precise budgets or target dates for project implementation are set in an organisation. Alternatively, the budgets and targets that are set are, for a variety of reasons, either unduly 'tight' or 'loose' and consequently, do not provide a good basis for assessing project success. Equally, though, it is often difficult meaningfully to compare project costs and timescales of implementation across organisations since schemes

vary in terms of their complexity and the specific circumstances sur-
rounding their development and implementation are also likely to vary.
Therefore it is best not to rely exclusively on either one or the other
approach, but rather, to use both approaches as a basis for arriving at a
more balanced evaluation of the efficiency of a process of change.

In brief, the proposed approach to efficiency evaluation combines
a goal achievement with a comparative perspective to the analysis of
inputs. It looks at the timescale and cost of implementation and
assesses efficiency by relating these inputs to project success, measured
in terms of the extent of implementation of an initiative and the
performance of the new technology once introduced.

Summary of framework

The main elements of the proposed framework for the evaluation of
technological change are summarised in Figure 5.1. Although open
to further refinement and elaboration, this framework provides a
useful starting point for assessment and can be used as a guide or
checklist for the evaluation of technological change.

As is evident from the above discussion, the comprehensive evaluation of technological change can be a daunting task involving the collection of a large body of both quantitative and qualitative data, and the
use of a variety of research instruments and methodologies, including,
for instance, in-depth interviews to assess reactions to change, attitude
surveys, conventional cost-benefit analysis, statistical techniques to
assess changes in performance outcomes, and the analysis of documentary material as a basis for reconstructing decision-making processes and examining the history and development of change initiatives.
In principle, the comprehensive evaluation of technological change
requires an assessment of all three dimensions of a change process,
particularly since, as we have seen, there may be trade-offs between the
nature, output and efficiency of the process. In practice, however,
because of the complexity of the task involved, it may not always be
possible to examine all three dimensions of change in the same amount
of detail. Nor, is a detailed evaluation of this kind always required.
When examining the case of the introduction of word-processors in
British Rail we will concentrate mainly on an analysis of the nature and
the efficiency of the change process, partly because these issues have
not received systematic attention in the literature on the evaluation of
technological change, and partly because the data for the study were
originally collected with a view to looking at the problem of the achievement of change in the industry. The following case study, therefore, is
essentially an analysis of the decision-making process associated with
the development of the initiative in BR and of the steps and blocks
along the path to implementation.

94

Type of evaluation	Focus	Criteria
OUTPUT	outcome/effectiveness of change	balance sheet, of costs and benefits (economic, social, physiological, psychological, industrial relations) for each interest group
PROCESS	nature and quality of change process	rationality, bureaucratisation, centralisation, participativeness and degree of conflict of decision-making process
EFFICIENCY	ratio of inputs to outputs in change process	extent of scheme implementation, performance of new technology, speed of implementation, cost of implementation

Figure 5.1   Framework for the evaluation of technological change

The development of the VWP initiative in BR – a brief case history

British Rail introduced video word-processors (VWP) in typing bureaux at British Railways Board (BRB) Headquarters in London and in three out of five Railway Regional Headquarters in early 1981 for a total outlay of approximately £450,000.

Word-processing equipment consists essentially of three units; a central unit for processing and storing information, a keyboard and visual display unit used by an operator to produce a communication in place of a conventional typewriter, and a high speed printer unit. VWP equipment is available in two forms, so-called Stand Alone Machines (SAM) and Shared Logic Systems (SLS). In the first case the keyboard/display and processor/storage units are all combined in one workstation. In the case of Shared Logic Systems several keyboard/display units share a common processor/storage unit. In either case the word-processors can be equipped with 'networking facilities' which enable the VWP units to be linked with each other and/or to existing computer facilities, thus making it possible to set up an integrated communications network. The VWP systems introduced by BR at Board HQ and in the Regions are 'Shared Logic Systems' equipped with networking facilities and comprising between 12 and 14 workstations each. (In addition BR also introduced several 'Stand Alone Machines' in a number of departments at Board HQ.)

In tracing the history of the VWP initiative we rely both on documentary material (e.g. internal management reports and correspondence on the scheme and records of union-management consultative meetings) and on information obtained from in-depth interviews with managers and union officials in the industry directly involved in the development of the scheme. The history of the initiative is summarised schematically in Figure 5.2.

Background to the initiative

The origins of the VWP initiative can be traced back to October 1975 when the Management Services Department decided to look into the applicability and usefulness of video word-processors for BR and prepare a feasibility study on the subject. This initiative was prompted by a number of factors and has to be seen in the light of the major economic and technological changes and developments taking place in the railway industry in the early 1970s. More specifically, the VWP initiative must be seen against the background of BR's worsening economic performance during the first half of the 1970s. Despite increased financial support from the government, the industry made steadily growing losses during this period. As a result, by the mid-1970s there were strong pressures from both outside and inside

Figure 5.2 Schematic representation of development of VWP initiative October 1975–October 1980

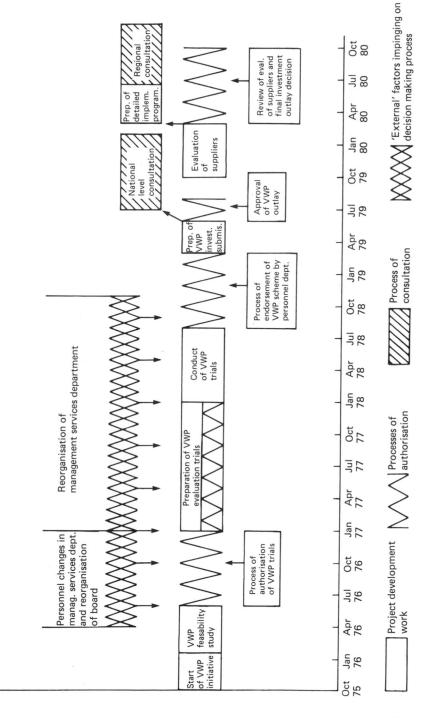

the industry to improve performance by increasing productivity and/or cutting costs. This emphasis on the need to cut costs and increase productivity applied to all areas of BR including administration and the exploration of the potential for word-processors was one of a number of initiatives. At the same time new technologies and particularly the new microprocessor based technologies, such as VWP promised in the long-term to revolutionise the whole area of administrative communications, and in the short-term promised to provide significant benefits for management in the form of increased productivity in the office services area. The new technology was therefore seen by management as providing a major new opportunity to tackle the problem of administrative costs in BR.

Feasibility study

Following the decision to prepare a feasibility study on video word-processors Management Services raised the issue with senior managers from the Signal and Telecommunications Department at meetings of the Teleprocessing Committee held in October and November of 1975. As a result of these discussions it was decided to broaden the scope of the study and carry out a general review of administrative communications systems in BR, emphasising in particular the need to relate any new initiative in this field to other major communications schemes currently being undertaken in the industry, such as the National Teleprinter Network being developed by the Signal and Telecommunications Department.

In line with these decisions Management Services in late 1975 prepared a paper on 'Administrative Communications Strategy'. The basic aim of this paper was to take stock of administrative communications in BR and to formulate a coherent strategy for the future. After reviewing the state of administrative communications in the industry, in terms of methods and equipment, the paper went on to emphasise the need to impose a greater degree of integration and centralised control over administrative communications and to improve productivity in the office services area by means of new technology and the elimination of unnecessary methods. As part of this overall strategy the paper recommended continuation of the investigation into video-typing systems, considered to be one of the most promising areas of new technology, with a view to 'commence (trial) implementation (of VWP) by the end of 1976'.

The 'Administrative Communications Strategy' paper was presented to the Teleprocessing Committee in January 1976. At this stage the Teleprocessing Committee, having accepted the recommendations put forth in the strategy paper decided to set up a joint study team to review VWP requirements in BR. This team, known as the 'Word

Processing Technical Study Group', consisted of five people, two from the Signal and Telecommunications Department, two from the Administrative Systems Group of Management Services and one from the Computing Division of the same department. The team was placed under the overall command of a member of the Management Services Department, with a member of the Signal and Telecommunications Department acting as team leader. In essence, the Word-processing Technical Study Group was to continue the investigation into VWP started by the Management Services Department in late 1975. Its main task was to carry out a product survey, assess likely increases in productivity and identify possible areas of application for VWP in BR.

The VWP Study Group completed its feasibility study by the early summer of 1976. The results of this study, presented in a discussion paper submitted in June 1976, indicated that it would be possible for BR to obtain significant productivity improvements through the use of word-processors in the office services area (productivity increases of between 125 and 200 per cent). Consequently, the June paper concluded by strongly advocating the introduction of VWP in BR and proposed that management start by introducing Shared Logic Systems at Railway Regional HQs, with a view to extending the system at a later date and linking up the various workstations into a communications network covering the whole industry. It recommended that formal evaluation trials be carried out as soon as possible in a number of Regional typing bureaux as a first step towards the implementation of the proposed scheme.

Process of authorisation of evaluation trials

The recommendation to carry out evaluation trials was endorsed by the Management Services Department in September 1976. Before work could begin on setting up the trials, however, the proposal had to be endorsed by the Personnel Department (i.e. the department with direct responsibility for administrative staff in the office services area), and cleared with three separate standing committees, the Teleprocessing Committee, the Railway Productivity Steering Group and the Computer Steering Group. This process took several months to complete. The proposal to hold trials was cleared by the Teleprocessing Committee, from a technical point of view, in September 1976. Following the endorsement of the Personnel Department, the proposal went to the Railway Productivity Steering Group and was approved in October 1976. The final authorisation to proceed with the trials was obtained in January 1977 when, following the restructuring of the Board, the proposal was cleared with the Chief Executive in office.

Setting up of the trials

The work involved in setting up the trials was carried out by the Administrative Systems Group with the support of the Computing Division and of the Signal and Telecommunications department, and in consultation with the Personnel Department. This work was spread out over a period of approximately twelve months. The trials themselves, in fact, did not commence until January 1978. During this period a considerable amount of planning and preparation had to be done by management (e.g. systems development work, deciding which equipment to use, getting experience of the equipment, deciding where to hold the trials and how to progress them etc.). At the same time the trials were cleared with the unions (TSSA and NUR) at national level, and discussions and consultations were held with the management and staff who were to take part in the trials at selected locations in BR.

In this context it is worth noting that the task of setting up the trials may have been rendered more difficult by the fact that a number of the people who had been directly involved in the early stages of development of the VWP scheme left the industry in 1976–77.

Reorganisation of the Management Services department

The setting up of the VWP trials coincided with a major process of reorganisation of the Management Services department. This process of reorganisation commenced in 1977, following the restructuring of the Board, and was completed in late 1978. As part of this reorganisation, the Management Services department was split and two separate departments were created. Internal Consultancy Services (incorporating the old Administrative Systems Group) and Computing Services and Operational Research.

Once the Management Services department was split, day-to-day responsibility for the VWP project passed into the hands of Internal Consultancy Services. Formally, however, no clear-cut demarcation of responsibility appears to have been established between Internal Consultancy and Computing with respect to the VWP project and both departments shared responsibility for most major decisions and recommendations made on the project.

The trials

The trials themselves started in January 1978 and lasted eight months. They were held in two locations, Eastern Region HQ in York and BRB HQ in London, using equipment from different firms. In

September 1978, immediately following the completion of the trials Internal Consultancy Services prepared a paper reviewing and evaluating the results of the trials. As pointed out in this paper productivity gains of between 75 and 100 per cent were obtained during the trials, lower than foreseen in the 1976 feasibility study, due mainly to problems encountered in the London typing bureau (inappropriate mix of work and apparently at times also a certain lack of cooperation from the local management involved in the trials). Apart from these productivity gains, the paper also emphasised a number of other benefits which might accrue from the introduction of VWP, including (a) a possible increase in job satisfaction for the staff involved, resulting in lower staff turnover rates and a general improvement in the climate of industrial relations in typing bureaux, and (b) the establishment in the longer term of a more effective system of management communication through an extension of the scheme to other parts of the organisation and the creation of an integrated administrative communications network in BR. On this basis the September paper recommended that BR should proceed to install VWP in all five Regional Headquarters typing bureaux as well as at BRB Headquarters in London.

Endorsement of the VWP scheme by the Personnel department

The recommendation to proceed with the installation of word-processors in BR was underwritten technically by the Teleprocessing Committee in late September 1978. Before Internal Consultancy could proceed with the scheme however, the project had to receive the official backing and approval of the 'user' department, which in thise case, was Personnel. More specifically, before an investment submission could be put to the Planning and Investment Committee the VWP scheme had first to be endorsed by the Personnel Conference, consisting of the senior members of the Personnel department from Board Headquarters, the Regions and BR's subsidiary companies. This process took approximately six months to complete due mainly to scheduling problems and the fact that at this stage there already were a number of other important items for consideration on the Personnel Conference agenda. It was not until March 1979, in fact, that the VWP scheme recommended by Internal Consultancy in September 1978 was eventually discussed and endorsed by the Personnel Conference.

The VWP investment submission

Once the Personnel department officially decided to endorse the scheme, Internal Consultancy started preparing an investment submission for six 8-station Shared Logic Systems (one for each region plus one for BRB HQ), for a total outlay of just under £500,000. During the evaluation trials, as we have seen, productivity gains of around 75 to 100 per cent were obtained. On this basis, it was calculated that the proposed scheme would enable BR to save approximately 45 typing posts. These projected manpower reductions amounted to a saving of £160,000 p.a., less running costs. On this basis, investment submission was prepared stressing the major benefits to be derived from the scheme in the medium and longer term (possibility of extending the system throughout BR and development of a comprehensive administrative communications network resulting in less costly and more effective management communications and giving a break-even of just over three years). This submission, jointly supported by the Internal Consultancy and Personnel Computing Service Departments was submitted to the Planning and Investment Committee in June 1979. The outlay for the VWP was officially approved in August 1979 subject to the continued availability of investment funds and provided the scheme was first successfully cleared with the unions concerned at national level (TSSA and NUR).

National level consultations with the unions

The process of consultation with the unions started in August 1979. At the consultative meeting held in August the TSSA representatives stressed the need to introduce national guidelines designed to protect the health and welfare of the staff operating video processing equipment and informed the Board that unless agreement was reached on such guidelines (e.g. minimum rest periods, workstation design and environment, provisions for eyesight testing and for training, etc.) the union would refuse to progress the VWP scheme through the machinery of consultation. At the same time though, the TSSA undertook to let the Board have a specific proposal on the subject at an early date.

By September the TSSA had drawn up a set of detailed guidelines concerning the installation and use of video word-processing equipment in BR. These guidelines were rejected by management. At this stage, in fact, the Board, arguing that 'the position (on VWP) would be covered by the guidance notes it was intended to issue to Managers', took the view that 'a formal agreement' on the lines proposed by the TSSA was unnecessary, and advised the unions to this effect in November 1979. The TSSA, in turn, rejected the Board's position and, together with the NUR, requested a further meeting with management in January 1980. In the meantime though, the TSSA advised its members that 'until a proper agreement was reached they should refuse to co-operate in the use of VWP and VDU (Visual Display

Unit) equipment where operation exceeds one hour continuously or four hours in aggregate a day'. The management, anxious to make progress on the VWP scheme, agreed to meet the unions in January in order to discuss the draft guidelines drawn up by the TSSA in September. At this meeting management proposed a number of changes and amendments to the TSSA document. Following a further round of discussions in early February 1980, management and unions reached agreement on a detailed set of guidelines for the introduction and use of 'visual information processing equipment in office systems'. The consultation process, in other words, took about six months, from August 1979 to February 1980, when the VWP scheme was successfully cleared with the unions at national level.

Evaluation of suppliers and the choice of equipment

Parallel to the process of consultation was the process of evaluation of suppliers. This process of evaluation, based on the specification requirements drawn up at the end of the VWP trials, was carried out by Internal Consultancy Services in the five month period from October 1979 to February 1980. During this time a systematic evaluation of equipment from seven different suppliers was conducted. Four suppliers were shortlisted. In late February 1980, after a further careful assessment, it was proposed that BR purchase Wang equipment.

There were a number of reasons why Internal Consultancy opted for Wang. Wang was one of the leading companies in the field of word-processors and of the three shortlisted suppliers it was the one which was best able to meet BR's VWP specification requirements. From a technical point of view Wang equipment was judged to be the most efficient and reliable. It was also seen as technically compatible with BRs major mainframe computer supplier. At the same time the cost of this equipment was considerably lower than that of its main competitors. A final point in favour of Wang was that it supposedly provided faster and better after sales service than either of its other two competitors.

The recommendation to purchase Wang equipment was eventually accepted by the Board but only after a delay of several months. This delay was due to the fact that, at this stage, there was a difference of opinion between Internal Consultancy and Computing about the choice of which firm from which to purchase. Any formal recommendation to the Board with regard to suppliers had to be jointly endorsed by the two departments. Computing, however, tended to favour BR's traditional supplier of mainframe Computers. The proposal to purchase Wang word-processors, therefore, raised the issue of future equipment incompatibility in BR. This was seen as a potentially major problem by the Computing department, particularly since

BR, at a later stage, was planning to link the VWP to the computer system. (The possibility of leasing the equipment was considered but rejected on cost grounds.) The Computing department, while apparently still retaining certain reservations, eventually accepted Internal Consultancy's view concerning the purchase of Wang equipment and its compatability. Given these differences of opinion and the issues at stake, however, it is not surprising that the final decision about suppliers took several months to make. In September 1980, after a further review of the shortlisted suppliers had been carried out at the request of the Chief Executive's office, the Board finally decided to go ahead with the purchase of Wang equipment.

Implementation programme and last minute investment problems

Following the successful conclusion of national level consultations with the unions in February 1980, and while the supplier debate was still in progress, Internal Consultancy, with the help of the Personnel department, prepared a detailed implementation programme for the VWP scheme. The programme provided for the installation of five Shared Logic Systems comprising between 12 and 14 workstations each at principal typing bureaux in the Eastern, London–Midland, Western and Scottish Regions and at Board HQ. (The Southern Region, having failed to prepare an adequate brief for the introduction of VWP was, for the time being, left out of the scheme.) The implementation programme provided for the initiation of regional level consultations with staff representatives in June 1980. The delay in choosing a supplier caused some temporary problems of coordination in the implementation programme at regional level but did not significantly affect the consultation process which started on schedule in June in the Western Region.

In April 1980 the Board, in the light of BR's critical financial situation, decided to freeze all investment funds for the fiscal year 1980/81. In line with this decision, and acting on general instructions from the Chief Executive's Office, the Investment Office, in June 1980, queried the availability of funds for the VWP project for the current fiscal year. While accepting the need to keep investment down, the Internal Consultancy Department asked for the release of at least part of the funds for the project, arguing that it was important for BR, if it was to reap the full benefits of the VWP scheme, not to postpone the entire programme for a year for this would risk undermining the momentum of the whole initiative. On this basis a compromise solution was reached, with the Board eventually authorising approximately £225,000 (or about half the original outlay) to be spent on the VWP programme in the 1980/81 fiscal year. This more limited VWP investment outlay was formally cleared by the Investment Office, acting under instruction from the Chief Executive's Office in July 1980. In the event, however, BR was able to proceed with the implementation of the full VWP programme in the 1980/81 fiscal year since Wang, under request from Internal Consultancy, agreed to supply all the equipment by early 1981 but agreed to BR's postponing payment on part of the equipment until the beginning of the next financial year. The VWP scheme was formally introduced at regional level in the winter of 1981. A few months earlier, however, despite strong pressure from management, Eastern Region staff representatives had refused to agree to the introduction of word-processors at Regional HQ. As a result, when the scheme was finally implemented in early 1981, word-processors were introduced in only three out of the five BR regions. Not long after this, there was progress in the discussions in the remaining two Regions, so that it was possible for them to introduce word-processors before the end of 1981.

Discussion

The reader will no doubt have been confused by the range of committees, the number of organisational changes and the complexity of the bureaucratic context of the particular technological change. Such confusion is understandable and serves to highlight the importance of taking full account of the organisational environment in evaluating such changes. Taking such considerations fully into account, the success of the introduction of VWP in BR can now be briefly assessed from the three perspectives of output, process and efficiency. In doing so we will highlight a number of more general evaluation issues emerging from the case study.

A general assessment of the VWP initiative based on the evidence and analysis presented in the previous section is shown in Figure 5.3.

For reasons of space it is not possible to discuss each of the assessments in Figure 5.3 in detail. There are, however, a number of general points worth noting about the VWP initiative. In the first place, management, almost without exception, viewed the initiative as a success. Often, in fact, the initiative was presented to us as a major example of the successful achievement of technological change in the industry. Two of the regions, as we have seen, had to be left out of the scheme at least for a while when it was eventually introduced in early 1981. Despite this, the scheme was generally viewed as effective in the sense that it was seen by management as providing important benefits to BR. The new technology was judged to be reliable and to work well. In the short term it helped reduce administrative costs and improve productivity and efficiency in the office services area. The

Type of evaluation	Criteria	Assessment
Output	Balance of Cost/Benefits For *Managerial Groups*: Senior Management Technical Department User Department For *Non-managerial Groups*: Operators Trade unions	Positive Positive Positive Mixed/Positive* Mixed/Negative*
Process	Rationality Bureaucratisation Centralisation Participativeness Degree of conflict	Medium/High High High Medium/High Medium/Low
Efficiency	Extent of Scheme Implementation Performance of New Technology Speed of Implementation Cost of Implementation	Partial Good Slow Medium*

* Assessments which are not based on 'hard' or systematic evidence and which are therefore more impressionistic in nature.

Figure 5.3   Summary evaluation of the VWP initiative

introduction of the scheme was also seen as an important step towards the creation of an integrated administrative communications network in BR and, therefore, was seen as providing potentially even greater benefits in the future.

On the worker/union side, reaction to the scheme was mixed. Thus, most of the operators we had occasion to interview at BRB/HQ were, initially, apprehensive about the new technology. After an initial period of adjustment, however, they tended, on the whole, to view the new technology in a positive light since it made jobs easier, more varied and less monotonous. The possible long term effects of the new technology on health and employment, however, remained an important source of concern for operators, a concern which was shared by the trade unions and which, in the case of the Eastern Region, was used by staff representatives as a basis for opposing the scheme.

Given these strong positive or, at worst, mixed judgements about the scheme, the VWP initiative could, on balance, be regarded as having been essentially successful from an output point of view. Assessed from an efficiency perspective, however, the initiative would show up in a less positive light, as evidenced, in particular, by the length of time it took management to develop and implement the scheme — over five years. Judged in relation to other major technological change initiatives undertaken within the organisation, five years is not an inordinately long time, BR being used to long timescales of implementation. A number of other large companies in both the private and public sectors, however, were swifter at implementing change than BR, introducing word-processors into their organisations two or even three years before the railway industry (e.g. B.P., British Airways, the NCB and the GLC), although usually on a more gradual basis and perhaps significantly on a less ambitious scale than BR. The introduction of new technology is, in any case, an expensive, and often risky proposition, and there usually are compensations for not being first in the field. Thus, by the time the VWP scheme was actually introduced in BR equipment costs were down and the technology was also more reliable and sophisticated. On the negative side, however, it meant that BR was slow in taking advantage of the economic benefits associated with the introduction of the new technology, and the possible financial as well as the political/public relations repercussions of this must clearly be given considerable weight in any overall evaluation of the initiative.

The reason why the VWP initiative was relatively 'successful' in one respect (output), but less 'successful' in another (efficiency), can be adequately understood only by reference to the nature and quality of the decision-making process associated with the development and implementation of the scheme. This process exhibited a relatively high degree of rationality in that major decisions relating to the scheme were not, on the whole, taken without being given careful prior thought and consideration. This was reflected in the general quality of the project which was produced. At the same time, though, the decision-making process was highly centralised and bureaucratic in nature. The actual task of preparing and elaborating the scheme from a technical point of view, including the task of drawing up particular proposals or recommendations for action, as we have seen, involved a number of different stages or steps including the preparation of a feasibility study, the setting up, conduct and monitoring of formal evaluation trials, the preparation of an investment submission, the evaluation of suppliers and the preparation of a detailed implementation programme. Before the technical staff responsible for developing the project could proceed from one stage to the next, however, the action, in almost every case, had to be cleared with a number of different departments and/or formally authorised and approved by top management. Overlaying the process of project development proper, therefore, was a formal process of hierarchical and inter-departmental vetting, endorsement and authorisation which, particularly in the early stages of the initiative, appears to have been unduly slow and cumbersome − thus, in effect, seriously delaying and retarding progress on the scheme. Progress on the initiative was also slowed down to some extent by the need for management to clear the scheme with the unions at various stages, by occasional disagreements between technical departments, and by processes of internal reorganisation of departments. The relative lack of efficiency of the change process, however, can be ascribed mainly to the highly centralised and bureaucratic nature of the management decision-making process in BR. In this context, it is worth bearing in mind however that after 1979 the scope of the project was extended and progress on the scheme was accelerated. At the same time, British Rail had not stood still. Since 1981 there has been major restructuring designed to focus, accelerate and decentralise decision-making around the main areas of business. Steps have also been taken to reduce the degree of compartmentalisation.

Conclusions

In conclusion, therefore, the VWP study helps to draw attention to some of the hidden costs of centralisation and bureaucratisation. As such, it serves to highlight the need for management to look more closely at the way in which change initiatives are normally dealt with within the organisation and at the value and utility of some of the organisation's existing decision-making practices, procedures and routines. It also serves to highlight the fact that the evaluation of technological change is a complex task and the pitfalls, therefore, of trying to analyse and assess different dimensions of change in isolation from each other.

References

Burns, T. and Stalker, G.M., *The Management of Innovation*, Tavistock: London, 1961.

DIO (Decisions in Organizations), 'Participative Decision-making: A Comparative Study', *Industrial Relations*, 18, 3, 1979.

Goodman, P.S. and Kurke, L.B., 'Studies of Change in Organizations: A Status Report' in P.S. Goodman and Associates, *Change in Organizations*, Jossey-Bass: San Francisco, 1982.

Goodman, P.S., Pennings, J.M. and Associates, *New Perspectives on Organizational Effectiveness*, Jossey-Bass: San Francisco, 1977.

Hage, J., *Theories of Organizations*, John Wiley and Sons: New York, 1980.

Hesseling, P., *Strategy of Evaluation Research*, Van Gorcum: Assen, 1966.

Industrial Democracy in Europe (IDE) International Research Group, *Industrial Democracy in Europe*, Clarendon Press: Oxford, 1981.

Jacobs, E., Orwell, S., Paterson, P. and Welty, F., *The Approach to Industrial Relations*, Anglo-German Foundation: London, 1977.

Lawler, E.E. III, Nadler, D.A. and Cammann, C., *Organizational Assessment*, Wiley-Interscience: New York, 1980.

Mintzberg, H., Raisinghani, D. and Theoret, A., 'The Structure of "Unstructured" Decision Processes' in *Administrative Science Quarterly*, 21, June 1976.

Mirvis, P.H. and Berg, D.M., *Failures in Organizational Development and Change*, John Wiley and Sons: New York, 1977.

Mumford, E., *The Computer and the Clerk*, RKP: London, 1967.

Perrow, C., *Complex Organizations: A Critical Essay*, Scott Foresman: Glenview, 1972.

Pettigrew, A.M., *The Politics of Organizational Decision-Making*, Tavistock: London, 1973.

Seashore, S., Lawler, E., Mirvis, P. and Cammann, C. (eds), *Assessing Organizational Change: A Guide to Methods, Measures and Practices*, Wiley-Interscience: New York, 1982.

Simon, H.A., *Administrative Behaviour*, The Free Press: New York, 1957.

Thurley, K. and Wirdenius, H., *Supervision: A Reappraisal*, Heinemann: London, 1973.

Wilson, D.C., Butler, R.J., Cray, D., Hickson, D.J. and Mallory, G.R., 'The Limits of Trade Union Power in Organizational Decision-Making' in *British Journal of Industrial Relations*, 20, 3, 1982.

6 Company employment policies and new technology in manufacturing and service sectors

Sheila G. Rothwell

Introduction

What is a company employment policy? There can be no universally acceptable definition of such a concept any more than of a 'financial policy', 'product policy' or 'market policy'. Yet these terms are more commonly used (despite some confusion and even interchangeability between the terms 'policy', 'strategy' and 'plan') and the gap indicates that employment issues are either less central or else less susceptible to policy formulation. Managers usually talk in terms of personnel policies or industrial relations policies or, in transatlantic style, of human resource programs, but from a theoretical point of view it is possible to infer an organisation's employment policy from the sum, not only of its manpower plans, training activities, payment systems, recognition agreements and the way in which they are implemented, but also of its whole 'people' management style and organisation of work.

One definition can be found in a long-forgotten government publication 'Positive Employment Policies' (Ministry of Labour, 1958): 'From the management's point of view an employment policy is an integral part of the whole managerial and production policy of the firm. It has as its objective the creation of a co-operative, responsible

* The research on which this chapter was based was financed by a grant from the Manpower Services Commission and undertaken 1981–3 at the Centre for Employment Policy Studies, The Management College, Henley.

111

and efficient working force. Regard must be paid to existing agreements and established practices in the industry and to the essential role of the trade union. It must be understood and applied at all levels of management. From the employees' angle the policy must provide not only fair conditions of employment but satisfaction on the job, opportunities for advancement and reasonable security'.

'Employment Policies' in the government's current Industrial Relations Code of Practice are also defined in terms of their objectives: 'they help management to make the most effective use of its manpower resources and give each employee opportunity to develop his potential'. Reference is made to the avoidance of discrimination and the main topics covered are 'planning and use of manpower' (including redundancy handling) and 'working conditions' (Department of Employment, 1971). Communication and consultation, collective bargaining, employee representation and grievance and disputes procedures represent separate sections of the Code, although for the purpose of this chapter they will be included in the definition of employment policy. One definition adopted at the Centre is that an employment policy is 'a comprehensive employment strategy which integrates the organisation's various personnel policies, manpower plans and procedures for implementation. It should enable the organisation to meet and absorb the changing requirements of technology and markets in the foreseeable future' (Henley Centre for Employment Policy Studies, 1980).

This policy may be written and explicit in a few instances but may only be implicit in the traditional ethos and climate of an organisation in many others. In most medium and large companies there will be a mixture of written statements of principle and of formal procedures with a lot of unwritten tradition, custom and practice governing 'the way we do things here', for 'subjective' and 'objective' reasons. Thus a company employment policy may be said to exist in that even the absence of a policy represents a policy (Bachrach, 1962), but the more explicit it is the more likely it is that an organisation is employee-centred as well as profit-centred (Cuthbert and Hawkins, 1971).

The key features of a company employment policy therefore are seen to be:

1 a relationship to business strategy;
2 a long-term future planning orientation;
3 a significant role for the personnel function;
4 an employee-centred philosophy;
5 a range of component personnel policies and procedures which are consistent with each other and with the business policy.

These five features of an 'ideal-type' employment policy are unlikely to be found in absolute form in any instance, and even for purposes of theoretical analysis it is more helpful to conceptualise each as a continuum from 'high' to 'low'. Thus each organisation would have a different employment policy profile which would relate to such factors as its market position, size, organisational structure, environment and technology. Since the employment policy is itself inter-related with and partly a product of these major variables, analysis of the relationship is inevitably a complex process and explanation difficult. Nevertheless this chapter will attempt to explore the relationship between employment policies and one of these variables — technology — since such significant technological changes are currently taking place. It will attempt to see how far the new technology influences any or all of the identified dimensions of company employment policy.

Technology

Technology is an even broader concept than 'employment policy' with more dimensions and definitions available. The concept of 'new technology', 'information technology', 'computerised technology' only narrows one dimension of the definition, that emphasising the machinery used, to the extent that a computer or microprocessor is involved somewhere in the process; it adds little to the definition of the other major dimension — the 'control' system or the way in which the work is organised, the means by which the 'input' is transformed into 'output' (Woodward, 1958, 1970; Perrow, 1970). Yet the very scope and scale of the 'new' technology machinery (both hardware and software), the massive reduction in size and cost of components, the vast increase in performance and reliability, the ever-extending range of applicability, has such qualitative as well as quantitative implications that some changes in work-organisation and socio-technical systems are almost implicit (Trist, 1981). The form of these changes may not, however, necessarily be determined by the equipment: human choices still exist in its design and implementation which have effects at the level of the primary work group, the organisation and society (Child, 1972, 1980). The focus of this chapter is primarily that of the primary work system in the context of the whole organisation: to explore the extent to which the installation of 'new' technology in one section affects the employment policies there and directly or indirectly of the whole organisation.

It might thus be hypothesised that the application of new technology to manufacturing processes has different effects on employment policies there from its application to office information systems (and different again where the microprocessor is incorporated into the product, although this was not covered in our research). Nevertheless, two major features of new technology are (a) the fact that each instalment of it tends to demand another and (b) its integrative effects in breaking down previous distinctions, as for example, between the shop-floor and the office (Sleigh, 1979). Some of the systems we studied such as automated packing and warehouse systems, or quantity control systems, as 'conversion' processes are both part of the 'production process' and the 'information system'. A materials management system may begin by replacing paper-based stock records or customer orders but may develop into integrating the whole process by including not only customer accounts, warehouse supply and distribution, but also the whole movement of materials and work in progress throughout the factory to the extent that it is 'driving' the production system.

Research methodology

In order to get a wide view of the effects of technological change on organisational employment policies, the case study method was used and the companies chosen to give a range of applications of computerised technology, in different industries and in different parts of the country. The eight cases studied in the first year of the research covered a broad range of applications and of industries, including the customer service system of a public utility, the life assurance policy section of an insurance company and some automated manufacturing processes. The fifteen cases in the second year focussed more narrowly on stock control and material management systems in both manufacturing and distribution industries, but included a few quantity control applications. In the second phase, the study concentrated more on job design and supervisory role issues (see Figure 6.1).

Data was obtained through background publications, company documentation and a series of company visits and in-depth interviews, following a semi-structured brief. This covered the following topics:

1   firm's activities and market position;
2   reasons for technological changes;
3   implementation responsibilities and methods;
4   changes in job design and organisation structures;
5   redundancy, redeployment and recruitment;
6   training and skills;
7   industrial relations;
8   supervisors;
9   hindsight.

114

Figure 6.1   Summary of case studies

Industry/case	Application of New Technology	Employees in Case Unit	Trade Unions Recognised
Engineering			
Electronics	Materials and production control	590	X
Heaters	Manufacturing	450	√
Print	Manufacturing	200	√
Engines (2)	Assembly working	1200	√
	Manufacturing	670	√
Power Tools	Materials and production control	1400	X
Food Drink & Tobacco			
Confections (2)	Chocolate bar manufacturing	1800	√
Packet Food	Automated warehousing and packing	75	√
Liquid Food (2)	Quality control	330	√
	Accounting	70	√
Chemicals and Pharmaceuticals			
Photo Products (2)	Materials and production control	250	√
	Order processing	160	√
Tablets	Quality control	300	√
Infusions	Materials and production control	900	X
Allergens	Materials and production control	450	√
Drugs	Materials and production control	2800	√
Wholesale Distribution			
Agent	Stock control and order processing	111	√
Wholesaler	Order processing	300	√
Own Distributor	Stock control	3500	√
Mail Order	Automated warehousing	1200	√
Stationer	Order processing	3500	√
Finance & Banking			
Insurance	Order processing/ accounting	500	√
Computing	Sales & service of computers	60	X
Public Utility			
Utility	Customer service/ order processing	4000	√

The method generated little readily quantifiable data but did give considerable insight into the context of change and managers' own frames of reference. Inevitably, however, organisations were at different stages of the change process — some were only just starting computerised applications at all, others were well into a second or third phase of an advanced system which was in itself a development of previous fragmented systems. The size of the unit of study therefore varied considerably according to the stage of the technological change being implemented, as well as the degree of access available.

In most cases it was not the whole organisation, although in some cases the 'ripple' effects of change were very widespread. Thus, even if the number of employees directly affected was usually limited, the indirect repercussions were considerable, from senior management to shop floor, from sales and marketing to design engineering, purchasing and stores, production, distribution services and accounting. Almost no activity was unaffected in some instances of the cases that were studied.

Effects of new technology on employment policy

Relationship to business strategy

The extent to which an employment policy relates to the major business policy — springing out of it and contributing to its implementation is a crucial aspect of an employment policy: it is in this respect that it is — or should be — more than the sum of the existing personnel policies which were often formulated at different times to meet different needs (such as a crippling shortage of labour in many instances). This aspect of employment policy is the most difficult for practitioners to realise: time and again personnel managers, corporate planners, senior line managers and managing directors complain of the difficulty of relating employment policies to business policies (Galbraith and Nathanson, 1978; Tichy et al., 1982). In some instances this is a sheer problem of timetabling: if corporate plans (with manpower implications) are not approved until February/March, to come into effect from April, then the timelaps inherent in many manpower policies are inadequate for more than *ad hoc* adjustments to be made. Policy makers in the publications of the National Economic Development. Office (1978), Commission on Industrial Relations (1973), Manpower Services Commission (Hunter, 1978) and academics have all called attention to the need for greater integration (and for more manpower planning) but with seemingly little effect so far (Beardsworth et al., 1982; Taylor and Hawkins, 1972).

If a major strand of business strategy is the application of new technology, then it is necessary to examine how far this was explicitly, or implicitly, related to employment policy, by looking at the decision to innovate, and any modifications of that decision. The purpose of introducing new technology was in the majority of our cases market-led — 'to improve customer service', 'to monitor or improve our competitive position', 'to respond more flexibly to changes in demand', 'to take advantage of new market opportunities', were the reasons given.

Linked closely with these was another main group of reasons relating more directly to profitability: 'achieve economies of scale', 'improve productivity', 'reduce costs (of materials and/or labour)' were frequently mentioned. It was here that employment policy seemed more central since *'headcount reduction'* was usually envisaged as a major area of saving and a justification for technological change. Some care must however be taken in the interpretation of this since the whole issue of investment justification in this area is uncertain. The scale of it was in many cases too great to meet traditional company standards involving return on investment within 3–5 years (and many British companies have failed to innovate for these reasons) so that the figures had to be 'adjusted' to demonstrate quick potential savings or else the decision to go ahead was taken on the basis of other assessments of 'intangibles'. Thus, whether expectations of labour-costs savings were realised was not necessarily evaluated or even seen as highly significant (nor were any 'savings' necessarily offset against the recruitment of more expensive 'management services' staff). Savings due to improved manpower utilisation are particularly tangible, especially when realised by another department. Moreover at a time of rapid change in the economy and world markets, higher costs or greater benefits are difficult to attribute directly to a particular new investment. The reduction of numbers employed, for whatever reason, was tending to be seen as a 'good' in itself, in corporate terms, whatever problems it might create in practice. In many of our cases, manpower reductions (see below) appeared to be more closely related to the product market — decline in demand — than the introduction of a new technology (although this may have been because of the early stages of introduction).

A third group of reasons for introducing new technology was related to the second, but also to specific circumstances of the organisations, in that they more explicitly mentioned efficient methods, such as 'promoting high standards of manufacturing practice', 'obtain more up-to-date and more accurate information', 'use the most advanced technology available', 'save the quantity of product packed', or just 'remove long-tolerated inefficiencies' (which related more to the management of work and information flows). The indirect employment policy implications of these goals were only dimly per-ceived initially although they were sometimes realised with hindsight – in respect of job design, or training.

The few examples that we found of any modification of the decision to innovate tended to be related to product market demand or major technology problems. In the past, however, one of our companies had abandoned plans to introduce a materials management system largely because of conflict between various interest groups (including management). It was largely in the process of implementation, how-ever, that employment policies could be said to have become more closely linked to business policy, if only by having to react to it more directly than before.

The problems of time-tabling reveal the assumptions that employ-ment policies are of a 'lower order': that priorities are to meet the needs of customers and thus of shareholders, rather than employees; and that human resources are a means to these ends like other resources. The fact that employees can adapt, or even be hired/fired, at less than optimal speeds is thus either overlooked, or, increasingly seen as a reason for either doing without them or else for increasing the type of organisational controls over them. In many of our cases, it was seen as more important to get the system running somehow, than to complete the training needed for its effective use.

The long-term planning orientation of employment policy

This dimension of employment policy is closely related to the first, since the problems of integrating business policies and employment policies relate particularly to timescale. Other studies have shown that 'long-term strategies are not widespread and even where they exist the relationship between them and day-to-day formulation of demand is not clear' (Beardsworth, 1982).

The timescale of new technology investment could in many instances allow – and even facilitate – manpower planning since preliminary feasibility studies may take up to two years, and from approval of capital investment to the first stage of implementation is likely to take another 2–3 years. However the novelty of the technology makes the uncertainties very high, in terms of both the people and skills likely to be needed, and of the time schedules. 'Slippage' of 6–8 months was fairly normal among our cases, so that those organisations that had attempted to plan their redundancy or training programmes well ahead sometimes tended to face new problems. Planning ahead in terms of 'awareness training' for managers, or for other employees or in simply communicating what was happening and what was planned was, however, found in some of our cases. Moreover a few of the senior managers whom we interviewed were grappling with the need to plan ahead and did have some vision of the medium-term (3–5 years) manpower future – even if no explicit strategy existed to achieve it. This lack of strategy might be a function of lack of ability or experience in this type of management, or it might be the reverse – the experience of the futility of employment planning in the past, reinforced by a current situation of doubly high uncertainty – unproven technology and volatile markets. More often it arose out of lack of awareness, or lack of responsibility, resulting partly from organisational structures and functional roles: there was no clear-cut responsibility for devising and implementing organisation-wide employment policies; line managers had responsibility only for their own departments, while personnel managers may have had a wider remit but no powers of implementation.

The significance of the personnel function

The changing role of the personnel function has been a continual topic of discussion within the professional and academic literature. There seems to be some broad consensus emerging about it being 'advisory' rather than 'executive' and also about the personnel manager becoming more of the 'organisational consultant' with responsibility for planning organisation change and organisation structure (Thomason, 1979). Whether there is a functional definition of the role has also been questioned: if emphasis is also put on the importance of an appropriate relationship between the business policy and the personnel policies of an organisation then the position of the personnel director may be organisationally rather than functionally determined. Recent London School of Economics research has tended to show this (Thurley, 1981; Guest and Horwood, 1980), and it fits in more easily with the 'contingency' role envisaged by Legge (1978) and others who have sought to examine what personnel managers actually do (Watson, 1977; Guest and Horwood, 1980). This approach is, however, subject to some of the other unsatisfactory aspects of any contingency approach to organisations (Wood, 1979) if it ignores the realities of power and interplay between interest groups in shaping organisation roles and policies.

While the needs of implementing technological change would seem to call for the planning, consultancy and 'OD' skills of the personnel specialist (IPM, 1981) – and the fact that she/he exists in a company may mean that no-one else sees themselves as responsible for this – yet at the same time, because she/he is seen in an advisory capacity, she/he cannot make the executive decisions that are often needed to ensure redeployment and obtain more effective utilisation of manpower.

Thus in many of our cases the role of the personnel function was still reactive rather than proactive, concerned more with implementing redundancy or resourcing training than planning ahead and setting employment policy criteria which those responsible for the design and implementation of new technology would have to take into account. Even these specifically 'personnel' activities become the responsibility of line or systems managers in some instances.

The usual pattern adopted once the investment decision had been taken (frequently after a preliminary feasibility study, at the initiative of the Board, the Managing Director or a marketing director) was for a detailed system design to be undertaken and application programmes developed, followed by a phased implementation programme. In most of our cases there was a senior cross-functional coordinating committee overseeing those stages with a much smaller team responsible for the actual application design and implementation process (Kochhar, 1979). The personnel director was usually represented on the top level committee but the implementation team was mainly 'management services' or 'systems' staffed with either the line manager responsible or another manager specially seconded to it for liaison purposes. In some cases a trainer might be brought in at a later stage or the personnel manager invited to attend but in several cases the driving force remained the systems specialist or line manager. If the personnel manager, or training officer, did not have sufficient 'systems' understanding (or even personnel credibility) there seemed little point in training them first — it seemed more practicable to train employees directly.

Occasionally they may have seen themselves in a 'mediator' role (Francis and Willman, 1981) — achieving a rought 'fit' between the decisions of systems analysts and engineers and the existing patterns and practices of work, but this seemed as likely to relate back to the strength of trade unions as to the power or ability of the personnel manager (Batstone, 1980).

In a few cases personnel managers seemed so sensitive to trade union reactions as to block the preference of some line managers for more direct and open communication with employees because of their fears of provoking confrontation, or at least negotiating claims, from unions. Thus in non-unionised companies the personnel manager was less likely to play a central role in implementing technological change.

An employee-centred philosophy

Appropriate indicators of the extent to which new technology influenced employment policies in this respect may be derived from managerial statements, analysis of the way in which communications were handled, and the approach to systems design and job design.

Most of our unionised companies had a strong paternalist tradition which had over the past decade evolved to a cautious pluralist style (Poole et al., 1982). The non-unionised companies we studied tended to have a more explicit employee centred philosophy and to work at employee communication. But some unionised companies were also giving more attention to direct communication and in some instances the implementation of new technology appeared to be either the impetus, or the means, since the 1982–3 climate of 'industrial relations wisdom' in which the managing directors and personnel managers operate stresses this. Companies studied in the second phase of our research thus tended to be more likely to give attention to communication than those in the first phase (1980–81), although sometimes this was because companies themselves were into a second or third phase of technological change and had learnt from their earlier mistakes. Experience in handling change tended to increase confidence in communicating: otherwise a philosophy that 'communications must go down the line' means that if the top of line waits to say anything until it has sufficient knowledge, there is considerable delay before information percolates through to those most directly affected, even if rumours abound.

Some companies made major efforts to inform, and even consult with employees from an early stage (confections, electronics, allergens, heaters, engines, print, utility, insurance) by means of an address by top management, video, letter to employees, company newspapers, etc. Sometimes this was only done in the early stage, followed by a gap as delays arose in implementation. A few made further efforts at keeping managers and supervisors informed and helping them to communicate regularly with employees, others left responsibility for doing this to the implementation teams.

In some respects communications policies merged with training policies (see below) if companies defined 'training' in broad terms to include 'education', 'attitude change', 'understanding' or even 'propaganda'. At electronics, for example, a training officer was given some systems training herself and then made responsible for a broad policy of communications and training which ranged from writing employee booklets (one introduced the system as a new employee) to arranging in-house and suppliers courses. This company gave particular attention to management communications and involvement since the Managing Director saw this as critical to wider employee attitude change, and made an employee-centred philosophy explicit (although not at the expense of profit orientation). Another US-owned company which was seeking to work gradually towards a long-term programme of technological change, was emphasising an 'OD' approach, and in one plant the planning of both technical and manpower aspects of change (mainly new layout of the production line and movement of parts) were the responsibility of the workgroup.

The extent to which there is an employee-centred approach may also be seen in the way in which systems — and then jobs — were designed. When asked how employees' needs affected their work, most systems designers admitted 'little or none'. This seemed common, regardless of whether a 'bought-in' software package or an 'own design' system was being used. Although it is fashionable for everyone to aim to design a system to be 'user-friendly' this could in practice mean many different approaches depending partly on whether it was assumed that users were morons or intelligent people. This was reflected in the extent to which users were consulted before and during the design process, so that suggestions could be incorporated (i.e. photo products). At allergens considerable time was allowed for discussion with employees since the aim was to design the application of the system (a bought-in package) to fit with current practices, but this had to be abandoned when it was eventually found that nine different ways of booking goods-received were in existence. At drugs, a paternalistic employee-oriented company, a new quantity control system was developed in a very 'mechanistic' style by the Technical Services department, almost single-handed with little or no employee contact, although care was later taken with employee training and familiarisation.

Similarly in many of the office-based information systems also affecting mainly female employees (Murgatroyd, 1982; Crompton and Reid, 1982), there was little user involvement in design or implementation — merely a few hours instructions and practice, before (with luck) and after the system went 'live'. At power tools there was a philosophy of employee involvement, but supervisors (who were to be critically affected by the new materials management system) only became involved in the planning teams half-way through, at their own request.

The extent to which consideration was given to the design of supervisory jobs could be treated as a separate dimension of employment policy as it raises many other issues. The very ambiguity of this role (which has been well documented — see Thurley and Wirdenius, 1973; Child and Partridge, 1982), tended to mean that management gave insufficient thought to it, although in some instances the role was dwindling (and foreseen at electronics) while in others it was changing to become either more technically oriented or else to have more 'team-building' or cost-accounting responsibilities. Companies that gave insufficient training to enable supervisors to meet these new demands, or trained employees before supervisors tended to find problems of supervisory resistance or lack of credibility later: they were beginning to realise this and to take action (e.g. photo products) on it, however, so it is arguable that the introduction of new technology was pushing companies to deal with long-neglected aspects of employment policy.

In office areas, however, and in some warehouses, the main role of supervisors seemed to be in keeping the old system running while the new was implemented.

Managers who were questioned about job-design and job satisfaction admitted that they did not really think in these terms so that such factors would hardly be seen as criteria for implementing new technology (Work Research Unit, 1982). On the other hand they did aim at greater employee flexibility and responsibility so that more emphasis was put on group-working (Kelly, 1980). Office practices had already been reorganised in this way in the customer-service function of utility and the new computerised system was designed to ensure that this was maintained. Elsewhere it was sometimes a function of the way in which training was organised on a modular basis with employees gradually acquiring a wider range of task-skills.

Office employees tended to express greater satisfaction with their new jobs in that they were cleaner, there was less paper-chasing and less inter-personal aggravation. If they were more boring there seemed a fatalistic acceptance of the fact (liquid food). If there was scope for more direct contact with customers, as at insurance and photo products (office section) this was welcomed. Those who did not want to cope with the change of felt their old skills of familiarity with customer 'idiosyncracies', 'fixing things', or knowing the snags in the product were now useless so that they lost status were probably the ones who left of their own accord. In some cases the change was too recent to be fully evaluated, and what managers claimed as evidence of greater employee satisfaction could have been merely 'Hawthorne' effect, which would disappear a year or two later (Blumberg and Gerwin, 1981).

Some attempt was made to look at new jobs along the usual dimensions of variety, autonomy, feedback, social contact and progression (Davis and Taylor, 1972), but management had given very little thought to such questions as whether people would be more tied to their desks or have opportunity for social interaction. Nor was it easy by observation and interpretation to reach general conclusions as to whether jobs had 'improved' in these respects. Thus a greater variety of tasks might well be performed by one individual, such as speaking to a customer, processing an order, and then linking to engineering services, or sending out an insurance policy, but it would all be done at the one desk and through the VDU or telephone. A process operator might be monitoring dials controlling a whole line of different operations rather than one work process on it but not be expected to move far away from the controls. These job changes could also give a sense of autonomy and task identity as well as feedback yet scope for discretion and innovation would be limited — changes needing to be referred to higher authority, even head office.

Forklift truck operators who also input data might have much greater task variety but less autonomy or social contact if their pick-up and distribution routes were optimally determined by computer. In some instances the fact that fewer operators were needed reduced opportunities for social contact, even if interpersonal recriminations were also reduced.

Further 'attitude survey' research is probably needed to explore employee responses to job changes, not only by comparison with what they did before but by the way in which they were beginning to make their own 'adaptations' of the new system. Examples of clerks short-cutting the procedures, making the systems do things that were technically 'impossible', were often quoted to us, occasionally as examples of ingenuity and initiative but more often in managerial terms of 'not realising the new "discipline" needed'. This is supportive of the growing body of evidence in 'the labour process' literature that employee as well as managerial strategies need to be taken into account in analysing any deterministic de-skilling tendencies inherent in the latest wave of technological innovation (Wood, 1982).

Manpower, pay and industrial relations policies

The extent to which new technology influenced employment policies might be expected to be seen most clearly through the effects on the various component policies and the details of their application. Manpower policies — including redundancy, recruitment, utilisation and training — together with pay, trade union relationships and grievances are the most significant of these. Organisational structures and career development processes (Tichy et al., 1982) are among other relevant aspects covered in the research but which are only touched on in this chapter.

Manpower   The stated aim of many companies was to reduce labour costs, chiefly by reducing headcount. Although only two quality control cases experienced no redundancy, the extent of redundancy found was more limited than expected. Where it occurred on a large scale (to the extent of closure, eventually, at heaters), it was more as a result of restructuring or market changes (falling demand) than for technological reasons, although it is not always easy to disentangle these factors and managers preferred to play down technology and redundancy: it seems likely that in some instances redundancies which took place prior to these changes were not entirely unconnected with them. 'Zero-based' reviews in two pharmaceutical companies were already leading to reduction of 'indirects' for example. It also seemed likely that further redundancies lay ahead: in many instances it takes 2–3 years for technology to be fully implemented, 'learning-curves' to take effect and new efficiencies economies realised, before

124

surplus labour is clearly visible. If the market simultaneously increases considerably (as at insurance) numbers may remain stable. The largest anticipated redundancy (20% of the total workforce) was at a pharmaceutical wholesaler where the direct data capture system might replace 300 telesales order takers.

Invariably there was a preference for traditional reliance on natural wastage (particularly of female clerks or packers) and voluntary redundancy, with generous schemes, aimed at attracting early retirement first. Confections was a company that undertook detailed manpower planning projections of the change, anticipating that the new production and packing line would be manned by 46 people out of the 180 on the three lines being replaced. Over the factory as a whole 800 were identified as being likely to be surplus to requirements by 1989. The plans were scheduled to maximise 'natural wastage' reductions, but up to 100 were scheduled for compulsory redundancy in 1982. In view of the very depressed local labour market, and the strong paternalist traditions of the company, it was decided to phase this over a longer period.

Redeployment was envisaged by most companies as a means of avoiding compulsory redundancy, but this normally seemed to mean training people to do their old jobs in a new way. Otherwise it meant greater flexibility of labour, so that workers could be transferred between jobs on a temporary or permanent basis. Sometimes the training programme, or the 'flux' created by change facilitated this and managers who envisaged 'flexibility' as one of the main manpower 'aims' of new technology (as at electronics) looked for opportunities to further it. Those with a more *ad hoc* approach were likely to miss the opportunities — confections only really began to tackle the issue of increased inter-craft (electrical and mechanical) flexibility rather late in the day, gradually achieving the negotiating persistency and providing the training that was needed.

Few examples were found of transfer and retraining for different occupations or departments. This was partly because of lack of management direction (resulting from the 'segmentation' of organisational structures and internal labour markets) (Osterman, 1983; Loveridge, 1983), but it was also a result of pay problems in one case (of clerks who felt they should be paid extra for retraining), or of employee preferences — some older foremen (at electronics) preferred to leave rather than go back to the bench (despite pay protection). At agent older women clerks were encouraged to leave while two young men were taken on to operate the microcomputer (involving some shift working). However, at insurance a few clerks were transferred from accounting to data processing; at power tools six surplus winding shop workers were transferred into assembly.

Recruitment was 'frozen' in most companies we studied with the exception of those who had chosen to start the new technology on a new site (photo products, packet food, mail order) with minimal transfer from old sites, in order to get away from traditional 'job demarcation' attitudes there. Otherwise the only major area of recruitment was that of data processing staff (programmers and analysts in particular) and a few technologists. The costs of these must have more than offset the savings of office staff in some instances, although this type of calculation seems rarely to have been made explicit, partly because of the firms' segmented views of their internal labour markets.

Some companies were deliberately avoiding building up large DP departments by making much more use of bought-in software packages and agency staff. This could be expensive and did not obviate problems caused by key (contract) staff leaving at a critical point in the project. Similar problems could also be found when training was contracted out to consultants or bought in with an equipment or computer suppliers' 'package'.

The extent to which these different methods were used probably related as much to company costing procedures or time pressures for implementation of new technology as to conscious company employment policies. Nevertheless they do provide illustrations of Osterman's thesis (Osterman, 1983) of the coexistence of different labour markets within firms — 'industrial', 'craft' and 'secondary' — and the preference employers have for creating more 'secondary' workers who have broad general skills and are easily redeployed, hired or fired, being tempered by the organisational needs for stability, predictability and realisation of training investment, as well as by employees' own preferences and strategies, so that an 'industrial' labour market of key workers is maintained. In some of the manufacturing companies, for example, considerable thought was given to the selection of those who would work on the new automated lines. On the other hand, some managers who were obtaining 'systems' and 'project implementation' expertise — a new 'quasi-systems manager' were tending to move from an 'industrial' to a 'craft' labour market having acquired more new non company-specific skills. Use of computer contract staff represented unconscious recognition of the occupationally mobile 'craft' features of this segment of the labour force.

Attitudes to *training* thus reflected these internal labour market distinctions. For although training for new technology was often talked of in advance as a major aspect of the innovation, it tended in practice to be treated as a very subordinate issue. As implementation schedules slipped, so the pressures increased for a 'quick and easy' training solution to an anticipated shortfall in skills. And the minimal keyboard, input and 'computer conversation' skills were often acquired remarkably quickly by people of varying ages and skill levels. On the other hand, the mental knowledge, adjustment and understanding required often lagged behind the 'technical' skill requirement and the ability to 'problem-solve' through the system instead of by manual adjustment to the machine or the paperwork, or by a combination of new and old skills (telephone conversation, typing, and interpretation of stock availability data on visual display unit) took a very much longer time than anticipated. In some cases remedial training was provided, in others the shortfalls were only realised in retrospect after a period of stress and errors, both human and technical. The need for extensive training in new technical engineering skills was not always realised until too late, but was beginning to be looked on as a different scale from that of operators or clerks. Successful acquisition of expertise seemed to relate both to existing skills and experience and to the willingness to accept training as well as the method adopted. Practical, problem-oriented instructions followed by some theoretical explanation tended to be much more effective than more traditional classroom approaches. A major development in the training of technicians, operators and clerks at various levels was, however, the compilation of detailed manuals of all aspects of the operation and the likely problems. In some cases this was supplemented by data on visual display units and in general more attempts were being made to use computer based teaching. The shortage of interactive packages and the time and expense of devising in-house ones tended to curtail this, however, unless there was a major programme of sequential implementation at every district office in a region, as at utility. There a mobile caravan training unit could be set up as a training office at each site in turn and clerks given practice on a simulated system.

Management as an 'industrial' labour market in Osterman's categories might normally have been expected to acquire firm specific expertise through internal development and progression: since the scale of new technology innovation supercedes much of this previous learning new 'generalist' appreciation courses, and even 'specific' technical courses were realised to be needed in some instances. At insurance new junior management courses in the skills of the business – actuarial and commercial – had to be developed since they could no longer be expected to acquire the understanding through working their way up through the business and different departments; the day-to-day expertise was in the system and could be acquired by a school leaver within a matter of weeks as a clerk.

Questions of 'deskilling' and 'reskilling' are thus no more easily answered than those of job design and are closely related to it (Braverman, 1974; Wood, 1982). The four factors of 'task', 'technology', 'skill' and 'training' can be combined in many different ways, depending on a range of other variables such as scheduling, individual preferences or values about 'men's' and 'women's' work to name but a few. Definitions of 'skill' like those of 'training' were rarely made explicit but obviously included both objective and subjective criteria, such as 'techniques', 'understanding' and 'the right sort' (Oliver and Turton, 1982). Thus whether new jobs are seen as 'more' or 'less' skilled will depend on the definition of the observer or the actor. More simplistically, it is perhaps helpful to speak in terms of 'horizontal' and 'vertical' dimensions of skill: an engineering maintenance craftsman may acquire more 'vertical' skills by adding 'electrical', yet have a narrower range of 'horizontal' skills if these are only performed within one particular department. In this respect managerial goals of 'flexible labour utilisation' may also have inherent contradictions. Similar problems could be found with pay: to avoid increases in labour costs through parity claims, occupational differentiation between even low skilled work groups was sometimes deliberately protected by management, suggesting that control of labour costs was more important than labour flexibility in most circumstances. Employees too tended to put more emphasis on protecting or improving the 'extrinsic' rather than 'intrinsic' benefits of work in the last resort, if it came to be a negotiated issue.

Pay   Management principles stressed 'we don't pay for change', 'no payment for training' (particularly when the job became 'easier') but individual managers often admitted that it seemed fair that employees should get some share in the benefits of higher productivity. (At engines, OD savings were split three ways between customer, company and worker; site assembly workers got £8 a week extra.) Thus in practice some small increase was awarded in many cases although in some it was combined with the annual increase, or in one it was calculated as an overtime supplement during the training period, since training was done in addition to normal working (even if no overtime was actually worked). Where there were likely to be large 'knock on' effects in terms of claims based on traditional comparability, or differentials, with other occupational groups, then management tended to take a harder line, as in one dispute between packers, assemblers and materials controllers. The job description was changed significantly to evade the issue of regrading as a result of changed technology.

In several cases, new job evaluations were needed and some innovatory practices were found in the new linkages then established between training and skill standards achieved and career progression (though limited) to slightly higher pay grades. New shift working patterns necessitated by new process technology at one manufacturer led to a prolonged pay dispute with the craft unions, but hardly any other examples were found of changes to working hours, associated with the new technology, being introduced.

Industrial relations Apart from redundancy, pay issues were the major concern of trade unions involved in negotiating change, in so far as they were aware of and/or involved in what was happening. Their traditional (apart from craft unions) lack of involvement in task, training and job design issues meant that they could easily be out-manoeuvred by management's gradual introduction of new equipment (Tipton, 1979; Robins and Webster, 1981). No examples were found of total refusals to work the new system although threats were made and some short-term stoppages experienced. In most cases these were resolved by agreeing a 'price', and but for the exigiencies of recession, this would probably have been much higher, and more examples were found in 1981 than 1982. Thus managerial prerogatives and a strategy of opposition to new technology agreements, on the grounds that the principles of them were already included in existing agree-ments, were successfully maintained (except in the public utility, where there was a much more 'pluralistic' approach). Consultation with unions tended to be differently interpreted from consulting with employees, by limiting its extent.

In general, therefore, as a result of recession as much as managerial competence one suspects, industrial relations problems were not widely experienced, and non-unionised companies do not seem to have had any major advantages. They saw their chief advantage as being able to implement change more quickly yet they were often more willing to consult employees than the unionised companies did. The Board of packet foods was so concerned to avoid 'industrial relations' knock-on effects in the new plant from redundancies at another (unionised) plant in a different part of the country, that recruitment and training were delayed to an extent that nearly jeopardised the whole implementation programme.

Grievance and disciplinary disputes tended to diminish once the automated systems were operating, although the scope for management control was greater. While it took some time for new 'work disciplines' to be instilled and the serious repercussive effects of mistakes in data-entry to be realised, employees seemed less resentful of being blamed for their own (attributable) errors than for faults that were largely the responsibility of others and which caused a general climate of recrimination and poor industrial relations.

Conclusions

New technology has undoubtedly had some impact on company employment policies in necessitating a closer linkage with the business and a more future oriented planning dimension. It has done little to enhance the significance of the personnel function but has made some more sophisticated systems and line managers give greater attention to 'employment' issues: whether this necessarily means a more employee-oriented philosophy may be doubted — but at least some of their original technico/rational assumptions appear to have been modified. Some changes have been stimulated in the manpower practices of the cases studied so that different labour force profiles are emerging with fewer low skill clerks and operatives (whose training is highly instrumental and largely aimed at increasing their interchangeability), far fewer 'indirects', and a core of experienced operators, technicians and managers who can think in systems terms and for whom organisational career progression is envisaged. Where it is not, contract skills are hired. The size and dimensions of the organisations' various internal labour markets are thus showing signs of change as new 'ceilings and floors' of different occupational groups are being constructed.

On the other hand, some of these changes — the reduction in numbers, and particularly in 'indirects' can be seen to be as much the result of 'cost' and 'market' as of 'technological' pressures since similar patterns are seen in non-innovative organisations. And in many respects the lack of change and innovation that was found in employment policies generally, despite high technological innovation, was striking in view of their reactive rather than proactive nature. It would seem either that the technology is unimportant, or that causality is in the reverse direction: that on balance it is employment policies that are more likely to determine the way in which technological change is implemented, whether by intention or default (Loveridge, 1983; Wynne, 1983). If there is a strong employee centred philosophy then attention is likely to be given to issues of communications and training, job design and redeployment and to either advance planning for them or awareness of the implications of certain implementation packages. If there is not, the technological imperative is likely to take priority and considerable stress be experienced in the process of change (Wynne, 1983). On the other hand, the continuation of traditional employment policies may have some advantages in providing a measure of needed stability and continuity at a time of threatening change and high uncertainty (Gerwin, 1982). A major managerial aim may be to reduce uncertainty: as one manager remarked, 'If I can get away with changing three things, rather than six, I'll do that, because people can't take too much'.

Yet one suspects that opportunities for beneficial innovation are being missed through the lack of a strategic employment policy perspective. Pouring new wine into old bottles has long been a risky practice.

References

Bachrach, P. and Baratz, M.S., 'Two Faces of Power', *American Political Science Review*, 56, 1962.

Batstone, E., 'What have Personnel Managers done for Industrial Relations?', *Personnel Management*, June 1980, pp.36–9.

Beardsworth, A. et al., 'Employers' Strategies in Relation to their Demand for Labour', *Industrial Relations Journal*, 13, 1982, pp.44–55.

Blumberg, M. and Gerwin, D., 'Coping with Advanced Manufacturing Technology', IIM/LMP: Berlin, 1981, pp.81–112.

Braverman, H., *Labor and Monopoly Capital*, Monthly Review Press: New York, 1974.

Child, J., 'Organisation Structure, Environment and Performance: The Role of Strategic Choice', *Sociology*, 6, 1971, pp.1–22.

Child, J., 'Culture, Contingency and Capitalism in the Cross-National Study of Organisations', in Staw, B.M. and Cummings, L.L. (eds), *Research and Organisational Behaviour*, vol. III, 1980, JAI Press.

Child, J. and Partridge, B., *Lost Managers*, Cambridge University Press: London, 1982.

Commission of Industrial Relations, *The Role of Management in Industrial Relations*, Report no. 34, HMSO: London, 1973.

Crompton, R. and Reid, S., 'The De-skilling of Clerical Work', in Wood, S. (ed.), *op cit.*, 1982.

Cuthbert, N.H. and Hawkins, K.H. (eds), *Company Industrial Relations Policies*, Longmans: London, 1973.

Davies, L.E. and Taylor, J.C. (eds), *Design of Jobs*, Penguin, Modern Management Readings: Harmondsworth, 1972.

Department of Employment, *Industrial Relations Code of Practice*, HMSO: London, paras. 24–50.

Francis, A. and Willman, P., 'Microprocessors: Impact and Response', *Personnel Review*, 9, 1980.

Galbraith, J. and Nathanson, D., *Strategy Implementation: The Role of Structure and Process*, West Publishing: St. Paul MN, 1978.

Gerwin, D., 'Case Studies of Computer Integrated Manufacturing

Systems: A View of Uncertainty and Innovation Processes', *Journal of Operations Management*, 2, 1982, pp.87–99.

Guest, D. and Horwood, R., *Role and Effectiveness of Personnel Managers*, Nancy Seear Fellowship Personnel Management Research Programme, Report no. 1, London School of Economics, 1980.

Henley Centre for Employment Policy Studies, *Employment Policies and Company Planning: The Role of the Personnel Director*, (unpublished Workshop manual), 1980.

Hunter, L.C., *Labour Shortages and Manpower Policy*, Manpower Services Commission, HMSO: London, 1978.

Institute of Personnel Management, *Personnel Policies and New Technology*, IPM: London, 1981.

Kelly, J., 'The Cost of Job Redesign', *Industrial Relations Journal*, 11, 1980, pp.22–35.

Kochhar, A.K., *Development of Computer-Based Production Systems*, Edward Arnold: London, 1979.

Legge, K., *Power, Innovation and Problem-solving in Personnel Management*, McGraw Hill: Maidenhead, 1978.

Loveridge, R., 'Sources of Diversity in Internal Labour Markets', *Sociology*, 17, 1983, pp.44–62.

Ministry of Labour and National Service, *Positive Employment Policies*, HMSO: London, 1958.

Murgatroyd, L., 'Gender and Occupational Stratification', *Sociological Review*, 30, 1982.

National Economic Development Office, *Case Studies in Manpower Planning*, NEDO: London, 1978.

Oliver, J.M. and Turton, J.R., 'Is there a Shortage of Skilled Labour?', *British Journal of Industrial Relations*, 20, 1982, pp.195–200.

Osterman, P., 'Employment Structures within Firms', *British Journal of Industrial Relations*, 20, 1983, pp.349–61.

Perrow, C., *Organisational Analysis: A Sociological View*, Tavistock: London, 1970.

Poole, M., et al., 'Managerial Attitudes and Behaviour in Industrial Relations', *British Journal of Industrial Relations*, 20, 1982, pp.285–307.

Robins, K. and Webster, F., 'New Technology: A Survey of Trade Union Response in Britain', *Industrial Relations Journal*, 13, 1982, pp.7–26.

Sleigh, J., et al., *Manpower Implications of Micro Electronic Technology*, Department of Employment, HMSO: London, 1979.

Taylor, B. and Hawkins, K., *Handbook of Strategic Planning*, Longmans: London, 1972.

Thomason, G., *A Textbook of Personnel Management*, IPM: London, 1979.

Thurley, K., 'Personnel Management in the UK — A Case for Urgent Treatment?', *Personnel Management*, 13, 1981, pp.24–9.

Thurley, K. and Wirdenius, H., *Supervision: A Reappraisal*, Heinemann: London, 1973.

Tichy, N. et al., 'Strategic Human Resource Management', *Sloan Management Review*, Winter 1982, pp.47—60.

Tipton, B., 'The Quality of Training and the Design of Work', *Industrial Relations Journal*, 13, Spring 1979, pp.27—42.

Trist, E., *Evolution of Socio-Technical Systems*, Quality of Work Life Center, Ontario: Occasional Paper, no. 2, 1981.

Watson, A., *The Personnel Managers*, Routledge and Kegan Paul: London, 1977.

Wood, S., 'A Reappraisal of the Contingency Approach to Organisations', *Journal of Management Studies*, October 1979.

Wood, S. (ed.), *The Degradation of Work?*, Hutchinson: London, 1982.

Woodward, J., *Management and Technology*, HMSO: London, 1958.

Woodward, J., *Industrial Organisation: Behaviour and Control*, Oxford University Press: London, 1970.

Work Research Unit, 'Key Human Factors in Manufacturing Industry', Reg Sell, *WRU Occasional Paper*, 21, 1982.

Wynne, B., 'Redefining the Issues of Risk and Public Acceptance', *Futures*, February 1983, pp.13—32.

7 Training for automation
Peter Senker

Introduction

The British Government has pointed out that 'New technology offers us the chance to become more productive and to create new and better jobs selling goods and services to the rest of the world'. They have initiated a 'Programme for Action' designed to create 'a better educated and more adaptable workforce' in order for the country to be able to take that 'opportunity' (Department of Employment, 1981). This programme is based on the Government's acceptance of the main objectives set out by the Manpower Services Commission earlier on the same year. In summary, the aims of this 'New Training Initiative' are:

1   To reform skill training, including achievement of training based on standards rather than time, to create flexibility in the age of entry into apprenticeship.
2   To create more opportunities for people under the age of 18 to continue in full-time education, or to combine training, work-experience and education.
3   To create widespread opportunities for adults to retrain.

The main emphasis so far has been on the second objective — specifically providing training for unemployed teenagers. The Government has allocated a very substantial sum — about £1 billion — to fund the MSC's plans for a Youth Training Scheme (YTS) to provide training to about 460,000 unemployed teenagers.

One of the principal problems British industry faces in its struggle to become more competitive is learning to use automation more effectively. This chapter examines some of the problems of relating training programmes to the needs of industry, with particular reference to manufacturing industry's needs for skills to cope with automation. Service industry skill needs are of growing importance – and in quantitative terms at least – of even greater importance than the needs of manufacturing industry. Nevertheless, some of the issues considered here are likely to be relevant to service industries, if only because, increasingly, they too need to learn to live with automation.

What is automation?

The term 'automation' was originally used by the Ford Motor Company to describe sophisticated handling and transfer mechanisms. Its use has been extended to include all uses of mechanisms and electronics to perform the information-processing functions of the control cycle associated with a process. One of the most important applications has been in the machining of batches of metal components. Numerically controlled machine tools (NC) were introduced in the 1950s. An NC machine is controlled by punched tape which activates relays and electrical circuits which instruct the cutting tool to shape a piece of metal in accordance with the punched tape program. Computer numerical control machine tools (CNC), introduced in the early 1970s, are controlled by a minicomputer which can be programmed either by specialist technicians or by operators themselves (manual data input).

Direct numerical control (DNC) involves linking groups of machines to a central computer which receives data – e.g. on work completed and interruptions of production – which can be used for computer scheduling and production control. A whole series of operations involved in the production of a component can be completed one after another, avoiding the need to store part-finished components while they wait for successive operations. Components can be made in sets rather than batches. Soon after a set of components has been made, it can be assembled into a final product. This means that metalworking factories no longer need to be littered with bins of finished and part-finished components waiting to be processed and assembled. The savings in terms of work-in-progress can run into millions of pounds. Probably the most advanced DNC system in Britain is at Normalair Garrett in Crewkerne, sponsored by the Department of Industry. The system was installed to produce ejector release units for ordnance and fuel tanks for the Tornado military aircraft. Very complex, precisely machined components are produced in sets. At the end of a machining cycle, a complete set of parts is available for assembly into an ejector release unit. There are plans to convert this into a flexible manufacturing system (FMS). An FMS system is one in which workpieces are transported automatically — by robots or pallet transfer — between DNC controlled machine tools.

Industrial robots can be programmed to manipulate and transport parts or tools through a variable sequence of movements. They are already used in car body welding, for paint spraying and for handling workpieces into and out of machine tools, presses and plastics injection moulding machines.

Engineers have used computers to assist with design calculations for a long time. The use of computer-aided design (CAD) began to increase rapidly in Britain in the late 1970s when relatively cheap 'turnkey' interactive graphics systems began to become available. In principle, a 'turnkey' system is one which the user can buy, install, plug in, 'turn the key' and obtain useful production drawings. It is never anywhere as easy as this, but suppliers have made substantial progress in making systems easy to use by designers or draughtsmen without computer experience.

Skill implications of automation

Management

Evaluation of the costs and benefits of investment in new technology has presented managements with serious problems continually. There were reports of such problems in the 1970s in relation to individual numerically controlled machine tools. But advanced automation offers firms increased flexibility and responsiveness to changing demand patterns. Such benefits are often not confined to the department in which automated machines are installed: for example, increased responsiveness can enable a firm to offer a given standard of delivery service while carrying a much smaller inventory of work-in-progress and finished goods stocks.

In relation to CAD, Arnold and Senker (1982) found that very few companies had recognised its full strategic implications. In most companies, CAD investment proposals had been approved on the basis of anticipated short-term savings in draughtsman employment costs. But potential savings in the time necessary for design or redesign were frequently of considerable strategic importance. Failure to get a new product range to market in time could put a substantial amount of business in jeopardy. Many firms realised that it was most important to gain experience with CAD, and then to benefit from its use. Nevertheless, the majority of those who had to prepare formal investment appraisals justified the proposed purchase in terms of potential savings of the costs involved in employing draughtsmen directly or on contract. Such appraisals often relied heavily on information provided by systems suppliers generally envisaging draughtsman productivity gains of the order of 3:1 compared with manual draughting. They were often prepared by design management who were not in a position to appraise its strategic significance for the firm as a whole. Investment appraisals generally made no allowance for the time it might take for firms to learn to use CAD, but we found that it generally took some time to learn to use CAD effectively.

When once a CAD system was ordered, establishments went through three fairly distinct stages in learning to use it. In stage 1, the CAD system was delivered, installed and used for experimental purposes. In stage 2, the system was used for production drawings, but not yet very efficiently. In stage 3, the system was used at today's state of the art — i.e. typically, operator productivity improvements of the order of 3:1 compared with manual methods were achieved on production drawings. On average, firms took about two years to reach stage 3 and all the firms which had had their first system delivered more than three years before had reached stage 3 by the time of the interview in 1982. However, if no undue delay was experienced, firms could often reach stage 3 in about a year.

Managerial inefficiency was a significant factor in delaying effective use of CAD, particularly in the mechanical engineering industry. Other factors besides managerial inefficiency were important in causing delays: for example, CAD system suppliers sometimes failed to deliver adequate software. In addition, in the motor and aircraft industries, in particular, delays were often caused by industrial relations problems: some were partly the result of design office management's lack of training and experience in dealing with industrial relations, but not all.

Managing a computer system was often a new experience for drawing office management. In addition to the need to deal with training and industrial relations, the workload, access to the machine and housekeeping all needed to be organised. In order to get good use out of the system, a data-base of standard components and standard procedures must be set up and the instruction 'menu' adapted to the firm's particular needs. Many users found it helpful to appoint one individual to be responsible for this. CAD often provided an impetus to reorganise drawing and related activities. At one firm, a new drawing numbering system was adopted for use on both the CAD system and the firm's mainframe computer. This permitted parts list processing to be done on the mainframe computer. Several firms failed to get full benefits as quickly as they might have done because of slowness or failure in these respects. For example, one firm had not yet put standard parts into their data-base; it was also severely hampered in the first six months by its failure to appoint a CAD manager.

In principle, the output from CAD equipment can be used to control production processes directly. This has already been done extensively in the electronics industry, where techniques of using the output from CAD processes to drive manufacturing processes is the only way of making very intricate but very small products. In particular, generating masks for complex microelectronics circuits — large scale integration and very large scale integration (LSI and VLSI) — and manufacturing printed circuit board artwork involves manipulating light or laser beams to produce and superimpose 2D designs. But progress in linking CAD with production processes in mechanical engineering has been much slower. This is partly because this involves adding other data — feeds, speeds, tool offsets and so on — to the output from CAD terminals; and partly because implementing such links involves the purchase of new, expensive, computer-controlled machine tools in toolmaking departments, so that these departments are equipped to use CAD output. Not only does this involve heavy capital expense, it also involves closer coordination between design and toolmaking departments. This strategic need has not generally been appreciated yet by senior managements in British companies. Design managers were heavily involved in the initial selection of a CAD system supplier. Particularly in the mechanical engineering industry, it is probable that insufficient weight in selection was accorded to the future need to use the output from CAD to control manufacturing processes. Design managers may not have been aware that some suppliers' CAD equipment could be used more readily for this purpose.

Strategic benefits offered by CAD are, therefore, reductions in design lead-times and the possibility it offers for future integration with manufacturing processes. Use of CAD can result in substantial increases in drawing productivity. But there is a danger of according insufficient attention to the long-term benefits of CAD/CAM, in comparison with possibilities of making short-term reductions in design costs.

Design skills

Further rapid diffusion of CAD is likely for several reasons: several existing users have found that CAD offers significant benefits for their competitiveness, including substantailly shortened lead-time, increased draughtsman productivity and better tender documentation prepared more quickly. Such users are likely to add substantially to

138

their CAD installations. Knowledge of successful applications is spreading rapidly through the industry via personal contacts, journals, exhibitions and conferences and particularly through the marketing efforts of systems suppliers. Over time, CAD is becoming increasingly good value for money. As more and better software is written, systems are becoming more versatile and efficient.

Until recently, CAD was being installed in an environment of a continuing shortage of draughtsmen. But recession reduced the demand for most skills — including those of draughtsmen — and resulted in the disappearance of all but isolated regional shortages of them. The status of the drawing office and its role in engineering career progression have changed considerably over the past thirty years or so. In the past, the aspiring apprentice tried to get into the drawing office because it offered white collar status together with a good chance of promotion and entry into management. But, it is generally believed in the industry now that promotion out of the drawing office has become more difficult. More widespread use of CAD is likely to reduce the need for more junior detail draughtsmen. Increasingly, engineers and design draughtsmen can themselves produce detail drawings as by-products by utilising the strengths of CAD in routine and repetitive drawing.

As well as junior draughtsmen, other lower level drawing office jobs are also threatened by CAD. During the last twenty years or so, technical changes in drawing materials, reprographics and microfilming have gradually eroded tracing jobs, and most remaining tracers' jobs are likely to be eliminated by CAD. The data processing capabilities of CAD (parts-listing, etc.) threaten clerical jobs.

Although these trends are fairly clear, it has to be admitted that it is extraordinarily difficult to predict the longer term implications of CAD for the organisation of design activities and for the jobs of draughtsmen, engineers and others involved in the design process. It is even more difficult to predict the skills needed to link CAD with production processes successfully. Very little thought has been given to such problems so far — the adoption and use of CAD has involved a substantial amount of 'muddling through'. Far more careful thought and analysis will be necessary if appropriate training programmes are to be developed.

Production, programming and supervisory skills

British managements have been too inclined to look to new technology to dispense with the need for workforce skills, rather than as providing an opportunity for developing those skills and using them more effectively. The same problems recur regularly in Britain as firms struggle to come to terms with each successive generation of automation. British management often use new technology as an ally in their struggle to organise work so as to deskill craftsmen. In contrast, West German engineers and managers are more inclined to utilise and develop their craftsmen's skills in order to use new technology effectively.

Some British managements use automation to try to wrest control of production from shopfloor workers. Barry Wilkinson (1981) quotes the works manager of a plating firm: 'some operators use the manual override if you don't watch them . . . it's a bad habit. It's difficult to get it into their heads that automatic is the best way . . .'. Workers prefer manual partly because they believe they can produce a better quality job and partly because it gives them some relief from machine pacing. 'We can slow down a bit when they are not looking'. A machine shop production engineer suggested that: 'The further use of CNC in the machine shop will reduce the need for operator skill . . . by taking the control of the machining away from the operator, a more consistent performance will result'. An operator agreed: 'They're paid to program, we're paid to operate, and the two should be kept separate unless they want to pay me more'. Wilkinson admits that not all managers want to deskill work so as to gain more control over it. A production manager of an optical company complained to him about new machinery 'there's no training needed to operate this, so it's deskilling the job and I don't like that, I like to train somebody'.

A few British machine shop foremen and superintendents are keen not to waste operators' skills. Some CNC machines are specifically designed for shopfloor manual data input. CNC machining centres, designed for 'office' programming, can, with a little ingenuity, be programmed on the shopfloor using tape editing facilities. A foreman thought that it was 'a waste of operators' skills if they just stand and watch'. Operators often want to 'use skills', 'gain work satisfaction', 'maintain self-respect'. The British tradition of using automation in the attempt to wrest control from workers frustrates such natural desires and results in lower productivity.

German firms often assign the task of programming CNC machine tools to skilled shopfloor craftsmen. British firms more often use specialist white collar planning departments (Sorge et al., 1983). Craftsmen at one British firm had changed programs on the shopfloor. Management reaction was to lock off the controls to stop operators 'tampering' with them. In contrast, management in two German firms stressed the need to make use of shopfloor intelligence to speed jobs up, to reduce downtime and maintain quality. German foremen were heavily involved in the introduction of CNC, while in Britain, they tended to be bypassed. In Germany, foremen are expected to know all about operating, programming, speeds and feeds, while in Britain, a foreman's lack of knowledge about what was going on could result in turnround times three or more times longer than they should be.

Exceptionally, a British foreman was sent on a course and said that 'by fiddling around, by modifying things a bit, I can get out of 75% of my problems'.

Maintenance skills

In a study of 48 engineering plants, Senker et al., (1981) found that maintenance was becoming increasingly important. In one factory about one in twenty people were employed in maintenance. By the mid-1980s, as the number of people engaged in production and in other functions decreases, maintenance employment could represent as much as a fifth of much smaller total employment. There are also likely to be relatively more people employed in maintenance in another factory. 'At one time, there used to be an electrician on every floor of a factory, sitting down and smoking most of the time until something went wrong. This was stopped as labour became more expensive. Now, with extremely expensive capital equipment, we are getting back to the point where maintenance labour is relatively cheap'.

The more the production system is automated, the more important it is to avoid machines breaking down — or, if they do break down, the more vital it is to repair them and get them back into production quickly. Manufacturers of automated machinery are very conscious of this and are increasingly relying on cheap, sophisticated electronics to provide automatic diagnostics for machine breakdown. But the trouble is that often the automatic diagnostics does not work properly: or, if it does it only covers a small proportion of the things which could go wrong on a complicated machine. Early experience with DNC systems has demonstrated that faults are difficult to locate — they may occur in machine tools, computers, materials handling systems or in parts being processed.

A senior manager at a firm making large electric motors told us that they had very sophisticated diagnostics on their new computer-controlled machine tools. Some of the diagnostics are carried out by telephone direct to a computer in the US, but the diagnostics only cover the computer controls and their interface with the machine. Many other aspects — bearing vibration, microswitches and solenoid valves, etc. are not yet covered. Forecasting failures is even further off — the manufacturers themselves do not know the life of components. Closer to the shopfloor, a senior maintenance engineer was sceptical: 'The management think that diagnostics are all built in. Just press the button and it will tell you what is wrong'. In practice, only a hundred or so out of a thousand or more items can be checked by the diagnostics.

The electrical foreman at an aerospace plant does not have much faith in automatic diagnostics either. For one fault they had the service engineers down. They ran a diagnostics tape through the control, but this failed to locate the fault. Eventually the service engineer hit upon the fault, but this was despite the diagnostics not because of them. 'The men can find the faults better than the diagnostics can'. The foreman reckons that automatic diagnostics are a sales gimmick rather than of practical use to the maintenance men.

Too often, British managements look to automatic diagnostics to deskill work and to remove the need for training. But successful implementation of automatic diagnostics and associated developments in automation usually demands extensive new training programmes. For example, a modern British motor assembly plant includes in-process monitoring on all overhead conveyors. Digital readouts indicate to maintenance people whether a stoppage is a normal programmed production stoppage or a fault. Automatic equipment incorporating visual display units monitors weld quality. When weld quality deteriorates below acceptable levels, maintenance people are called in. Programmable logic controllers (PLCs) are used throughout. The two principal advantages of PLCs are that they can control processes close to theoretical optima and they facilitate the collection of data — for example on production quantities and control settings. Electricians have been taught to program them at this plant. Fitters have been trained to use electronic diagnostics equipment for fault-finding, and have had to be trained in pneumatics and hydraulics. In the past, several individuals — setters, operators, maintenance engineers — were responsible for keeping machines in operation. If one machine broke down, another could be used. Now, with the total output of a particular plant highly dependent on specialised expensive and complex machines, any downtime is very expensive and very disruptive. The new pattern could be for each machine to be looked after by an individual technician. He would be responsible and accountable for setting, programming, operating and maintaining one machine.

In general, however, British managements are reluctant to face up to the possibility that the use of more complex automated production systems will result in the need for highly trained maintenance people with multiple skills.

The Japanese example

In 1979, impressed by Japanese economic success, the Finniston Committee of Inquiry into the Engineering Profession advocated a major national programme of training and retraining of employees of all ages and at all levels to develop the skills and support needed to implement and sustain new technologies. Since 1979, education and training relevant to industrial needs has been cut sharply in Britain. Since 1973, Japanese industry, its competitiveness bolstered by its world lead in the use of automation, has increased its share of world exports of manufactured goods from 13% to 18%. Even Japan has been affected by the slowdown in world trade since 1973, and their industrial output has only grown by 3% per year since then — but this is much faster than other industrialised countries. As a result of the slow rate of growth of the world economy, Japanese employment in manufacturing is about the same as in 1973 and unemployment has increased but only somewhat.

Britain has automated much more slowly than Japan, partly because we lack the necessary skills. Competitiveness has deteriorated as a result and our industrial production is still below 1973 levels, even though British industry has sold vast quantities of equipment for the development of North Sea oil. We have retained our 9% share of world exports of manufactures, but imports have grown fast. Since 1973, Britain has lost over 2 million jobs in manufacturing — a major element in the quadrupling of unemployment to over 12%.

The Japanese example demonstrates that successful planning and implementation of major automation schemes is dependent on the availability of engineering skills. The Japanese success in gaining economic advantages from the use of advanced FMS machining systems is now well known. But, Blumberg and Gerwin (1981) found that firms in the UK, West Germany and the US all had difficulty in implementing such systems. In these countries, the skills, systems and procedures availabe to firms were inadequate to support new, sophisticated manufacturing systems. In contrast, Yamazaki in Japan invested 100,000 hours in planning their successful 18 machine system, far more than anyone else. The FMS Report (1982) found that Yamazaki were much happier with their systems than were US firms who invested far less in planning.

Widespread use of robots in automatic assembly is on the horizon. Intensive research has been going on in Japan and in major corporations in the US such as IBM, Ford, General Motors, General Electric and Westinghouse, in some cases supported by the National Science Foundation. But getting from the research laboratory into a production environment demands large teams of highly educated and trained computer experts, mechanical and production engineers. In Japanese companies such as Hitachi, such people move with their projects into production, and later move back into research, making possible extensive cross-fertilisation of ideas. Japanese companies deploy and redeploy graduate engineers on a scale inconceivable for most British companies (Swords-Isherwood and Senker, 1980).

Investment in training by large Japanese firms has been described as 'massive' (Ball, 1980). Japanese firms regard technically qualified people as their most valuable asset: 'no effort is spared in ensuring that they are properly equipped to carry out their tasks'. They second their own key people for short periods to their training departments as instructors for various groups of employees, from production line workers to senior managers.

British engineering education and training policy

In Britain there have been powerful advocates of the need to adapt the educational system to the needs of industry for more than a hundred years. This is almost entirely a history of attempts to change the supply of education and training, not the demand for it. Scientists and engineers on successive government committees have advocated substantial increases in scientific and technical education at all levels. Economists have criticised the work of such committees as being motivated by engineers' self interest. Most economists believe that price movements always succeed in bringing supply and demand into equilibrium, and that shortages are generally temporary. If employees needed more expertise, then firms would be prepared to pay for it: the salaries of those possessing this expertise would rise and people would be encouraged to acquire it by the high pay offered. Mace's attack on the Finniston Report is a recent typical example of the conventional economic analysis (Mace, 1980), and such analysis has been a powerful influence on policy. In brief, economists such as Mace assume that businessmen − individual entrepreneurs − know what is the best technique of production to use in order to maximise their profits. They select and buy inputs (land, capital, various grades of labour) which will enable them to achieve this result. Underlying this theory is the assumption that businessmen have perfect knowledge of market conditions and that they select production techniques from a known range of options. This takes no account of firms' needs to use skills to develop new production technologies (and products). It assumes that new technologies are available 'off the shelf'. As firms are assumed to maximise profits in the short term, there is neither scope nor need for strategy. Strategies essentially involve the sacrifice of short-term profits in the hope of long-term benefits − for example, expenditure to build up markets now in order to achieve profits later; expenditure on research and development, education and training now in order to achieve the capability of designing better products or using better production processes later.

Japanese economic success depends partly on the implementation of just such strategies. British training policies seem to be based, in large part, on analysis which denies the necessity − or even possibility − of strategic behaviour by firms. Employers' requirements have become increasingly dominant influences in training policy. This despite the mounting evidence of British employers' short-sighted attitudes towards skills and training (Swords-Isherwood and Senker, 1980).

Several Industrial Training Boards have been abolished. Employers are paying the costs of those such as the Engineering Industry Training Board which remain and have more say in their policies. The Engineering Employers' Federation wished to retain the EITB and approved of employers having a greater say in running it, but wanted it to concentrate exclusively on the training of craftsmen and technicians. Such views are likely to be influential on training policy, although it has been shown in this chapter that the training of engineers and managers is a crucial element in successful adoption of automation.

The British Government is keen to see the implementation of schemes to base the accreditation of craftsmen and technicians on the attainment of standards rather than on the basis of time served by 1985. It will still take a 16 or 17 year old at least three years to attain the knowledge and experience required of a craftsman, although an adult with experience might attain the required standard somewhat more quickly. As the main emphasis of the Government's plans has been on the Youth Training Scheme (YTS) which lasts only for a year, it is difficult to envisage any substantial contribution to fulfilling industry's needs for skills to cope with automation. Pat Dutton (1982) has suggested that the YTS is no substitute for the successful schemes which operate in Germany and other parts of Europe, involving planned and regulated periods of training and study lasting two to four years during which prescribed skills are acquired: when the training is completed successfully, competence is recognised by employers and unions.

Conclusions

The British Government's New Training Initiative may represent a step in the direction of attaining the goal of a 'better educated, better trained and more adaptable workforce'. It will, however, require substantial supplementation if it is to achieve its goals at all fully. A large measure of responsibility for Britain's industrial decline is due to managerial failure to demand the skills necessary to implement technical change. Several examples have been given of deficiencies in firms' ability to implement automation. With rare exceptions, few analysts — whether scientists, engineers or economists — have considered seriously the possibility that deficiencies in industrialists' strategies and demand for skills could be partly responsible for British manufacturing industry's declining competitiveness. Although many enquiries have perceived the need for more technical expertise if industry was to be modernised, governments have not yet made serious, sustained efforts to address the problem of inducing manufacturing industry to demand and train the people it needs to become more competitive.

References

Arnold, E. and Senker, P., *Designing the Future — The Implications of CAD Interactive Graphics for Employment and Skills in the British Engineering Industry*, EITB Occasional Paper no. 9, 1982.

Ball, G.F., 'Report on Vocational Education and Training for Employment in Engineering in Japan', British Council/EITB, 1980.

Blumberg, M. and Gerwin, D., *Coping with Advanced Manufacturing Technology*, IIM/LMP, Berlin, 1981.

Department of Employment, *A New Training Initiative: A Programme for Action*, HMSO: December 1981.

Dutton, P.A., *The New Training Initiative: What are its Chances?*, Institute for Employment Research, Discussion Paper no. 18, May 1982.

Finniston, Sir Montague, (Chairman), *Engineering Our Future*, Report of Inquiry into the Engineering Profession, HMSO: London, January 1980, Cmnd. 7794.

Ingersoll Engineers, *The FMS Report*, IFS (Publications) Ltd: 1982.

Mace, J., 'The Finniston Report: An Economist's View', *Education Policy Bulletin*, 8, 1, Spring 1980.

Senker, P., Swords-Isherwood, N., Brady, T. and Huggett, C., *Maintenance Skills in the Engineering Industry: The Influence of Technological Change*, EITB Occasional Paper no. 8, 1981.

Sorge, A., Hartmann, G., Warner, M. and Nicholas, I., *Microelectronics and Manpower in Manufacturing: Applications of Numerical Control in Great Britain and West Germany*, Farnborough, Gower Press, 1983.

Swords-Isherwood, N. and Senker, P. (eds), *Microelectronics and the Engineering Industry: The Need for Skills*, Frances Pinter Ltd: London, 1980.

Wilkinson, B., 'Technical Change and Work Organisation', Ph.D. Thesis, University of Aston, 1981.

PART TWO

MANPOWER CONSEQUENCES OF NEW TECHNOLOGY

8 Management-union participation during microtechnological change
Annette Davies

Introduction

The repercussions of technological change tend to spread across many traditional subject areas of collective bargaining, such as manning levels, payment and working conditions, and a number of technological change-induced problems are likely to become the focus of management/union concern or conflict. Such 'change' may therefore be viewed as a political and problematic process with the different interest groups in the organisation attempting to achieve their 'preferred outcomes'. The consequences of such change to some extent will depend on or rather will be, those the main interest groups want to have.

This 'indeterministic' quality of technological change is supported by a large number of studies which have examined technology as an important contingency of organisations, and revealed quite different findings. Whereas many may be found to support the position that automation leads to close and coercive supervision (Dubin, 1965; Gruenfeld and Foltman, 1967), there are also an equal number that have suggested that supervision was becoming more participative, open and democratic with the introduction of increasing automation (Blauner, 1964; Woodward, 1965). Similar conflictual findings may be outlined from an examination of the impact of technology on skills (Haselhurst, Bradbury and Corlett, 1971; Wedderburn and Crompton, 1972), work behaviour (Mann and Hoffman, 1960; Goldthorpe et al., 1968) and organisational structure (Janowitz, 1959; Burns and Stalker, 1960; Woodward, 1965). Thus, given a certain

149

technology there are many different ways of organising the work, each of which giving different work situations and optimising different criteria. But, in this 'optimisation' process, the interaction of decision-makers' discretion both in the design of new technologies and the organisation of jobs, requires detailed examination (Davis and Taylor, 1975; Child, 1972; Cooper, 1972).

Technological choice and the discretion of decision-makers

Decision-makers have wide discretionary powers both in the design and implementation of new technologies, and in recent years, there has been a strong movement urging that such discretion be directed towards improving the quality of working life. A number of studies have sought to highlight the social principles which should underlie technological designs, and the type of manpower policies to be utilised during the process of introduction, in order to achieve this objective.

It has been stated that engineers should consciously provide individual workers with opportunities for increased skill, problem-solving, control, personal development and social relationships (Mumford, 1977). One needs to ascertain the psychosocial purposes and assumptions that are incorporated into technological systems, for as pointed out by Davis (1971), 'the engineers' assumptions about man, which underlie their designs, are often horrific'. There are also a number of policies and strategies which management may use to solve the manpower problems that technological change may give rise to, and to aid the labour transition from one technical system to another. For example, the Department of Employment, in a paper on the employment effects of micro-technology, emphasised quite strongly the availability 'of alternatives to labour reduction', and, like others (Dey, 1980), point to the Japanese as a notable example of how maximum exploitation of new technology can be combined with reasonable guarantees of continuing employment for the labour force. Also, manpower planning is seen as an essential element of any future integrated personnel policy dealing with the types of changes which are likely to be produced by microprocessors (Thornton and Routledge, 1980). Its importance was illustrated in a comparative study between British and German companies, which showed how a 'crisis' model of change seems to have been commonly adopted by British companies. The custom of 'letting things drift' and the accumulation of years of neglect, forced drastic changes which could only be carried through by confrontation (Jacobs et al., 1979). Other policies such as retraining, worksharing and the reduction of hours and overtime are also believed to be subject to management discretion,

150

and while such schemes may not initially appear cost-effective, it is argued that they hold many advantages for management. Retraining for example, would help to reduce the number of employees surplus to requirements by preparing them for redeployment into other jobs and situations, and it could also reduce the need for the employment of outside specialists, who may be in short supply and very expensive. Worksharing schemes may also be beneficial to management in terms of reduced absenteeism and turnover and greater manpower flexibility (Blyton and Hill, 1981).

However, any suggestions that managerial discretion during technological change will be concerned with the retention of labour and the improvement of the quality of working life, are strongly refuted by those who point to the 'social bias' of technological change in a capitalist society. According to Braverman (1974) and Friedman (1977), the development of new machinery is shaped by a desire to increase managerial control, which is achieved by the separation of conception from the execution of an activity. Knowledge of the machine becomes a specialist trait segregated from the actual machine operators. The pace at which the machine operates becomes a clearer managerial prerogative, as control over that pace is centralised and often removed from the site of production to the planning office (Friedman, 1977). Indeed, there are both historical and contemporary examples of how manufacturers of new technologies have attempted to sell their products by emphasising these aspects of control.

In the *Philosophy of Manufacturers*, written by Andrew Ure in 1835, there are vivid descriptions of how manufacturers oppressed by militant unions and unable to control workers by reducing wages, were led to use technological innovations for this purpose. One example of this was the development of the 'self-acting mule', when factory strikes in various towns in the Midlands led local factory owners to ask a firm of machinists in Manchester, 'to direct the inventive talents of their master to the construction of the self-acting mule, in order to emancipate the trade from galling slavery and impending ruin'. More recently, Noble (1979) believed that there was no question that management in the United States saw in numerically controlled (NC) machines the potential to enhance their authority over production and seized upon it. For example, in one trade journal article entitled, 'How can new machines cut costs?', the Landis machine company stressed the fact that with modern automatic controls, the production pace is set by the machine, not by the operator. Also, in relation to the new micro-electronic equipment, an IBM official has been quoted as saying: 'People will adapt nicely to office systems if their arms are broken, and we are in the twisting stage now'. The implications of these findings alert us to the fact that the new technologies may be used to reduce rather than enhance the quality of working life.

However, managerial discretion in these matters does not operate in isolation, and as well as economic and technological restraints, trade union interest has been shown to have an important influence (Lazonick, 1979; Hunter, Reid and Body, 1969). There are many examples of various kinds of workshop restrictions which may be imposed by unions on management and which significantly affect the development and utilisation of new technologies. These restrictions, which include rules regulating the manning of machines, inter-union job allocations, the nature and scope of work study, the recruitment of skill dilutees and levels of output and earnings per employee, form part of a considerable literature which now exists on the industrial relations aspects of technological development (Abbott, 1978; Scott et al., 1956; Jacobs, 1980).

Trade union interest

Since the late 1950s the British trade union movement has attempted to establish technological change as a major issue for collective bargaining. A special report on automation issued by the Trade Union Congress (TUC) in 1956, stated,

> 'Benefits from automation will not come automatically, nor can problems be left to sort themselves out as best they may, or from the trade union point of view be left to management to deal with. There is a strong insistence by the unions therefore, that all questions pertaining to automation — as with any industrial matter — must be discussed and negotiated through the appropriate machinery in each industry.'

In 1965, the TUC issued a further statement on automation and technological change, demanding that full consideration be given to the effect of these proposed changes on working conditions and conditions of employment. It insisted that threats to job and income security should be minimised, that there should be adequate facilities for retraining, and that union representatives should be consulted at all stages.

The most recent TUC report published in 1979 and dealing with the introduction of micro-electronics is in many ways very similar to these first two documents. The latest report, adopts like its predecessors, a positive attitude towards new technologies, confident of its contribution to the productive capacity of the UK industry. It lends support to evidence which suggests that high productivity growth leads to high economic growth and improved employment prospects. Second, again there is the belief that new technologies will offer great opportunities for increasing the quality of working life, and for providing working people with new benefits. Third, it is seen as the responsibility of the government and the trade union movement to face the challenges of technological change, and ensure that the benefits of this change are distributed equitably. A number of policies are referred to which may be used to smooth the process of adaptation, such as job and income security, reduction in working hours, improvements in working conditions, monitoring of health and safety implications and full opportunities for training and retraining.

However, there is one important difference between the earlier statements on automation and the more recent document. The new micro-technology seems to have provided a focus for union attempts to extend their ability to influence and control key areas of decision-making at a formative stage. The 1979 report argues that the trade union response should widen the debate about new technology into the area of industrial democracy, insisting on trade union involvement in the decision-making over technological change at an early stage through collective bargaining. The report includes a 'checklist for negotiators' covering such procedural issues as the level at which bargaining should take place, the nature of the discussions, the stage at which negotiations should begin, the use of a trial period, the information that should be available and the development of monitoring machinery. Thus it may be concluded that the trade union movement is fully aware of the potential 'costs' of micro-technological change, but with increased participation they argue that these 'costs' will be reduced.

Management/union participation

Some support may be found for the hypothesis that a participative, consensual approach between management and unions is a major factor in facilitating change in organisations (Coch and French, 1954; Scott et al., 1956; Gallie, 1978; Jacobs et al., 1979). In relation to micro-technological change, the Department of Employment study group concluded 'that consultation is not merely an inevitable requirement of trade unionists but something that management will decline only at their peril'. There are also now a few empirical studies of joint change efforts, although mainly carried out in the United States, which examine the potential for a collaborative management/union relationship in settings where clear structural sources of power and conflict are an inherent feature (Kochan and Dyer, 1976). In a time of rapid technological change, there would seem to be an obvious importance for empirical work which outlines the effectiveness of alternative types of change strategies in situations characterised by conflicts of interests, shared power and a high potential for conflict. Also, given the limited development of formal industrial democracy in Britain, policies for the management of change will have great significance in determining whether a consensual or conflict based approach develops (Williams and Moseley, 1982).

In the research initially carried out at Henley, I was interested in focusing on the degree of 'integrative bargaining' or problem-solving which occurs between management and unions during technological change. The emphasis of the trade union movement on achieving 'mutual benefit' from the new technologies would seem to indicate an openness for an integrative, rather than a distributive win/lose approach. A major work by Walton and McKersie (1965) gave the first comprehensive account of the necessary behaviours and conditions for integrative bargaining to occur. For these authors, integrative bargaining functions to find common or complementary interests and to solve problems confronting both parties. They distinguished this from distributive bargaining, which they believe deals with pure conflicts of interest. However, a study by Peterson and Tracy (1976), has shown that respondents find it difficult to distinguish between 'issues' and 'problems', some even maintaining that there is nothing that is non-distributive. They argue that Walton and McKersie's suggestion that problem-solving and a more participative approach cannot deal with 'conflict issues' fails to appreciate the true nature of management/union relationships. Therefore, in the present research also a wider definition of problem-solving was used. The study was based on the assumption that a more cooperative orientation may be adopted by the parties on an issue, where bargaining tactics may be equally appropriate. Also a more 'objective' view of the extent of problem-solving was sought, by a thorough examination of variables which have been shown by previous research to be important.

The study

The overall aim of the research was to assess the impact of management/ union participation on technological choice. More specifically, three empirical questions raised by the preceding discussion were examined. These were:

> First, to what extent have the trade unions been successful in influencing managerial discretion and establishing technological change as an issue for collective bargaining?

Second, is there evidence of a consensual, problem-solving approach between management and unions in the potentially conflictual context of micro-technological change?

Third, what impact does such an approach have in contrast to a more conflictual/distributive approach?

'Technological impact' was tested in relation to a number of substantive trade union demands which are included in the policy statements towards new technology of many different trade unions. These include issues regarding pay, work-sharing schemes, retraining, job enrichment, job satisfaction and redundancy.

Methodology and sample

Information was collected from a sample of managers and trade unionists, who had recently been involved in negotiations or discussions with the other side concerning the introduction of micro-technology. The research consisted of two main studies which enabled both qualitative and quantitative data about micro-technological change to be collected.

The brewing study

This first study was conducted solely within one particular industry, namely brewing, utilising case-study, interviews and questionnaire research techniques. An industry-specific study has obvious methodological advantages especially in relation to the fact that the substantive effects of advanced technologies may vary considerably from industry to industry, and a meaningful discussion of the impact of the management/union relationship during technological change needs to take into account these substantive variations.

The brewing industry was chosen as an appropriate area of study because of a number of its distinctive features, important both to micro-technological change and management/union participation. The significant economic activity of the industry provides a strong impetus for technological investment. In 1975 gross output was valued at almost £2 billion, the industry contributed some £575 million to the Exchequer in excise payments and gave employment to approximately 69,000 people. In relation to the manufacturing industry as a whole, the industry accounts for slightly less than 2% of net output, 1% of employment, and almost 5% of capital investment. The industry is also one which has been able to maintain its profitability in line with that of manufacturing as a whole (Price Commission, 1977), and despite the recent downward trend in sales, demand for the product is still fairly stable. Also, there are indications that micro-technological applications in the industry have great potential for reducing capital and labour costs, improving quality and exerting greater control.

In terms of labour relations, despite the fact that the industry is historically paternalistic, union membership in the production and distribution areas is very strong, with a large number of closed shop, post-entry agreements. The Transport and General Workers Union is thought to have about 45% of the workforce, the General and Municipal Workers 30%, the Association of Scientific and Managerial Staff 15%, and the Union of Shop, Distributive and Allied Trades most of the rest. Another significant feature is that plant negotiations and regional comparisons have a far greater impact than any national suggestions or industry guidelines, attributable to the way the industry has developed on a local pattern.

The brewing study was carried out in two parts. The first consisted of an analysis of the micro-electronic potential of the industry, along with a national survey of current and planned micro-applications. A list of the major breweries in the country was obtained from the Brewers' Society and 130 questionnaires were sent out to different operating companies, enquiring about micro-applications in 12 different areas of the brewing process. Of these 101 were returned, making a response rate of 78%. From this sample, 50 breweries were selected for the second part of the study, selection being based on the likelihood that the technological changes would have had manpower implications. In these breweries data concerning the process and outcome of micro-technological change was collected from managers and trade unionists. 46 out of the 50 management questionnaires were returned, but a union response was only able to be obtained for 18 of the 50 breweries. The majority of managers were unwilling for trade union representatives at their workplace to answer the questionnaire and therefore assistance had to be sought from the district officials of the relevant trade unions. Interviews were also conducted with key decision-makers in 25 of these breweries, approximately 35 people in total being interviewed. The breweries visited covered the whole of the country from Scotland to South Wales, and were chosen because they had carried out the greatest degree of micro-applications over the last few years.

The 'general' study

Whereas the brewing study has a number of advantages in being industry-specific, it also has limitations especially in the degree one can generalise from the results. In an attempt to overcome this problem, this second study involved a questionnaire survey amongst a selected sample of managers from within the food, drink and tobacco industrial sector, and a similar survey with full-time trade union officials of 10 different unions. 42 usable questionnaires were returned from managers, and 88 from full-time officials. In addition, 15 trade union officials, chosen from those who had completed and returned the questionnaire, were interviewed concerning their involvement in the introduction of micro-technology.

Results

The following analysis of the results is based on the information obtained from managers and trade unions in both studies. Interestingly, very few significant differences were found between the responses of the two management samples, and in only three areas did the brewing study differ significantly from the more general sample of managers. In the brewing industry, there seemed to be less formality in the management/union relationship, less conflict between the two sides and fewer redundancies during the introduction of micro-technology. A greater number of significant differences however, were found between the shop-floor union representatives in the brewing industry and the sample of full-time officials. The latter indicated significantly more success in achieving a greater degree of problem-solving in their relationship with management, less redundancies and more pay increases. There were also more formal negotiations and agreements concerning the introduction of micro-technology. As 88% of the total sample of trade unionists are full-time officials, conclusions based on this sample should be viewed as an optimistic assessment of what probably occurs in most companies at shop-floor level.

Managerial discretion during micro-technological change

In the introduction, it was shown how the influence of key decision-makers during technological change may be evident both in the psycho-social assumptions about man in the designs of the new equipment, and in the choice of manpower adjustment policies during the process of implementation. Thus, the first question which needs to be answered is 'what are the assumptions which lie behind the designs of the "new brewing technology"?' A survey of the advertising literature of brewing equipment manufacturers, showed that in most, emphasis is being placed on the elimination of the dependence on the human factor in most operations, and thereby reducing risk in 'error', and variation in the process constants. The essential elements, as outlined by one major manufacturer, were 'the replacement of the intelligent functions of man by instrumentation and engineering.

The brain is replaced by the control unit, the eye by the sensing device, and the hand by the operating device. An automated installation thus embodies control equipment that receives instructions on the process and ensures that they are carried out correctly'. The managers interviewed also fully realised the potential for increased control with the new technology. One manager commented, 'that there was no longer a reliance on individual expertise', and that 'discipline was easier when a computer dictates orders to the operator'. Similar sentiments were expressed by many others, and it was felt that the new technology gave a greater certainty 'of getting things right'.

These statements are far removed from the principles put forward by Davis (1971) and Mumford (1977) which embodied the notion that workers should control the technology and not vice-versa. Evidence was also found of the isolation of tasks and the breakdown of social relationships at work in situations where micro-technology had been introduced on a large scale. In many companies managers reported that workers complained of loneliness, and it was felt that the isolation of jobs had reduced any feeling of team spirit among employees. Despite these problems, many managers were confident that the new technology demanded greater initiative and sense of responsibility from the operators. This results from the fact that with the reduction in numbers that the new equipment affords, one operator will supervise far more process operations, and therefore the knowledge required is greater. In a few companies, it was envisaged that such changes would eventually lead to a brewery team made up of a few highly skilled operators, with the flexibility to carry out a wide range of functions. In the study, 61% of managers in brewing indicated that 'job enrichment' has resulted from the introduction of the new micro-technology, and a couple of managers indicated that manual aspects had been purposely maintained or built into the new process 'to prevent boredom and improve job satisfaction'.

Thus, it may be concluded that the designs of the new brewing equipment have given rise to more controlled and formalised working environments, where the manufacturers' aim is to make the intelligent functions of the human operator redundant. However, there are examples of managerial discretion being used to increase worker responsibility, prevent boredom and improve job satisfaction. In the next section the influence of the trade union movement on such discretion will be examined.

Trade union involvement and influence

Trade union involvement in eight different areas of decision-making relating to micro-technological change were investigated. Management and union respondents were asked whether they felt the union had been involved in these decisions, and if yes, whether the management/union relationship had been one of joint decision-making, bargaining or consultation. Five decision-making areas may be outlined where the unions are not involved in any meaningful way, i.e. either no union involvement was indicated or the unions were only informed of management decisions. These decisions related to the initial investment, the cost-benefit analysis, the type and extent of technology to be implemented, any job redesign and the selection and training of employees. More evidence of joint decision-making and bargaining were found in the three other areas studied namely, redundancy, pay and grading and health and safety. Such findings are what would be traditionally expected, and provide further support for the relative lack of trade union influence in decision-making, especially in strategic decisions (Heller et al., 1977; Edwards, 1978; Wilson et al., 1982).

However, interesting differences were found between managers and trade unionists in their perceptions of the types of relationships which were stated to have occurred in the various areas of decision-making. The most notable were in decisions regarding the initial investment, the cost-benefit analysis and the type and extent of technology to be implemented. Not one manager in the sample indicated that the trade unions had been involved in a joint decision-making or bargaining capacity with respect to the first two of these decisions, and only 3 managers indicated that any such involvement had occurred in the third decision. As for the trade unionists, 9 indicated involvement in joint decision-making or bargaining in the investment decision, 15 in a cost-benefit analysis, and 36 in decisions concerning the type and extent of technology. Very little evidence of such union involvement was found either in the case studies or in the interviews conducted with full-time officials. In all cases decisions were finalised by management committees before they were put to employees and the unions. In one instance where the union was thoroughly satisfied with their involvement, discussions between the two sides still had not begun until approximately four years after the initial management decision to invest.

Two important reasons were consistently given by managers during the interviews to explain the limited involvement of the trade union movement during technological change. First, it was felt that the unions lacked knowledge and expertise in this area, and would be unable to provide much feedback in the conceptual stages of the introduction of new technologies. One manager stated that an almost *fait accompli* should be presented to the workforce, and whereas there should be a willingness to change the plan if there was good reason, it should also be feasible in its own right. In four cases it was explicitly stated that the original plan had not been changed at all after discussions/consultations with the employees or unions. In contrast to this lack of union expertise, many examples were found of companies actively involved in the setting up of managerial expertise in this area. This either revolved around one person who had been specifically employed to look at various applications, or there would be a project team with the requisite skill to make such decisions. Management expertise is an often quoted objection to arguments for increased shop-floor involvement in decision-making, and as pointed out by Marchington and Loveridge (1979), the idea of non-useful and generally destructive contributions from the shop-stewards would appear to exert a particularly pervasive influence over British management thought. In one company it was also stated that the aim was to get people into the 'right frame of mind', so that information presented to them could be manipulated by management, and statements loaded in such a way that the right questions are asked by employees. The influence of specialists in controlling decision-making has also been well documented by many others such as Pettigrew (1973) and Winkler (1974).

A second reason outlined by management for the lack of union involvement was the fact that the position of the union in times of economic recession was very weak. In a number of instances, employees were threatened with the closure of the plant if the union did not reach agreement, and many trade unionists outlined the difficulty of getting support for industrial action, from employees who were increasingly concerned about keeping their jobs at a time of high unemployment. Only 33% of the management sample indicated that there had been a threat or occurrence of an industrial dispute during technological change, and in the 25 companies visited, only 6 instances of industrial conflict were found. These were caused mainly by grievances over substantive issues such as pay, reduction in hours or increased status, rather than procedural issues such as the lack of union involvement in decision-making.

Many managers also pointed to the usefulness of what was termed a 'softly, softly approach' to technological change, in order to reduce the drama of the situation and deter union involvement. In one company, the plan followed was to deal firstly with those areas which were 'least contentious', i.e. those with limited manpower implications. After these so-called innocent changes had been implemented, more controversial changes would then be made, and obviously the position of employees to resist would be weakened. The implications of minor changes carried out in a gradual way may be difficult to appreciate in the short-run, and they may not initially appear dramatic enough for the trade union organisation to attempt or succeed in gaining benefits for their members. In one company information was given

160

concerning a five-year plan of separate individual micro-applications, and gave an interesting insight into the cumulative effect such changes could produce. It was envisaged that there would be a 25% reduction in manpower and movement towards the 'flexible operator'. Many trade unionists were found to be ignorant about plans for future applications of micro-technological change, and at times such ignorance resulted in an unwarranted complacency on their part. This was illustrated in the brewing study, where in one company, the trade union official dismissed the issue of technological change in the brewery as being 'of no great consequence' and 'something which happened all the time'; while his management counterpart spoke of his plans to eventually 'automate everyone out of the process'. In relation to these findings, it is interesting that in 6 out of the 25 companies visited, the manager interviewed was surprised at the lack of trade union reaction, and their apparent lack of concern about future plans and applications. For example, one manager commented that the trade union did not seem to realise the implication of production being increased by about 65% to 70%, with no extra jobs being created, and in most of the companies there had been no initiatives from the trade unions for any formal agreements on new technology. Most managers felt that the trade union strategy had lacked expertise and preparation, and that their reaction could at most be only described as suspicious or defensive.

Thus, in view of the above findings, it must be concluded that any trade union influence on managerial discretion during micro-technological change will indeed be slight. In the vast majority of cases the trade union movement has effectively been excluded from the important stages of decision-making, and when they are finally consulted, the scope left for discussion, and their ability to change management decisions is very limited. 55% of the trade union sample indicated that their ability to change the decisions of the other side was slight, and 68% felt that the trade unions had not been involved at an early enough stage in decision-making. However, let us now turn to the incidence of consensual problem-solving between the two sides, and analyse the impact such union involvement has in the limited occasions that it occurs.

Problem-solving between management and unions during the introduction of micro-technology

Problem-solving was defined in the questionnaire as a 'participative process between management and unions in dealing with issues or problems such as new technology, in searching for alternative solutions and arriving at a mutually satisfactory agreement'. It is significant that 20% of the total sample indicated that there had been no such process in the management/union relationship. The majority of both managers and trade unionists (60% of managers and 54% of trade unionists), indicated that less than 25% problem-solving had occurred between the two sides during micro-technological change. In the companies visited, there was also very little evidence of joint problem-solving, but when it did occur it was felt to have been very useful. In one company, the joint management/union job evaluation exercise was outlined as one of the most interesting features of the whole programme. Management believed that it helped the individual trade union representatives and managers to overcome the pressure from their respective interest groups, and to give a result generally felt to show fairly the relative weights of the different jobs. It was only after achieving this by a joint approach that management and unions took up their separate roles for negotiations to 'price' the system.

Most of the trade unionists interviewed welcomed a participative relationship with management during the introduction of micro-technology. The most common complaint was that they were being involved too late in the decision-making. It was felt that if the employer came to the union open-minded and willing to discuss issues, any bitterness and a win/lose situation would be avoided. In keeping with these findings, the questionnaire data revealed a strong positive correlation between union satisfaction with the technological change and the occurrence of problem-solving in the management/union relationship ($r = \cdot 55$, sig.at $\cdot 001$). No such correlation was found in the management data, and indeed, many managers interviewed felt that it was impossible for both sides to participate fully in this situation. As one manager stated, even if the unions did recognise the need for the new technology, 'they will not be a party to a reduction in manpower and will fight hard to get the best terms'. The main reasons outlined by management, both in the questionnaire and in the interviews, for the introduction of micro-technology was the reduction or avoidance of labour costs. Such managerial rationality was not open to debate or discussion with the trade unions. The interviews with the brewery managers highlighted their resentment in having to bargain over technological change, and analysis of the total management sample showed a strong correlation between the occurrence of bargaining in the negotiating relationship and managerial dissatisfaction with the change-process ($r = \cdot 21$, sig.at $\cdot 007$).

Factors influencing problem-solving between management and unions during technological change

Table 8.1 illustrates the variables showing significant correlations with problem-solving in the management and union data. While some consensus may be found between the two samples in relation to the importance of various procedural issues for problem-solving in this situation, more interesting are the differences which were found between the management and union respondents.

For the trade unions, perceptions of the occurrence of problem-solving seems to have a strong effect on their cooperative attitude to the management side, tending to heighten feelings of trust, respect and legitimacy for the other team. Also variables describing the strength and expertise of the union team, such as clarity of objectives, a well prepared decision approach, knowledge about new equipment were significantly correlated with problem-solving. No such significant correlations were found in the management data in relation to problem-solving. The only significant positive relationship found for management was between a well prepared decision-approach for their team and a mainly consultative relationship with the other side, i.e. one where management does most of the decision-making and the unions are kept informed (r. = ·18, sig.at ·01). Thus, from such findings it may be concluded that when the management team is strong it will choose to involve the unions in only the slightest way. As the management team was shown to have significantly more confidence in the clarity of their objectives, and in the fact that they had a well planned and prepared approach to decision-making, the weak degree of union participation is due to their lack of team strength and expertise in this area.

The trade union data in this research provided some support for the factors hypothesised by Walton and McKersie to be associated with problem-solving. This relates mainly to variables describing a cooperative relationship and frequency and openness of communication between the two sides. The management respondents however seemed to lack the motivational orientation for problem-solving during technological change. Therefore, it can be argued that if they indicated that problem-solving had occurred, it was not because both sides wanted it (an assumption of Walton and McKersie), but because one side had enough expertise or procedural advantages to demand it.

163

Table 8.1

Correlations of perceived variables in the bargaining process with perceived degree of problem-solving for union and management negotiators

Variable	Management	Union
Cooperative working relationship		
Friendliness of other side		0·21
Trust of other side		0·27
Legitimacy of other side		0·32
Respect for other side		0·28
Constructiveness of other side		0·25
Procedural issues		
Clarity of other side in stating issues	0·21	0·28
Availability of information from other side		0·31
Uncommitted exploration of problems	0·30	0·33
Degree of informal contact		0·22
Degree of formal contact	0·22	0·23
Extension of collective bargaining	0·18	0·26
Ability to change decisions of other side		0·28
Involvement of trade unions at an early stage	0·15	0·36
Decision-making at plant level		0·35
Pressure exerted by other side	0·20	
Team Strength and Expertise		
Clarity of own team's objectives		0·16
Well prepared decision-approach		0·29
Team knowledge about new equipment		0·21
Technical ability to respondent		
Support from colleagues at head or regional offices		0·17

* Kendall Tau correlations significant at the 0·05 level or greater.

The impact of problem-solving on the outcome of micro-technological change

It was hypothesised that the more the trade unions would be involved in a problem-solving process with management during micro-technological change, the greater the degree of employee benefits they would achieve. First, however, it must be concluded that certain of the trade union substantive demands were consistently not being achieved. These included a reduction of working hours, increases in holidays, earlier retirement and job sharing, all schemes which could prevent labour loss during the introduction of micro-technology. Management is not choosing or being persuaded to adopt such schemes, and there is very little evidence that the trade unions are being able to prevent job loss and redundancy. One explanation for such apparent trade union weakness is the difficulty in tracing manpower reductions to techno-logical change, and one manager interviewed even admitted that there was an obvious attempt not to associate manpower savings with micro-applications. There were a number of indications that changes such as the reduction in numbers may occur sometime after the techno-logical change from which it results; and also in the present economic climate, redundancy may easily be blamed on the drop in sales, after or before micro-technological change has occurred. Also the more common 'gradual and piecemeal introduction' of micro-technology enables companies to reduce its labour force in a less dramatic fashion through natural wastage. Department of Employment figures show that most brewers have reduced their labour over the past years, with a substantial loss of 8,000 between 1980–81. This has also been a time of rapid micro-technological change, and there is much evidence in the present research to link these two factors.

The above types of 'employee benefits' (no job loss, work-sharing) are those which one would have hypothesised as emerging from greater management/union problem-solving during the change process. Although very little problem-solving did take place, interviews conducted with unionists who 'felt' they had fully participated in this way, provided some interesting information as to why this hypothesis might not necessarily be supported. These unionists showed a marked difference in their attitudes towards 'new technology' from those who had been less involved, and adhered closely to what could be described as the 'managerial rationality' in this situation. These unionists fully embraced the introduction of micro-technology, outlining the advantages that would result, rather than any of the drawbacks. One emphasised the strong financial side of his union, which looked closely at the cost/effectiveness of various computer technologies. It was stated that the union would always support the most 'efficient' technology, rather than a less efficient one which may save jobs.

Finally, there were also strong feelings amongst many of these unionists that the adoption of work-sharing schemes to preserve jobs was not cost-effective. These findings are similar to those of a recent study (by Wilson et al., 1982) on union participation in strategic decision-making, which concluded that the unions only get their way when this is congruent with management's way. In the present study there is also some evidence that unions involved in problem-solving during the introduction of micro-technology do not pose a threat to management's 'way of thinking'.

In both the management and union data, it was found that the occurrence of distributive bargaining between the two sides was correlated to an improvement in terms and conditions of employment as a result of the change (union $r = \cdot195$, sig.at $\cdot02$, management $r = \cdot197$, sig.at $\cdot05$). In the union data distributive bargaining was also related to a number of individual benefits such as an improvement in skills (chi-square $= 6\cdot22$, sig.at $\cdot05$, better health and safety (chi-square $= 4\cdot08$, sig. $\cdot05$); increases in pay (chi-square $9\cdot96$, sig.at $\cdot005$); reduction in working hours (chi $-$ square $= 4.17$, sig. $\cdot05$) and a reduction in overtime (chi $= 6\cdot61$, sig. $\cdot05$). However, in the companies visited, the only employee benefit which the unions seemed to have been able to achieve with any consistency has been an increase in pay, and in four cases this was only after substantial strike action. The full-time officials interviewed also stated that increases in pay had only been achieved at the expense of most other things. A few agreements were referred to, where in return for slight pay increases, companies had been given 'carte blanche' to do what they want. Such findings must be evaluated in the context that in most companies production was increased by between 25% to 70%. Thus, it may be concluded that in the majority of the cases surveyed, the benefits of micro-technology are *not* being equally distributed between the company and its employees.

Conclusions

While it has been argued that 'choice' does exist both in the design and implementation of technology, there is much evidence in the present study to show that the new micro-electronic equipment is being designed and implemented in a very 'determined' way. Principles of managerial control were prominent in the designs of the new brewing equipment, and cost-efficiency and labour reduction focused strongly as the main reasons and guidelines for implementation. It is true that some decision-makers did wander from this 'determined' way, introducing job enrichment schemes, improving skill levels and attempting to make work more satisfying with micro-technology.

166

However, more innovative manpower adjustment policies such as reduction in hours, job sharing, increased holidays are consistently not being adopted. Managers, to a large extent, have attempted and succeeded in disassociating improvements in terms and conditions of employment with the introduction of new equipment, and have prevented technological change from becoming a negotiable issue.

But what about the trade unions? While a conclusion of the 'unfettered triumph of capital over labour' could not be justified, as there was evidence of conflict, dispute and struggle, as well as some participation between the two sides, the real impact of trade unionists on management decision-making was very limited. The design and choice of technology are still unquestionably managerial prerogatives, and in no instance did discussions with the trade unions start until such decisions had been made. By that time, the scope for union influence has been severely narrowed, and the main achievement during the process of implementation has been a slight pay increase, usually at the expense of everything else. The imbalance of power between management and union negotiators was very evident in many of the cases studied and confidence in their own team strength and expertise was very much higher among the majority of managers surveyed. While the impact of the recession cannot be dismissed as a causal factor in explaining many of the trade union weaknesses found, the present research nevertheless raises a number of important questions concerning the effectiveness of trade union policy and structure in dealing with the new micro-technology.

It has been shown that a reactive, defensive strategy can only have limited impact when faced with well-formulated management plans, and a management team with the expertise to implement them. Trade unionists also lacked vital information about probable technological advancement in their industries, and there was very little evidence of alternative plans and suggestions put forward by them. It is interesting that the Norwegian National Union of Iron and Metal Workers (MWU) seems to have recognised this problem, and is providing educational courses for its members to enable them to present an informed point of view when company policy decisions on the use of technology are being taken (Nygaard and Bergo, 1975). In addition, insufficient attention is being devoted to the issue of technological change due to the work overload of many union officials, and the lack of intra and inter union communication leads to localised responses, which are ultimately inadequate. There is also certainly a need for a greater concentration by unionists on strategies of job redesign, and policies for reducing hours and other work-sharing schemes. Job loss and redundancies will certainly be main problems in a future with micro-technology, and ones which will not be solved by unions continually battling for pay increases, only achieved to the detriment of all else. Finally, it could be argued that for the trade unions to be really effective in the micro-technological debate, their influence needs to be felt beyond the shop-floor or the boardrooms of companies, in the area of design and manufacture. A major contribution to such thinking has come from the shop stewards of the British aerospace company, Lucas.

To conclude, the present research raises many issues which are in need of further investigation. The trade unionists surveyed indicated greater involvement and participation during technological change, than was ever attributed to them by any of the managers surveyed. Also, many unionists who were satisfied with their involvement, adhered closely to a 'management' appreciation of the change. A more detailed case study approach would seem to be needed to examine the factors which affect union perception of involvement during technological change, and the extent to which such perception is 'manipulated' by management. One trade unionist, when asked about management/union participation during the introduction of micro-technology, replied that 'management don't want it, and the unions are not ready for it'. On the basis of the research carried out, there is no better statement with which to conclude this chapter.

References

Abbot, L.F., *Social Aspects of Innovation and Industrial Technology*, HMSO: London, 1976.

Blauner, R., *Alienation and Freedom*, The University of Chicago Press: Chicago, 1964.

Blyton, P. and Hill, S., 'The Economics of Worksharing', *National Westminster Bank Quarterly Review*, November 1981, pp.37–45.

Braverman, H., *Labor and Monopoly Capital*, Monthly Review Press: New York, 1974.

Burns, T. and Stalker, G.M., *The Management of Innovation*, Tavistock Publications: 1961.

Child, J., 'Organizational Structure, Environment and Performance: The Role of Strategic Choice', *Sociology*, 6, 1972, pp.1–22.

Coch, L. and French, J.R.P., 'Overcoming Resistance to Change', *Human Relations*, 11, 1948, pp.512–32.

Cooper, R., 'Man, Task and Technology', *Human Relations*, 25, 1972, pp.131–57.

Davis, L.E., 'The Coming Crisis for Production Management: Technology and Organisation', *International Journal for Production Research*, 9, 1971, pp.65–82.

Davis, L.E. and Taylor, J.C. (eds), *Design of Jobs*, Penguin Modern Management Readings, 1972.

Department of Employment, *The Manpower Implications of Micro-Electronic Technology*, HMSO: London, 1978.

Dey, I., 'Making Redundancy Redundant – or How to Save Jobs Without Really Trying', *International Journal of Manpower*, 1, 1980, pp.15–20.

Dubin, R., 'Supervision and Productivity: Empirical Findings and Theoretical Considerations', in Dubin, R., Homans, G.D., Mann, F.C. and Miller, D.C. (eds), *Leadership and Productivity*, Chandler: San Francisco, 1965.

Edwards, C., 'Measuring Union Power: A Comparison of two Methods Applied to the Study of Local Union Power in the Coal Industry', *British Journal of Industrial Relations*, 16, 1978, pp.1–15.

Friedman, A., *Industry and Labour*, Macmillan: London, 1977.

Gallie, D., *In Search of the New Working Class*, University Press: Cambridge, 1978.

Goldthorpe, J.H., Lockwood, D., Bechhofer, F. and Platt, J., *The Affluent Worker: Industrial Attitudes and Behaviour*, University Press: Cambridge, 1968.

Gruenfeld, L.W. and Foltman, F.F., 'Relationships among Supervisors' Integration, Satisfaction and Acceptance of a Technological Change', *Journal of Applied Psychology*, 51, 1967, pp.74–77.

Hazelhurst, R.J., Bradbury, R.J. and Corlett, E.N., 'A Comparison of the Skills of Machinists on Numerically Controlled and Conventional Machines', *Occupational Psychology*, 43, 1969, pp.169–82.

Heller, F.A., Drenth, P.J.D., Koopman, P. and Rus, V., 'A Longitudinal Study in Participative Decision-Making', *Human Relations*, 30, 1977, pp.567–87.

Hunter, L.C., Reid, G.L. and Boddy, D., *Labour Problems of Technological Change*, George Allen and Unwin Ltd: 1969.

Jacobs, E., 'Open Letter to Management', *Industrial Society*, January/February 1980, pp.9–10.

Jacobs, E., Orwell, S., Paterson, P. and Weltz, F., *The Approach to Industrial Change in Britain and Germany*, Anglo-German Foundation: 1978.

Janowitz, M., 'Changing Patterns of Organisational Authority: The Military Establishment', *Administrative Science Quarterly*, 3, 1959, pp.473–93.

Kochan, T.A. and Dyer, L., 'A Model of Organisational Change in the Context of Union-Management Relations', *The Journal of Applied Behavioural Science*, 12, 1976, pp.59–78.

Lazonick, W., 'Industrial Relations and Technical Change: The Case of the Self-acting Mule', *Cambridge Journal of Economics*, 3, 1979, pp.231–62.

Lucas Aerospace Combine Shop Steward Committee, *Corporate Plan: A Contingency Strategy as a Positive Alternative to Recession and Redundancies*, unpublished, 1976.

Mann, F.C. and Hoffman, L.R., *Automation and the Worker*, Henry Holt and Co: New York, 1960.

Marchington, M. and Loveridge, R., 'Non-participation: The Management View?', *Journal of Management Studies*, 16, 1979, pp.171–84.

Mumford, E., 'The Design of Work: New Approaches and New Needs' in Rijnsdorp, J. (ed.) *Case Studies in Automation Related to the Humanisation of Work: Proceedings of the IFAC Workshop*, Pergamon Press: Netherlands, 1977.

Noble, D.F., 'Social Choice in Machine Design' in Zimbalist, A. (ed.), *Case Studies on the Labor Process*, Monthly Review Press: New York, 1980.

Nygaard, K. and Bergo, O.T., 'The Trade Unions – New Users of Research', *Personnel Review*, 4, 1975, pp.5–10.

Peterson, R.B. and Tracy, L.N., 'A Behavioural Model of Problem-Solving in Labour Negotiations', *British Journal of Industrial Relations*, 14, 1976, pp.159–73.

Pettigrew, A., *The Politics of Organisational Decision-Making*, Tavistock Publications, London, 1973.

Scott, W.H. et al., *Technical Change and Industrial Relations*, Liverpool University Press: 1956.

Thornton, P. and Routledge, C., 'Managing the Manpower Aspects of Applying Micro-electronic Technology', *International Journal of Manpower*, 1, 1980, pp.7–10.

Trades Union Council, *Employment and Technology*. Report by the TUC General Council, 1979.

Walton, R. and McKersie, R., *A Behavioural Theory of Labour Negotiations*, McGraw-Hill: New York, 1965.

Wedderburn, D. and Crompton, R., *Workers' Attitudes and Technology*, University Press: Cambridge, 1972.

Williams, R. and Moseley, R., *Technology Agreements: Consensus, Control and Technical Change in the Workplace*. Paper presented to EEC/FAST Conference, 1982.

Wilson, D.C., Butler, R.J., Cray, D., Hickson, D.J. and Mallory, G.R., 'Union Participation in Strategic Decision-Making', *British Journal of Industrial Relations*, 20, 1982, pp.322–41.

Winkler, J.T., 'The Ghost at the Bargaining Table: Directors and Industrial Relations', *British Journal of Industrial Relations*, 12, 1974, pp.191–212.

Woodward, J., *Industrial Organisation: Theory and Practice*, University Press: Oxford, 1965.

Ure, A., *The Philosophy of Manufacturers*, Knight: London, 1835.

9 Consultation and change: new technology and manpower in the electronics industry

Howard Rush and Robin Williams

Introduction

The electronics industry is arguably the first to be affected by its own technology. Although variations exist between different sections of the industry the pace of technological change is widely credited with being the principle influence behind a dramatic shift in skill requirements. Since 1978, for example, firms producing computers, components, electronic capital equipment, consumer electronics, office equipment and telecommunications supplies have employed an additional 10,000 scientists and technologists; their expertise being used to develop both new products and processes for an industry whose R&D budget has grown to £1145 million (in 1981).

This increase in highly skilled labour has been restricted more by the supply of qualified, often at degree level, individuals than by any inherent limits to demand. At the same time, however, the introduction within the industry of new technology, from computer-aided-design through automated insertion equipment is, to a large extent, responsible for the decline (1978–81) of assembly and operator personnel by some 40,000, or 21% of the industry's workforce (NEDO, 1982).

The efficient introduction of new technology within the electronics industry and the responsible management of change, given such dramatic changes in labour requirements, is ultimately dependent upon the participation of the workforce and active consideration of industrial relations issues. The effects of the introduction of micro-electronically based technology on productivity and the nature of work has, for example, already resulted in substantial changes to matters predominantly subject to collective bargaining (e.g. numbers and grades of people employed, remuneration) as well as a wide range of issues over which consultation has been less well developed. Within this latter category are changes in working methods and workflow, skill and training requirements, career structures, working hours and job satisfaction. Moreover, the type of technological change which the electronics industry is currently experiencing frequently blurs the demarcation between different categories of labour.

Within the newer 'high technology' sections of the industry in particular a 'culture of change' has emerged which has led to a smoother and more continuous process of change. Where the transition has involved a major shift, e.g. from electro-mechanical or electrical to electronic products and processes, the potential for dispute has been much greater. As rates of technological diffusion increase the impact on job content and boundaries is likely to raise further questions about the adequacy of the consultative mechanisms employed to introduce change and the potential benefits of effective consultation.

These concerns are, of course, not limited to those employed in the electronics industry and have been the subject of national debate since the late 1970s. In 1979, for example, the Trade Union Congress (TUC) backed by many individual trade unions, published a comprehensive policy document calling for joint bodies to be formed to deal with information about corporate planning and projected technological developments resulting in 'New Technology Agreements' (see Robbins and Webster, 1982). While welcoming technological change, the unions sought to 'maximise its benefits and minimise its costs and ensure that its benefits are equitably shared' (TUC, 1979). The costs and benefits were recognised as not being predetermined but rather influenced by the way in which new systems and equipment were introduced. The greatest scope for influencing this process was seen as through the provision of information and consultation from the earliest stages of decision-making over technological change.

The Confederation of British Industry (CBI) subsequently issued a call for 'full and systematic consultation' over technological change (CBI, 1980). Improved consultation and communication with the workforce were seen as bringing benefits to management, not only by overcoming resistance to change that might develop if employees perceived technology as threatening their position, but also by gaining the cooperation and utilising the experience of the workforce to ensure

172

that the sometimes difficult and uncertain process of change would be successful. In July 1980, TUC and CBI representatives agreed on a text of a proposed join statement on a framework for technological change which suggested that 'improvements in information provision and consultation are most likely to succeed if supported by the creation, or improvement of joint machinery between management, their employees and their trade unions'. The representatives also agreed that access to information from the earliest possible stages of the decision-making process is vital to a successful approach to technological change. However, despite apparent areas of consensus between the TUC and CBI positions the statement, while agreed by the TUC, was not accepted by the CBI membership (TUC, 1980).

Whether or not a formally agreed statement would have greatly influenced the pace or direction at which early consultation and information has become institutionalised is difficult to say. The pattern of development of consultative mechanisms in workplaces has certainly been uneven, due in part to differential rates of change between and within industries, the relative perspective of trade unions and companies, as well as the impact of the recession on the industrial relations climate. Although a substantial number of employers have signed technology agreements (Labour Research Department, 1982), the vast majority of these have been signed by four unions – APEX, ASTMS, NALGO and TASS, representing clerical and technical staff (Williams and Moseley, 1982). These have frequently fallen short of union guidelines on both procedural and substantive matters and typically cover only part of the workforce. Furthermore significant differences between industrial sectors have been noted. The engineering industry, for example, accounts for about half of all technology agreements (primarily in the high technology sectors of electronics, aerospace and capital goods) followed by local government and the insurance industry (Williams, 1982).

The great majority of the technological changes affecting the majority of the workforce are handled through well established, conventional consultative procedures. Some firms continue to adhere to restrictive approaches to consultation and the provision of information and have adopted a strategy of unilaterally imposing technological change (Levie and Williams, 1983). Many have, however, attempted to improve their overall framework for consultation and communication without formal technology agreements by increasing employee involvement on a wide range of issues of which technological change is but one (CBI, 1981).

That the development of effective consultative mechanisms is vital for the technological and economic success of British industry is agreed by a wide range and increasing number of commentators from industry, government and academia (see Evans and Wilkinson, 1983;

Sleigh, 1979; Peltu, 1980; NEDC, 1980). However, the arrangements and procedures under which early consultation and the provision of information should occur remain the subject of much, often heated, debate. As a means of aiding informed discussion and decision-making two surveys are described which provide more of the picture of the mechanisms for change employed in the electronics industry.

Both surveys were conducted for the Electronic Economic Development Committee's (EDC) Employment and Technology Task Force. The Task Force and the EDC have published the results of these surveys and recommendations in a NEDO (1983) publication, upon which this chapter draws heavily. The survey on the more established arrangements are based upon a postal questionnaire with personnel managers in the industry while the survey on Technology Agreements canvassed the views of both managers and union representatives through both postal questionnaires and in-depth follow-up interviews. The range of issues covered and the questions asked were designed to be complementary. The analysis and interpretation of survey results are, however, the sole responsibility of the authors and do not necessarily represent the views of NEDO or any member of the committees for which the surveys were done. The authors wish to thank NEDO for permission to use this work.

The first survey examines the established procedures adopted by 46 firms, producing electronic capital equipment, components, information technology and electronic consumer goods. A second complementary survey concentrated on 9 firms, also from the electronics industry, which had been party to specific 'technology agreements'. This chapter reports the results, in turn, of the two surveys focussing on issues which were subject to consultation, the stage at which this occurred during the introduction of change, and the range of information which was disseminated to the workforce. In our concluding section, the perceived benefits or costs of the adopted arrangements are discussed together.

Established procedures

A large majority of electronics firms which participated in the survey on conventional procedures for introducing change agreed that employee involvement is fundamental to the efficient introduction of new technology. The personnel managers canvassed, described a wide range of micro-electronically based 'new technologies' introduced in the last several years, predominantly in the broad category of 'design, manufacture and test technologies' which included automatic insertion and assembly equipment as well as computer-aided-design

(CAD) and computer-numerically-controlled machine tools (CNC). Of the 82 technologies listed by the respondents 61 came from this category. A further 21 were categorised as office systems and a relatively minor number (4) from warehousing and stock control. The commitment to both technological change and to employee participation was indicated by the high proportion (nearly 90% of the 46 participating firms) who reported that they had employed some form of consultation during the process of change. While accepting the need for consultation and the provision of information to assist informed involvement, many managers argued that this could best be achieved through the already well established mechanisms adopted by firms for consultation on a wide range of issues. However, no single model of consultation emerged from the survey, which covered 14% of those working in the industry, with practices varying according to the size, value and needs of each business, the type of technology employed, as well as the prior history of industrial relations.

Formal consultative arrangements were found to exist in the form of 'joint consultative committees', 'works committees' and 'joint staff-union councils', all of which bring trade union representatives and management together on a regular basis, be it quarterly, bi-monthly or monthly. In addition, 'Briefing Groups', often at the departmental level or 'Participation Meetings', usually on a company basis, are held once or twice each year in many firms. On a less formal basis companies referred to liaison with shop stewards, discussion groups and have meetings with those individuals directly affected by change. Several firms, both large and small, mentioned a 'reasonably open' style of management as part of building an atmosphere where consultation is the rule rather than the exception.

The degree of involvement, the stage at which it occurs, and the extent to which information is provided differs widely between companies as well as between firms within the same group. The degree of consultation practiced can also vary according to the nature of the change, some of an evolutionary or incremental nature and others more radical in their impact on job content and job boundaries. Assessing the stage at which consultation occurs is difficult not least because the process of decision-making is far from straightforward, with few clear distinctions drawn between the planning of change and its implementation. The survey has, however, divided the process of introducing change into three separate stages, for the purpose of quantitative assessments. These cover the initial planning for technological change, followed by the choice of equipment or systems, and the resulting implementation of the chosen technology. As shown in Table 9.1 the overwhelming amount of consultation practiced by these firms occurred at a relatively late stage, after initial planning and the choice of technique had been established. Of the 46 firms concerned only

11% reported no employee involvement during any of the three stages and only 13% encouraged participation throughout the entire process. Overall, 50% of the firms restricted involvement to the implementation stage.

Table 9.1

Stage of employee involvement/representation

Totals		Per cent	Number of firms
I	Planning	32.4%	(15)
II	Choice	19.5%	(9)
III	Implementation	86.9%	(40)
	No involvement/ representation	10.8%	(5)

While a large number of firms encouraged employer involvement, the consultation takes place on a wide and varying number of issues. Table 9.2 shows, in descending order of frequency, the topics covered by these consultative arrangements. Health and safety, job content, remuneration, redundancy and the monitoring of the introduction of new technology were all listed as topics for discussion by over 50% of the plants surveyed. The pacing of work was least often subject to consultation.

Table 9.2

Major areas of discussion under established procedures

	No.	%
Health and safety	32	69.5
Changes in job content	30	65.2
Remuneration	28	60.8
Redundancy	26	56.5
Monitoring the introduction of new equipment and related systems	24	52.1
Pacing of work	13	28.2
	N = 46	

Commitment to wide ranging and early consultation, while adhered to by some of the more progressive firms in the industry, could obviously be substantially improved upon. However, efficient participation is unlikely to occur unless it is based upon readily available and easily understood information. In general, data on the health and safety aspects of new technology are most frequently made available to the employees of the electronics industry. This should not be entirely unexpected given that it is the only area in which legislation currently exists and more than 90% of the samples are found to provide the relevant information, with half disseminating details during the planning stage and half electing to wait until implementation had begun. Table 9.3 lists a range of additional issues and the stage at which the information is first made available. The category least often referred to at either planning or implementation was 'costing' with dissemination practiced by only 24% of responding firms. Aside from 'health and safety' information has not been made available as a matter of course by more than one-third of the firms on any issue before a decision on a specific technology is made. When the implementation stage is included, three-quarters of the firms disseminated information on issues of 'manning and skill levels' and 'training' and by more than half of the sample on 'setting and timing of equipment', 'workflow and methods' and 'remuneration'. Although a number of firms did not take the initiative in supplying information on any of the topics listed, several indicated a willingness to provide information on request.

Table 9.3

Information is first made available on the following issues
at the planning stage, the implementation stage, or not at all

	Planning stage		Implementation stage		
	No.	%	No.	%	Total %
Setting and timing of equipment	7	15.2	26	56.5	71.7
Workflow and methods	13	28.2	15	32.6	60.8
Manning skill levels	15	32.6	25	54.3	86.9
Training	14	30.4	26	56.5	86.9
Remuneration	10	21.7	22	47.8	69.5
Costing	5	10.8	6	13.0	23.8
Health and safety	21	45.6	21	45.6	91.2

Most of the information was provided through regular union/ management consultative meetings, with other forms of communication including management meetings with those directly affected, departmental meetings, newsletters and noticeboards somewhat less frequently employed. The majority of firms (61%) channelled their information primarily to those sections of the workforce considered (by management) to be those most directly involved with the technological change. Only one-quarter of those surveyed undertook to disseminate information concerning the change to all employees.

Technology agreements

As the survey described above implies, many firms in the electronics industry prefer to integrate their discussions over technological change into their established procedures. However, 18 firms have signed specific 'New Technology Agreements' which mirror those signed in other industries and fall into two general categories. 'One-off' agreements, primarily signed by TASS related to a specific technological change, particularly computer-aided-design. These agreements have derived from established patterns of wage and productivity bargaining and tend to focus on wage levels, conditions of employment and training. All were concluded in 1978–9 prior to the publication of the TUC ten-point 'Checklist for Negotiators of New Technology Agreements', and do not establish any general procedures for handling subsequent technological change. A second category of agreements are of a more 'procedural' nature as they establish consultative arrangements for technological change in general. These, signed primarily by APEX do not specify change in wage levels, job content or related conditions of work, but rather were designed to establish the methods for handling these and other issues. Such 'procedural' agreements were specifically intended to increase early consultation and the scope of information provision. Consultation has, for the most part, remained within the framework identified as previously existing in the industry (i.e. on works councils or joint consultative committees) although in several instances joint union/management technology committees have been established to monitor a company's programme of technological change.

The second survey conducted for the NEDO focussed on 9 of the Technology Agreements signed in the electronics industry of which 4 were 'one-off' agreements signed by TASS and 5 were 'procedural', 4 of which were signed by APEX alone and one jointly by APEX, ASTMS, TASS and EESA. Of the 18 agreements identified 4 had been signed too recently to assess, 2 were no longer in force and the other remaining firms declined to fill in the questionnaire (although they agreed to participate in interviews). The 9 agreements were signed in 8 plants which employed 22,700 workers of which 5,486 operated micro-electronically based equipment. In all, 3,705 of these employees were covered by the 9 agreements. The questionnaire responses revealed significant differences between the two broad types of agreement, on their influence in stimulating early consultation and disclosure of information. Furthermore, the follow-up interviews indicated that the approach to consultation taken by different occupational groups vary across the workforce and with the history of industrial relations. Amongst production workers, for example, consultative mechanisms for discussing change were well established with substantial changes subject to formal or informal agreements which had many similarities with the TASS 'one-off' agreements mentioned above. These agreements are seen as a pragmatic response to a specific technological change that would not be repeated or continued; longer term developments received little consideration. On the other hand, 'procedural' agreements have been signed predominantly by clerical workers with whom consultative mechanisms for change had previously been less well developed. In contrast to both production and clerical workers those technologists with responsibility for the design, development and installation of computer-based or electronically controlled equipment had not generally sought collective procedures of either type even though they were frequently trade union members (in ASTMS). This was explained by the fact that the current and future work of these groups was tied to the existence of 'new' technologies.

Taken as a single group, the 9 technology agreements can be seen as as having a significant impact on the timing of consultation of the introduction of new technology described earlier. As shown in Table 9.4 they resulted in consultation taking place at an earlier stage in the process of change than had previously been the case. For example, the incidence of consultation from the planning stage more than doubled.

The shift towards earlier employee involvement, as illustrated in Table 9.5, is seen as being primarily the result of procedural agreements. In general, those firms with 'procedural' technology agreements appear to have started from a position of somewhat later consultation than was observed in those firms surveyed without specific agreements. After agreements were concluded the firms concerned moved to a position either equal to or slightly higher than the norm (as established by the survey on conventional agreements.

In documenting the influence of agreements on technological change on the extent of consultation, five approaches were identified

Table 9.4

Stage at which unions are first consulted

Stage at which unions first consulted	Agreements on technological change	
	Before Agreement Signed (n=9)	After Agreement Signed (n=9)
Planning new equipment systems	1.5	3.5
Choice of equipment systems	1.5	1
Implementation	5	4.5
None	2	

Source: In 4 firms where we had replies from both the union representative and personnel manager and in one plant where two unions responded, we used the average of replies.

Table 9.5

Effect of clauses on advance notification stage at which unions are first consulted

Stage at which unions first consulted	5 Agreements stipulating advance notification etc.		4 Agreements not referring to advance notification	
	Before Agreement	After Agreement	Before Agreement	After Agreement
Planning new equipment/ systems	0	2	1.5	1.5
Choice of equipment/ systems	0	0.5	0.5	0.5
Implementation	3.5	2.5	1.5	2
None	1.5	0	0.5	0

Source: In 4 firms where we had replies from both the union representative and personnel manager and in one plant where two unions responded, we used the average of the replies.

Table 9.6

Major areas of discussion under technology agreements

	Agreements on technological change	
	No. (n=9)	%
Monitoring the introduction of new equipment and systems	7	78
Pacing of work	1.5	17
Changes of job content	7.5	83
Remuneration	6.5	72
Health and safety	8	89
Changes in employment levels	7	78

Source: In 4 firms where we had replies from both the union representative and personnel manager and in one plant where two unions responded, we used the average of the replies.

Table 9.7

The scope of information provision

	Agreements on technological change			
	Before agreement signed		After agreement signed	
	No. (n=9)	%	No. (n=9)	%
Setting and timing of introduction	3.5	39	8	89
Workflow and methods	3	33	6.5	72
Manning and skill levels	2.5	28	4.5	50
Training	5	55	8	89
Remuneration	5	55	6	67
Costing	1.5	17	2	22
Health and safety	6	67	8.5	94

Source: In 4 firms where we had replies from both the union representative and personnel manager and in one plant where two unions responded, we used the average of the replies.

including *mutuality* where no change occurred without mutual agreement; *negotiation* where there was no change until negotiation procedures were exhausted; *consultation* in which changes were discussed in advance with unions but were not linked to dispute procedures or 'status quo' clauses; *individual representation* in which changes were discussed with the workers involved; or finally *no representation* at all. The proccedural agreements either provided for 'prior negotiation of change' and included use of the normal disputes procedures or 'prior consultation', while 'one-off' agreements did not usually specify consultative procedures. Following implementation of the agreement 6 firms practiced prior negotiation, 2 consultation and one did not institute change without 'mutual agreement'. In 5 of the cases these arrangements merely continued previous practice, while in the rest they reflected an increase in the extent of consultation from 'no representation', 'individual representation' or 'consultation'. The principal level of consultation in the firms with agreements was with the representative committee for the union at plant level. This continued previous practice for those plants in which 'one-off' agreements were signed. Where 'procedural' agreements had been signed, this represented a shift, in all but one case from lower level discussions usually with the shop steward or the operative. In the firm with the joint staff union agreement, a joint new technology committee met with management on a fortnightly basis and the unions had observers on the management committee that was coordinating the company's programme of technological change.

The pattern and range of issues covered by firms having signed Technology Agreements are also broadly comparable with our findings for general consultation in the industry. The most frequently cited issue, as shown in Table 9.6, was health and safety, while the pacing of work was rarely mentioned. The research indicates that on average a wider range of issues were covered under Technology Agreements than under 'conventional' arrangements although once again there exist considerable differences between categories of agreement. 'Procedural' agreements, for example, were twice at likely as 'one-off' agreements to cover monitoring the introduction of new equipment and systems. Remuneration, on the other hand, was less likely to be the subject of consultation resulting from 'procedural' agreements than would be the case in 'one-off' agreements.

The similarities between many firms' already established procedures and those with technology agreements is also evident in the range of information provided to the workforce. Once again we find that information on 'health and safety' is most often disseminated while 'costings' were referred to infrequently. However the process of formulating and signing an agreement has resulted in those firms with a previously inadequate flow of information significantly increasing the amount of information made available.

As Table 9.6 shows, the number of firms supplying information on the 'setting and timing of introduction' and on 'workflow and methods' doubled. This increase is principally a consequence of those 'procedural' agreements which incorporate specific clauses on information provision. Table 9.7 indicates that with the signing of 'procedural' agreements the range of topics covered were subsequently extended and are now on a par with many of the more 'open' firms in the electronics industry. Those firms who had signed agreements without specific clauses on information provision ('one-off' agreements) had already been providing union representatives with a broad range of information which increased only marginally while the agreement was in force. It would appear that the inclusion of clauses concerned with information provision was a response to such information disclosure not having been part of the firm's industrial relations tradition.

In considering the contribution made by information provision to the joint handling of technological change the quality of information is as important as the quantity. In nearly all cases this was considered to be satisfactory although one union representative pointed out the need for more time to study this information. Concern was expressed, however, on the limitations of the information in understanding the longer term implications and the possibilities for extending and linking systems that might emerge over the longer term.

Conclusions

The responses to the two surveys indicate that within the electronics industry there are firms which recognise the benefits to consultation and disclosure of information, both in terms of directly increasing the efficiency with which new technologies are introduced and, more generally, in creating a more conducive climate for good industrial relations. When asked to elaborate on the benefits to established arrangements managers referred to general considerations such as 'increased commitment through involvement', 'greater appreciation of the nature of commercial and technical decisions by those on the shopfloor', and a 'better understanding by managers of the issues related to change'. In addition more specific advantages included the 'reduction in the time involved in introducing change', 'the readiness to accept redeployment' and 'improvements to the design of the product'. While the number of such firms is undoubtedly growing others remain unconvinced, leaving much room for improvement. In those firms responding to the first survey on established procedures over half (29 of the 46 firms) unequivocally stated that current arrangements had facilitated the process of change. Of those firms which were less sure and indicated only the occasional benefit, we find that only a small proportion (1 in 12) encouraged consultation during the planning stage or provided any information before implementation (2 in 12). Although the relationship between the two factors, early in consultation being a prerequisite to good industrial relations is accepted by some, for many firms, the 'penny has yet to drop'. Nearly all the firms in the sample were content to maintain the status quo with some expressing the concern that increased consultation could delay the rate of technological change. Such an attitude is unlikely to serve the industry well in the future. If anything, the pace of technological change which has ushered in such dramatic shifts in labour requirements is more than likely to continue if not increase. The scale of change required in the electronics industry (EDC, 1982; IT/SWP, 1983) if it is to maintain a share of the world market cannot possibly be successful if it is based upon the unilateral introduction of change. Such an approach is likely to result in resentment and resistance to change or at the very least will leave thorny demarcation problems particularly between 'white' and 'blue' collar functions which can arise during the introduction of new technology. A case in point has been the conflicts in several plants between technical staff and electricians about the maintenance of computer-based systems. In one example, the enhancement of skill and grading levels of electricians had in turn led to tensions over differentials with engineering craftsmen.

As mentioned above the bulk of technological change in the workplace has been handled through 'normal consultative procedures', with 'normal' representing a wide range of possibilities. The desire by managers not to single out technological change as an issue to be dealt with outside conventional arrangements has led to Technology Agreements becoming a more emotive subject than the evidence would suggest is warranted. Although trade union representatives and managers emphasised different benefits accruing from Technology Agreements the reaction based on our limited samples, has been primarily positive. In general, while satisfaction with 'procedural' agreements was expressed more frequently than with the 'one-off' variety the latter were also perceived as a pragmatic response at the time to a specific technological change. As might be expected given their concentration on specific issues such as remuneration, arrangements for operating the system, or training, their value was seen by respective signatories on the balance between concessions and achievements and some found this style of agreement inflexibile in resolving disagreements. With hindsight the union signatories to 'one-off' agreements on computer-aided-design would have amended the arrangements by changing the training and selection procedure, improving

184

conditions of employment (i.e. better pay, shorter hours, while trying to avoid shiftwork), better information and earlier consultation. These agreements have been recognised as being too narrow in scope and unable to deal with many problems unsuspected before implementation. The suggestions on how agreements would be changed with hindsight also indicate that the procedures for solving problems established may not have been fully effective. In fact, two of these 'one-off' agreements have subsequently been amended. In one, provision has been made for closer consultation with local shop stewards on day-to-day problems and in the other a new agreement had been signed at the initiation of management along the lines of procedural agreements. In comparison to 'one-off' agreements, procedural arrangements on general technological change were seen as a useful tool for improving industrial relations. Rather than replacing existing procedures these agreements are employed as a supplement which tend to cover a similar range of topics for consultation and information provision as included within conventional procedures.

As expected the perceptions of different parties to change, although coinciding to a larger extent than often imagined, are subject to different aims and expectations. Personnel Managers generally sought to gain union commitment to the introduction of new technology (through better information provision) and to establish mechanisms for handling change without confrontation on a planned basis. Most of the managers felt that these expectations had been largely achieved in that unions accepted new technology readily, resulting in increased flexibility and productivity, and that discussions on change were more constructive because the union was confident that it was going to be consulted and had less fears of redundancies.

One respondent noted a marked difference in resistance to change between the signatory union and the others in the firm. Another manager confirmed that as a result of the agreement, the machinery for introducing change has been regularised, speeding up the process of technological innovation although another remained concerned that prolonged consultation might delay the introduction of change. This fear was similar to that expressed by some managers who preferred to maintain more informal procedures for change and with those who claimed that the technology advanced 'too rapidly' to be tied to specific procedures. To some extent, satisfaction with the agreements is dependent upon the degree to which local practice at the firm level adheres with policy preference at the group level. In one case, management expressed some concern, not with the practical effect of the agreement within the plant, but rather with the potential conflict with what had since become corporate policy. In another example, however, where both corporate and local policy were more in tune, management expressed surprise that the union model agreement was not stronger and the agreement presented little problem for the firm.

Trade union representatives expected and reported a wider range of benefits from technology agreements than did their counterparts in management. Most welcomed the opportunity to participate in early consultation particularly where it occurred before the company had made a final decision on the introduction of a system and in those cases where the agreement included the possibility for monitoring and extension of subsequent innovation. Union representatives saw the agreements as a chance of slowing or in some cases stopping redundancies, although no direct correlation between job loss and satisfaction with the agreements were observed. In general, the agreements were seen as a means of improving working conditions from health and safety through to training. Satisfaction and dissatisfaction with 'one-off' agreements was closely associated with the concrete experience of the specific impacts of the technologies introduced on pay, elimination of mundane tasks, or even improvements to the product. The major concerns were with the implementation of the agreements (the suspected lack of commitment by management) and the complacency of the unions after agreement was reached.

Overall, the agreements were seen as representing a shift from an adversarial and reactive approach to a more participatory arrangement with noticeably less suspicion. However, such agreements, while useful should not be viewed as a universal panacea to industrial relations problems. For example, rarely (only two cases found) have the technology agreements, either 'one-off' or 'procedurals' increased multi-union consultation with management. Although there are examples of some increased inter-union meetings, this does not appear to cross traditional 'white' and 'blue' collar boundaries, even though the technologies have an impact across job boundaries. In one firm, management had offered to sign a procedural agreement with each of the other unions but this is likely to increase uniformity rather than integrate mechanisms for handling change.

Two surveys while not intended as a comprehensive review of the industry's practice, provide a fairly representative indication of the extent to which UK electronics companies are involved in consultation and what information is made available to employees. The surveys do not provide sufficient information to evaluate objectively the different forms of consultative mechanisms adopted by individual firms or groups. In particular the limited, although increasing, number of technology agreements signed in the industry should be compared with the over 200 signed in other industries and sectors of the economy. However, the surveys do illustrate that among both the formal and less formal means of introducing change there exists a considerable amount of room for improvement. The results also suggest that perhaps a greater importance than the differences, between those firms which sign technology agreements and those which have developed their existing procedures to incorporate discussion of technological change, are the similarities. Both forms of arrangements require the commitment of managers and unions together and the important feature is early consultation and wide ranging availability of information regardless of the degree of formality of the approach.

One respondent commented that improved consultation with and the increased involvement of employees in the process of change is necessary in order to match the higher expectations of today's population to participate in and influence decisions that affect their lives. The potential of micro-electronically based technological change to be both labour and capital saving will assure a rapid pace of innovation and diffusion of new technologies in the electronics industry. In order to benefit both the individual and the firm the responsible and equitable 'management of change' required informed consultation and participation of decision-making at the earliest possible stage.

References

Bamber, G., 'Microchips and Industrial Relations', *Industrial Relations Journal*, 11, no. 5, November 1980, pp.7—19.
CBI, 'Job Facing the Future', London, 1980.
CBI, 'Current Employee Involvement: Practice in British Business', London, 1981.
Evans, A. and Wilkinson, T., 'How to Introduce New Technology', Institute of Personnel Management, London, 1983.
Labour Research Department, 'Survey of New Technology', *Bargaining Report*, no.22, October 1982.
Levie, H. and Williams, R., 'User Involvement and Industrial Democracy: Problems and Strategies in Britain', in Brief, U., *et al* (ed.), *Systems Design for, with and by the Users*, North Holland, 1983.
NEDC, 'Policy for the UK Information Technology Industry', London, 1982.
NEDC, 'Manpower and Training in the Electronics Industry' report to the Electronic EDC's Employment and Technology Task Force, EDC/ELEC (82) ET39, mimeographed, 1982a.
NEDC, 'Policy for the UK Electronics Industry', London, 1982b.
NEDC, 'The Introduction of New Technology in the Electronics Industry', London, 1983.

Peltu, M., 'In Place of Technological Strife', *New Scientist*, 13 March 1980.

Robins, K. and Webster, F., 'New Technology: A Survey of Trade Union Response in Britain', *Industrial Relations Journal*, 13, no. 2, Spring 1982, pp.7–26.

Sleigh, J. *et al.*, 'The Manpower Implications of Microelectronics Technology', HMSO: 1979.

TUC, 'Employment and Technology revised report, London, 1979.

TUC, 'Technology Change', a joint TUC-CBI statement, August 1980.

Williams, R., 'Technology Agreements – Report to the Electronic's EDC's Employment and Technology Task Force', NEDO EDC/ELEC (82) ET16 mimeographed, 1982.

Williams, R. and Mosely, R., 'Technology Agreements: Consensus, Control and Technical Change in the Workplace' in Bjorn-Anderson *et al.*, (ed.) *Information Society for Richer for Poorer*, North Holland, 1982.

10 Industrial relations, new technology and the BL Metro

Graham Winch, Arthur Francis, Mandy Snell and Paul Willman

Introduction

The British Leyland Motor Corporation, now BL plc, was formed in 1968, and is unique in the British car industry in being the product of a series of post-war mergers and rationalisations. Vauxhall and Ford have expanded through growth rather than amalgamation and the Rootes Group, now owned by Peugot Citroen, was largely formed before the war. The two companies which came together in 1968 — British Motor Holdings and Leyland — were themselves loosely integrated and the new corporate structure exacerbated this fragmentation. This merger was greatly eased by the Industrial Reorganisation Corporation, and the company has since held a special position as the only remaining major motor manufacturer which is British owned.

During the 1950s the British motor industry enjoyed an unprecedented boom in which companies could sell all that they could produce. Production at full capacity in an easy market, coupled with full employment and hence a tight labour market meant that the employers' concession costs were low and resistance costs high in collective bargaining. The post-war shop steward movement easily established itself in the motor industry, and managements failed to invest adequately in the modernisation of their production processes (see Bhaskar, 1979; Dunnett, 1980; Turner, 1973 for detail). The crisis broke in the early 1970s as the world market moved into recession and import-penetration grew. In these respects, the British car industry presents a case study in the more general phenomenon of the process of 'deindustrialisation'. This can be defined as the failure of an advanced manufacturing country to provide the wealth to support the desired level of imports in a socially acceptable way.

During 1974 the financial position of BL worsened rapidly as it ran up to the limit of its overdraft facilities with little prospect of further funds being made available. The Government responded by appointing the Ryder Committee in December 1974 to analyse the 'present position and future prospects' of the company. The Report was presented to the Secretary of State for Industry in March 1975 (Ryder, 1975). It covered all aspects of the company's operations, and concluded that BL should remain a producer of cars and commercial vehicles throughout the product range. In order that this be successfully accomplished, the injection of £900m, largely from state funds, for capital investment was recommended. This was to be supported by extensive rationalisations of the product range, operating facilities and engineering resources. In the area of industrial relations, recommendations were made in three areas — payments systems, industrial democracy and collective bargaining. This chapter will analyse the inter-action between the developments associated with the implementation of these recommendations, and those associated with the development of the product range and modernisation of manufacturing processes. The company is in a continuing organisational flux, and the descriptions below are accurate up to the middle of 1981. There have also been two industrial engineering exercises since then which have significantly reduced direct and indirect labour levels.

BL Cars, Longbridge

The complex at Longbridge near Birmingham — the old Austin works — is one of the major manufacturing sites of BL Cars, and it saw substantial investment in the biggest single project launched by the company since the publication of the Ryder Report. This was the Metro project which cost £275m in total. The car was launched in October 1980, and its success was seen as crucial to the continuance of BL Cars as a volume car producer. The largest single element of investment was the £106m spent on the West Works No.2 for the assembly of the Metro body, or body-in-white as it is called in the industry. Details of the production process are given in Butler (1980), but the key points to note here are that two main operations are involved — handling and fastening, the latter operation being performed by seam welding, spot welding and bolting. The majority of

190

seam welds and all the bolting are performed manually — the £80m spent on production technology went largely on the handling and spot welding operations. In contrast to the publicity attracted by the plant, robots perform only 9.5% of the welds, while 70.9% are completed by multiwelders and 19.6% are applied manually.

For organisational purposes the site at Longbridge is divided into six units:

Unit 1 . . . Body-in-white and paint
Unit 2 . . . Car Assembly Buildings (CAB) and trim manufacture
Unit 3 . . . Power — Train manufacture A Series
Unit 4 . . . Power — Train manufacture E Series
Unit 5 . . . Power — Train manufacture O Series
Unit 6 . . . Central Engineering Services (CES)

Units 1, 2, 3 and 6 are those concerned with Metro manufacture; the West Works No.2 is within Unit 1. Daily industrial relations issues are handled by industrial relations (IR) managers in each Unit; they are supported by a central IR department, and all report through the industrial relations manager for the hourly paid to the site personnel manager. The personnel manager has a direct line responsibility to the Operations Director, Birmingham, and a functional reporting relationship through the regional employee relations director to the Cars Group Employee Relations function.

There are 10 unions representing hourly paid workers at Longbridge, and they form the Austin Joint Shop Stewards Committee (JSSC). The JSSC elects on an annual basis the Works Committee which consists of seven members plus a minutes secretary. Four places go to the Transport and General Workers Union (TGWU), three to the Amalgamated Union of Engineering Workers (AUEW), and the remaining place to one other which represents the remaining unions. The TGWU and AUEW are the numerically predominant unions on the site, with the TGWU having the largest membership due to its organisation of around three-quarters of the direct production workers. The JSSC also elects a chair and secretary, and the secretary is designated works convenor. At present the convenorship is held by the TGWU and the chair by the AUEW. There are no senior stewards recognised by management within the production units, but within Unit 6 a senior steward represents each of the four trade groups. The millwrights and machine tool fitters are both organised by the AUEW, the electricians by the Electrical, Electronic, Telecommunications and Plumbing Trade Union (EEPTU), and the pipefitters by the National Union of Sheetmetalworkers, Coppersmiths, Heating and Domestic Engineers (NUSMW). The chair and convenor are full time lay officials. For negotiation purposes, the Works Committee is expanded to involve

191

a wider cross-section of unions to form the Negotiating Committee of around a dozen members.

BL left the Engineering Employers Federation (EEF) in June 1980. This organisation bargains annually with the body representing those unions organising manual workers in the industry, the Confederation of Shipbuilding and Engineering Unions (CSEU). These negotiations provided for basic pay and conditions of employment in BL, but as in most companies, major enhancements were negotiated at the local level. Piror to 1979 there was very little bargaining for hourly paid workers above plant level in BL Cars; pensions were negotiated at company level, and corporate security of earnings and sick pay agreements had been negotiated in 1977 and 1978 respectively. Although the company had made an identical pay offer to all plants under the auspices of incomes policy in 1978, November 1979 was the first time that negotiations on the full range of topics took place at corporate level.

In 1975, the Longbridge Operations Direct Workers and Indirect Workers Agreement was reached. These agreed a two-grade structure for direct workers, and a seven-grade structure for the indirect workers. The latter structure had been established through a job evaluation process (see Ogden, 1971 for the background to this). Other items covered by the agreements were the use of industrial engineering techniques, mobility, and conditions of employment. A notable feature of the agreements is that they embodied the principle of mutuality — for instance the application of industrial engineering techniques was to be preceded by full discussion with shop stewards and the membership, and mobility was based upon the 1968 plant mobility procedure agreement which specified discussions between the supervisor, and the members and shop stewards concerned as the first stage. These two agreements formed the basis of negotiations at Longbridge on pay and conditions until they were superseded by the 1979 corporate document. The Longbridge procedure agreement was negotiated in 1976. It provided for union recognition, the role of shop stewards, and Works Committee, and procedures for negotiations and the settlement of disputes. The only formally recognised demarcation within the plant for production workers is included in the terms of this agreement. It reserves a number of sheet metal working jobs on the finishing line in West Works No.1, which makes the bodies for the Mini and Allegro, for members of the NUSMW, and door hanging on that line for members of the TGWU.

This formal system of plant agreements was supplemented by a large number of local agreements throughout the plant. These were negotiated at sectional level, without control from the site IR function, yet were written agreements which could be 'held up against' management. Most of these agreements were for special payments

192

of one kind or another, but many covered working practices, such as the 6A agreement which specified that if there were to be lay-offs on the night shift, they had to occur before 10 o'clock, and the 6 and 2 agreements which specified the day shift and night shift ratios for maintenance workers. There were also around 50 groups of workers listed in the Direct Workers Agreement who qualified for some form of fixed supplementary payment on the main grade rate. Such fragmentation led to very complex and time-consuming bargaining – one line manager estimated that he used to spend 45% of his time on industrial relations issues. It also militated against mobility of labour because the agreements were not compatible between different areas. Again, perhaps the crucial feature of this informal system was the emphasis upon mutuality and the role of the shop stewards – management would always approach the workforce through the shop steward.

The 'principle of mutuality' is long established in the British engineering industry. Payments by results began to be introduced into the industry towards the end of the 19th century with the aim of enabling employers to gain greater control over the effort and output of their workforce. In order to exclude trade union officials from the setting of piece-work prices, the engineering employers imposed the principle of mutuality after the 1898 lockout (Jeffreys, 1946). The essence of the principle is that 'piece-work prices and bonus or basic times shall be fixed by mutual agreement between the employer and the worker who is to perform the work' (CSEU, 1979). However, the other workers in the plant clearly have an interest in the prices agreed by individuals, and so the setting of prices quickly became the subject of workplace negotiations; indeed this bargaining was the origin of many of the shop stewards' committees that arose during World War I (Goodrich, 1975). Thus, in times of full employment and workplace trade union strength, the principle of mutuality became a major source of workplace bargaining. Any changes in working practices, particularly measurement of the job, have an impact upon bonus earnings, and so mutuality rapidly extended to most aspects of job control on the shop floor and became enshrined in formal agreements as the power of workplace organisations grew during the 1950s and 1960s. Clack (1978) gives the flavour of such bargaining in a plant which later became part of BL Cars.

Payments systems

It is often argued that the installation of automatic machinery means that payment by results systems are no longer viable, because the operator has no control over output, and that the job requirement is consistency of effort rather than maximisation; this point has been made with reference to the motor industry by Turner and his colleagues (1967). The company had begun to implement a corporate policy of moving away from incentive systems to Measured Daywork (MDW) in the early 1970s, and Longbridge had switched in 1972. Although there had been significant increases in manning consequent upon this change, the Ryder Report recommended that no changes be made initially. Therefore, there were no problems associated with payments systems consequent upon the implementation of the new plant. The principle of mutuality survived this change to MDW to become mutuality over the effort bargain, in that standard times were bargained over on the shop floor. Beynon's (1975) account of Halewood describes bargaining under Ford's MDW scheme.

Industrial democracy

Following upon the policies advocated by the incoming Labour Government in 1974, there were a number of experiments in industrial democracy in Britain (see Elliott, 1978 for an overview). The participation scheme at BL Cars was one of the more comprehensive examples. The scheme started in January 1976, and continued until September 1979 when the unions withdrew (the overall structure is shown in Figure 10.1). The terms of reference of the scheme were to review corporate performance, and to examine ways of improving the competitiveness of the company; issues that were normally discussed in the collective bargaining forum were excluded.

The two most important levels for the Metro project were those of the Council, and the Longbridge Joint Management Committee (JMC). At each level, a Metro subcommittee was formed which handled the discussions. The Metro, code-named ADO 88 until 1978, was reconceptualised as the LC 8 thereafter (see Robson, 1982). In early 1976, the Council had, however, approved a presentation of the overall concept of the Metro, which included an evaluation of the production technology to be used. This evaluation covered both the efficiency of the technology proposed, and personnel aspects such as cycle times. This evaluation had been undertaken during 1974 and 1975. The decision to go for high technology contained an element of faith in that the financial appraisal did not fully justify the technology chosen. This is a common problem in justifying automation in that a number of the supposed benefits are not quantifiable — for instance quality and reliability. However, it was felt that high technology was where the future lay, and that all the other car companies were going down the same road. Thus the questions of whether high technology was the best way to produce a competitive small car, and the most appropriate forms of high technology, were not placed before the union side.

The company had been placed under the control of the newly formed National Enterprise Board (NEB), the state holding company, in 1975. When approached for finance for the project in 1976, the NEB expressed grave reservations about its viability, and the company promised to provide more detailed figures. To gain union involvement in providing these figures, the Metro subcommittee was set up, and owing to the very limited amount of time available, the union side were allowed complete access to the manufacturing planning meetings. The outcome of this access was that the union side fully supported the management recommendations on the targets for the new car; and in particular, the targets that were laid down for productivity. These targets were the outcome of a management survey of the operations of competing companies.

At the end of 1976 the discussions were handed down to the plants that were to produce the car. At Longbridge a special subcommittee was also set up. The early meetings were dominated by discussion of the working practices that would be required to meet the productivity targets specified. The key areas were industrial engineering; mobility of labour; and restrictive practices, particularly amongst the maintenance trades. A rest allowance target of 12% was also stressed by management. The major proposal on work organisation was the implementation of team working. The idea was to combine flexibility of labour with increased job satisfaction — teams made up of material handlers, on-line maintenance workers, operators and quality controllers reporting to team supervisors were to cover production zones. The concept also involved the amalgamation of the existing maintenance trades into two — electrical and mechanical. These proposals from management met the approval in principle of the trade union side, although the maintenance trades' representatives were not involved because they were not co-operating as part of their campaign for toolroom autonomy. The background to this campaign is described by Scullion (1981). Once agreement had been reached on these issues, the discussions settled down to a routine of the presentation by management of the various aspects of the production facilities, followed by union questioning. Only in the area of manpower planning did the union side make alternative proposals. This was over proposals for the removal of some trim manufacture from Longbridge to Castle Bromwich. On the other hand, the union side turned down a request from management to put forward proposals for shift patterns.

The participation scheme at BL Cars, unlike many others of that era, did have genuine commitment from the management involved, at least for the first two years, and the trade union leadership was also supportive. However, line management and the trade union membership became increasingly hostile to the scheme. In October 1977 Sir Michael Edwardes was appointed, and he turned first to a re-appraisal of the Ryder plan in the light of continuing failure to meet its targets. The Edwardes plan, announced in February 1978, reorganised the company, reducing sales targets and cut parts of the expansion and modernisation programme (Bhaskar, 1979; Edwardes, 1983). This new policy included redundancies and closures, most notably the closure of the Speke No.2 plant (see Beynon, 1978), and meant that the trade union side were put into an increasingly difficult position, and the scheme began to break down. However, all levels of manager and trade unionist interviewed agreed that the Metro subcommittees did some of their best work under the auspices of the scheme. Insofar as the subcommittees were used by management as 'persuasion arenas', they were highly successful, and major commitments were made by the union side on working practices. On their part, the unions gained major insights into the way the company was managed and the dimensions of the problems it faced.

Collective bargaining

It has been argued that the seventies have witnessed a shift towards the formalisation of bargaining, the spread of job evaluation, and a move to pay bargaining at the level of the single employer (Brown and Terry, 1978; Brown, 1981). In these respects, BL Cars represents a classic case study in the problems implicit in these developments when starting from a highly fragmented base which was the result of amalgamations over a long period of time. So far as the Metro project was concerned the developments associated with the centralisation of bargaining within BL Cars acted as an important constraint upon bargaining over the new technology; but at the same time, that bargaining made a significant contribution to the final shape of the corporate agreement.

In October 1976 the Longbridge JMC was asked to commit itself to the recommendations of the Council subcommittee. The negotiating committee were brought into the discussions on this commitment, and the hourly paid representatives expressed particular concern over the productivity recommendation. They tried to write assurances on mutuality into the commitment, but this was rejected by management who reported a failure to agree with the NEB. The response was 'no commitment — no AD088'. The JMC met again, after balloting the workforce on management's proposed form of the commitment;

the result was in favour. The manual unions backed down and gave their support to this form of the commitment, while stressing that they would be seeking payment for the changes in working practices proposed. A notable feature of these negotiations is that management, driven by the NEB, wanted a commitment to the achievement of productivity targets from the unions before they, and therefore the unions, knew how they were going to be achieved in any detail.

Early in 1978, management made a presentation of the new working practices that they were seeking to the trade union negotiators — again the issues were industrial engineering techniques, team working, mobility, and 2-trades maintenance. Later in the year management tried to open negotiations for the areas affected by the Metro project, however the unions replied by stressing the importance of payment for change and the negotiations covering the whole site. Management's proposals would have meant two bargaining units on the Longbridge site, a move that was against company policy of the centralisation of bargaining: it would also have opened them up to comparability claims. The problems associated with a separate agreement on working practices for the Metro, and the union pressure for a single site agreement meant that management changed their minds, and by the summer of 1978 had drawn up a draft agreement covering the whole site.

The 1978 draft marked a radical departure from the 1975 agreements. The protective clauses on mutuality in the earlier documents were removed, and the range of industrial engineering techniques fully specified while the extent of mobility was broadened. Clauses on the method of team-working and the operation of 2-trade maintenance were also included. No negotiations took place on this draft, but the 'Management of Change' negotiations which finally took place in May 1979 were based upon a similar document. The main issues at these negotiations were payment for change, and the grading of team workers. Discussions on both issues were constrained by the negotiations on the centralisation of bargaining. Management's proposals for payment were based upon the incentive scheme then being negotiated centrally, and the completion of the job evaluation exercise for the establishment of the corporate grade structure. This meant that no money was payable immediately. To avoid this problem the union side demanded a payment in a lump sum upon the reaching of agreement, but this gave management no means of ensuring the achievement of the agreed productivity targets. On team working, the union side wanted grade 2 under the job evaluation scheme for the team operative, and management tried to split that job into two so that it would attract grade 3. This was because management feared comparability claims throughout the company as grade 3 was the main grade for procution operatives.

The 'Management for Change' negotiations were inconclusive, but in many respects they were just a holding operation while the corporate negotiations proceeded. As a matter of policy management were trying to get away from the notion of payment for change; such a concept is inherent in mutuality but is incompatible with a job evaluated grade structure unless the actual job content changes. Moreover, team working was not supported by many managers at Longbridge — it was seen as something imposed from head office smacking of behavioural science and not relevant to those who considered themselves as 'hard men who knew how to make motors'.

In drawing up the draft of the agreement for the 1979 corporate negotiations management invited submissions from all the plants in BL Cars. Longbridge had spent the last three years thinking about new working practices in relation to the Metro, and the ideas developed in that forum were largely incorporated into the draft which was presented to the trade unions in the form of the so-called '92 Page Document'. Although the clauses on team working and 2-trades maintenance were greatly toned down, those on mobility and industrial engineering remained as forceful as before. Amendments were made to the draft during the ensuing negotiations which re-admitted an element of mutuality, but these were little more than cosmetic in effect. The central place that mutuality had held in the 1975 agreements was completely overturned.

The negotiations on the '92 Page Document' dragged on for five months until management imposed the draft, together with those amendments that had been agreed, in April 1980. In doing this, the company was greatly aided by the weakening of the trade union strength consequent upon the sacking of the Longbridge Convenor, Derek Robinson, in November 1979. The formal reason for the sacking was that Robinson had led the campaign against the BL Cars Recovery Plan announced in September 1979 which involved substantial redundancies and plant closures, although one manager argued that the sacking 'reflected a completely new determination on the part of management to manage the business in the only way it could be successful'. Sir Michael Edwardes argues that the sacking was the 'last chance of gaining manageability of Longbridge' before the Metro was launched (1983). In terms of new working practices, management concerned with the Metro project argue that they got all they wanted from the successful imposition of the '92 Page Document'.

While these developments were taking place, the issues of demarcation in maintenance working were being resolved. In July 1977 a Unimate robot was installed on the Allegro line to test the reaction of the workforce. As expected this provoked a demarcation dispute, and the use of the Programmable Logic Controllers (PLC), which control the multiwelders and conveyors, for maintenance diagnostics

198

caused similar problems. The dispute was between the electricians and the two mechanical trades over programming and the accessing of information. The issue finally went to a national conference under the engineering industry procedure, and an interim agreement lasting one year was reached in February 1980 which gave the electricians responsibility for both jobs. However, in practice the working has been much more fluid; the demarcation has not been maintained and the issue has not been raised again. The maintenance trades also refused to undergo training as part of their long-running dispute over differentials and toolroom autonomy, and it was only in April 1980 that full training commenced. On both these issues, however, management claim that there was little impact on the overall project – they had foreseen both problems and had allowed themselves plenty of time to sort them out before they could affect production of the new car. There seems little doubt that the main reason for installing the Unimate on the Allegro line was to allow the demarcation issue to be raised and resolved in good time.

Sir Michael Edwardes has stated that '1978 was the year in which the industrial relations nettle was grasped' (cited Chell, 1980). In June 1976 there had been 58 bargaining units for hourly paid workers in BL Cars; in November 1979 there was one. Against these developments the unions had been unable to mount an effective opposition. The long standing weaknesses of the Leyland Combine Trade Union Committee meant that the shop steward organisation had no means of co-ordinating their activities above plant level, and this vacuum was filled by the CSEU. Bargaining over the new technology was constrained by management's concern to maintain the integrity of the new bargaining structure and meant that they were not prepared to make concessions for the Metro project. The unions fully supported the implementation of the new technology, but demanded payment for change and the retention of the traditional protection of mutuality, their weaknesses meant that they could not enforce these demands.

The positive aspect of management's strength was the credibility of the Edwardes team which took over in November 1977; the negative aspect was the desperate financial situation of the company (Chell, 1980). For personnel management at Longbridge, the role of Edwardes was quite fundamental. They felt that the company was now being managed from the top, and that tough decisions would get support from senior management in a way that they never had before. The belief that the company was on the brink was shared by the CSEU Executive and the membership. The former's interventions were always to move the trade union side toward the acceptance of the company's proposals. The membership demonstrated their views in the series of ballots on the key aspects of the centralisation proposals, and thereby supported the belief amongst management that the rank and file leadership did not represent the voice of the membership (Chell, 1980). These views were strongly influenced by company propaganda, the statements of the CSEU, and the threats by the government and the NEB to withhold funds. The divisions on the union side and the twin strengths of management meant that the company had made remarkable progress in the restructuring of the industrial relations system by the time the new car went into full production.

The system at Longbridge after April 1980

The imposition of the '92 Page Document' in April 1980 had two distinct impacts. Firstly, the main level of bargaining was moved sharply upwards. Except within closely defined areas, all bargaining now takes place at the corporate (BL Cars) level. This shift in levels upwards is dependent upon the removal of mutuality from the shop floor and has meant a great reduction in the amount of time spent by shop stewards and line managers on industrial relations. One manager reckoned that the time he spent on industrial relations dropped from 45% to 5%, and management initially reduced the number of full time shop stewards to the seven on the Works Committee, and have more recently cut this to two. Secondly, on working practices, management claim to have successfully removed a high proportion of restrictive practices and special payments. In Unit 1, management drew up a list of the practices they wanted to remove, informed the shop stewards in April, and largely implemented the changes in June. However, the demarcations in production and maintenance still remain − there has been very little progress towards 2-trades maintenance at the level of the Longbridge plant overall, and there is still the demarcation on the Mini and Allegro lines in the West Works No. 1.

Perhaps the major impact of the imposition, at least in the short term, has not been in the area of bargaining levels or working practices, but in management style. The Ryder Report recommended that line management should take a greater responsibility for industrial relations. Although the range of bargaining at local level is severely constrained by the new framework there has been an increase in the authority of local management in the implementation of policy. In the past, central industrial relations at Longbridge was the 'lynchpin through which everything to do with the employees' was handled; it is now much more passive and co-ordinating in its role.

The key to the new style has been a re-assertion of what one industrial relations manager described as 'management's responsibility to manage'. This can be seen most clearly over the issue of communication with the workforce. In the past, management spoke to the workforce through the shop steward, but as the centralisation of bargaining developed and the crisis of 1979 was overcome, the means of direct communication with employees were developed. At plant level, this means direct mailing to the employee's homes; on the line it means a policy of briefings with the whole workforce where possible. As the Metro line was being manned up, there was a deliberate policy circumventing the shop stewards in communication, and at the launch, the whole workforce received a briefing. These changes in style were codified by a statement issued in December 1979 on 'Management in BL' (see Chell, 1980: Appendix VIII) which emphasised the necessity for firm and consistent leadership, backed by senior management. Longbridge management see themselves as more forceful and determined than they used to be, and more than one manager stressed the importance of the fact that they could now rely on support from senior management for firm action. The success of such a strategy depends, in the end, upon the suspension of mutuality – the shop stewards are now informed of changes when they would have been asked about them in the past. The changes were described to us by management as deliberate and dramatic.

In the run-up to the Metro launch in October 1980 there were no particular industrial relations problems. The main concern of industrial relations management in Unit 1 was to ensure that the disciplines imposed through the imposition, and the gains made were not jeopardised under the pressure for output as the launch date approached. The pre-launch pressures were very high and a new operations manager was brought in from another BL Cars plant to ensure production targets were met. Although the main problem did not lie with the workforce, he met the Works Committee and negotiated increased production rates. The Works Committee agreed to the working of unlimited overtime, despite the opposition of the local AUEW District Committee which argued that in a period of high unemployment, more workers should be taken on instead.

Although the thinking around the working of the new body-in-white facility in West Works No.2 was the source of many of the provisions of the corporate document, there were no special provisions that applied to the new facility. However, management saw the facility as an opportunity to start with a clean slate in an area where no tradition of custom and practice had built up. On the production side, the manning of the new works took place in two stages. At first, volunteers were requested, and later compulsory transfers taking into account seniority were then made. When selecting amongst the volunteers, management picked those whom they considered to be flexibly minded, and those with 'bad records' were not selected. However, as the volume of production increased management could not afford to be so choosy, although the seniority rule meant that younger workers tended to be transferred. Recruitment for maintenance workers took place outside the company. The problems that the company faced during the seventies due to skill shortages were considerable, and a nationwide recruitment drive was launched. The result of this is that many of the maintenance workers have only ever worked for BL in the new West Works.

Partly by luck and more by judgement, therefore, the workforce in the new facility was not steeped in the trade union traditions of Longbridge. The established trade union hierarchy within the Unit remained in the old No.1 Works. Although the company does not formally recognise senior stewards within the Units, the informal senior stewards for both the TGWU and the AUEW remained in the old West Works, and management recognise that the general level of experience of the stewards in the No.2 Works is low. The stewards in the new works are also poorly organised − there are 20 production stewards for 1400 men in the new works, as against 24 for 600 men in the old works (figures for January 1982). On the maintenance side there are two shop stewards for each trade group with the exception of the machine-tool fitters who have four. These stewards are split across the two shifts.

Five shop stewards from the West Works No.2 were interviewed − three production workers and two tradesmen. All five complained about the lack of communication between stewards, particularly with opposite numbers on the other shift. There are no regular meetings between stewards in the new West Works, and few contacts with other stewards in the Unit. The forum for such meetings could be the Unit Committee, but that is almost defunct at the moment, as it is in the other Units. The only forum at which the production stewards can meet with others is the JSSC meetings. The craft workers are better off in that they have their regular trade group meetings. The reasons for this recognised state of poor organisation were mainly laid at the door of the selection procedure by the stewards. As one put it − when they selected the volunteers, they chose the worst trade unionists, and the good shop stewards who were moved in the compulsory transfer took the attitude that they were not going to help out those who had failed to back Derek Robinson. Also, as the groups were moved across, management did not at first recognise shop stewards, but appointed spokesmen. Management had a deliberate policy of not talking to the shop stewards, trying to build up the role of the supervisor as the means of communication with the workforce. Against these tactics, the trade unions found it difficult to build up a workplace organisation. The unions were also refused facilities, such as a room for meetings, which they have in the old works. The shorter lunch breaks and faster pace of working were also blamed for less effective meetings by one steward.

None of the shop stewards interviewed felt that there had been a particular attack upon them in the new works — they were ready to place the problem at the level of the plant, or even the mood of the country, but management have built upon this situation to make further progress on implementing new working practices than in other parts of the Longbridge complex. On the production side, the demarcation between the NUSMW and TGWU has not been established, and the Metro line is generally considered by management to present few industrial relations problems. It is on the maintenance side that working practices in the new facility have most changed. Although there is still 4-trade maintenance, a compromise has been reached in the form of 2-trade response. As the equipment was being installed, maintenance management decided which two trades were most suited to the particular maintenance problems of each machine. In practice, this meant the electricians and one other trade were allocated to each machine. The pipefitters were not really involved as they tend to be allocated to site services, but each machine was allocated to either the machine tool fitters or the millwrights — the latter tended to get the heavier work such as the conveyors. The shop stewards were then informed that, for intance, the KUKA multiwelder would be an electrician and machine tool fitter job. There was a certain amount of diplomacy involved in that while management saw the Unimate robots as more appropriate to the skills of the machine tool fitters, they did give those used for material handling to the millwrights. The electricians and fitters have also been moved out of their maintenance pens and they are now permanently allocated to a machine; this has reduced maintenance response times, which was considered to be the major advantage of team working from the maintenance point of view.

There are no aspects of the new working practices which particularly stand out for the workforce — the shop stewards interviewed all considered the general regime to be more of a problem. Both the maintenance stewards interviewed — an electrician and a millwright — stressed the amount of co-operation that there was between the two trades on the machines. The millwrights need the assistance of the electricians to use the PLCs, and the electrician argued that the problems were so closely linked that they had to work together. The general success of the 2-trade response arrangement in generating co-operation between the trades was confirmed by both the members of the Works Committee interviewed, and management. However, the millwright shop steward did report that his members were not too happy with having the machine tool fitters around. The issue here is that the type of work required for these automated machines is closer to the skills of the machine tool fitter than the millwright.

Thus management have made major gains in implementing new working practices in the Metro body-in-white facility. The opportunity to start from scratch with a new facility coupled with the general tenor of industrial relations in the company allowed management to break with previous working traditions. Although much of the thinking behind the new working practices was stimulated by the challenge of implementing a major capital investment in automated equipment, none of the working practices implemented are in any sense determined by the technology, with the possible exception of 2-trades response. The new working practices apply equally across the Longbridge site, and it was the newness of the technology rather than its intrinsic information processing capabilities which allowed the more successful implementation of the working practices in West Works No.2. On 2-trades response, however, the greater size and complexity of the equipment, together with diagnostic facilities provided by the PLCs does seem to have generated a more co-operative approach independently from the benefit of the workers being largely new to Longridge and BL. The fitters need the information generated by the PLCs in order to tackle their jobs, and the logic of those doing the actual repair work on the robot hardware also doing any reprogramming that might be necessary has also been informally accepted. The placing of the workers together on the machines, rather than together with their own trade in the maintenance pen may also have helped generate this atmosphere. Again, the newness of the technology, with the challenge of tackling new problems may have been an element in generating the more flexible approach.

Employment levels in the new West Works

Considerations of both employee numbers and job satisfaction played a key role in the early planning of the project. The productivity target set in October 1976 was effectively an employee numbers target which was progressively tightened as the project developed. The specific productivity targets set for the Metro line were included in the overall target of 2000 direct workers for Unit 1 as a whole. Since the launch, this target has been progressively reduced through industrial engineering programmes. One manager has estimated that only 10% to 15%

204

of the direct labour productivity increase at Longbridge is due to new technology (Fryer, 1982).

There were no redundancies directly associated with the new technology — it was a new facility and hence provided extra capacity. In fact around 1000 workers were taken on at Longbridge in late 1980, mainly to work in the final assembly area and maintenance function. However, there has been a long term cost in jobs, which is detailed in Table 10.1. The overall loss of 942 jobs is a theoretical figure based on comparing the planned direct labour on the automated line with the levels of direct labour that would be required to produce the Metro body with the same technology as the Marina body. Such a loss pales into insignificance in comparison to the loss of 24,000 jobs in BL Cars during 1980 alone.

Conclusions

Broadly, the Metro project went through two distinct phases so far as industrial relations is concerned. The unions had long supported the principle of investing in high technology to make the company competitive in world markets, and management in 1976 and 1977 displayed a genuine commitment to participation as the way of solving the company's long-standing industrial relations problems. The early discussions over the Metro were therefore conducted within a co-operative atmosphere and a broad measure of agreement on priorities was reached. The situation may therefore be described as one of 'bargained acceptance' by the workplace organisation (see Francis and Willman, 1980), or, more precisely, that of a 'productivity coalition' (see Streeck and Hoff, 1981). From the beginning of 1978 the mood in the company changed, and the trade unions found themselves increasingly powerless and divided as management imposed its plans for restructuring the company. By the time the Metro was coming into full production, the trade unions were unable to resist the imposition of new working practices and to press for payment for change.

The role of Sir Michael Edwardes in bringing about this situation is crucial — he provided direction and gave management the confidence to act at the local level, a credibility that was reinforced greatly after the sacking of Derek Robinson. The dire financial situation also greatly strengthened management's hand. In this later confrontational period, management built upon the commitments that had been given by the unions on the Metro project during the cooperative phase. The earlier phase provided a crucial sounding board for management to establish how far the union side were prepared to go, and it is doubtful that management would have been as successful in the imposition of new working practices and the removal of mutuality from the shop floor if they had not been able to build on the base of the earlier period. This of course begs the question of whether the project would have reached its successful conclusion without the shift to confrontation. These considerations suggest that it is more sensible to talk of the impact of industrial relations on technological change than the reverse so far as the Metro project is concerned. The new technology may well have provided a lever for changes in working practices, but the overall developments in the industrial relations system in BL Cars, had a much more profound impact on the project, than the project had on these developments.

References

Beynon, H., *Working for Ford*, E.P. Publishing: Wakefield, 1975.

Beynon, H., *What Happened at Speke?*, 6-612 Branch TGWU, Liverpool, 1978.

Bhaskar, H., *The Future of the UK Motor Industry*, Kogan Page: London, 1979.

Brown, W., *The Changing Contours of British Industrial Relations*, Basil Blackwell: Oxford, 1981.

Brown, W. and Terry, M., 'The Changing Nature of National Wage Agreements', *Scottish Journal of Political Economy*, 125, 1978.

Butler, R.D., 'Modernisation of a Car Plant', *British Association*, Section G, 1980.

Chell, R., *BL Cars Ltd – The Frontier of Control*, MA Thesis, University of Warwick, 1980.

Clack, G., *Industrial Relations in a British Car Factory*, CUP: London, 1967.

CSEU, *Handbook of National Agreements*, CSEU: London, 1979.

Dunnett, P.J.S., *The Decline of the British Motor Industry*, Croon Helm: London, 1980.

Edwardes, M., *Back From the Brink*, Collins: London, 1983.

Elliot, J., *Conflict or Cooperation*, Kogan Page: London, 1978.

Francis, A. and Willman, P., 'Microprocessors: Impact and Response', *Personnel Review*, 9, 1980, pp.9–16.

Fryer, J., 'How they worked a Miracle at Longbridge', *Sunday Times*, 21 March 1982.

Goodrich, C., *The Frontier of Control*, Pluto Press: London, 1975.

Jeffreys, J.B., *The Story of the Engineers*, Lawrence and Wishart: London, 1946.

Table 10.1

Direct labour levels
New West Works vs. Theoretical Conventional Assembly

	New West Works	Conventional
Typical manpower savings in subassembly (per shift):		
Bodyside assembly (m/welder)	10	58
Dash assembly (ASEA robot)	1	5
Underframe floor assembly (m/welder)	11	76
On framing line(s):		
Manual welding vs. ABF plus Unimate Robots Robots	1 operator per line	80 operators

Conventional Metro body build: 942 jobs more than present method

Figure 10.1   BL cars participation scheme*

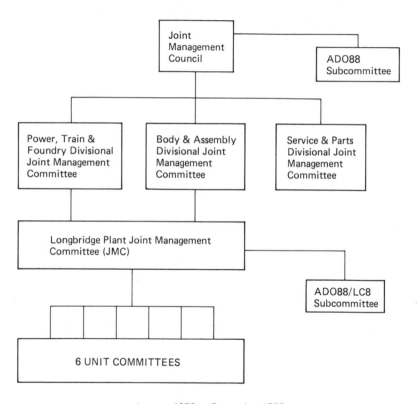

January 1976 to September 1979

---

* The Metro was codenamed ADO 88 until 1978, when the car was reconceptualised and codenamed LC8. See Robson (1982) for details.

Ogden, S., *The Indirect Workers Wage Agreement at Longbridge, Birmingham*, MA Thesis, University of Warwick, 1971.

Robson, G., *Metro: The Book of the Car*, Patrick Stephens: London, 1982.

Ryder Committee, *British Leyland: The Next Decade*, HMSO: London, 1975.

Scullion, H., 'The Skilled Revolt Against General Unionism', *Industrial Relations Journal*, 12, no. 3, May–June 1981, pp.15–28.

Streeck, W. and Hoff, A., *Industrial Relations and Structural Change in the International Automobile Industry*, International Institute for Management: Berlin, 1981.

Turner, G., *The Leyland Papers*, Pan Books, London, 1973.

Turner, H.A., Clack, G. and Roberts, G., *Labour Relations in the Motor Industry*, Allen and Unwin: London, 1967.

11 The Post Office, the unions and the new technology

Vivien Walsh

Introduction

Electronic mail is increasingly being seen as an alternative to conventional forms of communications, especially by businesses. The Mackintosh Report (Mackintosh Consultants Ltd., 1977) forecast a 600% increase in electronic mail terminals in western Europe between 1978 and 1987, while more recently Butler, Cox and Partners (1982) predicted that the UK market for advanced office systems would grow from £48m in 1983 to £320m in 1987.

Conventional mail deliveries will increasingly be competing with electronic mail, and the Post Office faces a potential loss of business as a result. British Telecom's Telecommunications Systems Strategy Department (1977), for example, suggested that '25% of postal mail could be lost to electronic mail systems as the advanced services are used more widely'. It is business-to-business mail that is most likely to be affected.

The Post Office itself, however, is optimistic. It believes that by introducing new services itself, by automating existing work and by 'aggressive marketing', it will be able to compete successfully with electronic mail services provided by other enterprises. As a result of an analysis of Post Office Business Plans and interviews with personnel, we concluded (Walsh *et al.*, 1980 and 1982) that the Post Office's optimism was unjustified. The Post Office has since amended some of its forecasts and assumptions. This chapter will attempt to evaluate current strategies for competing with electronic mail, the likely

210

impact on jobs and services and the factors, within and outside the Post Office's control, which are likely to influence the outcome.

Evaluation of earlier Post Office forecasts

In its 1978–9 Business Plan, the Post Office made a 10 year forecast of postal business volumes, taking into account the likely impact of all telecommunications services, including the telephone as well as electronic mail and electronic funds transfer. The estimate was that the impact of these competing services would be fairly limited in the 1980s, increasing from zero to 5% annual reduction in letter mail by 1988–9. This contrasts with the forecast by the Telecommunications Systems Strategy Department (TSSD) (then still part of the Post Office), mentioned above, that a loss of 25% of postal traffic was foreseen, as a result of the effects of facsimile and communicating word-processors.

The 1978–9 Business Plan also forecast the number of staff likely to be employed in handling this business. The estimate was that there would be a reduction of 14,600 jobs by 1989. Our report (Walsh *et al.*, 1980) was commissioned by the Union of Communication Workers (UCW), the largest of the Trade Unions representing Post Office employees: it was then the Union of Post Office Workers. The authors of the report were at that time all members of the Science Policy Research unit at Sussex University. The UCW's National Executive Council commissioned the report as a result of the following resolution being carried at the Annual Conference of the Union in 1979:

> 'Conference agrees that it is deeply concerned at the effects on the Post Office and its services, and the members of the UPW in particular, of the growing development of the silicon chip and other technological advances in the field of electronics. It agrees that a searching enquiry and review be undertaken to establish the future effects of these advances, to ensure that the pay and working conditions of the membership, as well as Post Office services, are not placed in jeopardy, and that a report be made to Annual Conference 1980, taking into account the motions herein composited. The Executive Council is instructed accordingly'.

The EC took the decision to commission us to carry out the study for them, rather than the union's research department or a private consultancy company. The research department did not have sufficient resources to carry out a study such as this in addition to its normal workload without recruiting extra personnel; and private consultants would have been too expensive. Our terms of reference were:

> 'to prepare a report on the impact of technological advances in the field of electronics on Post Office services and on the grades represented by the Union of Post Office Workers. This would include an assessment of the business environment within which the Post Office was operating'.

We considered that the union's requirements would be met better by a general review of the major technological and organisational changes which could affect employment opportunities in the Post Office, rather than in-depth studies of one or two areas such as electronic mail or postal mechanisation. Rather than conduct our own surveys and forecasts, we decided to rely largely on information already available, as time and resources were limited. We concentrated on collating and analysing existing information from a variety of sources and on questioning the assumptions made by the Post Office in its projections of trends of business volume and staff levels.

The majority of the union's members had not been able to see this information before; some of the Post Office's reports we used had been tucked away in the files of the union's representatives on the Post Office Board and had not been seen even by the other members of the Executive Council. None of the members or officers of the union had had the opportunity to consider the material all together in the context of the overall impact of new technology on employment.

We aimed to use all available data to provide as coherent a picture as possible of the implications of technological change for union members' employment. This revealed and made explicit some serious contradictions between the various Post Office projections and between some such projections and their published statements.

On the basis of Post Office plans and forecasts, interviews with Post Office research and development staff and management, and reports prepared by other bodies, we assessed the total business available to the Post Office and the number of people likely to be needed to carry it out. We attempted to assess the effects of organisational changes, such as the split of Posts and Telecommunications into two businesses and the ending of the monopoly; and the effects of technical changes on both the volume of business available to the Post Office and the number of staff likely to be required for the work.

The task was made all the more complex by the inter-relationships of various factors involved. For example, if economic growth is faster than forecast, the volume of mail may grow faster; on the other hand faster economic growth could lead to more rapid investment in computerised office equipment with electronic mail capabilities, which in turn could give rise to reduction or slower growth in letter mail volume.

We concluded that there were some factors which would tend to increase business volumes and/or employment levels (or reduce their decline) – such as a reduction in working hours, slower or less efficient mechanisation than planned or the diversification of Post Office business into new areas. On balance, however, the likelihood was that postal business volume and employment levels would be a lot lower than forecast. We suggested that, if the maximum possible effect of factors not taken into account by the Post Office's forecast were included, and if the Post Office's assumptions were all mistaken by the maximum amount at the same time, then job losses could be in the region of 40,000 compared to the Post Office's prediction of 14,600.

We did not predict that there would certainly be 40,000 job losses over 10 years, but that there would be up to that number if a conjunction of the worst alternatives occurred. The actual levels of employment will depend not only on the factors we considered, but also on the strategies and tactics adopted by the Post Office and by the Post Office unions, and on social and political changes that may take place. So far, for example, the Post Office is attempting to diversify, the unions are pressing for a shorter working week and the government, by reducing capital investment funds available, has caused the slow-down of mechanisation, all factors likely to reduce the rate of decline of employment.

The Post Office, whose comments on our report were also published by the union (UCW, 1980), were critical of some of our findings. However, many of our reservations about Post Office Business Plan assumptions have been justified. The Post Office has now ceased to include forecasts of business volumes or employment levels in its Business Plans. For example, in 1978–9, forecasts were based on the use of a mathematical formula (never revealed) which assumed that every 1% increase in GDP led to a 0.59% increase in postal business volume. The Post Office's latest Business Plan now says that the relationship is more complex and that trends in the two variables cannot be related by an equation of this sort. Furthermore, the wildly optimistic forecast of a 2.9% average annual increase in GDP to 1989 has since been revised to a still optimistic 2.3% increase to 1991, and the qualification that the current recession may, in fact, be more than a temporary downswing.

In 1978–9, no inclusion was made in the Post Office's forecasts of the impact of Optical Character Recognition (OCR) equipment in sorting, or of increased computerisation. Both OCR equipment and computerisation of Post Office counters have now reached the stage of trial operation.

The Post Office was particularly critical of the attention we drew to the two forecasts of the impact of electronic mail: the TSS6 forecast that 25% of postal traffic was likely to be lost and the Business Plan forecast that there was likely to be an increase of zero to 5% annual reduction in letter mail by 1988—9. These forecasts are not necessarily contradictory, since the TSS6 forecast does not estimate any date by which the reduction is likely to have taken place. But the existence of two forecasts is certainly misleading. And N.N. Walmsley of Postal Headquarters, when asked about the 25% forecast reduction said: 'As you know from the Business Plan our appraisal of the risk over the next 10 years is far more modest . . . losses are estimated at around 5% of total inland letters by the end of the period.' (Walmsley, 1979). Walmsley does not make it clear that the Business Plan's forecast was for 5% *a year* by 1988—9, a very different matter from 5% over the whole period, the amount implied in his letter. Since then, however, the Post Office has publicly revised its assumption of likely impact of electronic mail, referring to the likelihood of mail volume declining by 25% as a result of new technology (Dearing, 1981).

The 1978—9 Business Plan did not take into account the effect of dividing the Post Office into two independent public corporations, which has since been carried out. Nor did it take into account the ending of the monopoly, although a separate document suggested that the impact of this could be a reduction of up to 10,250 staff. So far the telecommunications monopoly has been affected; and the Government is to review the postal monopoly at regular intervals, its continued existence being dependent on satisfactory performance by the postal business. Reductions in Government agency work as part of counter business volume were seen as a possibility in the sensitivity analysis of the 1978—9 Business Plan, but it was not made clear that reductions would be as large as they have been in such a short period of time.

We did, however, suggest that a reduction in hours worked could lead to fewer jobs being lost. For example, 117,000 mail handling staff were employed in 1979—80. These people did the equivalent of 142,000 people's jobs by working overtime. The forecast for 1988—9 was that 101,500 mail handling staff would be employed, and would do the equivalent of 117,500 people's jobs. Thus, the 'staff equivalents' in 1988—9 are forecast to be just over the actual number of staff employed when the forecast was made. Thus, in theory, according to Post Office forecasts there should be enough jobs in 1989 for all the staff employed in 1979. The Post Office, however, did not allow in its 1978—9 Business Plan for any reduction in hours worked over the following 10 years despite a campaign by the Post Office Engineers, for example, for a 35 hour week. This too, has been amended in subsequent business plans. Our report commented that Post Office Managers, when interviewed, had said that the Post Office was, in fact, privately working on the assumption that a 30 hour week would be worked by 1990: but that they could not state this publicly in case it led to an immediate union demand for those conditions now. This was a point that the Post Office did not deny, or even mention, in its comments on our report.

Post Office strategy for competition

Since the completion of our study, the Post Office has been implementing a strategy for competition with the electronic mail services offered by other organisations. The main aspect of Post Office strategy has been to enter the electronic mail business itself. It has introduced hybrid electronic mail systems like Intelpost, launched January 1981, and Electronic Post, launched in December 1981. Hybrid systems are intended to exploit the Post Office's national network of conventional delivery to some 21 million addresses as well as the potential of rapid electronic transmission over long distances. A number of premium services like Datapost and Special Delivery, which rely on conventional methods of transmission but guarantee (for a price) next day delivery, have also been introduced or more actively marketed. Intelpost now operates from 60 UK post offices. It is a facsimile (or remote photocopying) service, whereby the sender takes a message on an A4 sheet to an Intelpost centre, it is transmitted using the telecommunication network, and enveloped and delivered with the conventional mail the next day or collected the same day by the recipient. Alternatively, a courier service is available for collection and/or delivery of messages. Messages to any of the 5 centres in the USA or 8 centres in Canada are sent via satellite. Intelpost may also be sent to Holland or Sweden and the Post Office is negotiating with the West German and French postal services to make a similar service available to those countries this year. The inland cost is £2 for the first page and £1 for subsequent pages: it is double that to North America. The courier service costs an extra £4.50 in London, £2.50 elsewhere in the UK and £1 in the USA or Canada. The Post Office hopes to open a further 40 centres before the end of the year.

Between April and September 1982, 5000 pages were sent inland and about 4000 to North America by Intelpost. Clearly, the Post Office will have to attract a far greater volume than this if it is to be a successful competitor to alternative forms of electronic mail. The Post Office likes to quote the case of a businessman who received a telephone call from New York in response to an Intelpost letter sent just 23 minutes earlier, but it has yet to make many of its own staff, never mind the public, aware of the service.

Electronic Post is the Post Office's equivalent to E-COM in the USA. It is a mass mailing system aimed at large companies and other organisations who send out hundreds or thousands of standard letters, statements, subscription renewal notices or bills. At the moment there are centres in Manchester and London. Four more, originally planned to open in 1982, should be in operation this year. The sender takes a computer tape containing a list of names and addresses and the message (which can be standard or variable) to the local centre. The Post Office's computer sorts the addresses into those for the north and those for the south, in postcode order. In the case of messages sent from Manchester, details of those for the south are sent to the Mount Pleasant computer via the telecommunication network. Each computer then prints out the texts on A4 sheets of paper, the messages are enveloped, still in postcode order, and delivered with the ordinary mail. The cost per item is the same as a first class letter, and some 400,000 had been sent out by November 1982. The users are generally mail order and direct mail companies and messages are usually sent out in groups of 200 or so.

The Post Office was aiming to have reached a million such mailings by the end of 1982, and to have established a network of 20–25 centres by 1985–6. Several public utilities are currently developing automatic billing, which will enable a meter reader, for example, to read a meter and deliver the bill on the spot. The Post Office has forecast a possible loss of 150m items of mail a year as a result of automatic billing, and Electronic Post was introduced partly to compete with developments of this sort. Thus, the Post Office hopes to persuade major mail users like the gas and electricity boards to use Electronic Post for sending out their bills, rather than use automatic billing.

Direct mail, 92% of which is handled by private companies, is estimated by the Post Office to account for 10% of the letter market (25% in the USA). The Post Office hopes to attract some of this business to Electronic Post, too. Clearly, however, the Post Office will have to achieve a volume of business from Electronic Post considerably greater than a million items a year if it is to maintain its volume of business in the face of such competition.

The Post Office is optimistic that it can fight off the threat to its business by introducing these new services, by introducing new technology to modernise its existing services and by 'aggressive marketing'.

216

The latest Business Plan comments that the recession has provided the Post Office with an advantage, in that companies have been investing in electronic equipment less rapidly than might have been anticipated. Butler, Cox and Partners (1982), for example, in a survey commissioned by the Department of Industry and five electronics companies, say that the arrival of the 'electronic office' has been delayed, despite the large sums invested by suppliers and 'strong latent demand for new technology from customers'. This has meant that private electronic mail services, replacing part of the most profitable business-to-business sector of the postal business, have not yet had much effect on mail volume, and it has given the Post Office a breathing space in which to launch its own hybrid systems.

However, the signs are that it is precisely the recession that is now encouraging some firms and public sector organisations to invest in new technology, especially in offices, in order to reduce costs in the long run. In 1979 the Post Office based its forecasts of competition from electronic mail partially on the relatively high cost of sending messages electronically rather than by conventional mail. The successful use of electronic mail certainly involves an organisation in a considerable investment, but in comparing costs it is the **total** costs of producing a message that are significant. Organisations are likely to invest in, say, communicating word processors (CWPs) to reduce the cost of *preparing* a message (typing, filing, correcting) so that the additional cost of using the same CWP to transmit the message becomes relatively low (Communications Studies and Planning Ltd., 1978).

Secondly, if economic recession has provided a temporary delay in the growth of electronic mail systems, it has equally hit the Post Office's major investment plans. The Post Office has a capital investment programme of around £700 million over the next 3 years. However, the effect of the Government's External Financing Limit has been to reduce the funds available. The Post Office is one of the more profitable public enterprises, but it has a negative cash limit: it must pay over to the Government a share of its profit, it is not allowed to keep surplus profits and it cannot invest reserves accummulated in earlier years. If the EFL continues to be applied in the present way, the Post Office could be facing a 30–40% cut in investment. The Letter Post Plan, for example, for mechanisation of sorting, has already fallen well behind target as a result of cut-backs in investment funds. Fourteen years after it was initiated, the programme is still less than two-thirds complete. Last year, the House of Commons all-party Select Committee on Industry and Trade reported: 'It is clear to us that the Government's financial policy towards the Post Office is the main factor delaying and reducing the investment programme'.

Competition from British Telecom

Meanwhile, British Telecom, now a separate business from the Post Office, is also moving into electronic mail not only in order to compete with the postal business but, more significantly, to compete with the private companies from which it is no longer protected by statutory monopoly. Since the Telecommunications Act (1981) was passed, British Telecom has been facing competition in provision of terminals of all kinds and Value Added Network Services. Mercury Communications Ltd., for example, is currently installing a telecommunications network due to come into use this year.

The convergence of computing and telecommunications (telematics) is now well established and British Telecom alone have supplied more than 90,000 of the data terminals now in use. Terminal-to-terminal electronic mail was identified in British Telecom's Business Plan as the major new market into which they should move. CWPs, facsimile equipment or computers can all be linked together via the public switched telephone network or by private wire. British Telecom's strategy is to attract traffic onto the public networks by directing their attention to 'medium sized businesses which need to communicate widely with others and which have less incentive to build up private, in-house systems' and 'those services that depend on universal availability to fulfil their potential'. In order to do this, British Telecom set up Telecom Gold in March 1982 as an independent company to market electronic mail systems. Telecom Gold, which is wholly financed by BT, currently markets the Dialcom system, originally developed in the USA by Dialcom Inc. Organisations which subscribe to Dialcom receive electronic 'mailbox' codes for the employees they nominate. Mailbox olders' terminals are linked to the Dialcom service via the telecommunications network. There is no fee to join the system, but subscribers pay for the amount of time they are on-line. Firms which originally became subscribers for their own internal communications are now finding that they can also use Dialcom to send electronic mail to customers, suppliers and others outside their organisation who also subscribe to the system, although a directory has not yet been published.

Dialcom is due to be linked up shortly to the telex, telemessage and radio paging services so that subscribers will also be able to send messages to people without electronic 'mailboxes'. So far there are 140 subscribers to Dialcom in Britain and 2000 'mailboxes'. Clearly this, too, is only a small beginning, compared to the number of users of conventional methods of communications; but Telecom Gold are optimistic about the potential of Dialcom and point to the 40,000 'mailboxes' in the USA. Westinghouse, for example, has 'mailboxes' in 37 countries.

218

Where the Post Office hopes to exploit its universal coverage of every address in the country, British Telecom are relying on their 'strength as a ubiquitous provider of services' which may not be as widespread as the postal service, but could be a lot more convenient in the long run. Once System X digital transmission and switching is installed, a wide range of electronic devices will be able to transmit messages via the telecommunications network without the need for modems, and at least as efficiently as the telephone. Already printers and TV screens are available to be used for such messages. Current forecasts are that installation of System X will be 85% complete by 1995, but this, too, depends on the rate of investment and Government limits on public spending. The Government's £16m grant to Plessey and GEC for adapting System X for export, announced in October 1982, will effectively kill off British Telecommunications Systems (BTS), owned equally by British Telecom, Plessey, GEC and STC, which was set up in 1979 to market System X abroad.

British Telecom has also introduced a public electronic mail service, Bureaufax. It has now been on trial for two years and is about to be established permanently. Bureaufax has only 15 UK offices compared to Intelpost's 60, but operates a service to 30—40 countries. However, Bureaufax, like Intelpost, is not only not very well known to the public but not known to many of British Telecom's staff either.

British Telecom has identified Electronic Funds Transfer (EFT) as another example of the potential opened up by combining tele-communications and data processing, which will be 'a key area in ensuring the future prosperity of the Business'. Here, too, British Telecom aim to attract users to the public network and to provide terminal equipment. The Post Office envisages providing point of sale debit/credit EFT facilities in the future, together with Girobank cash dispensers similar to those already provided by the clearing banks. On balance, however, EFT is more likely to reduce Post Office business, both as a result of reduced business and reduced postal mail.

A study carried out in the USA (PTT1 1978) estimated that each cheque generates one item of mail; each cheque replaced by EFT would eliminate half a mail item. It was forecast that 5—15% of first class letter mail would be eliminated by 1985, but the impact is not likely to be as rapid in Britain. Already the less frequent payment of DHSS benefits has reduced counter traffic, and alternative payment of pensions (less frequent payment or payment direct into bank accounts) is likely to reduce business by a further 6%. In order to maintain counter business, the Post Office hopes to diversify into, for example, sale of Railcards, tickets and energy stamps and to accept credit transactions, for example for TV licenses and road tax.

Post Office automation

In addition to new serivces the Post Office has plans to further modernise existing services. Whereas the Post Office unions have so far supported moves by management to expand business by adopting new technology, they have been more reluctant to co-operate in implementing technical changes that may reduce costs by reducing staff levels.

Optical Character Recognition (OCR) equipment reads addresses (up to 3 lines) and sorts mail without the need for a human coding desk operator. By 1978 the Canadian, Japanese and United States postal services had installed OCR equipment able to process up to 40% of mail (PTT1 1978). The British Post Office had intended to install its own prototype in 1980, laboratory tests of which had been conducted by the end of 1978. However, at the same time it was considering equipment developed by private firms and the prototype that was finally delivered in October 1982 came from AEG Telefunken. Trials have not yet started in Britain although the German postal service has begun to test the equipment. The British Post Office 'aren't saying a great deal at the moment until we've come to an agreement with the unions'. In fact the Union of Communication Workers are refusing to co-operate in the trials. The union has submitted to Post Office Management a New Technology Agreement approved by its Annual Conference in May 1982. So far they have not received a response from management and it looks as though trials with OCR equipment will not begin until they do.

OCR machines are only capable of reading a limited number of addresses, even assuming maximum efficiency. AEG Telefunken claim that their equipment can even read handwriting in some cases, and the Post Office's long term plans have certainly included equipment capable of reading handwritten addresses. However, the main use of the equipment waiting to be tested is likely to be in handling uniformly addressed bulk consignments of mail from large posters. Complete elimination of coding desk operators will not, therefore, be possible and the Post Office's informal estimates of the reduction in staff they hope to achieve is at the most half. However, in the UCW's view, having the number of coding desk operators means a loss of 3000 jobs on top of the 6000 being lost by mechanisation of sorting. There was already a reduction in staff by 3146 during 1981. OCR equipment currently costs about £400,000 per machine, although a large order and further development work could reduce the figure.

As a result of a productivity deal the UCW has agreed to co-operate in trials of computer equipment at Post Office counters. This year four post offices outside London will begin the 18 month £400,000 experiment in counter automation. Counter staff in building societies have been using computer terminals for some time, but computerisation of Post Office counters has proved to be a more complex business since post offices handle more than 200 different sorts of transaction: at the beginning of 1983 a Post Office working party was still discussing the equipment it will recommend for the trial and exactly which four post offices should carry it out. The experiment was announced in 1982 by Kenneth Baker, Minister of Information Technology, but the working party was expected to take a year to report.

The Post Office has also begun to instal LOCUM (Letter Office Computer Monitor), a computerised information system to provide data on traffic flows and workloads in mechanised letter offices (MLOs). LOCUM is on trial in MLOs such as Manchester and Leeds while TRIPOS, a similar system for Parcels Concentration Offices (PCOs), will be in the new Glasgow PCO and is already on trial in Leeds and elsewhere.

The trade union response

The New Technology Agreement the UCW wishes to secure with management would allow for co-operation with the introduction of new technology provided the union was kept informed of proposed developments at least once a quarter, and that no new equipment was introduced without negotiation and agreement with themselves. In exchange for their co-operation, the UCW are asking the Post Office to agree to the introduction of a 30 hour week and up to 6 weeks' annual leave (after 20 years' service) by 1990, voluntary retirement at age 55 and no compulsory redundancies. The UCW does not, however, appear to be particularly optimistic about the outcome of negotiations over the New Technology Agreement, having made qualifications such as 'the claims we are making on the Post Office are ambitious', 'The immediate reaction of the Post Office will be to resist' and 'it will not be achieved quickly or easily' (UCW, 1982). The more left wing members of the Union (Communique, 1982) have been critical of the draft Agreement and of these qualifications in particular. Their influence, though growing, is still a long way from having an effect on the National Executive Council, though increases in the rate of unemployment nationally, or more explicit Post Office plans for staff reduction, may well push the UCW into taking a more militant stand in relation to staffing levels and acceptance of new technology. For the time being, however, it looks as though most of the technical changes planned by the Post Office will go ahead and agreement reached between union and management. Innovation is more likely to be held up by the Government, as a result of limits on capital investment in the public sector.

Conclusions

The Post Office faces competition from electronic mail services provided by British Telecom and by private firms, as well as from conventional telecommunications. Forecasts of Post Office business volume and employment levels, made in the late 1970s, failed to take into account several important technical and non-technical factors including the division into two corporations, The Post Office and British Telecom, the possible change in the monopoly, the introduction of computerisation and the introduction of optical character recognition in sorting. They also underestimated the impact of electronic mail, changes in Government agency business and the general effect of the recession.

However, the Post Office has attempted to face all these threats to its volume of business by diversifying its services, especially into hybrid electronic mail services; by increasing the rate of automation of existing services; and by a more active marketing policy. The marketing policy still has a long way to go before many Post Office staff, never mind the public, are fully aware of the new services. The trade unions are so far pursuing a policy of limited co-operation: co-operation with strategies which increase the business but not with those that may reduce jobs even further, calling instead for a reduction in hours worked.

A shortage of capital for investment by private firms has delayed the impact of private electronic mail systems, but this is likely to be temporary, while the completion of British Telecom's System X and related developments is likely to make BT a serious threat. On the other hand the Government's hard line on public spending means that mechanisation will be completed at least 3 years late, and other capital investment plans may be delayed, thus reducing the Post Office's ability to compete with new services.

The example of technical change introduced by the Post Office, its customers and its competitors, demonstrates that the impact of innovation on jobs depends less on the nature of the technology itself than on non-technical factors such as Government policy on innovation and on public and private industrial sectors, the Post Office's strategies for fighting off the competition and the activities of the trade unions, which themselves change in response to social, economic and political developments.

References

Butler, Cox and Partners Ltd, *The Market for Office Technology*, London, 1982.

Communications Studies and Planning Ltd, *Post Office Telecommunications — The Way Ahead*, 1978.

Communique, Journal of the UCW Broad Left, May 1982.

Dearing, R., Post Office Chairman, quoted in *The Times*, 20 February 1981.

Mackintosh Consultants Ltd. and Communications Studies and Planning Ltd, *Electronic Mail in Western Europe and North America 1978–87*, London.

Post, Telegraph and Telephone International, *PTTI Studies*, no.21, Winter 1978.

Telecommunications Systems Strategy Department (TSS6), *Long Range Intelligence Bulletin*, no.16. Formerly part of The Post Office, now British Telecom, 1977.

Union of Communication Workers, *Posts, Telecommunications and the New Technology*, a Commentary on the Report of the Science Policy Research Unit, 1980.

Union of Communication Workers, *The Post*, April 1982.

Walmsley, N.N., letter to Tom Jackson, General Secretary, UCW, dated 4 December 1979.

Walsh, V., Moulton Abbott, J. and Senker, P., *New Technology, The Post Office and the Union of Post Office Workers*, UCW, London, 1980.

Walsh, V., Moulton Abbott, J. and Senker, P., 'New Technology and The Post Office — A Research Project for the Union of Post Office Workers' in *Proceedings* of International Council for Science Policy Studies and University of Manchester Programme of Policy Research in Engineering, Science and Technology Policy and Trade Unions, 1982.

12 New technology in banking: the impact of autotellers on staff numbers*

Paul Willman and Rowena Cowan

Introduction

Concern over the impact of automation both on the numbers of staff employed in the banking industry and on their career prospects has been expressed in a number of quarters. The most vociferous statements come naturally enough from the Banking, Insurance and Finance Union, the largest in the industry, (BIFU, 1980, 1981, 1982), who conclude that 'further automation is making it easier for the banks to man their expanding business with a smaller labour force' (1982). However, some support for their views, albeit in the longer term, comes from government investigations (Sleigh *et al.*, 1979) from assessments of technological impact in other countries (Nora and Minc, 1980) and from recent projections of retail banking prospects in the 1980s (Shaw and Coulbeck, 1983) which imply a 12% reduction in clearing bank staff numbers by 1990 specifically as a consequence of automation.

The changes which are alleged to effect their reduction include existing developments which show a potential for expansion, such as the use of counter terminals, stand alone computers, word-processors, automated payment systems and autotellers. They also include technologies in very early stages of development such as point-of-sale systems, memory cards and home banking systems based

* The research on which this chapter is based was supported by a grant from the SSRC.

on current viewdata facilities or on home computers. A third category of changes is technologically more mundane, but perhaps more significant in the short-run and includes those systems or organisational changes which might generate staff savings, such as till sharing, credit scoring and cheque truncation.

However, those who argue that staff reductions will occur on these bases face at least three different sets of problems. Firstly as the Director of the Federation of Clearing Bank Employers recently noted: 'just because something is technically feasible it is not necessarily economically viable', and it is not inevitable that it will be introduced (IOB, 1982). For example, fairly thorny legal problems surround liability on electronic funds transfer and it is not clear that all parties would benefit from point-of-sale terminals (ibid.). Secondly, and in consequence, the time-scale of change may be more protracted than envisaged: the evidence we present below indicates that some of the more esoteric changes may not be on the agenda for several years. Thirdly, the *direction* of impact of technology may not be as envisaged. Even if the labour content of particular tasks is reduced, alternative products and services may develop on the basis of change which absorb existing labour time. The basis for this argument is partly historical. Table 12.1 gives employment and productivity figures for insurance, banking, finance and other business services from 1965–75. Over this period, a steady growth both in employment and productivity was experienced in the SIC as a whole. Significantly, this was also the period of relatively rapid development of computerised systems within banking itself (MLH 861). The development of integrated computer networks incorporating on-line terminal systems dealing primarily with mainframe batch-processing computers enabled the handling of rapidly increasing transaction volumes which could not have been handled manually. In MLH 861 overall numbers increased by 49.1% over the period, and Robertson *et al.*, predict continued growth of employment numbers on variable GDP growth assumptions on the basis of this historical data. They conclude that 'EFT (Electronic Funds Transfer) will have virtually no impact on employment in the next five years' and that 'there is every reason to suppose that technology, output and employment will be positively correlated' (Robertson *et al.*, 1982). More recent evidence lends some support to this. Table 12.2 indicates that clearing bank staff numbers since 1976 have continued to increase, although there was a substantial down-turn in 1981. Moreover between 1979 and 1981 the number of items handled per member of staff increased by 18.7% and the number of accounts per member of staff by 6.3% (Shaw and Coulbeck, 1983).

Table 12.1

Employment and productivity
SIC Order XXIV 1965–75

Employees* (000's)		Productivity index
1965	803	91.8
1966	819	92.3
1967	827	101.0
1968	858	96.1
1969	893	96.3
1970	956	95.5
1971	976	100.0
1972	996	102.8
1973	1058	103.7
1974	1116	103.3
1975	1103	107.7

Source: Robertson *et al.*, 1982.
Notes: *Includes part time staff

However, one cannot assume that past relationships will necessarily hold through the 1980s. Most financial institutions face rising costs within a very competitive personal market. Although only 64% of the UK working population has a bank account, only 4% have no account of any kind: competition between different types of financial institution may be expected to increase. Moreover, as cost pressures increase, pressure on staff costs within a labour-intensive industry will also rise. About 60% of staff are engaged in relatively easy-to-automate money transmission operations. Automation may thus hold the key to the transformation of cost structures within the industry (Shaw and Coulbeck, 1983), but it is not clear that technological change plays any well thought-out role in corporate strategy. As one recent bank observer notes:

> We have complained frequently of the high cost of cash handling, and yet provide ATMs to encourage its use: we have similarly expressed a desire to limit cheque growth and substitute EFT, and yet provide cheque guarantee cards that encourage the use

of cheques: we have trained staff to cross-sell in branches, but yet provide "through-the-wall" ATMs so that many customers no longer need the branch' (IOB, 1982).

Given that technological changes may be adopted either to take advantage of market opportunities or to minimise costs, these confusions may be inevitable. But there remains a dearth of knowledge about the staffing implications of new technology which feeds in part off an ignorance of the strategic intentions behind particular innovations. The remainder of this chapter will seek to shed light on a small part of this problem, by looking in detail at the strategy for implementation and operation of Autoteller Machines (ATMs) within a particular bank. We hope to show that assessment of staffing consequences is extremely difficult, but must take account of the *growth* in work volumes which follow ATM installation.

Autoteller machines

The first ATMs — more accurately cash dispensers) were introduced in the 1960s. They were simple machines, usually dispensing only £10 in cash and retaining the customer's punched card, but from the beginning they were the subject of discussion, particularly between the banks and BIFU (then NUBE). From the outset, ATMs were seen by the latter as relatively sinister developments, substituting for the cashier and simultaneously frustrating the union's policy on opening hours.

The Midland Bank introduced its first cash dispensers in late 1969, but the limitations soon became apparent, not only in the facilities they offered, but because the machines were unreliable. Other banks experienced similar problems, the limitations being compounded because some banks had placed their cash dispensers within the banking hall. The Clydesdale Bank began to look at more sophisticated machines at the same time as the Midland. Within the Midland, experiments took place with in-branch Chubb machines and through-the-wall NCR machines. Clydesdale began its evaluation with Chubb machines and finally adopted them. Midland Bank chose an NCR 1780 machine and along with other banks, began phasing out the £10 cash dispensers. Table 12.2 shows the number of ATMs installed by the major high street banks by June 1981. Nearly all banks, with the exception of the market leaders, Lloyds, doubled the number of ATMs installed within the year. With a total number of branches of around 12,700, there is currently an ATM for every 3—4 branches.

Table 12.2
Clearing bank employment 1970–82

31 December	Number	Change from previous total
1970	174,033 (171,568)	—
1971	172,201	− 1.1% (+0.4%)
1972	174,116	+ 1.1%
1973	182,048	+ 4.6%
1974	197,448	+ 8.5%
1975	192,598	− 2.5%
1976	195,122	+ 1.3%
1977	200,967	+ 3.0%
1978	207,341	+ 3.2%
1979	216,633	+ 4.5%
1980	231,451 (227,703)	+ 6.8% (+5.1%)
1981	223,237 (219,539)	− 3.5% (−3.6%)
1982	227,594	+ 2.0%

Notes:
1 Figures in brackets exclude National Westminster non-clerical staff who were within the poll vote totals for 1970, 1980, 1981 and thereafter. Between 1971 and 1979 National Westminster non-clerical staff were excluded from the poll vote total.
2 The 1970–1980 increase was 33% (32.7% excluding National Westminster non-clerical). The 1970–1981 increase was 28.3% (28.0% excluding National Westminster non-clerical).

Source: Federation of London Clearing Bank Employees.

One of the reasons for this rapid growth is that ATMs can be relatively cost-effective and that they are seen to improve quality of service. An ATM (NCR) cost £20,000 to buy and £10,000 to install in 1982: this may be broadly compared to the current average earnings of staff in banking of £114.0 (female) and £219.5 (male) per week (New Earnings Survey, 1982). But proper evaluation of cost-effectiveness depends on the philosophy of each bank in introducing ATMs.

In many banks, ATMs were cost-justified on the grounds that transactions would be displaced from the counter and fewer cashiers would be needed. In Lloyds, for example, 30 million transactions through

ATMs dispensed £700m in 1980. On the Friday before Christmas in the same year over 200,000 transactions were recorded. Without automation, it is estimated that this would have required an extra 3000 cashiers (*Banker's Magazine*, November 1982). However, what is not known is the number of transactions that are created by ATMs. A recent analysis by Chemical Bank of their ATM network revealed that it has created many new transactions — particularly balance enquiries and low value cash withdrawals — but the marginal reduction in transactions over the counters has been very small. Similarly, Barclays found that for every transaction displaced from bank counters two or more transactions were originated on ATMs (IOB, 1982). Nevertheless, they estimate that 100 installed machines saves 50 staff (0.5 per machine) whereas Lloyds estimate a saving of 290 staff with 750 installed machines (0.4 per machine).

However, these proposed savings must be considered against the backdrop of Table 12.3: staff numbers actually increased while ATM numbers expanded rapidly. Either the savings have not been taken or business has expanded to encompass the displaced cashiers. Some evidence of this, and of the alternative justification for ATM installation — that of improved quality of service — can be gained by examination of the patterns of usage of ATMs.

Table 12.3
ATMs in service: June 1982

Bank	Supplier	Total	Through wall	Special lobby	Customer area	Stand alone
Nat West	NCR	628	590	1	11	26
Barclays	NCR/IBM	363	349	–	2	12
Midland	NCR	427	423	–	2	2
Lloyds	IBM/Chubb	1315	391	55	787	82
Will/Glyn	IBM	82	78	2	1	1
Roy Scot	IBM	241	230	6	2	3
Bank Scot	IBM	168	164	–	–	4
Clydesdale	Chubb	128	114	4	1	9
TSB (Eng)	Burroughs	10	4	–	6	–
TSB (Scot)	Phillips	46	43	–	3	–
Yorks	NCR	58	57	–	–	1
All banks		3466	2443	68	815	140

Source: Banker's Magazine, November 1982.

Figure 12.1 ATM workload: Midland Bank, 1981

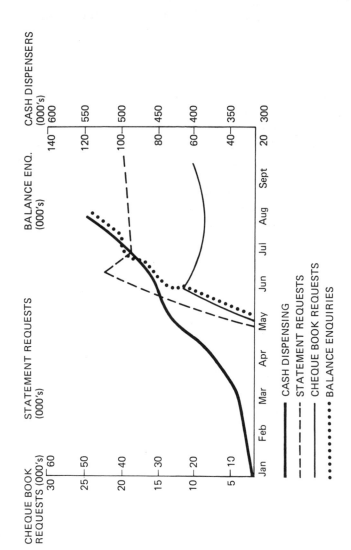

Source: Midland Bank Newspaper December 1981

230

Figure 12.1 shows the mix of transactions conducted through Midland Bank ATMs in 1981. From May onwards, facilities were available on the ATM which would involve further clerical work in pursuit of cheque books or statements. National Westminster and several major Scottish banks provide similar facilities while TSB 'Speedbanks' allow leaflet requests. Two different trends are visible here: one, for example, that of the Royal Bank of Scotland, is to restrict ATM transactions to cash withdrawal and notice enquiry (*Banker's Magazine*, November 1981). The alternative, pushed by a number of banks in the USA, is to expand services by offering up to 125 options on ATMs. In strict cost terms, the comparative advantages of ATMs favours a restricted approach — as Table 12.4 shows — unless quality of service arguments are considered, the best use is as a substitute for cheque cash withdrawals.

Table 12.4

Relative costs of payment methods: 1980

Direct Deposit	100
Direct Debit	100–230
Cheque Payment	220
Cash Deposit	250
Cash Withdrawal ATM	250–320
Cheque	400

Source: Inter-Bank Research Organisation

Moreover, even if ATMs were restricted to cash dispensing, a second area of considerable cost is the issuing of cards. As Table 12.5 shows, the volume of cash withdrawals per machine can be relatively low, and the return on issue relatively small. However, this too must be related to the purposes of innovation. Lloyds see the primary objective of ATMs as being to reduce queues at peak times and to release/reduce staff on routine counter transactions so they have installed primarily 'in lobby' ATMs which are accessible only during banking hours (other reasons given for installing ATMs inside are security, customer comfort and avoidance of the need for planning permission) (Pactel, 1980). Because of this, the ATMs are used by customers for routine cash withdrawals in preference to counter service, and therefore experience a higher number of cash withdrawals per *card* than, for example, Barclays. However, as they have a more extensive network, they have issued fewer cards per machine (c.1727 as against 4862) and fewer weekly withdrawals per machine (Lloyds 718 against Barclays 1248).

Table 12.5

ATM workload

Bank	Total ATMs	Cards issued (000)	Weekly av. cash trans.	Av. value of trans (£)
Lloyds	1315	2271	718	26
Barclays	363	1765	1248	29
Nat West	628	1800	933	24
Midland	427	883	662	25

Source: Banker's Magazine, November 1982.

In contrast, Barclays see their ATMs more in terms of the provision of cash withdrawal services outside banking hours, with only one-third of withdrawals taking place while branches are open (Pactel, 1980).

This raises one of the major problems with ATMs. Restriction of functions is cheaper, but given the tendency of customers ot use available ATMs, rather than cashiers, there arises the problem of marketing the range of bank products. Both Barclays and Midland are beginning to experiment with lobby machines in order to 'lure' customers back into the banking hall.

In summary, then, the high street banks appear to have several goals for their ATM programmes: they want to improve quality of service both by reducing queue lengths and by providing banking 'out-of-hours': they want to use a cheaper method of dispensing cash than cheque transactions: simultaneously they want to attract new customers. The pressure to expand and market services goes along with the desire to reduce costs in such a way as to imply the positive correlation of output and employment referred to above.

The case study

Implementation

The bank concerned is in the 'second rank' of UK banks, having a total of 1500 branches in the UK in 1982. It has had some twenty years of experience of computer systems and counter automation and currently operates from four major computer centres covering different areas of the country. All four centres offer on-line systems operating through the use by cashiers of VDTs on the counter itself;

enabling immediate provision of statement and standing order information, as well as cheque encashment. The bank first introduced ATMs in England in 1977, operating a pilot scheme in which ATMs were sited in city centre and suburban locations and both through-the-wall and in the lobby. At the end of the scheme, the 10 ATMS had a card-base of 25,000, an average number of 370 withdrawals per week with an average amount of £30.

An evaluation of the scheme took place in 1979/80. The financial evaluation model produced by the computer division stated two prime points for consideration: serviceability and operational cost-efficiency; in the latter context, they concluded that a severe problem existed in identifying the transaction displacement involved. The evaluation was concerned primarily with equipment reliability, and little consideration was given to staff or cost considerations. The eventual decision was to purchase 400 ATMs. There appears to have been so little work done on the cost-effectiveness of ATMs because it was felt that the major competitors had done enough work to prove that ATMs were economically viable. The installation of the first two hundred ATMs in large city-centre branches was seen as straightforwardly necessary, although the financial evaluation procedure was spelt out in some detail. In fact the following rules-of-thumb produced in 1980 appear to have been more effective influences on siting decisions. The receiving branch must have:

a)   a minimum of 3000 active cheque accounts;
b)   a minimum of 2,000,000 counter transactions per year;
c)   a suitable catchment area;
d)   suitable premises.

The bank operates ATMs from three of its four computer centres. Regions have had considerable autonomy in the past in deciding whether to adopt ATMs and where to site them, but early in 1983 the ATM operation came under the control of central marketing which decides on installation programme in conjunction with computer division. Table 12.6 indicates the progress of the programme date.

Table 12.6

Operational ATMs

	Planned by end 1982	Operational 1 April 1983	Planned by end 1983
England & Wales	123	86	310
Scotland	64	70	130
N. Ireland	—	14	14
	187	170	454

Source: Bank Records

Staffing implications

The background to the introduction of ATMs is an overall increase of 11.7% in staff numbers from 1977 to 1982: this overall figure conceals different regional growth rates. The projectional staff increase to 1987, based on expected growth in business volumes, is 2.9%; including an allowance for lower than expected growth, *and* for ATMs the projection is of a decrease of 1.6% over the same period. But the bank itself completed no detailed review of the employment consequences of the ATM programme: personnel department were not, in fact, involved in the decision, and in any event, key data such as the displacement of counter transactions and ATM work volumes remained unavailable.

In November 1982, the present authors conducted a survey of regional systems managers within the bank asking about the staff savings associated with planned new technology. Usable replies were received from 11 of the 16 regions; the principal notified savings are given in Table 12.7. Although ATMs gave the largest savings, the overall levels are quite small. Moreover, particularly for systems changes (i.e. the introduction of the on-line system to regions which had previously operated manual ones) the returns indicates that staff savings were notional, and the staff so displaced would be allocated other work.

Table 12.7

Principal staff savings 1982–7

	No. staff saved	% of total staff (1982)
ATMs	295	1.81%
Microfilming	269	1.65%
Systems changes	224	1.37%
Word processing	45	0.28%
Total	833	5.11%

Source: Imperial College Survey

Four regions offered variable projections of staff saved per ATM. As Table 12.8 indicates, these savings would imply very different consequences on the basis of an extensive ATM programme throughout the organisation. However, they are reasonably systematic estimates based on the measurement of known work volumes – rather than mere 'guesstimates'. The implication is that different savings may represent very different levels of usage and displacement of transactions, depending upon branch business, volumes and location.

Table 12.8

Staff saved per ATM

Region	No. saved/ATM	No. ATMs
4	0.27	26
8	1	60
10	0	3
11	0.35	60

Source: Imperial College Survey

ATM operation

This implication can be explained by analysis of the operation, a sample of 8 ATM branches in a single region of the bank. Table 12.9 outlines the basic usage figures for this sample for a 5 week period in Spring 1983. The Table gives the percentage of cheque accounts with cards issued, the proportion of overall counter transactions performed on the ATM, percentage downtime and notional staff displacement. A number of points need to be made. First, the proportion of ATM transactions varies from branch to branch, reflecting very different utilisation patterns, this does not simply relate to differential levels of downtime; nor is it simply a function of differential card issue. One important factor which relates also to the staff saving is the level of 'non-parent' transactions: i.e. the use of ATMs by customers from non-ATM branches. This varied from 0.6% to 19.4% of ATM transactions for different branches. All branches find that the overall level of transactions increased after ATM installation, but this varied with the propensity to attract non-parent transactions and with the capacity of ATMs to generate more transactions: an average 40.3% of ATM transactions were balance enquiries, statement and leaflet requests.

The notional staff savings are based on the assumptions:

a) that one member of staff has a workload of 30,000 transactions per year (the systems department figure) and less plausibly,

b) that all ATM transactions are displaced counter transactions.

On this basis, the introduction of one ATM per branch throughout the region would involve a reduction in branch staff of roughly 9.7% (8.4% if non-branch staff are included). However, the pattern of staff

Table 12.9

ATM utilisation and staff savings[1]

Branch	Installation date	ATM cards Cheque A/Cs	ATM transactions Total transactions	% Downtime	Staff saving[2] No.	%
A	Dec.82	40.92	47.90	11.1	2.21	10.3
B	Dec.82	43.52	46.90	16.4	1.49	11.5
C	Dec.82	64.11	68.50	12.7	1.35	16.9
D	Jan.83	39.22	50.42	9.2	1.02	7.0
E	Feb.83	36.36	25.29	24.9	0.81	6.8
F	Feb.83	27.87	29.18	19.3	0.75	7.9
G	Jan.83	37.50	37.70	8.5	1.17	10.2
H	Jan.83	43.60	24.89	12.9	0.99	6.8
Average		41.64	40.18	14.38	1.22	9.7

Notes:
1 Figures are for period 15.2.83–22.3.83.
2 Based on 300 transactions per staff.

change does not make this likely. In the 8 branches of the sample, staff numbers changed in the period prior to ATM installation, but in the brief period since they have remained static. From summer 1982 to January 1st 1983, staff levels in the 8 branches dropped by an overall 22%, as the region switched over to the on-line computer system: previously counter work had been handled manually. After ATM installation, up to April 1983, they decreased no further.

This pattern is of some general interest, since the bank has moved onto the on-line system on piecemeal basis throughout the 1970s. Staff numbers have continued to grow over this period, reductions in one region being compensated by increases in others. The ATMs are thus installed on the basis of a very efficient existing counter system. The scope for saving may thus be small (technologically speaking, the ATMs are simply an automated counter position in a large metal box): in fact, initially, workloads may increase.

The installation of ATMs is preceded by a marketing exercise in which current account holders are sold ATM cards on their visits to the branch by specially trained staff. These careds are then issued by the branch, and a personal identification number provided separately by the Computer Centre. Customers are given basic guidance in the use of ATMs, but a volume of 'retained cards' which must then be reissued is expected. Other measured workload elements related to ATMs involve routine filling of cash dispensers. Further work is involved in fault rectification. The result is that, at least initially, ATMs involve workload *increases* for the receiving branch. Given the installation dates outlined in Table 12.9, one might not expect staff reductions within this time period in any event.

In fact, analysis of measured work elements alone supports the view that ATMs are a product rather than process innovation. ATMs add elements to transaction workloads, without removing any routines. Potentially, the effect on high-volume activity − such as debit in and debit out − may be substantial, but other high volume elements − such as credit in and out, and mail despatch − remain manual. Other innovations, such as truncation and word processing, may reduce staff requirements in these areas, but ATMs essentially substitute for cheque transactions dealing with cash withdrawals at the parent branch. Since counter work involved only an estimated 30% of branch work, and such transactions are only a proportion of this, their impact is limited particularly where the extensive use of counter terminals has already reduced basic times for most counter operatives (see IOB, 1982). For example, in the region under consideration, postal items constituted 35% of workload in 1982, whereas till work comprised 14%; the projected loads for 1987 are 37% and 9% respectively. Less easily automated items will continue to be a large proportion of branch workload.

Conclusions

It is not always sensible to form generalisations on the basis of case study evidence, particularly when only one case study is involved, but the data presented here is of considerable interest. Banking is an industry which has already experienced considerable computerisation, and speculation about the possibility of a second 'wave' of change transforming cost structures and employment patterns within the industry has been rife. The evidence presented here both from the survey and from the case study branches encourages caution. No fundamental changes were considered by systems managers within the next 4–5 years. The largest single staff reduction was seen to follow from the ATM programme, but the analysis of the actual operation of ATMs does not support the view that massive staff reductions will follow. Restrictive assumptions about static business volumes and displacement of counter transactions are needed to support such a case. Other banks may plan very different patterns of change, but the history of technological change within the case study bank imply that it would be in the forefront of future developments.

This is not to say that no areas of concern exist. Changes to the internal organisation of money transmission — such as truncation — may lead to substantial job loss particularly in clearing houses. Automated transmission systems such as Chaps II may cause redundancies amongst bank messengers. More generally, changes in technology and organisation may alter job content and career prospects for employees in a thorough-going way. But the timescale of these changes is probably longer than some commentators envisage. Personnel policies within banks are focussing on the need progressively to develop skills in the marketing of new services as much as on the need rapidly to control costs. As one commentator has noted of banking generally:

> 'The enormous investment in property, systems and staff means that any major change in organisation structure will take place through a relatively slow process of evolution rather than through a process of revolution' (IOB, 1982).

References

Banking, Insurance and Finance Union, *Report of the BIFU Micro-electronics Committee*, 1980: 'Microtechnology: A Programme for

Action' (1981): 'New Technology in Banking Insurance and Finance' (1982), London.

Institute of Bankers, *The Banks and Technology in the 1980s*, Proceedings of the Cambridge Conference, London, IOB, 1982.

Nora, S. and Minc, A., *The Computerisation of Society*, MIT Press: Cambridge, Mass: 1980.

Pactel, *Automation in European Banking 1979–1990*, Pactel, London, 1980.

Robertson, J.A.S., Briggs, J.M. and Goodchild, A., *Structure and Employment Prospects of the Service Industries*, Research Paper no. 30, Department of Employment, London, 1982.

Shaw, E.R. and Coulbeck, N.S., *UK Retail Banking Prospects in the Competitive 1980s*, Stanilad Hall: 1983.

Sleigh, J., Boatwright, B., Irwin, P. and Stanyon, R., *The Manpower Implications of Micro Electronic Technology*, HMSO: London, 1979.

13 New technology and industrial relations in Fleet Street: 'New technology will make it possible for managers to manage'
Roderick Martin

Introduction

Few industries have seen more rapid and significant changes in technology since 1960 than the printing industry. Until the 1960s the industry had changed little since the introduction of linotype and monotype machines in the late nineteenth century, and some sectors still use hand composing methods derived directly from late fifteenth century technology. Since 1960 the industry has been transformed: the title of Anthony Smith's survey of newspapers in the 1980s, *Goodbye Gutenburg*, is not simply poetic licence (Smith, 1980). Major changes have already taken place in origination, in plate-making, in the press room, and in packing and despatch with the development of computerised photocomposition, direct printing, offset lithography, web-offset printing, and automated bundling, tieing and stacking machinery; further changes, involving increased computerisation, are likely in the 1980s. The transformation has been neither uniform nor complete; technological changes have affected different sectors of the industry differently; for example, offset lithography has been introduced extensively in general printing, but not in national newspapers. Moreover, the potential of new technologies has not always been fully realised, partly for industrial relations reasons.

The major focus of this chapter is on the relationship between new technology and management control. In view of the wide range of technological changes underway, and their different impacts, this chapter concentrates on one group of changes, the introduction of

240

computerised photocomposition, the replacement of mechanical linotype machines by computerised systems.

The chapter is divided into two parts. The first part outlines the basic structure of the industry and the policies of the major unions on new technology. The second part examines the specific issue of the effect of the introduction of computerised photocomposition upon management control: will new technology make it possible for managers to manage, as some senior managers have claimed?

Basic structure of the industry — policies of the unions

National newspapers comprise one of three major sectors of the printing industry, the others being regional and local newspapers, and general print. The sector employs about 37,000 workers, fewer than each of the other two sectors, the majority in London, but with a substantial minority in Manchester. The industry produces 10 national morning newspapers and 8 national Sunday newspapers: in addition, the London evening newspaper is conventionally regarded as part of the national newspaper industry. In 1980 total revenues amounted to £789,066,000. Revenue is derived from two sources, direct sales and the sale of advertising space; in 1980 56% of the revenues of national dailies was derived from sales revenue, the proportion being considerably lower — probably about 30% — for the 'quality' newspapers. Although the sector is relatively small in employment terms, it is a major political force. The national press plays a major role in defining the political agenda, and has substantially colonised television and radio, both editorially and commercially. Its industrial relations system, with its high level of trade union power, has also attracted considerable public interest.

Historically, there have been four major production unions in the industry — National Graphical Association (NGA), Society of Lithographic Artists, Designers and Engravers (SLADE), National Society of Operative Printers Graphic and Media Personnel (NATSOPA) and Society of Graphical and Allied Trades (SOGAT) — together with the National Union of Journalists (NUJ), AUEW(E) and EETPU. However, there have been major recent changes at national level, with the merger of the NGA and SLADE to form NGA '82 and of NATSOPA and SOGAT to form SOGAT '82. The significance of changes in national trade union structure for plant level industrial relations has so far been limited; their future importance will depend upon the extent to which national changes lead to changes in chapel arrangements at plant level. At the time of writing (June 1983) national level changes have led to changes in branch structure, but not in chapel.

Computerised photocomposition can only be introduced into Fleet Street by negotiation, owing to the strength of trade union organisation. The unions in the industry have adopted different attitudes towards new technology (which I have examined at length elsewhere: Martin 1982). On the whole, NATSOPA has been generally more favourable towards the introduction of new technology than the NGA, since new technology increases job opportunities for NATSOPA members in the clerical area; for the NGA new technology involves major difficulties, with little prospective reward. The NATSOPA General Secretary, Owen O'Brian, saw new technology as a means of ending the craft exclusiveness of the NGA, to the advantage of his own members: 'speaking realistically, the lines of demarcation (between NATSOPA and NGA members) will not be blurred, they will be *obliterated*. The sooner practical people in all unions come to terms with reality the better for all concerned . . . instead of trying to maintain an out-moded guild mentality that should be interned in peace'. NGA leaders recognised that new technology could not simply be rejected, but were unenthusiastic. The NGA policy remains as it was outlined to the Association's Biennial Delegate Meeting in Douglas in 1978: maintenance of NGA jurisdiction over typographic input; no compulsory redundancy; reductions in the working week; extension of annual holidays; improved pensions and sick-pay arrangements. Although there are differences in detail, SOGAT's policy on new technology is aligned with that of NATSOPA, and SLADE's with that of the NGA.

In addition to print production workers, journalists are substantially affected by the introduction of computerised photocomposition. Their involvement is obvious if computerised photocomposition is associated with direct journalist in-put, with journalists directly keying editorial matter into the computer. However, only one regional newspaper, the *Nottingham Evening Press*, has adopted a direct-entry system, after a major strike resulting in the company becoming a non-union shop. (In addition, the Portsmouth and Sunderland Group of regional newspapers has reached agreement with the NGA on a gradual move towards direct-entry, phased over 3 years.) Even 'back-end' systems, in which editorial matter is in-put into the system by compositors (retitled more accurately as key-board operatives), have important implications for journalists, most notably earlier deadlines. The NUJ policy is to refuse to undertake work previously carried out by members of other unions unless the other union has voluntarily surrendered the work involved. Moreover 'any NUJ chapel has the right to refuse to enter into negotiations on new working methods and will have the support of the Union in such a refusal . . . any agreement

242

reached must include a clause guaranteeing existing chapels' members and freelances the right, if they so wish, to continue working on traditional lines without prejudice to pay and promotion'. The NUJ policy specifies in detail the issues negotiators are required to attend to, and the objectives to be achieved: editorial quality and safeguards; working conditions; health and safety; provision of information; manning levels, recruitment and training. Requirements for new equipment are specified in detail; for example, function keys are to be arrayed according to frequency of use, to avoid confusion between frequently used keys, like the cursor, and infrequently used ones, like 'kill text' (NUJ, 1980). The NUJ is sceptical about claims that new technology will lead to enhanced editorial control: 'engineers designed these systems with a view to cutting costs by using less labour, simplifying routines and work patterns, ensuring cleaner and neater copy. Editorial requirements are for spending money to get more or later information, staffing-up to guarantee capacity at peak times, bringing copy-flow as close as possible to deadlines, and providing for the greatest possible number of editorial checks and balances' (ibid.).

Two alternative strategies are available for introducing new technology in the industry: industry level negotiations to provide a framework agreement, with implementation at company level according to agreed general principles, or one-off company level negotiations. An initial attempt was made to negotiate an industry-wide framework agreement on new technology, *Programme for Action*, in 1975—6. The agreement provided for improved pensions, voluntary redundancy and an 'agreed strategy' for decasualisation. It was signed by the employers and the union General Secretaries in 1976. However, the agreement was rejected by a majority of members involved in all unions except the NUJ, who accepted it by a small majority. It was therefore impossible to proceed with the industry-wide scheme. Since 1976 individual newspaper managements have therefore negotiated the introduction of new technology on a company basis, in the absence of a national framework agreement.

Since the failure of *Programme for Action* several newspaper companies have outlined schemes for the introduction of computerised photocomposition. The most progress in implementing the schemes have been achieved at Mirror Group Newspapers and Times Newspapers, although major changes are underway at other newspapers, including *The Financial Times* and *The Daily Telegraph*. A comprehensive account of technological developments in the industry is impossible in the space available here. Moreover, it is too early to assess the implications of the new technology in a number of companies where the process of implementation is continuing. However, it is possible to use the experience of the 'first generation' of computerised photocomposing systems in Fleet Street to assess the issue of the extent to which new technology makes it possible for 'managers to manage', where they had not been able to do so before.

The introduction of photocomposition

Writers in the post-Braverman tradition of industrial sociology have argued that the development of new technology will increase management control, both of the production process itself and of labour (Wood, 1982). However, this has often been a matter of faith, or fear, rather than experience, based upon what new technology is technically capable of achieving, rather than upon how technology is used. New technology permits work simplification, previously manual skills being programmed into computerised equipment, as with CNCs; it also facilitates precise monitoring of individual task performance. However, the extent to which computerised systems increase managerial control depends upon two sets of factors. First, whether management wishes to increase its control. Second, whether management is able to implement the new technology in the way in which it wishes. The extent to which management wishes to increase control depends upon managerial values, and the extent to which management is willing to pay any increased costs incurred (for example, through increased supervisory and administrative costs): such aspirations are likely to vary. However, in the Fleet Street context there is little doubt that management wishes to increase its control over the labour force. The extent to which it is able to do so is the issue examined in the remainder of this chapter.

In the exaggerated rhetoric which has characterised changes in Fleet Street, management is out to 'smash the unions'. However, it is necessary to examine the issue more precisely. What is management concerned to control? How might new technology increase management control? How does new technology in practice increase management control? How does the effect of technology on management control relate to other factors influencing management control?

At the most general level, management control systems have been defined as 'the formal means by which organisations decide what ought to be done and ensure that it is doen both in the sense of goal-setting and goal achievement' (Purcell and Earl, 1977). This implies detailed managerial specification of tasks, setting of performance norms, and monitoring of performance in relation to the norms specified. In this formal sense management control systems are scarcely

244

relevant to the production of national newspapers; management neither specify individual tasks in detail, nor establish performance norms, nor monitor individual performance (outside management itself). However, management is concerned with control in a less deterministic sense, in the context of bi-lateral job regulation: although control is unlikely to be ever achieved, management is concerned to increase its influence over specific issues in the direction of achieving control. There are four major areas in which newspaper management is concerned to increase its control: labour costs, work allocation, performance evaluation and recruitment.

By far the major concern is to reduce labour costs, which represent the major element in variable production costs: in 1975 labour costs represented 40% of the average cost of producing a quality daily newspaper, and 44% of the average cost of producing a popular daily newspaper (Royal Commission on the Press: Final Report, 1977). The distribution of labour costs between different parts of the production process differs between different types of newspaper: quality newspapers have especially high 'first copy' costs (i.e. origination costs), and therefore have the major incentive to introduce computerised photocomposition as a means of reducing labour costs. At the same time as reducing labour costs, on a once-for-all basis, management hope to establish firmer control over wage costs for the long term. In comparison with the interest in reducing labour costs management's interest in other aspects is limited. Management hope to increase control over work allocation and to monitor work performance more accurately than had been done in the past. It also hopes that, in the long run, managerial involvement in the selection of personnel might become possible. The way in which computerised photocomposition enhances management control in each area is examined in turn.

The simplest effect of computerised photocomposition is to reduce the number of compositors required. In theory, computerised composition provides the potential for eliminating composition completely, through the introduction of direct editorial and advertising in-put. The labour savings involved would be substantial – at *The Times* probably almost £3 million a year at present earnings and manning levels, unless substantial increases in staff elsewhere absorbed the savings made. However, direct editorial in-put is less advantageous than implied, because of the high level of copy produced outside the company, which requires key-boarding in-house; direct in-put of advertising material – especially classified advertising material – offers higher financial returns. In addition, elimination of the composing room involves obvious major industrial relations difficulties. Less radically, the introduction of computerised photocomposition on 'back-end' principles provides the opportunity for a major reduction in manpower and the achievement of 'more realistic' manning levels. For example, under the new technology agreement at Times Newspapers it was agreed that a manning level for the new composing room of 186, 50% below existing levels under traditional methods, would be achieved over three years. The 186 are to produce both *The Times* and *The Sunday Times*; under the initial agreement the same staff were also to produce weekly supplements (*The Times Educational Supplement, The Times Higher Educational Supplement, The Times Library Supplement* and *The Times Health Service Supplement*) but it was subsequently decided to set the three supplements outside the company. At the same time, new technology agreements at Mirror Group Newspapers and at Times Newspapers provided for the buying out of the London Scale of Prices, a piece price payment system, and the establishment of a common composing room time rate for all composing room staff. By doing so management enhanced its control over wage costs — and reduced rivalries between linotype operators previously paid on the LSP and 'stab hands' paid on time rates. New technology thus enabled management to increase its control over labour costs by a once-for-all negotiated reduction in manning levels and the establishment of a more predictable payments system.

The second management concern is to increase management control over the allocation of work. Traditionally, operations in the composing room have been based upon *de facto* labour only sub-contracting, the Chapels being the sub-contractors, with a high degree of internal self-regulation. When the division of labour in the composing room was fragmented the system operated successfully, if at the cost of friction and conflict. With the introduction of new technology the composing room became more unified, and the necessity for, as well as the possibility of, co-ordination increased. This co-ordinating role is performed by the composing room management, in conjunction with the Imperial FOC. However, the merging of jobs inevitably reduced commitment to the particular sub-group, and it is impossible for the Imperial FOC, responsible for the whole composing room, to perform all of the functions previously performed by individual FOCs when the composing room was fragmented. Moreover, the agreement providing for the introduction of new technology involved flexibility of manpower throughout the whole composing room, according to the needs of the flow of work. This inevitably involved an increase in managerial control on the shop-floor.

The process of the transition to the new system inevitably involved management in a detailed analysis of work under the old system, as well as precise specification of the new. At the same time, the training reuqired for the new system inevitably provided information on the capabilities of individual workers; some workers became experts in the system, and differences in key-board skills became obvious. Since the new method of operation involves flexibility, continuous monitoring of performance is impossible. But the process of change has, at the least, provided management with information about the abilities of individual workers.

A final way in which new technology might enhance management control is through its influence on recruitment. In production areas the unions in Fleet Street operate a pre-entry closed shop: recruitment is via the unions, the unions supplying labour for vacancies notified by management, with management reserving the right to reject nominees. In clerical areas management recruits actively. In the composing room recruitment is via the NGA. At the present time there is no recruitment in the composing area, since the level of employment is being reduced through natural wastage. Moreover, both management and unions expect that when recruitment resumes it will continue according to traditional methods, despite this resulting in the recruitment of compositors unfamiliar with the Qwerty keyboard, who will therefore require training in-house. However, the introduction of a standard keyboard, and simplification of keyboarding, obviously reduces the skill level required and widens the range of potential employees: operation of the in-put VDTs is no different, in principle, in Fleet Street from its operation in other types of organisation (although in practice the pressure at peak times, which recurs daily, is greater than in other standard circumstances).

New technology thus provides the potential for enhanced management control. However, it is not inevitable that the potential will be realised. In each area there are limitations on the extent to which management can increase its control: and the increased control obtained may prove to be temporary. New technology has undoubtedly reduced labour costs, and resulted in a simplified payments system. Moreover, the re-organisation of the composing room reduces the opportunities for increasing earnings through fractional bargaining. However, the extent to which this will result in enhanced control of labour costs remains uncertain. Earnings levels in the composing room remain high: in 1983 the composing room rate in one national newspaper was £279 a week. Basic rates in the industry remain high: national newspapers had the second highest basic rate for male manual workers in any industry (behind firemen) in June 1983. Simplification of the composing room rate increases the salience of composing room rates for other groups of workers, both in editorial and in production areas. At Mirror Group Newspapers the establishment of a composing room rate led to demands for parity from editorial staff; at Times Newspapers, workers in the process area succeeded in linking their rates to the composing room rate. Moreover, productivity bonuses have been negotiated following the introduction of new technology, re-opening the process which the new technology agreements were designed to end.

The relationship between the division of labour and changes in the distribution of power is ambiguous. On the one hand, the conventional scientific management view is that increased specialisation is associated with task simplification, and enhances management control. However, in Fleet Street the division of labour reduced management control in the composing room: Chapels used the opportunities for fractional bargaining provided by a complex but very tightly coupled production system to enhance their own earnings.

New technology and the flexibility of labour negotiated have increased managerial control over the allocation of labour. But this may prove temporary. Under the terms of new technology agreements composing room operatives are expected to do work as required. However, differences in task remain, at the request of workers and accepted by management as operationally convenient: at one national newspaper the division between keyboarding, photosetting operative and paste-up continues in practice, different employees specialising in each area. Moreover, there is pressure from the composing room to reduce flexibility by requiring operatives to be involved in one task for at least half a shift. The re-emergence of specialised work groups, with a claim to *de facto* exclusive jurisdiction over specific tasks, will reduce management control over the allocation of labour.

New technology provides the means for evaluating individual performance. But the significance of this depends upon the use made of the information required: if there is no possibility of sanctioning inadequate performance the information is of limited use. Moreover, the introduction of a composing-room rate has, in one way, increased the difficulties of management in ensuring adequate levels of performance — comparable to the difficulties experienced with the introduction of measured day-work in motor vehicles: the London Scale of Prices was an effective motivator, although it led to very high earnings for linotype operators. The link between effort and reward became less direct with the introduction of a composing room rate, requiring increased supervisory pressure to ensure output. In the particular circumstances of the newspaper industry this pressure is difficult to exert. In normal circumstances there is sufficient 'slack' in the system for edition requirements to be met: but in times of friction it is obviously easy for Chapels to make it difficult to achieve edition deadlines.

The effect of new technology in lowering the 'quality' of labour required is likely to be limited. Under traditional methods of production the level of skill *required* from linotype operators was limited:

high speeds were required, but the ability to achieve high speeds was not a pre-condition for recruitment, which was by seniority, and th complexity of the task was often less than required in general print. In other words, union control of labour supply depended upon solidarity, not upon the skill requirements of the task. This continues to be the case under new technology. If union solidarity remains unimpaired new technology will make little difference to union control over labour supply. The NGA recognises that its monopoly over keyboarding rests upon the maintenance of unity, both between different groups of its own members and, especially, with other print unions. It has therefore accorded high priority to bi-lateral agreements on jurisdictions in the short run and 'one union for the printing industry' in the long run.

Finally, the introduction of computerised photocomposition enhances the power of some groups of workers – especially the process department and electrical engineers. The dependence of the production system upon maintaining computers effectively enhances the importance of electricians. At one newspaper the introduction of computers led to an increase of 12 in the electrical engineers department, although the computers were used for accounts and management information as well as production. The introduction of an integrated computerised system led to the need to maintain 24 hour cover, and increased the need for rapid response time in dealing with repairs. At the same time, the introduction of computers led to demarcation 'hassles', both with compositors eager to carry out their own routine repairs (e.g. changing sockets) and with engineers over functions previously performed by mechanical methods but now electronic.

In short, computerised photocomposition provides the potential for an increase in management control in all four areas – labour costs, work allocation, performance monitoring and recruitment. Both the processes involved in introducing new technology – including the systems analysis and the retraining programmes – and the new technology itself potentially enhance management control. However, the potential is not inevitably realised: the process of collective bargaining over new technology can result in new technology resulting simply in changes in the methods of production, without changes in the distribution of control. Differences in the control implications can be seen in the approach to retraining. Retraining for work on new systems can be provided on the basis of assessed potential, with an assessment of achievement at the end of the training period. Alternatively, retraining can be made available to all employees in the relevant group, without an assessment of competence at the end of the training period. The former practice is likely to lead to an increase in management control, the latter not. The latter was more common than the former in Fleet Street.

Examination of the impact of new technology upon management control needs to be placed in the context of other factors influencing management control. There are four major sets of factors: political and social environment (including legislation); product market; labour market; and institutional arrangements governing relations between management and employees (especially the collective bargaining system). In addition, the attitudes and abilities of the groups involved affect the extent to which favourable conditions enhance the achievement of each side's objectives. The effect of introducing computerised photocomposition upon the level of management control is likely to be limited unless other factors also change. The structural relations can be summarised diagrammatically:

Figure 13.1   Model of technological change and control

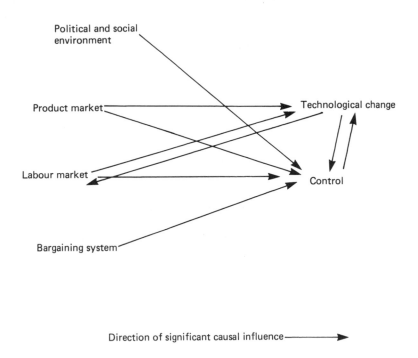

Hence the environment, product market, labour market, bargaining system and technological change all influence the level of control. Technological change is itself influenced by the product market, the labour market and the level of management control.

Conclusions

In Fleet Street the four sets of factors have changed since 1970, but the changes have not been permanent. Most importantly, the product market declined substantially in 1974–6, only to revive in the late 1970s. The effect of the decline in the product market was to give urgency to plans for new technology then being considered by newspaper managements, and to persuade union officers, especially at national level, that reduction in labour costs were necessary to improve the financial performance of the industry. The improvement in revenue in the late 1970s indicated the resilience of the industry's market, and reduced the pressure on union officers, especially at Chapel level, to accept new technology. The process of introducing computerised photocomposition was prolonged, the new systems finally operating in very different circumstances from those in which the plans were announced; by the early 1980s the product market was more similar to the position in the early 1970s than in 1974–6. Accordingly, technological change was not accompanied by major changes in other areas, and therefore had only limited impact upon management control, at least in the short run.

New technology can be both the cause, and consequence of changes in management control. In Fleet Street changes in external factors – the financial crisis in the whole industry in 1974–6, the change in ownership at TNL in 1981 – made it possible to introduce new technology. Some managers hoped that the introduction of new technology would facilitate the process of making permanent the enhanced control which other changes made temporarily possible. However, the argument of this paper has been that new technology in itself has only a limited role in increasing management control in Fleet Street; management control is determined by a wide range of factors – social and political environment, product market, labour market and institutional arrangements. Such factors continue to sustain union bargaining power in Fleet Street. The process of introducing computerised photocomposition will therefore have only limited impact upon management control, at least in the immediate future.

References

Martin, R., *New Technology and Industrial Relations in Fleet Street*, Oxford University Press: Oxford, 1981, chapters 3 and 4.

National Union of Journalists, *Journalists and New Technology*, National Union of Journalists: London, 1980, p.41.

Purcell, J. and Earl, M.J., 'Control Systems and Industrial Relations', *Industrial Relations Journal*, 8, no. 2, 1977, pp.41–54.

Royal Commission on the Press (Macgregor), *Final Report (Cmnd. 6810)*, 1977, p.42.

Smith, A., *Goodbye Gutenberg: The Newspaper Revolution of the 1980s*, Oxford University Press: New York, 1980.

Wood, S. (ed.), *The Degradation of Work? Skill, De-skilling and the Labour Process*, Hutchinsons: London, 1982.

PART THREE

CROSS-NATIONAL AND SOCIETAL IMPACT

14 A promethean change of industrial relations: a comparative study of Western European unions and technological developments *

Anders J. Hingel

Introduction

Not long after the first commercial computer was introduced in Great Britain, the President of the TUC in his address to the annual congress set out his views as to the necessary steps to take in order to face the suspected future development of automation:

> 'We should immediately set ourselves to the task of controlling these developments not restricting them; of turning them to our advantage and not to our disadvantage. If we are wise and see ahead, the new developments can be the tools with which we can remould our world as a home for man. To fear automation would be the cowardly approach − it could only arise from a sense of weakness' (TUC, 1964).

More than twenty years later, in 1978, a resolution was carried at the congress stressing the 'challenge and threat' that new technology poses to trade unionists; at the same time it put emphasis on the need for taking 'urgent steps' in formulating a 'policy on the social and industrial consequences of the growth of automation and computerisation' (TUC, 1978).

* This chapter was developed within the framework of the 'European Trade Unions *vis-à-vis* the New Technology' project which was financed by the Danish Council for Scientific Policy and Planning.

255

The technology-optimistic attitude, which was distinctive of the years of prosperity up through the sixties, could be found in all European countries: technology was unequivocally seen as a, and often the most important, remedy for securing full employment and greater welfare for the union members. Certainly various 'disadvantages' existed, but they were considered as 'the exception more than the rule' (Kern, 1979), and at worst, the reaction of the trade unions would more than counter-balance them. Certainly technological developments in the prosperous sixties also initiated substantial alterations in employment and qualification structures, as innumerable scientific studies at that time testify (Bright, 1958; Reynaud, 1956, Blauner, 1964; Friedrichs, 1963—65) but almost as certain was the possibility for each expelled or 'dequalified' employee to find a new job on the market that corresponded to his or her qualifications. The economic expansion 'absorbed' the disadvantages of the technological development. It was thus possible for the greater core of union membership to find, what has been named, an *individual arrangement with society* (Hörning, 1971). For less organised wage-earner groups, more marginal to the unions — as for example foreign workers, women and young workers — the situation was often different (Hingel, 1982; Kern, 1979).

In the sixties, unions in their policy making and action concerning technological development derived great advantage from these 'individual arrangements' of their members with society, and concentrated on taking technological developments for granted and securing a satisfactory relationship between wage-levels and productivity increases. It was the time of union demands for an 'Aktiven Lohnpolitik' in Germany (Bergmann, Jacobi and Müller-Jentsch, 1975), for 'productivity agreements' in Great Britain (Clegg, 1979) and for 'des contrats de progrès' in France (Reynaud, 1975).

By taking technological developments for granted throughout the sixties, unions therefore paid little attention to the fact that in general a *dichotomous* or *contradictory understanding* of the consequences of this development for working and living conditions, was actually general among their members. A number of scientific studies showed in fact, that workers on one hand considered the *individually* experienced negative consequences of the introduction of new technology in the firm as surmountable, and often even as a chance that could be turned into their personal advantage, but on the other hand that the *general* technological developments in society were perceived, by the very same workers, as bringing about unemployment and falling standards of living (Reynaud and Touraine, 1956; Popitz, Bahrth, Jüres and Kesting, 1956).

One of the first labour movements to integrate a more *critical* view of these general technological developments in their policy making was the German. The recession in the years 1966–67, and numerous major strike movements in 1969, 1971 and especially in 1973, in which technological change played a prominent role, had obliged the unions, and especially the Metal Workers Union, IG-Metall, to present a more radical response to the 'negative aspects of progress'. This situation resulted in a trade union involvement in the political regulation of research and development within the frame of the actions of the Ministry of Technology and Research – which included the notorious programme for the 'humanisation of working life'. A trade union demand for a say in the numerous other technological development programmes of this ministry – the humanisation programme covers only about 1% of the budget of the ministry – in order to carry forward demands for a 'qualitatively different type of growth' based on an alternative technological mode of development, was never to be satisfied (DGB, 1977; Hingel, 1982). The general problem of technological development in society remained uninfluenced by union actions.

European unions thus encountered the rapid introduction of the new technologies of the seventies (i.e. the introduction of semiconductors and their application in technics like robots, NC, CNC and DNC machine-tools, CAD and ETP etc. as well as in products) in a period of economic and social crisis and high levels of unemployment, holding only hesitant strategies. The breaking down of the conditions for 'individual arrangements with society' – the expelled and 'dequalified' blue as well as white collar worker did no longer find new jobs corresponding to his qualifications – threw light upon the lack of consistent union strategies in the field.

The resolution carried at the congress of 1978 demanding TUC to take urgent steps in order to formulate a trade union policy of influence on technological development and its social consequences, testified to the unsatisfied need and the difficult task trade unions in most countries were confronted with.

Trade unions' influence on technological development in six European countries

In this section we will outline the general features of the regulatory system of technological development in six European countries which represent different types of labour movements and different industrial relations systems: Scandinavia (Norway, Sweden and Denmark), Germany, France and England.

257

Norway deserves special attention in the case of Scandinavia. Indeed, the Norwegian experiences in the field have been the subject of attention in all European countries. A technology agreement was signed by the Norwegian LO and the employer confederation, NAF, as early as in 1975 aiming at regulating the introduction in firms of 'data based systems'. Outside the LO area since then we find the conclusion of similar agreements in the public sector, banking and insurance. The greater part of the private as well as the public sector is thus covered by such agreements. On this general basis a substantial number of technology agreements have been concluded on local, regional and national level. The 1975 agreement stated the following principles to be respected in cases of the introduction of data-based systems:

(a) employees, through their unions, have the right to get all relevant information about systems which may affect their interests. The information should be given sufficiently early to allow the unions to exercise a real influence upon the decisions made, and given in a language comprehensible to non-specialists. System descriptions shall also include information about the effect upon the interests of the employees;

(b) employees and their unions have the right to participate in the system's development;

(c) unions may elect an additional shop steward (data steward) with systems as his special field of responsibility. He has the right to get a proper education for his job (Nygaard, 1979).

The 1975 agreement has been renegotiated in 1978 and 1981, the latter covering 'technological change and data systems' and putting emphasis on 'local level as the appropriate level of conflict resolution'. In the 1981 agreement unions have also obtained the right of calling on external experts, paid for by the firm.

However, one should not underestimate the Norwegian unions in the cases of the other Scandinavian union movements, as to a certain degree, looking *beyond* technology agreements for a genuine say about technological developments. In fact, the Work Environment Act of 1975 (which took effect in 1977) constitutes more promising grounds for union influence on the introduction of new technology and on the regulation of social consequences. This law, which since 1977 actually has functioned as the legal basis for the technology agreements, demands a *'fully satisfactory work environment'*: a state of affairs which should be realised by means of 'work environment improvement programmes', negotiated between employers and the employee representatives. The long term benefits from this law are thus considered promising even though one has experienced 'an initial phase of hesitation and confusion' (Gustavsen and Hunnius, 1979; Elden *et al.*, 1982, EPOS. 1982).

258

In *Denmark*, we can see for the moment less than 100 local technology agreements. In 1981 a central agreement was signed by LO and the employer confederation, DA — which was in fact an additional agreement to the co-operation concluded in 1977 — and was followed by a definite reluctance among employers to discuss any further local agreements although one could observe that the number of arrangements signed by employers who were not members of DA increased. The same employer reaction was actually also registered in the Norwegian case, where the period 1976—79 was marked by a relatively low activity on the local level (Finansdepartementet, 1981). Similar to the above mentioned central agreement between LO and DA, a technology agreement has been signed in the public sector concerning State employees, whereas the municipal employees up to now have rejected such an accord. The unsolved problem has in the latter sector been the demand for information rights and employees' influence on the highly centralised cross-municipal development of computer systems.

In *Sweden*, workers' and unions' influence on the introduction of new technology has remained until now essentially regulated by the Act of Codetermination at Work of 1976. Consequently, the Act induced the conclusion of central agreements in the public sector, banking and insurance; more lately, LO and the employers' organisation SAF, have, after five years of fierce negotiations, agreed upon a so-called Development Agreement (May 1982). The latter is expected to engender local technology agreements in the near future.

However, although employees and their representatives have, in the three above mentioned Scandinavian countries, obtained, at least formally, a certain voice in technology matters by means of central/ decentralised technology agreements, the employers 'right to direct and distribute work' has been preserved. This is why unions presume technology and working conditions to be in the long run transformed primarily by means of the various work environment Acts and especially by the related directives and regulations, rather than by means of collective agreements.

In the case of the *Federal Republic of Germany*, agreements on the regulation of social consequences induced by technological change (rationalisation) have been signed since the end of the sixties on a national as well as on a regional level. A strong union demand for influencing State-programmes of R&D in the field of technology and working conditions, has throughout the seventies constituted the focus of unions' strategy *vis-à-vis* technological development. The programme for humanised working conditions represents, as mentioned above, so far the only German State-financed development programme in which the union and their members formally have a certain say — in so far as the employee representatives in the works councils (Betriebsräte) have a *veto-right* as to the state financing of such programmes in the company (IG-Metall, 1980; Janzen, 1980).

In spite of a highly centralised trade union movement and in spite of a fierce employers' reluctance to negotiate, local agreements on technology have been reached between works councils and employers within the plants and companies. The present possibilities for concluding agreements on decentralised levels are becoming still more limited owing to a reinforced co-ordination of employers' policies regarding technological development: in the so-called Taboo-catalogue, a treaty of policy coordination concluded by the members of the German employer organisation, BDA — it is thus clearly stated that new technology is not to be dealt with in local agreements (BDA, 1978). The most important central agreements on the regulation of technological development were concluded in Germany a decade ago: i.e. the 1973 agreement in the iron and metal industry (Nordwürttemberg-Nordbaden) which determined *minimal-norms of working conditions* — a demand, which the trade unions unsuccessfully have put forward ever since (Briefs, 1980).

Notwithstanding their shortcomings, the Co-determination Acts of 1951 and 1976 (covering respectively the coal, iron and steel industries, and large stock companies with more than 2,000 employees) and especially the Works Constitution Act of 1972 providing the works councils with numerous information rights and some influence rights on working conditions and social affairs in the firms, have contributed to enhance workers' influence on technology, but have also clearly circumscribed the bargaining scope on technology in plants and companies (Hingel, 1982).

In *France*, many industrial conflicts have taken place in which new technology was a central issue, but hardly any examples of technology agreements and negotiations in this domain have been seen. Nevertheless, the major union confederations (CGT and CFDT), as well as their respective engineer, technician and manager sections, representing the 'cadres' (UGICT/CGT and UCC/CFDT), have developed elaborate understandings and strategies for the regulation of working conditions, division of labour, technological change and industrial structure. At the annual fair on office technology in Paris 1979 (Sicob), the CFDT presented '*9 propositions*' concerning the conditions for investments in information technology (informatics) based on the principle that (to paraphrase): 'we will not, in the case of the new information technologies, accept the same type of approach as the one followed by scientific management' (*Le Monde,* 27 September 1979). CFDT thus presented a critical attitude to new technologies and demanded workers' control over investments (CFDT, 1977; CFDT, 1980). In

260

more recent discussions, the CFDT has developed a less critical policy mostly because of pressure from the members. The technology policy of the CFDT is of particular importance because the CFDT is reckoned to play a significant role in the elaboration and implementation of the industrial policy of the new socialist government in which 'strategic new technologies' play a major role (Boublil, 1977; Ministère de la Recherche et de la Technologie, 1982).

In the past, workers' influence on technology has indeed been rather limited in France. The new law on workers' rights within the firm – the 'Auroux Law' – which was passed in June 1982, is supposed to open up new possibilities. On the one hand, the individual worker now has a right to *a direct say* on working conditions in firms with more than 200 employees. This right is to be organised on the basis of homogeneous work groups, and its specific outline left to negotiations between management and trade unions within the firm. (In February 1983, 440 agreements had been concluded and negotiations took place in more than 90% of the remaining firms concerned (*Le Monde*, 22 March 1983). Owing to its imprecise legal context, the outcomes of this prescription remain however fairly uncertain for the moment (Lyon-Caen, 1981). On the other hand, the works council will have to be informed in the future before the introduction of new technologies if the latter have consequences for employment, qualifications, remunerations, training or working conditions (Auroux, 1982; Goetschy, 1983). The implicit aim of these reforms is, according to the Minister of Labour: 'to *reconcile workers with technological innovations* which are often perceived as an aggression' and further 'to create thus new investment opportunities' (*Le Monde*, 6–7 June 1982).

In *Great Britain*, numerous technology agreements have been concluded at plant and at company level between single unions, or groups of unions, and employers – e.g. the agreement between ASTMS/ACTSS and the firm CPC Ltd., prescribing 'joint discussions at each stage of the company plans for the investigation and introduction of electronic data processing equipment', or the agreement between the Joint Shop Steward Committee (TASS, ASTMS and ACTSS) and the Ford Company on the introduction of EDP, agreements signed respectively in 1979 and 1978. One reckoned, in 1981, that more than one hundred technology agreements had been concluded. Most of these were signed after the TUC had published 'guidelines' for union negotiators of new technology in July 1979 (TUC, 1979; ETUI, 1982). Whereas examples of national sectoral agreements can be mentioned – POEU and the Post Office; ACTT and the independent television companies, ITV – no agreement has been reached in the private sector at central confederation level between TUC and CBI. The breakdown of negotiations in 1981 was mostly due to resistance on behalf of the Engineering Employer Federation (EEF), but also the reluctance of certain unions to let the TUC play a too prominent role in these matters (*Intersocial*, November 1980). A central agreement has recently been concluded between the civil service unions and the government. This agreement will last for two years and work as a basis for local agreements in the public sector.

As mentioned above, the TUC congress had already declared as far back as 1955 that technological development should be controlled, not restricted. At the congress of 1968, it was confirmed as a TUC policy that all questions such as the introduction of new machines should be handled on a decentralised level. The *shop steward movement* thus remains of crucial importance for workers' influence on technological change and its social consequences in the firm.

The challenge of new technology for the labour movement

Apart from the fact that new technology has been given great attention in all the above mentioned countries, another common feature is that the technological issue has to a large extent been treated according to the specific industrial relations system existing in each country. One notices however that in each national context the technological issue has proved to be a challenge and threat to traditional, deeply rooted practices. This challenge is twofold. On the one hand, the concrete − but also the awaited − alterations of employment and qualification structures due to technological development change the modalities of organising the employees within each union, between unions and the relative importance of member groups, as well as the basis of employee solidarity. But, on the other hand, the challenge is not only due to the fact that unions are *affected by* technological developments, but also to the fact that unions want to *influence* these and their social consequences. Industrial relations systems are traditionally built up in order to set up rules and regulate the development of wages, working hours, health and safety items etc. To a certain extent, such a regulatory system is appropriate for the regulation of the *social consequences* of new technology. The elaboration of a *policy* involving the *choice* between alternative social consequences of new technologies and the choice of tactics towards its realisation can, therefore, often be observed to be the initial step for unions to take (Hingel, 1983). The limits of the industrial relations system becomes manifest, however, when unions envisage to formulate and practice not only a policy *vis-à-vis* the consequences of technological change but also a *technology policy* — involving the choice between alternative technologies and the choice of action for realisation: such a demand touches the very core of the relations of production (Piotet, 1983; Hingel, 1983).

It may thus be relevant to put forward the question whether technology, its mode of use, its development and its social consequences are not being treated as distinct matters compared to wages, health and safety items, working hours, etc. In other words, does not the complexity of the social process of technological development, and of the application of technology in the firm, and the speed of present technological change require the setting up of new regulatory structures and process (Brooks, 1981)? If one follows such a logic, the integration of the technological issue in union policies is bound to challenge elements such as:

union structure
inter-union relationships
the union relationship to research
the relationship between union and employers
the co-operation between unions at cross-national level
and union-state relationships

In no way do we here intend to support the argument of an international convergence of industrial relation systems as a result of technological developments: a debate (Kerr, 1960), which is now taken up again, this time by Marxist orientated authors (Claire, 1982). Neither do we believe that there is a 'one best way' for unions to deal with this 'promethean' challenge. But we do think that new technology constitutes a challenge common to industrial relations systems and that comparative studies can provide common experiences about the means, aims and consequences of various ways of confronting such a challenge. In the paragraphs below we intend thus to illustrate some of the transformations each of the previously mentioned elements is presently subject to, as a consequence of technological development and of the increasing union activity in the field.

Union structures

In most European countries we observe centralised as well as decentralised union strategies for the regulation of technological change and its social consequences.

Technology agreements at confederation level as we have seen them in Denmark, Norway and now also in Sweden, (and on federation level as it extensively is the case in Scandinavia, Germany and Great Britain) constitute mostly frameworks for further decentralised technology agreements to be signed at company and plant levels. Decentralised activities are thus often the result of centrally initiated actions, based on a twofold rationality (Hingel, 1982):

> a *technical, economic and social rationale* where the plant/company specific design, use and consequences of new technology make it necessary that 'those directly concerned' are actively involved in defining demands, and carrying out actions, founded on a knowledge of the specific technical, economic and social circumstances;
>
> a *union strategic rationale* based on the assumption that the increasing employer mobilisation at central levels in all European countries obliges unions to carry out at a decentralised level, what cannot be achieved centrally. As part of a long-term strategy, decentralised results are thus often considered as precedents for further union claims.

The respective importance of either level — centralised versus decentralised — can be presumed to influence internal power relations within the single union. Hence a different type of union representative can be seen coming to the fore as a result of decentralised activities regarding new technology. Local *'technology-awareness centres'* such as we observe in Norway and Germany, or *'trade union resource centres'* in Great Britain, are examples of new decentralised union bodies providing economic and technical expertise. The fact that the TUC, for instance, is opposed to such centres because of 'the fear of side-stepping established hierarchies' gives an indication of possible structural transformations (EPOS, 1982). The open conflicts between IG-Metall and parts of local works councils in two companies, Daimler-Benz and Siemens, to the discrepancy between the union policy and employees' claims concerning the introduction of new data-systems represent other examples of the sort (*Wechselwirkung*, no. 7, 1980; Hingel, 1982).

Besides, the *specialisation* of employee and union representatives (data-stewards, work environment representatives, company board and works councils representatives, etc.) — although justified somehow by the necessity of building up sufficient negotiation expertise required by a still more complex, centralised and confidential information system induced by new technology — will certainly cause a change in the role distribution within the union and its organisational structure. Such transformations might occur in three levels:

> between union 'experts' within the firm and the union members, where an *expertise gap* might emerge;
> within the hierarchy of shop stewards and experts in the firm;
> between shop stewards/experts who develop more and more

firm-specific expertise — and firm-specific orientations — and the union federation/confederation outside the firm.

The specific forms of such structural changes and their implications for the strengthening or weakening of union organisations will differ from one industrial relations system to another. In countries like Germany, with an industrial relations system characterised by union unity ('Einheitsgewerkschaft'), industrially organised unions and especially by highly centralised unionism, such modifications can be crucial and might well jeopardise the stability of the whole system (Streeck, 1982). In other countries like France or Great Britain, where union actions and practices have been marked in the past by a greater dispersion between central and decentralised levels, changes in the union structure will appear less clearly, although one will probably observe at firm level a trend towards more centralised negotiations with a shift from plant to company negotiations, due partly to the more central information systems brought about by technological development.

Inter-union relationships

New technology challenges also in different degrees occupational experiences, skills, employment conditions and career perspectives. For certain union members, new technology might induce new opportunities for higher salaries, employment security and requalification; whereas for others, it might represent a threat to each of these three items. Such consequences are experienced among employees within the firm, across firms (users and non-users of new technology) or branches (users and producers of new technology) as well as across nations each time new technologies are set up. As a consequence, rather narrow craft, industry or nationally orientated strategies have, for the reasons exposed above, caused open conflicts between union members and/or between unions, in numerous cases.

Such conflicts, resulting directly from technological changes, have occurred for example in Great Britain between APEX and TASS, or between TGWU and ASTMS. In Germany, similar fights have taken place between the printing union, IG-DruPa and the salaried employees' union outside DGB, DAG; the union of employees in banking and insurances, HBV, and DAG; the union of employees in wood and synthetic materials, GHK, and IG-Metall, etc. The conflicts between occupational groups, demarcation disputes etc., induced by the introduction of new technology, thus challenge established power and interest relationships between unions, and exacerbate the competition as regards the recruiting of members. Nevertheless, one also can see cases where the difficulties resulting from new technology have produced co-operation between unions. In Great Britain, technology agreements have been negotiated and signed by several union organisations: e.g. one agreement signed by TASS, ASTMS and ACTSS, another one by APEX, AUEW and TASS. In most countries, agreements between newspapers' owners and unions involve several federations: in Germany, for example, IG-DruPa and DJV, representing the journalists, have reached a common agreement. More recently in Denmark, the unions concerned (journalists, typographers, salaried employees) only accepted to negotiate a technology agreement *after* having agreed amongst themselves.

On the basis of a closer comparative approach, one could reasonably forecast that the higher the degree of multi-unionism − whether based on craft traditions (GB) or on political/ideological divergences (France) − the greater the likelihood of conflicts to occur and even to be exacerbated as a result of new technology. However, in countries where the principle of 'one plant, one union' is implemented (Germany, Sweden), conflicts about contradictory interests between occupational groups are not absent, but they come to the fore within the union organisation itself.

Moreover, the introduction of new technology may provoke the setting up of original union relationships. A complete re-organisation of union structures may in certain cases appear, as for instance with the creation of 'media-federations': following the example of Italy, certain countries have been envisaging such a change (IG-DruPa, 1980).

The search for a 'balance' between occupational groups' self-interests and the need for co-ordinated union actions will have to be found; failing this unionism could seriously be weakened.

Union links with research and researchers

Unions are more and more involved in research activities. Several confederations have created their own research and investigation centres such as the WSI centre (Germany) and the forthcoming Institute for Works and Technics, the new research centre connected to the Norwegian LO, the Center for Working Life in Sweden (set up in co-operation with the State, managers and unions) and the various independent research institutions working for the French unions (such as ARETE or BRAEC for example). Owing to the new requirements of collective bargaining, the unions' need for scientific knowledge becomes more and more evident. Indeed, new technology, in the same way as health and safety issues, require a high level of information and knowledge on behalf of union representatives − a knowledge which to a great extent becomes only accessible to them through union-researcher co-operation.

266

German unions have gained an extensive experience of 'working with' researchers through the various humanisation projects. The problem of researchers being often nearer to management than to workers' concerns, has especially been stressed, but also that these humanisation projects are co-operation projects, that their results constitute common knowledge and that they do not therefore strengthen unions' positions as such (IG-Metall, 1980I; Hingel, 1982).

The Scandinavian experiences of so-called 'one-party research' and of 'action-research' should not suffer from such deficiencies — researchers working solely with unions and on the basis of union-defined interests; further, the projects are often carried out in close co-operation with union members in specific firms and regions. But even in these cases a certain 'malaise' often characterises the relationship between researchers and unions (Sandberg, 1981; Stange, 1982).

If research and scientific knowledge become an inherent part of union activities, there is also a danger of weakening decentralised levels of the union and rendering the union's central structures more intellectual and more 'technocratic'. The so-called 'corrective co-determination right' in the German Betriebsverfassungsgesetz (par. 91) which provides the works council with a co-determination right in cases where changes in the workplace are contradictory to 'reliable scientific knowledge' on humanised working conditions, constitutes an example of how this 'intellectualisation' of the relationship between employers and employees has been formalised.

Seen from the point of view of union membership, the above mentioned need for a union involvement in research appears to lead towards an integration of new occupational groups in the labour movement. We refer here to the growing unionisation of engineers, technicians and researchers. Especially in France, the fact that these occupational groups are getting organised, is to a large extent now affecting union discussions and union viewpoints *vis-à-vis* new technology (Valerenberghe, 1981; Mentré, 1981).

Union-employer relationships

The consequences of the technological issue for the union-employer relationship will only briefly be evoked. The subsequent expansion of the scope of negotiation has led employer organisations to more clearly express their standpoints, preferences and strategies *vis-à-vis* new technology. We would like to refer here to the prominent place that technology occupies in the so-called 'Taboo catalogue' of the German employer organisation (BDA) (which includes the refusal to conclude technology agreements on a decentralised level and accepts only agreements on 'major' technological changes); another illustration of the above mentioned obligation of clarification on behalf of employers, can be seen in the mutual recognition of the employer's right 'to direct and to distribute work' which has been redefined in the Danish central technology agreement: unions consider it as a victory that this right has not been expanded: employers as a victory that it has been maintained (Dansk Metalarbejderforbund, 1981; Aktuelt, 16 March 1982).

The technological issue thus often serves as a *scapegoat* for a number of other conflictual items between employers and unions. The general awareness of the problem, its distinctive nature and the employers' clearly defined interest in the field makes technology an ideal domain for employers' mobilisation.

Co-operation between unions at cross-national level

The understanding of the technological development as a social process that crosses national frontiers appears obvious to most union organisations, though very few international activities do take place. International secretariats such as FIET or FIOM, regional organisations like ETUC and NFS are in varying degrees active in the diffusion of information related to experiences and policies in the field of new technology, but they are *not* policy-making bodies. the TUAC/OECD 'advises' OECD about union viewpoints, but it does not initiate policies.

International union co-operation as a strategy directed against the activities of multi-national firms which emerged at the end of the sixties seems to have withered away together with deepening of the economic crisis in the seventies. A certain co-ordination of industrial policies has been realised between European unions within the EEC (ETUI, 1981) and between Scandinavian unions *vis-à-vis* the Nordic Council of Ministers in recent years (NFS, 1982), but until now no cross-national industrial policy has been realised.

Cross-national co-operation is required if the intention is to contribute to increase unions' influence on technological development within each national context. Exchange of information across national borders, information on industrial development within various branches (data on the future state of international competition and on the development of production systems in a given industry as well as across industries), and information on unions' experiences in the field of technology regulations and of social consequences of technology, could well be a preliminary step in the building up of such co-operation. This development will no doubt challenge the autonomy of national unions and will demand their acceptance of union policy-making on an international level.

Conclusions

In most European countries, the State has actively supported R&D activities in the field of new technology. The French government's 'missions' for microelectronics, the British governmental 3–5 years programmes in the field of new technology and the consecutive German data-processing, microelectronic and technical communication R&D programmes have been (and still are) indeed developed, presented and carried out with hardly any union involvement. The possibilities of unions having a say in governmental R&D schemes have thus remained extremely rare, though they have, in most countries, been claiming such an influence in state bodies and in firms carrying out public-supported R&D activities (Vangskjær, 1980; SID, 1980; LO, 1981). The representation of union interests in governmental and ministerial boards and working groups of which we have seen numerous examples in Sweden, Germany and France, appears to have been evaluated in fairly negative terms (ETUI, 1981; Naschold, 1979; Vangskjær, 1980; Briefs, 1976; IG-Metall, 1980II).

In all Scandinavian countries, the unions' viewpoints were to a large extent embodied in the three respective Work Environment Acts. In fact, State regulations and directives of the work environment in relation to new technology (e.g. VDUs, robots) are demanded by most European unions (EPOS, 1982).

In the present economic crisis, where the bargaining power of the unions in front of employers has been weakened at all levels, resorting to the State is imperative. Given the low level of influence unions presently exert in State bodies, the question of whether increasing union involvement in their activities will, in the long run, contribute to weaken or enhance unions' power remains open (Crouch, 1979). Further, in order to equal out welfare between those employed and those 'ostracised' from social life, the need for higher integration of technology policies, employment and income policies, appears as increasingly urgent. New technology could thus induce a complete redefinition of industrial relations and the functions of trade unions in society.

References

Auroux, J., 'Les droits des travailleurs', *La Documentation Française*, Paris, 1982.

BDA (Bundesvereinigung der Deutschen Arbeitsgeberverbände), Katalog der zu koordinierenden Lohn — and Tarifpolitischen Fragen, BDA, 1978.

Bergmann, J., Jacobi, O. and Müller-Jentsch, W., 'Gewerkschaften in der Bundesrepublik', *Europäische Verlagsanstalt*, Frankfurt a.M., 1975.

Blauner, R., 'Alienation and Freedom', University of Chicago Press: Chicago, 1964.

Boublil, A., 'Le socialisme industriel', Presses Universitaires de France: Paris, 1977.

Briefs, U., 'Technologie — und Modernisierungspolitik im Spannungsfeld zwischen den Interessen der abhangig Beschäftigten und der Unternehmenspolitik', *WSI Mitteilungen* 12, 1976, pp.747—53.

Briefs, U., 'Arbeiten ohne Sinn and perspektive?', Gewerkschaften: und 'Neue Technologien', Pahl-Rugenstein: Koln, 1980.

Bright, J.R., 'Automation and Management', Harvard University Press: Boston, 1958.

Brooks, H., 'Science, Technology and Society in the 1980s' in OECD *Science and Technology Policy for the 1980s*, OECD: Paris, 1981.

Caire, G., 'Confluence', *Consommation-Revue de Socio-Economie* 3, 1982, pp.3—12.

CFDT (Confédération Francaise Démocratique du Travail), 'Les dégâts du progrès: Les travailleurs face au changement technique', *Edition du Seuil*, Paris, 1977.

CFDT, 'Le tertiaire éclaté: Le travail sans modèle', *Editions du Seuil*, Paris, 1980.

Clegg, H.A., 'The Changing System of Industrial Relations in Great Britain', Basil Blackwell: Oxford, 1979.

Crouch, C., 'State and Economy in Contemporary Capitalism', Croom Helm: London, 1979.

Dansk Metalarbejderforbund (DM), 'Debatoplæg: Den teknologiske udvikling — teknologien i menneskets tjeneste', DM: Copenhagen, 1981.

DGB (Deutscher Gewerkschaftbund), *Vorschläge des DGB zur Wiederherstellung der Vollbeschaftigung*, DGB: Dusseldorf, 1977.

EPOS (European Pool of Studies), 'Social Change and Technology in Europe', Information Bulletin no. 4-10, Commission of the European Communities: Bruxelles, 1982.

Elden, M., Havn, V., Levin, M., Nilssen, T. and Rasmussen, B., 'Good Technology is not enough', Institute for Social Research in Industry: Trondheim (Norway), 1982.

ETUI (European Trade Union Institute), 'Industrial Policy in Western Europe', ETUI: Bruxelles, 1981.

ETUI, 'Negotiating Technological Change', ETUI: Bruxelles, 1982.

Finansdepartementet (Ministry of Finance, Norway), 'Økonomiske og sosiale virkninger av ny datateknologi', Oslo, Norges Offentlige Utredninger (NOU 1981:14), Universitetsforlaget, 1981.

Friedrichs, G., 'Automation, Risiko und Chance', *Europäische Verlagsanstalt*, Frankfurt a.M., 1963—65.

Goetschy, J., 'A new Future for Industrial Democracy in France', *Economic and Industrial Democracy* 1, 1983, pp.85—101.

Gustavsen, B. and Hunnius, G., 'New Patterns of Work Reform — The case of Norway', Universitetsforlaget, Oslo, 1981.

Hingel, A.J., 'Den Europæske Fagbevægelse over for ny Teknologi: Tysk fagbevægelse i spændingsfeltet mellem statslig teknologipolitik og faglige aktioner i virksomhederne', Institut for Organisation of Arbejdssociologi, Handelshøjskolen i København, Copenhagen, 1982.

Hingel, A.J., 'Ny teknologis sociale funktion og konsekvenser', *Nyt Nordisk Forlag* (Spring 1983), Copenhagen.

Hörning, K.H. (ed.), 'Der "Neue" Arbeiter: Zum Wandel sozialer Schichtstrukturen', Fischer Taschenbuch Verlag: Frankfurt a.M., 1971.

IG-DruPa (Industriegewerkschaft Druck und Papier), 'Rationalisierung und Humanisierung — unauflösbare Wiederspruch oder gewerkschaftliche Aufgabe?', *Gewerkschaftliche Monatshefte* 4, 1980, pp.268—70.

IG-Metall (Industrigewerkschaft Metall), 'Beteiligungen der Betriebsrats bei betrieblichen Humanisierungsvorhaben', Schriftenreihe der IG-Metall 84, 1980I.

IG-Metall, 'Entschliessungen des 13 ordenlichen Gewerkschafttages der IG-Metall, Berlin, 1980II.

Janzen, K-H., 'Technologiepolitik und Gewerkschaften', *Gewerkschaftliche Monatshefte* 4, 1980, pp.256—62.

Kern, H., 'Kampf um Arbeitsbedingungen: Materialen zur "Humanisierung der Arbeit" ', Suhrkamp Verlag, Frankfurt a.M., 1979.

Kerr, C. *et al.*, (eds), 'Industrialism and Industrial Man', Harvard University Press: Cambridge, 1960.

Leontief, W., 'What hope for the Economy?', New York Review of Books, 12 August 1981, pp.31—34.

LO (Landsorganisationen i Sverige), 'Fackföreningsrorelsen och forskningen', LO: Stockholm, 1981.

Lyon-Caen, G., 'Une législation à adapter à la lutte contre le chômage', *Le Monde*, 5 November 1981.

Mentré, M., 'L'Informatique: Les technologies nouvelles, des question, des éléments de réponse', *Options 5*, 1981, Annex.

Ministère de la Recherche et de la Technologie, 'Recherche et technologie: Actes du Colloque National 13—16 Janvier 1982', La

Documentation Française, Paris, 1982.

Naschold, F., 'Probleme einer "sozialorientierten Forschungs – und Entwicklungspolitik" – Das Programm "Humanisierung des Arbeitslebens" am Scheideweg', Wissenschaftszentrum, Berlin, (IIVG/rp/79–209), 1979.

NFS (Nordens Fackliga Samorganisation), 'Industripolitiskt samarbete i Norden – politisk vilja och handlingskraft eller . . .?', Forlaget SOC, Copenhagen, 1981.

Nygaard, K., 'The "Iron and Metal Project": Trade Union Participation' in Å. Sandberg, *Computers Dividing Man and Work*, The Swedish Center for Working Life, Stockholm, 1979.

Piotet, F., 'L'expression des salariés dans l'entreprise', Projet 173, 1983, pp.214–23.

Popitz, H., Bahrdt, H.P., Jüres, E.A. and Kesting, H., 'Das Gesellschaftsbild des Arbeiters', J.C.B. Mohr: Tubingen, 1957.

Reynaud, J-D. and Touraine, A., 'Les ouvriers de la Sidérurgie et le Progrès Technique', Actes du III Congrès Mondial de Sociologie 3, Paris, 1956.

Reynaud, J-D., 'Les syndicats en France I, II', *Editions du Seuil*, Paris, 1975.

Sandberg, Å., (ed.), 'Forskning for förändring – om metoder och förutsättningar för handlingsriktat forskning i arbetslivet', Arbetslivscentrum, Stockholm, 1981.

SID (Specialarbejderforbundet i Danmark), 'Teknologiens udfordringer til fagbevægelsen', SID: Copenhagen, 1980.

SID, 'Ny teknologi – et løfte eller en trussel?', SID: Copenhagen, 1983.

Stange, J. and Ivarsson, O., 'Forskning för demokrati', ASF: Stockholm, 1982.

Streeck, W., 'Qualitative demands and the neo-corporatist manageability of industrial relations', *British Journal of Industrial Relations* 2, 1981, pp.149–69.

Vangskjær, K., 'Industriudvikling og Industripolitik – analyse og perspektiver', Arbejderbevægelsens Erhvervsråd, Copenhagen, 1980.

TUC (Trade Union Congress), 'TUC Report 1964', TUC: London, 1964.

TUC, 'TUC Report 1978', TUC: London, 1978.

TUC, 'Employment and Technology', TUC: London, 1979.

Vanlerenberghe, P., 'Le syndicalisme face aux changements technologiques', Cadres CFDT 297, 1981, pp.4–7.

15 Microelectronics and quality of working life in the office: a Canadian perspective

Richard J. Long

Introduction

No one will argue that the advent of microelectronics will not bring about revolutionary changes in the workplace. Indeed some suggest that microelectronics will bring to the office a revolution similar to what took place in the factory about a hundred years ago. However, what few experts will agree on is what the precise effects of this revolution will be. Some envisage a future that includes happy productive workers freed from the need to perform menial and repetitive tasks working in jobs which allow high discretion and full use of their abilities and skills. Others see a future where most people will be either unemployed or working as adjuncts to machines under tight control by an organisation in which only the top few have any power to make decisions.

The purpose of this chapter is to assess the implications of the new technology in a less polarised way, examining issues which have implications for the quality of working life — broadly defined. These issues include the implications for job and organisation design, health and safety, and security of employment.

This chapter focuses on Canadian research and policies in these areas, since other parts of the world have been dealt with in other chapters. In this regard, it is noteworthy that this chapter could not have been written three years ago, or even one year ago. The amount of Canadian research available on the topic has mushroomed during the past year and is increasing at an accelerating rate, as documented by

Sutton (1982). Governmental agencies are at the forefront of this. In the past eighteen months no less than five major reports have been produced or sponsored by governmental bodies — the Science Council of Canada (1982), Labour Canada (1982), The Province of Ontario (1981a), and two by the federal department of Communications (Plowright and Booth, 1982; Department of Communications, 1983). A recent survey by Kaye (1982) indicates that many Canadian universities are also establishing research programmes in this area, although most are still in a stage of infancy.

Since all parties agree that more empirical evidence is needed, a major set of 'field trials' have been initiated by the Department of Communications, in conjunction with the Department of Industry, Trade and Commerce, to be conducted in various government departments from April 1982 to 1985. The following statement illustrates the rationale and primary purpose of the programme.

> 'The Office Communications Systems (OCS) Program was established because of an alarming fall in the productivity growth rate of Canadian labor, and because the trade deficit in this electronic office industry could reach $20 billion by 1990. We in Canada have strength and potential, especially in word-processing and telecommunications equipment provided by Canadian companies. The OCS field trials are expected to provide Canadian industry with experience in developing and marketing electronic office systems while providing a market in the federal government for Canadian Products and Services' (Department of Communications, 1982:2).

In addition to these economic concerns, a great deal of attention is being focused on the human and social impact of office technology, and the field studies are being carefully designed in order to provide sound empirical evidence on these issues (see Trigon Systems Group, 1982).

In general, there are a number of different interest groups with views on this issue — and they can be arranged on a continuum ranging from optimism to pessimism. The optimists, of course, are led by the suppliers of the equipment, but often include some business and government leaders. Two groups are at the other end of the spectrum — organised labour and women's groups — who both fear loss of employment, deskilling of jobs, physical and mental health problems, and a tightly controlled work environment somewhat akin to scientific management gone wild. Arrayed in between are a variety of governmental agencies, each of which tends to reflect more closely the views of one constituency or another. The Department of Communications views office technology as one area where Canadians can develop and

274

apply sophisticated technological expertise on a world class level. The Department of Industry, Trade and Commerce sees development of a Canadian industry in this area as a source of jobs and a means of reducing potential trade deficits in this area. Labour Canada is concerned with the impact on workers and the quality of working life, which has become a major concern of the department in recent years (see Regan, 1981). Since the majority of the workers most affected are women, the Ministry for the Status of Women is concerned. Finally, because of a relatively high level of unemployment currently prevailing in Canada, elected government officials are particularly concerned with the employment effects.

Despite their differences, all of these groups are in agreement on one issue — the inevitability of the application of microelectronics to the office. What they differ on is the extent to which the changes which come about will be beneficial to society and the extent of the action required to ensure that the benefits will be maximised and the disadvantages minimised.

Most of the possible implications of office automation are somewhat paradoxical — they can be seen as having the potential for either positive or negative consequences. Thus, both pessimists and optimists can find evidence to support their arguments. However, at least part of this controversy can be explained by the fact that there are at least two distinct phases to the so-called office automation 'revolution', and various individuals may have one or the other aspect in mind when discussing the issue. Up to this time, the main impact of the new technology has been simply to facilitate office operations as they are now being carried out. For example, the text editor replaces the typewriter; the microcomputer replaces the filing cabinet. While significant, these innovations simply increase the efficiency of work as it is now done.

However, a second phase of application is now beginning, which portends revolutionary changes to the organisation. This stage involves the outright elimination of many intermediary functions and has been brought about by the convergence of the three technologies of electronic data-processing, telecommunications and office machines (Tapscott, 1982). To illustrate, take the example of a firm where field sales personnel need to frequently 'phone the central office for pricing and product information. Phase 1 automation would be illustrated by the adoption of microcomputers for storing this information, and the provision of video display terminals to the clerks answering the telephone calls from the sales force. In contrast, phase 2 would involve provision of portable terminals to the sales force, or even, conceivably, to the customer, thus eliminating the clerks and even some of the sales personnel. Similarly, managers would communicate directly with one another through 'electronic mail' and interconnected data banks.

Menzies (1981, 1982) has developed a useful distinction between two basic types of office worker. The first is the 'information worker' who is involved in the routine entry, recording, storage and transmission of information. These include typists, secretaries, clerks and data entry personnel and are primarily female. The second group consists of those who analyse and utilise this information. These are known as 'knowledge workers', and are primarily male. Phase 1 of the microelectronic revolution affects only the information workers, while phase 2 will affect the 'knowledge workers' as well. 'knowledge workers' as well.

Thus far most of the experience has been with phase 1 type applications of microelectronics and some empirical evidence exists on the effects of this application. On the other hand, widespread application of the phase 2 type is in its infancy so little empirical evidence is available to inform the debate about its effects. The balance of this chapter will reflect this dichotomy. The next section of the chapter will discuss the organisational and human implications of microelectronics over the medium run, while the later section will illustrate some of the concerns of the phase 1 revolution by examining perhaps the most widespread form of office automation – word-processing.

Organisational and human implications

This section will discuss the organisational and human implications in the near to medium term, a period when phase 2 of the microelectronic revolution should be taking place. These implications will fall under four categories – communications and decision-making, the hierarchy and managers, flexibility of work time and place, and effects on lower level personnel. Two important implications that are more properly related to the phase 1 revolution – computer monitoring and pacing, and physical and mental health – will be treated in the following section dealing specifically with word-processing.

Communication and decision-making

What will happen to communication and decision-making processes within the organisation? Will the efficiency with which information can be transmitted to key decision-makers lead to a centralised organisation structure where all but the top few people in the organisation will become information gatherers and order followers? Or will this same ease of transmitting information enable decisions to be made and discretion to be applied at lower organisational levels than hitherto possible?

Taylor (1982, a,b,c) suggests that there are two forces at work in society. The first, based on older 'mainframe' computer technology, is pushing towards centralisation. The second process, based on micro-computers, leads toward what he calls 'distributed intelligence' – a powerful force for decentralisation. It is based on the notion that key decision-making information is not best generated by feeding it into a central computer – but by the formation and reformulation of networks connecting a number of previously independent systems on a 'per occasion' basis. Utilising this system of distributed intelligence, he argues, will 'for the first time, take advantage of a modern educational system that is turning out literate, original and independent minded individuals . . .' (Taylor, 1982c: 179).

In support of his thesis he cites a study carried out by Leduc (1979). This study reports on the results of the application of electronic communication/computing technology to the Business Planning Group of Bell Canada. This technology linked the 14 individuals in the group to one another, as well as linking them to outside experts doing similar work. He found that the hierarchical pattern of communication hitherto present when the main medium of communication was the written memo tended to be replaced by a more open 'all channel' everyone to everyone network of links. This occurred because of the perceived informality of the electronic messaging system and the ease of transmitting duplicate copies to all group members.

Taylor is not alone (e.g. see Zureik, 1983) in his belief that decentralisation will occur. However, just because the technology will exist to support the free flow of communication throughout the organisation does not necessarily mean that managers will use it in this way. Indeed, top managers who possess classical values and beliefs about managing – and there remain many of these – can be expected to attempt to use the technology to centralise decision-making. For many top managers a radical shift in beliefs and values will have to take place before true decentralisation will occur.

Finally, Taylor himself (1982a) foresees some problems with regard to unrestricted flow of organisational communication. Aside from the risks of 'information overload', the organisation may lose its capacity to 'absorb uncertainty', which is now done by the filtering and interpretation of information by various organisational units before it reaches key decision-makers.

The traditional organisation structure is likely to be affected in a number of significant ways, depending on the extent to which automation is introduced. First, there will be fewer persons needed for the routine manipulation of information as electronic mail and other types of direct interconnections develop between the actual users of the information. Since there will be fewer lower level workers to supervise, there will likely be a reduction in the number of supervisors and lower level managers required, thus reducing the number of hierarchical levels in the organisation, as well as the size (Plowright and Booth, 1982).

Those supervisors who do remain can expect to have their roles changed from a control or surveillance type of function to a broader role definition, as computer monitoring takes over this role. Instead, they will focus on training and helping to implement new organisational systems as procedures and technology are continually improved, as well as performing 'boundary roles' — that is, linking the unit to the greater organisational system. Linkages between the relatively few workers still needed for routine data input and those who use the information may become electronic, rather than physical. Indeed, as will be discussed later, these information workers may not be physically located on organisational premises or even considered technically as employees. (However, it could be argued that even now, although they may be physically located on the same premises, there could not be much less interaction between routine information workers and decision-makers in most hierarchies.)

Overall, the picture this view presents is of smaller, flatter organisations where decision-makers communicate directly with one another and where authority is more evenly shared because of the free flow of information these devices will encourage. The surveillance and routine coordination roles will be substantially reduced or eliminated. However, there are others who argue that these types of predictions are based on a faulty understanding of a manager's true role. As Kasurak, Tan and Wolchuk (1982: 59) put it:

> 'Electronic systems certainly have the ability to overcome time and space barriers, but this capability is often overrated by persons who lack an understanding of the nature of managerial work. It is true that managers "plan, organize, direct, and control". More importantly, managers negotiate, conciliate, inspire and lead. These functions are not easily automated leaving more than one system designer puzzled at the "perverse" behaviour of managers who find their electronic system of little relevance to their work.'

In other words, organisations are much more than just devices concerned with the processing of concrete information, as many of the enthusiasts of the 'automated office' seem to imagine. Instead, they are also systems that generate power and influence which is then used to allocate resources and execute tasks, and are dependent for their success on a complex web of interpersonal relationships that often takes years to develop. Mintzberg (1973) notes that managers frequently need to base key decisions on information that is unsystematic, diverse, fragmented, and not highly amenable to codification or even recording. The environment of a modern organisation is exceedingly complex and it is still an art to select and correctly interpret what is relevant to the organisation. Furthermore, because an organisation is a political mechanism, managers may not always find it in their personal interest to share key information, even though this may be in the best interest of the organisation as a whole. All of these factors militate against the prospects for significant automation of managerial functions.

There is some empirical evidence to support this latter view. Brophy reported on an attempt to install an integrated office system into a head office department of Shell Canada. The objective (1981: 10) was 'to demonstrate the potential for professional and managerial time savings through machine dictation, word-processing and the delegation of work as well as the potential for new technologies, such as electronic mail'. The major emphasis was to attempt to push some of the more routine responsibilities of higher levels down the hierarchy, right to the lowest level which would then shift its most routine responsibilities to automated equipment, such as word-processors. Rather than being deskilled, these 'information workers' at the lowest levels received training in communications skills, problem-solving, decision-making and conflict resolution. The goal at this level was to create a semi-autonomous group, with responsibility for their own procedures, work allocation and vacation scheduling.

Implementation of the system took considerably longer than expected, and was accompanied by substantial resistance to the depth of change required. 'Managers seemed to experience difficulty both in delegating tasks and in redefining their roles to make the most productive use of time freed up through delegation. The redefinition of roles were also found to be time consuming and interfered with day-to-day business activities . . . .'. Cost savings during the first six months were about half of what was anticipated. Ironically this decentralisation process within the department was brought to an abrupt halt when a corporate reorganisation resulted in the decentralisation of much of the work performed by the corporate department. In sum, Brophy attributes the limited success of the programme to a failure to sufficiently consider the social factors involved and to take a socio-technical approach.

Greenberg (1981) supports this point of view in describing an experiment at Bell Northern Research where a group of '19 knowledge workers were given electronic work stations to help them with various aspects of their jobs, including electronic mail, word-processing, information retrieval, administrative support and data-processing'. Participants indicated increased job variety, accomplishment, creativity and satisfaction, according to quality of working life measures administered before and after the implementation. No changes were found in a comparison group.

Although he does not discuss any productivity gains or cost savings in quantifiable terms, Greenberg concludes that the experiment has been a success and attributes this to the socio-technical approach used in implementation. However, it should be pointed out that these workers were explicitly 'knowledge workers' (e.g. researchers) in the most complete sense of the term, and this type of function may be particularly receptive to the type of information made available under 'automated' systems.

Flexibility of working hours and place

One effect of microelectronics technology will be to allow work to be done away from the traditional office. A number of potential benefits of this immediately come to mind. Persons who are bound to the home by reason of handicaps, need to care for family members, or other reasons may now find it possible to gain employment. Time and money now wasted in commuting could be eliminated. Individuals may be able to optimise their work schedules and productivity by working as their own biological rhythms as well as other commitments dictate.

However, there are a number of concerns, particularly by women's groups. They point to the potential for reisolating women in the home and burdening those with responsibilities for care of family members with two jobs instead of one. This type of home work, they claim, is not only devoid of the opportunities for social interaction that most jobs afford, it also takes away the visibility with superiors that is important for promotion. Finally, they fear that such systems may allow employers to treat these employees as independent contractors − thus relieving organisations of the need to provide fringe benefits. The Labour Canada report suggests establishment of labour standards on these matters as well as on working conditions.

Another concern deals with the possibility of installation of VDTs into the homes of professional and managerial employees, thus placing implicit demands on them to continue their work outside of normal hours, perhaps to the detriment of their family lives (Phillips, 1982). On the other hand, if the alternative to work at home is work at the office, then the use of home computer terminals may actually increase time available for the family.

Effects on lower level employees

What will be the effects on the lives of lower level workers — the 'information worker' rather than the 'knowledge worker'? The previous material has already suggested that there will likely be fewer of them in the future, particularly as phase 2 of the microelectronic revolution takes place. However, it is unlikely that these effects will be as severe or as immediate as the pessimists fear. As will be seen, the word-processing revolution has not had the severe effects imagined even two or three years ago, which were largely based on 'optimistic' (to use a kind expression) claims by manufacturers of the equipment. Furthermore, phase 2 is not likely to progress as fast as either the optimists or the pessimists believe. This will be at least partly due to the inherent difficulty in automating management tasks, and not least of all by the resistance of managers concerned with not disturbing their hard earned power and status in the organisation. Ironically, to the chagrin of women's groups, one of the major saving graces will likely be the reluctance of executives to give up the status and convenience of a personal secretary. Nonetheless, some reduction in employment can be expected and programmes are necessary to encourage retraining for other positions within the organisation, or more likely, new occupations entirely.

If, in fact, total employment needs in the economy are reduced due to microelectronic technology (and this point is the subject of some debate — see Zeman and Russel (1980) for an overview) then the continuation of a trend toward a shorter working week would be one solution. Not only would jobs be spread among more individuals it would also spur continued creation of jobs in the leisure industry.

The effects on the task itself are not clear, and will likely vary from organisation to organisation. Clearly, a deskilling is not inherent in the technology, and there have been instances where introduction of microelectronics has improved the quality of jobs, as a study of bank tellers commissioned by Labour Canada (1982) found. Tellers reported increases in variety, use of skills and interest in their jobs due to implementation of microelectronic technology. On the other hand Menzies (1981, 1982) has documented cases where this has not occurred. This issue will be further discussed in the following section.

Electronic word-processing

Video display units, or as we shall call them, terminals (VDTs) attached to either micro or mainframe computers have become to many synonomous with the microelectronics revolution. As of 1978 it was estimated that there were some 18,000 full-fledged word-processors in Canada, with 65,000 projected by 1985 (Province of Ontario, 1981b). Use of this technology has sparked heated debate among a number of groups, and some empirical evidence is now available. In Canada, four main areas of concern have arisen. First, the employment effects. Will use of this technology lead to a net reduction in the number of clerical workers needed? If so, what is to be done about these 'surplus' workers? Second, are there physical or mental hazards related to the use of VDTs? Third, what will be the effects on job design? Will this technology create a new class of boring and meaningless jobs or will just the opposite occur? Finally, what will be the impact with regard to control and supervision? Does supervision and monitoring of an employee's work without his/her knowledge constitute a demeaning and/or unethical practice?

Employment effects

Estimates of the unemployment effects of introduction of electronic word-processing vary enormously. One early estimate suggested that 'between four and six jobs are eliminated every time a word-processor is installed in an office' (Brunet, 1980). In a study conducted in the head office of a large diversified Canadian corporation, Menzies (1981) found that despite an expansion in the head office's activities, the percentage of clerical staff declined from 78% in 1972 to 46% in 1980 due to the introduction of word-processing. Of some 130 clerical workers displaced by this process only two were able to retain their employment with the firm by advancing to professional or managerial positions. In a study by Wilkins (1981) of three municipal governments which introduced word-processing, he found that employment remained stable between 1975–80, while increases in workload were met through increased use of word-processing and related technology. A recent report by the Canada Department of Communications (1983) concluded that introduction of the new word-processing technology has reduced employment somewhat although layoffs have been avoided due to the process of attrition. However, the report (1983: 17) goes on to say that 'if the rate of diffusion of office automation increases and the range of functions affected also increases, it may no longer be possible to balance decreased demand against attrition'.

The balance of the evidence seems to indicate that the most dire predictions (often based on claims by suppliers of the equipment) overstate the short to medium run impact on employment, although all parties agree that some loss of employment among the affected workers can be expected. This trend is likely to accelerate over the longer run as 'phase 2' technology — which eliminates, rather than simply facilitates, many present clerical functions — comes into more widespread use. Particularly concerned are women's groups since women are the primary holders of the jobs likely to be displaced.

In order to counter these effects all of the government reports recommend improved government-sponsored training and retraining, with a particular emphasis on the needs of displaced or potentially displaced women. The Labour Canada report, particularly, stresses that legislative and other efforts must continue to be aimed at breaking down barriers which may retard the large scale entry of women into employment areas where they have traditionally been under-represented. They also suggest that organisations create more 'bridging' positions to enable a smoother transition for workers in administrative support jobs to positions offering greater opportunities for career advancement.

Physical and mental health

Ever since the widespread introduction of VDTs, there has been a rash of complaints from workers and unions about the possible health hazards associated with these machines (see DeMatteo, 1981). The most serious of these complaints deals with a disproportionately high rate of miscarriages and birth defects among pregnant VDT operators. For instance, the Canadian Airline Employees Association stated that seven of thirteen pregnant VDT operators at Montreal Airport miscarried in 1981. The Hospital Employee's Union of British Columbia, Local 180 reported that of six pregnant VDT operators, two miscarriages occurred and only one of the four babies was born normal. Four out of seven pregnant VDT operators at the Toronto Star newspaper gave birth to babies with congenital defects. Many of these groups theorised that some type of radiation leakage may be a contributing factor. However, despite extensive testing, there is absolutely no evidence to suggest any type of radiation hazard, as a report by the Radiation Protection Bureau of Health and Welfare Canada (1980) concluded:

> 'It can be stated unequivocally that video display terminals do not emit levels of electromagnetic radiation that could possibly be hazardous to the operator whether pregnant or not, and therefore do not present an occupational radiation hazard.'

283

Despite these findings, neither unions (DeMatteo, 1981) nor the Canadian Advisory Council on the Status of Women (Chenier, 1982) are entirely convinced that no radiation hazard exists, and contend that one must err on the side of safety. Possibly in response to these pressures, the federal public service, in a bulletin dated 17 June 1982, promulgated a policy providing pregnant VDT operators with the right to transfer to positions not requiring use of the VDT, if available.

One possible explanation for the disproportionately high number of problematic pregnancies among VDT operators has been suggested by Labour Canada (1982: 153). Citing a prominent physician, they point out that, 'while VDT operators' complaints of eye strain, fatigue, and stress do not, in themselves, lead to birth defects, they are very likely to result in increased smoking and the increased use of tranquilizers and other drugs — factors known to have an adverse effect on the unborn child'. There is some evidence reported by the United States National Institute for Occupational Safety and Health (1981) that VDT operators do suffer higher levels of stress than other office workers.

That VDT operators do experience physical symptoms in excess of those experienced by similar employees is quite clear. For example, in a carefully controlled study of 1,166 clerical employees at Ontario Hydro, Mallette (1983) found three symptoms that occurred more frequently among VDT operators than other clerical employees: (a) eye strain, (b) aches in neck and shoulders, and (c) blurred vision. He also found these symptoms to be related to the amount of time spent on the equipment in a given day as well as individual concern about possible radiation dangers. A review by Treurniet (1982) of prevailing literature on this issue produced virtually identical conclusions. He went on to note that the causes of these symptoms are, by and large, correctible. Reports of visual fatigue were related to improper ambient lighting, poor display quality and ophthalmalogical deficiencies, while muscle pain and fatigue were related to poor work station design, such as improper height of chair, keyboard and display screen, absence of source document holder and no support for the forearms and wrists.

Labour Canada (1982) concluded that there is a need for ergonomic standards to cover the physical environment and design of office equipment and furniture relative to VDTs. Until such standards are established, they suggest some guidelines for employers. These include right of reassignment for pregnant VDT operators, a maximum limit of five hours per day on a VDT, hourly rest breaks, and annual ophthalmic testing and provision of any necessary ophthalmic devices at the expense of the employer.

It is interesting to note that these guidelines also have some indirect implications for quality of working life. For example, if operators may spend no more than five hours daily at a VDT, employers must find other tasks to occupy the remainder of the work day, thus providing some variety and enrichment for the operators.

Job design

Views on the impact of introduction of this technology on the quality of jobs themselves cover both ends of the spectrum. Some (e.g. Johnson, 1983: 49) contend that 'there are few who will deny that . . . video display terminals . . . and other microimage equipment intensifies the pace of office work in the name of productivity, while increasing monotony and boredom in many jobs'. On the other hand, promoters of the equipment suggest that use of the new technology can improve and enrich jobs by automating many simple and routine tasks, thus freeing up time for the more complex and challenging tasks that cannot be automated.

What is the empirical evidence on this issue? In general, it appears that the initial reaction in many organisations was to create a central word-processing 'pool', where all VDTs and their operators were centralised. A major rationale for this was the desire by purchasers to amortise the high cost of this equipment by keeping it constantly in use. Another rationale was that personnel who specialised as VDT operators would become more proficient, and that this would result in minimisation of training costs. This Tayloristic approach, by all accounts, resulted in most of the problems feared by critics, such as narrowing of jobs, reduction of autonomy, variety and meaningfulness of jobs, as well as curtailing the ability for human interaction.

One empirical study of this type of arrangement was reported by Buchanan and Boddy (1982), who studied effects of conversion from conventional typing to word-processing at a British consulting engineering firm. They found (page 1) that the change to centralised pool has 'reduced task variety, meaning and contribution, control over work scheduling and boundary tasks, feedback of results, involvement in preparation and auxiliary tasks and communication with authors'. With regard to productivity, number of pages produced per typist increased tremendously – by a factor of five at least – and typing staff was reduced from 28 to 16 persons, despite a slight increase in work load. However, authors of the material were not entirely satisfied with the new system. Although the typists' output had risen, authors did not receive their material in less time than before and felt they spent more time correcting drafts. Furthermore, they were separated from their work by a new supervisory layer, the word-processing centre supervisor, and directly approaching the typist was discouraged – possibly causing authors to feel a loss of control of the work flow.

Interestingly, it was not found that application of the new technology in itself led to any 'deskilling', as many unionists (e.g. Mather, Stinson and Warskett, 1981) fear. Indeed, in some ways the new technology requried a higher skill level as typists needed to learn a complex set of codes and then keep updating their knowledge of them as programmes changed. The operators themselves stated (page 10) 'that they enjoyed handling the equipment but resented being pooled and remote from the authors'.

Despite writing from a Marxist-feminist orientation, Manchee (1980, 1983) agrees that moving from a typewriter to a word-processor cannot be considered deskilling – quite the reverse in fact – based on her four years of experience with the Canadian federal government both using word-processors and conducting training on them. She suggests major reasons for the myth that little skill is required are self-serving claims by suppliers about ease of implementation and a lack of actual experience with the equipment by most persons writing about the topic.

There seems to be ample evidence that the technology itself need not detract from the quality of working life, but if implemented properly, may actually enhance it. Mueller (1981) describes a change form a centralised word-processing pool at Shell Canada's head office to a more decentralised structure involving three semi-autonomous groups, each serving a specified number of authors/departments. The changes were designed primarily by the workers themselves, assisted by management and a specialist in quality of working life principles. As a result of the changes, plus upgrading of some equipment, output and turnaround have improved, and absenteeism has declined. However, there was also an unexplained decline in output quality.

Another example relates to two Canadian schools of business, which both implemented word-processing at about the same time. One school created a centralised pool, with faculty members feeding their input through a supervisor, while the other simply provided departmental secretaries (who work in decentralised work sites) with the equipment. In the first instance, output was so slow and of such poor quality that some faculty members resorted to paying outside typists for rush jobs. Satisfaction among operators in the pool also was low. At the other university, secretaries tended to regard the word-processor as a tool to facilitate their work, and many actually enjoyed working on it as long as they did not have to spend all day at it. Speed and quality of output was generally good, except for jobs of extreme length. Although there were times when inequities

286

did occur, with some secretaries being overloaded and others idle, the system worked satisfactorily for the most part, with absenteeism and turnover quite low. Interestingly, the pool at the first school is now being decentralised in an attempt to stem faculty and operator complaints.

Overall, it seems clear that the technology itself does not dictate any particular job design. Instead, as Buchannan and Boddy (1982) found, managerial values play a key role. In their study management believed that the opportunities for tighter control and increased specialisation posed by the technology would result in greater efficiency.

In their research Kasurak, Tan and Wolchuk (1982) make the same point about managerial choice. However, they are somewhat optimistic that the central pool may lose some of its perceived attractiveness as the real cost of this type of equipment continues to decline. Part of the original motivation for central pools, they point out, is based on the belief by managers that full utilisation of the equipment at all times is the only cost effective way of implementing it. Van Beinum (1981) is also hopeful that the growing Quality of Work Life movement in Canada will provide many managers with an awareness of the human issues involved with the implementation of the equipment as well as the knowledge that viable alternatives are available.

In recognition of some of the detrimental effects of pooling and narrowing of job scope, the Department of Communications (1983) recommended that 'the hidden costs of the centralisation of word-processing' be brought to the attention of those responsible for decision-making about centralisation or decentralisation. Furthermore, they recommended that (page 21) 'in choosing office automation equipment, management should be encouraged to opt for systems that encourage flexibility and enriched careers, and to avoid creating jobs that are associated with machines only'.

Computer monitoring of work

A major concern of various labour groups is the extent to which the new technology permits constant, close and surreptitious monitoring of employee performance (e.g. Mather, Stinson and Warskett, 1981). (Indeed, to some managers this ability to monitor performance and productivity may be one of the most attractive features of the new technology.) Johnson (1983: 150) argues that:

> 'The ability of the computer to provide a precise measurement of input is a constant source of tension between senior management and shop-floor workers. Workers complain of speedups, higher production quotas, and increased stress . . .'.

Related to this, arguments are made that these measures do not take into account difficulty of the work and quality of output, thus resulting in questionable validity. Employees may also be kept in the dark about what acceptable standards are and may not be provided with feedback on whether they are meeting them.

Aside from the stress that such constant monitoring can cause, civil libertarians have argued that electronic monitoring can be considered an invasion of privacy and may be in violation of the recently promulgated Canadian Charter of Rights. The Labour Canada Task Force (1982: 56) has concluded that the concerns on this issue are so serious that the process should not be allowed under law:

> 'The Task Force regards close monitoring of work as an employment practice based on mistrust and lack of respect for human dignity. It is an infringement on the rights of the individual, and an undesirable precedent that might be extended to other environments unless restrictions are put in place now. We strongly recommend that this practice be prohibited by law . . .'.

While the Department of Communications report (1983) does not go so far as to propose an outright ban on the use of such information, it does suggest that 'employees at all levels should be consulted and should be allowed to participate in decisions about the type of data collected and how it is used to monitor their productivity and to assess their performance'. Where possible, they suggest that use of evaluation systems that are not based on computer generated data be seriously considered.

Some federal government departments have already taken the lead in this. Thompson (1981: 15) reports that the Ministry of Transportation and Communications

> '. . . decided to use a measurement system that would not be tracked by the equipment. The measurement is taken for one week every five weeks. Operators now personally maintain their work measurement and supervisors summarise it'.

Other methods could also be used to control the effects of computer monitoring. For example, employees could participate in setting reasonable standards for production and would receive feedback on their productivity whenever they desire it. As long as their overall production falls within these norms over a specified time period, short term fluctuations in output would be irrelevant. A simple procedure such as this could reduce uncertainty and stress considerably.

Conclusions

One inescapable conclusion is that the microelectronic revolution will have an impact on the quality of working life. It can result in the enrichment of work and the creation of humanised work organisations through elimination of tedious and repetitive tasks, allowing employees to concentrate on tasks that require judgement and skill. Alternatively, it could create a type of organisation beyond the wildest dreams of Frederick Taylor — where machine controlled human automatons endlessly repeat identical tasks. Which of these scenarios will prevail? While it is clearly too early to tell for certain, there are a number of encouraging trends.

Clearly, the technology itself does not dictate one or another of these outcomes. Instead, managerial values and beliefs seem to be the most important determinant. After a false start towards Taylorism in the office, it appears that the forces away from Taylorism are gaining strength. Perhaps one of the strongest forces for centralisation — economics — is declining in importance as the real cost of the equipment continues to decline and the hidden costs of Taylorism become more evident. Interest groups concerned about the potential negative effects have been successful in publicising their views and gaining substantial public and governmental support. Through the publication of successful alternatives to Taylorism, managers are beginning to realise that they do have a choice in how to apply the technology (Van Beinum, 1981). Hopefully, the field trials now under way will provide a large quantity of high quality information on this. The growing popularity in Canada of the Quality of Working Life movement is helping to encourage acceptance of certain key values.

Nonetheless, as all of the major reports concur, there is still a crucial role for the government to play in bringing about the positive scenario. In recognition of this, on 4 May 1983, the federal government announced its intention to create, in conjunction with business and labour groups, a productivity and employment centre to ease the economic transition into the high technology era. Changes in certain labour standards may also be required in order to deal with certain concerns discussed earlier. In addition, governments must do all they can to encourage employers to consider the broader human issues involved with the implementation of the new technology and to consult with employees at an early stage in the adoption of such technology.

Aside from the impact on the quality of work life itself, great concern has been expressed about the employment effects of the technology, particularly for lower level 'information workers'. However, while there is little doubt that some jobs have been.lost, it does not seem the impact has been as rapid or as deep as many have feared. Much of this pessimism appears to have resulted from over-enthusiastic claims by sellers of the equipment. For example, Kusurak, Tan and Wolchuk (1982: 59) have found that 'the strategy of attempting to use electronic devices to achieve a reduction in numbers of clerical and administrative support personnel has not been very successful'. Some of the reasons, they suggest, include the fact that personnel savings are frequently distributed over several locations (saving one-fifth of a person a year in five locations does not equal a one person—year saving), the new capabilities create new demands, and the reluctance of managers to part with the status and convenience of a personal secretary.

As a result of these somewhat disappointing (by some standards) results, enthusiasts now suggest that the real savings will occur with the introduction of phase 2 of the electronic revolution and the 'automation' of managerial jobs. However, these individuals may not be recognising that organisations are more than merely information processing mechanisms, and are also systems of power and interpersonal relationships. Managerial work involves far more than simply collecting information, analysing it and making decisions and managers are more than just sophisticated 'calculators' — they are human beings with a variety of needs and motivations. As a result, managers and their tasks will likely prove less amenable to 'automation' than some might expect. Furthermore, managers will turn out to have a much high ability than lower level employees to successfully resist changes they perceive as threatening.

Thus, while microelectronics will be introduced into higher levels in the office, implementation and usage will likely be slower and more limited than believed by both the pessimists and the optimists. Nonetheless, certain types of jobs will be reduced or eliminated and both employers and governments must develop programmes to allow the affected workers (particularly women) to retrain for other jobs. Particularly important will be the need to help 'information workers', assume productive roles as 'knowledge workers', whose ranks will expand at five times the rate of 'information workers', according to one study (Department of Communications, 1982). The educational system must recognise changing needs within society and incorporate programmes designed to develop the general skills of analysis and problem-solving crucial to knowledge workers, as well as to encourage the flexibility that will be necessary in making two or three significant occupational shifts during one career. Finally, if an employment shortfall persists after taking these measures, the government can seiously consider the other options it has available, including possible reduction of the working week.

290

References

Brunet, L., 'Word processors: Source of Emancipation or Alienation for Office Workers?', *Quality of Working Life: The Canadian Scene*, 3, 1980, 4: pp.17–19.

Brophy, L.M., 'Office Automation in the Employee Relations Department Shell Canada Limited', *QWL Focus*, The News Journal of the Ontario Quality of Working Life Centre, 1, 1981, 3: pp.9–12.

Buchanan, D.A. and Boddy, D., 'Advanced Technology and the Quality of Working Life: The effects of Word Processing on Video Typists', *Journal of Occupational Psychology*, 55, 1982, pp.1–11.

Chenier, N.M., *Reproductive Hazards at Work*, Canadian Advisory Council on the Status of Women: Ottawa, 1982.

DeMatteo, B., *The Hazards of VDTs*, Ontario Public Service Employees Union: Toronto, 1981.

Department of Communications, Canada, *The Electronic Office in Canada*, Department of Communications: Ottawa, 1982.

Department of Communications, Canada, *The Human and Social Issues of Office Communications Technology*, Report of the Human and Social Impact Committee on Office Automation. Department of Communications: Ottawa, 1983.

Greenberg, M., 'Bell Northern Research applies Integrated Office Systems and the Quality of Working Life', *QWL Focus*, The News Journal of the Ontario Quality of Working Life Centre, 1, 1981, 3: pp.12–13.

Johnson, W., 'White Collar Wasteland', *Policy Options*, 4, 1: 1983, pp.49–52.

Kasurak, P.C., Tan, C. and Wolchuk, R., 'Management and the Human Resource Impact of the Electronic Office', *Optimum*, 13, 1982, pp.57–68.

Kaye, R., *Survey of University Research Activities in Office Automation*, Report to the Department of Communications, Canada, 1982.

Labour Canada, *In the Chips: Opportunities, People, Partnerships*, Report of the Labour Canada Task Force on Micro-Electronics and Employment. Labour Canada: Ottawa, 1982.

Leduc, N.F., 'La Communication Mediatissé par Ordinateur: Une Nouvelle Definition du Dialogue Groupal', *Memoire de Maitrises-Sciences de la Communication*, Department de Communication, Université de Montreal, 1979.

Mallette, R., *A Survey of the Attitudes and Perceptions of Video Display Operators in Ontario Hydro*. Human resources research report prepared by the Personnel Applied Research Branch, Ontario Hydro: Toronto, 1983.

Manchee, J., *Drowning in the Pool: Word Processing and the Organisation*, Institute of Canadian Studies, Carleton University, Ottawa, 1980.

Manchee, J., *Skill, Word Processing, and the Working Class*. Unpublished mauscript, 1983.

Mather, B., Stinson, J. and Warskett, G., *The Implications of Microelectronics for Canadian Workers*. A discussion paper for the Canadian Centre for Policy Alternatives. Canadian Centre for Policy Alternatives: Ottawa, 1981.

Menzies, H., *Women and the Chip*, Institute for Research on Public Policy: Montreal, 1981.

Menzies, H., *Computers on the Job: Surviving Canada's Microcomputer Revolution*, James Lorimer and Company: Toronto, 1982.

Mintzberg, H., *The Nature of Managerial Work*, Harper and Row: New York, 1973.

Mueller, M., 'Overview of the automation and reorganization of the word processing centre at Shell Canada Limited's Head Office', *QWL Focus*, The News Journal of the Ontario Quality of Working Life Centre, 1, 3, 1981, pp.7—9.

National Institute for Occupational Safety and Health, United States, *Proceedings of a Workshop on Methodology for Assessing Reproductive Hazards in the Workplace*, April 1978. U.S. Department of Health, Education and Welfare: Cincinnati, Ohio, 1981.

Phillips, D., *The Human and Social Impact of Office Communications Technology*. Presented at the 4th International IDATE conference (Institut pour le Dévèloppement et l'Amenagement des Telecommunications et de l'Economie), Social Experiments in Telematique, Montpellier, France, 1982.

Plowright, T. and Booth, P.J., *A Study on the Social Impacts of Office Automation*. Report prepared for the Department of Communications, Canada: Ottawa, 1982.

Province of Ontario, Canada, *Microelectronics: Report of the Task Force to the Government of Ontario*, Ministry of Industry and Tourism, Government of Ontario: Toronto, 1981a.

Province of Ontario, Canada, *Microelectronics: Background Papers for the Task Force to the Government of Ontario*, Ministry of Industry and Tourism, Government of Ontario: Toronto, 1981b.

Regan, G., 'Micro-electronics: The Human Element', *Quality of Working Life: The Canadian Scene*, 4, 1, 1981, pp.16—20.

Science Council of Canada, *Planning Now for an Information Society: Tomorrow is too Late*. Report no. 33, Canadian Government Publishing Centre: Hull, 1982.

Sutton, M.J.D., *Human Aspects of Office Automation: A Review of Published Information*, Department of Systems and Computer Engineering, Carleton University: Ottawa, 1982.

Tapscott, D., 'DP Professionals face Major Challenge in Automated Office', *Computer Data*, 7, 2, 1982, pp.22—32.

Taylor, J.R., 'Computer aided Message Systems: An Organizational Perspective'. In Neffah, N. (ed.) *Office Information Systems*, INRIA/North-Holland Publishing Company: 1982.

Taylor, J.R., *New Communication Technologies and the Emergence of Distributed Organizations: Looking Beyond 1984*. Unpublished manuscript, Department des Communications, Université de Montreal, Montreal, Quebec, 1982b.

Taylor, J.R., 'Office Communications: Reshaping our Society?', *Computer Communications*, 5, 1982c, pp.174–80.

Thompson, N., 'Word Processing: The Human Side', *QWL Focus*, The News Journal of the Ontario Quality of Working Life Centre, 1, 3, 1981, pp.14–15.

Treurniet, W.C., *Review of Health and Safety Aspects of Video Display Terminals*, Department of Communications: Ottawa, Canada, 1982.

Trigon Systems Group, *Field Trial Evaluation Guidelines*, Department of Communications: Ottawa, Canada, 1982.

Van Beinum, H., 'Organizational Choice and Microelectronics', *QWL Focus*, The News Journal of the Ontario Quality of Working Life Centre, 1, 3, 1981, pp.1–6.

Wilkins, R., *Microelectronics and Employment in Public Administration: Three Ontario Municipalities*, Institute for Research in Public Policy: Montreal, 1981.

Zeman, Z. and Russel, R., 'The Chip Dole: An overview of the Debates on Technological Unemployment', *CIPS Review*, January/February 1980, pp.10–14.

Zuriek, E., 'Canada and the Chip'. Forthcoming in *Queen's Quarterly*, Queen's University: Kingston, Ontario, 1983.

16 Automation and work design in the US: case studies of quality of working life impacts

Joel A. Fadem

Introduction

In assessing the prospective human aspects of increased automation in the workplace, two classes of problems emerge at the level of the firm. They can be stated in question form: What types of work and jobs will be eliminated? What kind of work will be required by the new systems?

Much deserved attention is being given to the job displacement effects of programmable automation, with robots dominating current attention. Predictions vary widely on the question of how many robots will be in use by the end of this decade and the net number of manufacturing jobs lost (Hunt and Hunt, 1983). As in the 1960s, when automation was the subject of widespread concern and national policy debate, there is no shortage today of gloomy and utopian scenarios.

The evolutionary nature of change towards integrated computer-based manufacturing notwithstanding, this writer has little doubt that serious technological unemployment will be a certainty in the absence of effective job training and retraining, supported on a long term basis. Such training can only thrive on the scale needed through co-ordinated policy and action at both the micro level of the firm and the macro levels of state and federal government.

* This chapter is a revised version of the author's contribution to the 'International Comparative Study on Automation and Work Design', commissioned by the International Labour Office, Conditions of Work and Life Branch, Geneva, 1982.

However, it is not the purpose of this study to address the question of technological unemployment, important as it may be. Rather, we shall focus on the issue of the qualitative nature of the work environment under conditions of automation — the second question posed above. We shall explore issues associated with the nature of automated production systems and their impacts on the quality of working life (QWL). The chapter will review selected North American experiences during the 1970s of the introduction and/or management of computer-based manufacturing technology. They represent varying degrees of responsiveness to what can be labelled the 'human aspects' of automation, ranging from negligible to substantial. More specifically, the case studies illustrate how QWL considerations were present or absent, either in the planning, introduction or management of technical change. Particular emphasis will be given to the relationship between technology and the processes by which work systems are designed.

Automation and work design

Prevailing approaches to work design for automated conditions have thus far not differed from those of traditional production systems. That is, the fundamental building block of the organisation continues to be the person-task ('job') rather than, for example, a system of roles largely enacted at the discretion of a work group ('self-maintaining organisational unit') (Davis and Taylor, 1978). Thus, with the person-task as the focal unit, the integrity of classical organisation design — job specialisation under hierarchical control — tends to be preserved. Organisational control systems are aimed at ensuring reliable worker performance. Most importantly, the implications of automation for organisational structure and the work environment are not usually explicit in the terms of reference of the technical design process. Instead, they tend to remain, tacitly or otherwise, unsanctioned areas of concern. Engineers and systems designers, themselves, must function within a framework of control, custom and practice and over-arching values which do not support the simultaneous consideration of technology, organisation and quality of work life factors. As a consequence, a deterministic quality informs the choice process in the evolution of factory automation. In this connection, the following remarks by a union official are germane:

'I feel that the manufacturing engineer plays an important role in determining the industrial relations climate in a particular plant . . . Specifically, when the manufacturing engineer is engaged in such activities as setting batch sizes, determining plant layout, establishing process specifications, ordering changes in the priority of work to be done, or when making any decision about matters involving shop operations, he influences the behaviour patterns on the shop floor . . . Typically, however, these production systems give too little consideration to the human beings who run the machines. All too often, it appears that these designers are guided by the feeling that technological advances in manufacturing engineering relegate the worker to the status of a machine, designed to perform small tasks, precisely specified on the basis of time and motion studies. He is assumed to be motivated primarily by economic needs and classified by a known degree of strength, dexterity and perseverence. The worker is often considered by management as incapable of dealing with variables in the production flow: any unplanned occurrences are to be handled by supervisory personnel' (Newell, 1975).

There have been exceptions, however. Some of the work restructuring efforts in a variety of US companies during the 1970s provided management and labour with insight into ways to improve poor working condtiions generated by technologies chosen without regard to the work environment. In these instances, technology, itself, remained unaltered, and the human system was adjusted to create a better fit. Also, as will be described later, further inroads into aligning technical and human considerations have been made through the design of innovative work structures in new organisations. Several reflect the application of 'socio-technical' concepts, where choices regarding the human and technical systems result from a process of reciprocal influence (Trist, 1981). Although increased attention has been given to these developments, they are comparatively small in number and tend to be isolated within their respective parent organisations. It is too early to discern the extent to which these innovations will diffuse and penetrate conventional orthodoxies of job design.

Manufacturing case studies

Increased attention is now being given to intensifying the introduction of automated technology in the mass and batch production of discrete parts (Gerwin, 1982). Using continuous process industries as a model, major US manufacturing companies have begun to invest heavily in computer-aided design and manufacturing equipment as a first step toward evolving integrated production systems, largely free (other than maintenance) of direct human intervention. This activity is being mainly undertaken by aerospace, automobile and heavy equipment companies, which already have extensive experience with unintegrated ('standalone') forms of computer-aided technology.

The case studies cover discrete parts manufacturing and illustrate different types of accommodations to computer-based automation. They represent variations on the central idea that the design of technical systems is, of necessity, governed by social choices which either restrict or nourish opportunities for improving the quality of working life on the shop floor. The implications of the case material will be discussed at the conclusion of the chapter.

Case one — numerical control

In mid-1968, plant managers at a major aerospace firm were exhibiting great alarm over low efficiency levels in the production of engine parts. More specifically, a crippling bottleneck existed in a shop where numerically controlled (NC) lathes were in use. Tension and ill feeling between workers and supervisors had been chronic in this shop, and were reflected in grievances — the highest in the plant. Other symptoms of disorder included high employee turnover, abnormally low production speeds, unreliable quality, high levels of scrap and rework, and frequent materials review enquiries. The NC section was especially strategic to the plant's highly integrated production system. If engine parts were not produced at sufficient rate or if quality slipped, schedules were delayed, other workers idled and contracts placed in jeopardy.

Resentment among workers was still nurtured from past struggles with management to upgrade the pay classification for the NC lathes. Strikes over this issue had seriously damaged the company, which remained steadfast in its position that hourly rates were commensurate with the skills required. The company contended that it was providing button-pushing jobs, purely and simply. In the words of one manager, 'Any monkey off the street can be trained to operate the computerised lathes'.

Realistically, however, button-pushing was not enough. Because of the close tolerances involved, the engine parts had to be absolutely flawless. In some cases, the tapes were not pre-programmed correctly, resulting in scrapped parts and fouled machines. Frequently, the tools would undercut from wear not compensated for in the tapes. Resets had to be made for second cuttings. Minor disturbances in the circuitry of the NC equipment were another regular occurrence. These disturbances were aggravated by the attitudes of operators:

'Look, I could slow it down, and it would look completely above board. Say the machine stops running. I go to the foreman and say "I pushed the button and nothing happened". He calls in the maintenance man who brushes some lint out of the machine. All that takes time. But if I had wanted to, I could have brushed the lint out myself' (Fadem, 1976).

The deteriorating situation resulted in a management initiative to begin a pilot programme of job enrichment. Management stated its rationale as follows:

'The principal reason for a good many of our difficulties is that our hourly employees are lacking in motivation. They perceive themselves as being treated as immature, irresponsible, incompetent people who are relegated to a button pushing status. A detailed analysis of their duties and responsibilities indicates considerable justification for their feelings. Because of the way their jobs have been structured, these men are not challenged; they have no sense of involvement in the total manufacturing scheme and they appear to derive little or no personal satisfaction from their employment . . .' (Fadem, 1976).

The union was initially apprehensive but, with management's offer of a 10% pay bonus for participation in the project, the union accepted the proposal and played an active role in overseeing the programme from its inception in October 1968.

The programme was launched in a section of the plant where 7 NC lathes were clustered. Recruitment to the project was voluntary subject to union security rules. Each operator was assigned to a single machine. Over the three shifts, this amounted to 21 men, including a single working leader per shift. The foremen and unit manager were transferred to other departments. The pilot unit reported to a single NC manager, assisted by a manager who co-ordinated the special programme, monitored its outcomes, and provided feedback. In the initial phase, the pilot programme had the following additional features: (1) flexible starting times; (2) elimination of timeclock punching for informal lunch breaks; and (3) extra responsibilities for operators, including preventive equipment care, minor machine adjustments and repairs, debugging new tapes, tools and fixtures, as well as troubleshooting existing ones.

The company sent a number of participants to programming school, in the hope that they would be able to devise their own tapes. This proved too ambitious and was scrapped, although training was given in record keeping and related management paperwork. The company's wish that the men carry out their own repairs was dampened by union job demarcation restrictions. During the first 3 months of start-up, productivity and machine utilisation dropped and accompanying attitudes were poor. There was confusion over roles and responsibilities. Absenteeism had not improved.

However, things changed for the better after January 1969. The next three months evidenced significant increases in machine utilisation and group productivity. Attitudes and levels of individual involvement also improved. The group became more cohesive as stable work roles were developed, understanding with management was established and team work assignments became harmonised. Group goals concerning machine utilisation, quality, scrap, rework and costs also began to develop. In general, the pilot group had improved its internal communications and level of mutual trust. It also received stronger support from outside departments concerning incoming quality, voucher integrity, machine maintenance and planning.

During the next 4 months, as activities became more routine and doubts faded about the continuity of the programme, operator attitudes became less clear, with a corresponding decline in machine utilisation and productivity. Contributing reasons for this were group conflicts about its informal leadership and discipline of members, diminished management attention to the project, the appointment of a new programme manager (there were 8 during the programme) and vacations. The unit's performance was also affected by a strike of maintenance workers in the plant.

From September 1969 through the beginning of a 100-day industry-wide strike in November, performance and attitudes in the pilot programme deteriorated rapidly. The strike marked the end of the experiment's first phase. Until then, it had yielded encouraging but unsettled results. Machine utilisation and productivity had increased only slightly, if at all. Scrap and rework had decreased significantly, as had the frequency of materials review disputes. Lateness and absenteeism had also been markedly reduced. The overall effect on unit cost, as traditionally measured, was unchanged.

With the return to work in early 1970, the pilot programme resumed with a different orientation. Whereas efforts were made in the first phase to enrich individual jobs within the context of relaxed supervision, the second phase focused on the collective group task. Rather than pursue job enrichment in isolation, attention was devoted to making the group a viable, self-maintaining unit, capable of managing its boundary relative to other groups and hierarchical levels. The group divided its labour to assume responsibility for various coordination and support funcitons. Group members conducted liaison duties with production control, planning, quality control and materials managers, as well as with maintenance engineers and payroll officers.

They also performed housekeeping and safety functions, training of new operators and record-keeping.

Internal production scheduling was managed by the workers, who also determined work assignments within and between shifts. When a bottleneck arose at the main tool crib, the workers set up their own and stocked it to fit their requirements. When breakdowns or equipment problems occurred, maintenance staff were usually required. But operators were often essential to a specific diagnosis, as in the case of programme faults, because maintenance men were spread over a ten-mile area and infrequently encountered the same machine. Some operators became proficient in programming. Greater interest also was kindled in tool fixturing and design. One instance of this was when operators developed methods of cutting two dimensions simultaneously, thereby saving time and set-up costs. In general, despite limitations in technical knowledge, pilot unit workers became highly motivated to meet the challenges raised by multiple role requirements within the group. An important feature of the pilot group was that individuals were not coerced into accepting responsibilities they did not want, aside from basic time and housekeeping duties. Peer discipline was applied to individuals who violated basic group norms.

By all reported accounts, the second phase of the pilot programme was a success. By September 1972, the project expanded to include 63 operators (it was to reach its peak at 72). That month a national newspaper featured a story describing the experiment. The company did not disclose details of productivity or cost savings to the newspaper, though it did acknowledge that scrap and rework had declined, accompanied by gains in product quality.

During this period, the union had assumed almost complete responsibility for monitoring performance and sustaining the programme, following local management's expression of concern about the implications of the programme and its wish to discontinue it. This was prompted, at least in part, by management's fear that the union would attempt to extend the pilot programme and the accompanying 10% pay bonus to other areas of the plant. This unsettled state of affairs persisted until the union actually stated its wish to negotiate for extension of the programme. This coincided with corporate management's apprehension about the pilot programme's implications for other plants. Its concern also included the following: (1) that they had not been adequately informed by local management regarding the project's expansion; (2) the 10% bonus scheme was disturbing the corporate pay classification system; (3) the notion of enriched jobs raised the issue of whether or not they could be fairly paid relative to other company jobs; (4) more fluid work group roles might not conform to National Labour Relations Board definitions of exempted jobs carrying management responsibilities; (5) they did not approve of flexible starting times and unclocked lunch breaks; (6) that longer term reliability of the pilot project as a means for securing better productivity had not been demonstrated.

Company management, having already los control over the programme's direction at plant level, unilaterally terminated it. The union took no official position on the programme's termination, and by early 1973, foremen had been re-assigned to the pilot programme area. The company had to continue payment of the 10% bonus until it was negotiated out of the contract 3 years later.

Case two – flexible manufacturing system

The next study was undertaken in the tractor-producing division of a large, diversified manufacturing firm. The plant is unionised, employs 1900 people, and in the 1970s introduced a flexible manufacturing system (FMS). During a 5-month period in 1980, a study was made involving direct observation, intensive interviews and survey questionnaires from a sample of foremen, machine repairmen, operators, loaders and tool setters (Blumberg and Alber, 1981).

The FMS essentially consists of a network of computer-controlled transfer lines which transport individual raw castings in wheeled pallets, and present them to work stations in the requisite order for processing. The workpieces are loaded onto the metal-cutting machines by shuttle carriages, whereupon a second computer initiates the direct numerical control transmission which causes the machine to process the part. After the processing sequence is completed, the pallet is extracted from the machine and routed to its next work station or returned to a loading station for removal of the finished part. This procedure is undertaken simultaneously for several dozen parts of various 'families' that may be in process at one time and routed in random order among the work stations. The system consists of 10 machines and 3 loading stations spread over approximately 100,000 square feet of floor area and joined by 12 tow chains which propel each 4-wheel cart.

System utilisation rates (hours actually worked relative to theoretical capacity) had been projected by the equipment suppliers to be on the order of 80–90%. Actual rates ranged between 50–60%. One source of underutilisation stemmed from the system's complexity and interdependence. Because all elements were indispensible, pressures to minimise downtime during the system's frequent failures prompted

301

hastily-made 'jury-rigged' repairs. As a consequence, each machine developed its own idiosyncrasies which eventually requried further rectification by the operators or maintenance workers. Workers also directly influenced system utilisation by controlling the pace at which they loaded and unloaded casting pallets. Finally, worker intervention was essential for monitoring the machines for dull or broken tools, responding to programme stops, and troubleshooting minor faults.

Analysis of the survey data provides insight into one of the underlying sources of sub-optimisation in the advanced FMS. Of the 20 employees working in the FMS, 18 participated in the study. The sample included responses from 2 foremen, 2 machine repairmen, 6 operators, 6 loaders and 2 tool setters. The questionnaire included items concerning the motivating potential of jobs and personal motivation of workers, as well as questions on job satisfaction and job stress. Results from the motivation questions were compared to data from a normative sample of 16 machine trade employees. Results concerning satisfaction and stress were compared to those of a national sample of over 1500 employee adults.

In general, the sample perceived work on the FMS as having low motivational attraction. For the combined sample of 18, the composite score on motivational potential was below that of the normative sample. This was the case for four of the five job classifications in the sample, especially the loaders and operators. With respect to particular elements of motivation, all five classifications rated opportunities to exercise discretion (autonomy) below the normative sample's score. Respondents in four of the five grades scored task identity (the degree to which the job requires completion of an identifiable piece of work) below that of the normative sample. In contrast, perceived needs for personal growth and development were higher for the combined sample, and for four of its five job classifications, relative to the normative sample's score.

Job satisfaction was measured in terms of co-workers relations, job challenge, resource adequacy, job comfort, promotion opportunities and financial rewards. The combined sample of FMS workers ranked below the national sample on every aspect with the exception of financial rewards, where there was parity. Of the five classifications, tool setters, operators and loaders were the least satisfied; foremen and repairmen felt reasonably satisfied.

Respondents from the FMS indicated that the work was stressful. Measures of stress were based on five factors: the extent to which conflict existed over how the job should be done, employees had skills they were not using, people did not know what was expected of them, resources to perform jobs were inadequate, and employees felt uncertain about their job security. The combined sample scored

302

below the national sample on all factors. With the exception of repairmen, every job classification had scores below the national sample on at least four of the five factors.

Finally, the absence of meaningful pay incentives, along with perceived earnings inequities relative to workers in the same pay grade operating conventional equipment were cited as further sources of dissatisfaction by a majority of the sample.

The above and other data from the open-ended questions indicated that the basis was lacking for generating worker commitment to the effective utilisation of the FMS. A familiar irony was manifest here; while the FMS was explicitly designed to remove the human element as much as possible from the manufacturing process, the precise opposite (human intervention) was required to bind the technical system together. By superimposing onto the FMS a traditional structure of specialised job classifications an essential source of flexibility appears to have been lost. This example typified the prevailing tendency to concentrate on maximising the technical properties of the work system at the expense of equally important social and organisation factors. The study concludes:

> 'Despite glowing statements that we are entering the new era of the automatic factory, available evidence indicates that such facilities are a long way from being a practical reality. The human element is still very much a factor to be considered, and appears to be making a significant difference in the utilisation of the few advanced systems which are now on-line. The major effect humans have on system performance appears to stem from the manner in which they respond to the system's requirements for raw materials, maintenance and the clearing of faults brought about by operating anomalies. Until equipment can be brought on-line which is totally automatic and completely reliable at acceptable costs, which can procure its own raw materials and dispose of its finished products, the behaviour of human beings will continue to be important' (1981: 1–20).

Case three – islands of partial automation and assembly

Packard Electric Division of General Motors Corporation manufactures a variety of automobile systems and employs 15,000 people in the United States and Mexico (Boyer, 1981). In 1972 the company was among the first in the corporation to build a new facility in a rural area of the southern US. The new plant employed approximately 500 people and provided an opportunity for experimentation with more participative management styles in a non-union setting. In retrospect, company managers candidly refer to this early effort as having been a 'benevolent dictatorship'. A second plant, built a few miles away, went further than its predecessor in developing an organisational philosophy which supported the creation of semi-autonomous work groups, a payment system based on demonstrated skills and knowledge, and related social mechanisms aimed at increasing worker job satisfaction, involvement and commitment to production objectives.

In 1977, a confluence of circumstances at the company's main complex in the North, employing 8,000 people in 3 adjacent locations, led to the following developments. First, sustained labour-management conflict in the presence of a declining working force, no new capital investment, and the conspicuous emergence of the corporation's anti-union 'Southern strategy' led to substantial pressure from local members of the International Union of Electrical Workers (IUE) to seek alternatives to a protracted union holding action. This found expression in the election of a new slate of local officers who advanced a platform of exploring possible areas for increased co-operation with management. Consequently, both company and union initiated a number of joint ventures during the following year, culminating in the formation of a top-level 'Jobs Committee' to search for more productive ways to operate and generate new jobs.

The second, coinciding element was the need, resulting from developments in product and process technology, for the creation of new manufacturing facilities. Based on a local decision to scale down the size of new plants, the company was faced with the requirement of spreading operations into four new facilities. Confronted with the choice of starting-up four new branch plants near the existing complex using employees from the same labour force, or starting afresh in a Southern state or Mexico, the company chose to remain in the area, given the labour-management co-operation attained. This was a significant achievement for the union and its members; 2,400 jobs had been retained.

The stage was thus set in 1978 for a collaborative planning process between local company engineers, line and personnel managers, union officials and shop floor workers. It consisted of a labour-management committee which guided the work of a 'design team' which applied socio-technical concepts to planning the new work systems. The principal design objectives were to reduce job fragmentation and attendant boredom, improve communication among workers and problem-solving capabilities between work groups, develop greater workforce flexibility, and control key production variance as close to their sources as possible in order to meet strict standards of volume, quality and cost.

The four branch plants commenced operations during 1980, each employing between 600–800 workers. Three plants manufacture wire harnesses for engine emission control systems. Each plant is self-contained, totally integrated operation with a one-day inventory system. The fourth facility is also totally integrated and produces other wire harnesses. The latter had actually begun operations in 1976, but its work structures were redesigned to be consonant with the 'branch concept', as it was known, at the other three plants.

Manufacturing in each plant is divided between two basic operations: the preparation of wire circuit leads ('lead prep') and final assembly, with a buffer area between the two. Each finished wire harness may contain between 60–100 wires, depending upon the unit. Before lead prep operations were significantly automated, wire circuits were prepared by six people in a series of short-cycle operations on different machines. A few batch process operations of this type remain, but the predominant mode is for a team of two operators per machine to load raw stock and take off prepared circuit wires. There are 113 of the lead prep, wire indexing machines spread over the 4 plants. The lead prep operators rotate at will, conduct their own inspections, and are responsible for troubleshooting their equipment and performing minor maintenance tasks. In contrast to the previous division of labour, all lead prep operators are in the same wage classification. Although these 'islands' of automated activity in lead prep represent the state of the art in manufacturing technology for this product, the overall technical system remains low on the automation scale. Labour accounts for 50% of total costs.

Final assembly operations are performed along 18–20 stations, each with an average job cycle of 60 seconds. In some areas, stationary fixtures are available off-line to permit the assembly of whole units. All workers in final assembly are cross-trained, and rotate on a regular basis. They are paid the same hourly rate (there were formerly 5 job classifications and rates). Final assemblers are also responsible for inspection, repair-work and servicing. Each assembly group is accountable as a whole for their unit's finished output.

In each plant, the production layout was designed to place workers in lead prep and final assembly in close proximity (12–15 feet) in order to expedite intergroup communication and error rectification. As of 1981, the possibility remained open for cross-training between the two production areas; its desirability and feasibility are presently unclear. Supervision was retained in all areas of the plants with control spans of approximately 1:25.

From the beginning of this venture, the company invested heavily in training. All 2700 workers (including foremen) received 8 hours of orientation to the new approach being pursued by labour and management, plus 40 hours of technical and social skills training.

It was also emphasised that each plant would be permitted to evolve its own form of accommodation to the general 'branch plant concept'. Much effort thus far has been devoted to socially integrated work teams and encouraging greater worker participation. Groups have developed different norms regarding job rotation and decision-making, and latitude had been provided for individuals to opt out of group-orientated production methods. More training and support will be devoted to developing greater technical co-ordination within and between work groups. Supervisors continue to receive training in participative management and group problem-solving. An inter-plant task force of managers, technical staff, supervisors and union officials was formed to identify and develop cost reduction projects.

Detailed information on the outcomes in human and financial terms is not available. The company has disclosed, however, that during the first year of operation, performance of the plants was sufficient to comfortably pay for all of the substantial training costs. The four branch plants also lead their company in cost reduction and for a 6-month period in 1980–81, were among the highest in quality within GM.

Accounts from the union have been positive in nature. Apart from preserving jobs locally, the improved working conditions have been acknowledged by the membership, in part, by the re-election of all local officers. Job cycles are still relatively short, but have been ameliorated to a certain extent by better environmental conditions and the participative climate that is being established. Individual differences regarding job rotation and involvement in teams will continue to require thoughtful accommodation. Each plant has thus far evolved unique customs and practices to address this and other issues. Difficulties have also arisen from some skilled trades groups, which felt their job territory had been eroded by machine operators. However, the elimination of routine, minor maintenance duties was conceded by many as an opportunity to engage in more challenging and important work. The job territory issue may remain thorny in the absence of more engaging and rewarding work for the skilled tradesmen.

Discussion

While the above discussion reveals the broad contours of the design and intended consequences of certain innovative work systems, it is more difficult to specify in detail the results obtained. Based on the few published reports extant, together with informal accounts, the following comments can be offered.

Because much responsibility for day-to-day management is delegated to work teams, corresponding pressures on their ability to function effectively can stem from a variety of sources. In some cases, inadequate advanced training and/or unforseen technical difficulties during early start-up phases of new plants have disillusioned their workforces. Regardless of the cause, when initial high expectations of management and workers have not been matched by reality, this has sometimes led to the imposition of management controls, such as more direct supervision, and retrenchment in multi-skilling programmes towards job specialisation.

Alternatively, early periods of crisis have often been successfully navigated through management's (and, where applicable, the union's) patient adherence to the original design philosophy and, where necessary, the renegotiation of performance expectations and standards, both internally and with the corporate organisation. A central dimension of effective team functioning is their ability to evolve internally and externally acceptable work norms. Because teams are responsible for work assignment, training and member discipline, among other functions, issues of equity, fairness and respect for individual differences must be continuously addressed. Predictably, these have been sources of strain. Groups have experienced difficulty in judging others in connection with pay raises, and in disciplining members. Tension arises when a member chooses not to broaden his or her skills and blocks another's training opportunity. Often, issues which cannot be resolved within a work group are referred to plant-level worker review bodies, and, if necessary, to management. In some cases, management has permanently absorbed these functions, either by design or default, leaving some form of multi-skilling as the core feature of the work system. In one company, multiskilling, a supporting payment system and mechanisms for encouraging open, two-way communication have been the main 'package' of techniques it has chosen to support in the design of other new plants.

In plants with first-level supervision, difficulties of role ambiguity, confusion over power and responsibility, and discomfort with the group dynamics of self-managing work teams have undermined the effective development of work norms which support the design philosophy. Management has contributed to this awkwardness by not adequately training supervisors for their new roles, and in those instances where first-level supervisors were assigned to a new plant on a mutually-acknowledged, short term basis the untenability of their position has been further increased. Some plants with formally-designated 'coordinators' and 'team leaders' as quasi-first-level supervisors have faced similar difficulties of role ambiguity and uncertainty about job mobility prospects.

Companies have started-up new plants with traditional management controls as a transition until production is smoothly running, phasing-in self-managing groups thereafter. Others have commenced operations with the rudiments of self-managing work units, some coping successfully, others requiring direct management guidance. Once operating on a stable basis, there are strong tendencies for work teams to become isolated within and between shifts, despite formal mechanisms of coordination. Correspondingly, management may neglect to develop or sustain plant-wide mechanisms for problem-solving, performance review, and goal setting. At work group level, production demands create pressures on their ability to attend to their own mechanisms of self-regulation.

Little objective evidence is available concerning the actual performance of the open job progression or multi-skilling systems. Depending upon the complexity of the technical process, optimal time-lengths for mobility between entry and top level jobs may range from approximately 3–8 years. Although theoretically all workers are eligible to progress to top pay rates, in practice skill profiles in the internal labour market are typically expected to resemble a normal distribution based on abilities and interest. Derived mutual benefits are viewed as preferable to those under strict job seniority systems. The decision to acquire more skill and knowledge is voluntary (however, hiring interviews usually stress that multi-skilling will be expected of everyone), but there can be strong pressures on workers to cross-train; this has led to labour turnover. In those plants where operators of the process technology are encouraged and in some cases required to develop maintenance skills, experience to date has suggested that this has taken considerably more time than anticipated. Nevertheless, the job progression systems appear to have significantly opened the range of opportunities for workers to enhance both financial and intrinsic job rewards.

In some organisations, the above and related problems have been accepted as teething troubles in an evolutionary process. In others, they have led to the deterioration and eventual abandonment of innovative work structures. Their continued existence and proliferation in a variety of North American companies suggests that at a minimum, the derived economic benefits have been satisfactory. Because there is a scarcity of published information of a detailed nature on the operation of the new plants, little is actually known on a systematic basis about how these work systems have matured and adapted to changing circumstances, such as economic downturn, layoffs, management and worker turnover, the levelling-off or peaking of opportunities to improve effort-reward ratios, shifts in political support from the parent organisation and, where applicable, the union.

Conclusions

The outpouring of literature on the 'factory of the future' and the role of programmable automation has primarily stressed its technological aspects. While choice of technology has historically been the single most influential management decision in determining the structure of the manufacturing enterprise and its internal work environment, it represents only half of the innovation equation. The other half is social and requires attention on a par with the purely technical aspects. This brings us back to the original question posed at the beginning of the chapter: What kind of work will be required by the new systems? The case material illustrates the point that there is nothing inherent in automated technology which makes a particular form of work organisation 'imperative'. Rather, if the notion of 'imperative' is at all relevant, it finds expression in the centralised control, bureaucratic hierarchy and task specialisation which underpins the design and management of most production systems — both manual and automated.

The pursuit of flexible manufacturing must not be concentrated exclusively on the massive application of automated technology. To do so would ignore the indisputable fact that higher levels of automation increase a system's dependence on people, albeit in smaller numbers. People, not technology, are the source of flexibility and adaptiveness. Automation's impact on job content and skill will vary, as will opportunities for enhancing human ability, rather than degrading it. While impacts of the future use of programmable automation remain uncertain, we can learn from experiences like those described in this study. These examples clearly demonstrate the existence of alternatives to the dominant and largely unquestioned acceptance of bureaucracy and scientific management as the 'state of the art' in the design, introduction and management of new technology in the workplace.

References

Blumberg, M. and Alber, A., *The Human Element: Its Impact on the Productivity of Advanced Batch Manufacturing Systems*, School of Business Administration, University of Wisconsin, Milwaukee and the College of Business, Bradley University, Peoria, USA. June 1981.

Boyer, C. and Crawford, L., Director of Organization Development Plant Manager, Warren, Ohio Operations, *Case Study of Packard Electric*, presentation to Tenth Annual Residential Course on 'Improving the Quality of Working Life and Organizational Effectiveness', Center for Quality of Working Life, Institute of Industrial Relations, UCLA, 24 September 1981.

Davis, L. and Taylor, J., *Design of Jobs*, 2nd edition, Goodyear: Santa Monica, 1979.

Fadem, J., *Fitting Computer-aided Technology in Workplace Requirements: An Example*, proceedings of the 13th annual Meeting and Technical Conference of the Numerical Control Society, March 1976.

Gerwin, D., 'The Do's and Don'ts of Computerized Manufacturing', *Harvard Business Review*, March–April 1982, pp.107–16.

Gerwin, D. and Tarondeau, J., *Uncertainty and the Innovation Process for Computer Integrated Manufacturing Systems; Four Case Studies*, School of Business Administration, University of Wisconsin, Milwaukee, Institute for Social Research in Industry, Norwegian Technical University, Trondheim: and ESSEC, France, March 1981. 1981.

Hunt, H. and Hunt, T., *Human Resource Implications of Robotics*, The W.E. Upjohn Institute for Employment Research, Kalamazoo, 1981.

Newell, R., International Association of Machinists, *Labor's View of Automation and Productivity*, Society of Manufacturing Engineers, Technical Paper Series, (AD75–766), Dearborn: Michigan, 1975.

Trist, E., *The Evolution of Socio-technical Systems: A Conceptual Framework and an Action Research Program*, Occasional Paper no. 2, Ontario Quality of Working Life Centre, Toronto, 1981.

17 Consequences of CNC technology: a study of British and West German manufacturing firms

*Gert Hartmann, Ian J. Nicholas, Arndt Sorge
and Malcolm Warner* ✶

Introduction

In particular, this chapter sets out to explore the ways in which the
new technology impacts upon organisation and manpower, and whether
it leads to greater de-skilling, or not. The effects of the new information
technology on organisation and manpower however depends on where
and how it is used (Francis and Willman, 1980; Francis et al., 1981). A
wide range of application may lead to a similar spread of effects, many
of which may be in different directions (Sorge and Hartmann, 1980).
A statement to the effect that 'electronics . . . will substantially condition industrial and service activities and the socio-political structure'
(Rada, 1980) is at least potentially misleading, for its consequences
may be more due to specific conditions prevailing in such industries
and societies. It is thus advisable to exercise great caution when examining predictions of the effects of information technology (Warner,
1981a).

   The way in which technology affects organisations (Woodward, 1965;
Pugh *et al.*, 1969; Gerwin, 1981), raises many difficulties and must
be first discussed before proceeding to a wider debate about its impact.
It is, in this context, that we have emphasised the interdependence
of organisation and task as central *vis-à-vis* the management and man-

* We gratefully acknowledge the support of the Anglo-German Foundation for the Study
of Industrial Society for this study, as well as the help of CEDEFOP, the European Centre
for Vocational Training. For professional dialogue and criticism, we have pleasure in thank-
ing Marc Maurice, Donald Gerwin, Georges Dupont, Michael Fores, Derek Allen and
Jonathan Hooker.

power consequences of the so-called 'new technology' in manufacturing industry. Recent technological advances such as the applications of microprocessors illustrate the conceptual and empirical problems involved in tackling this question. One of the most important of these applications is *computer numerical control* (CNC) of machine-tools (Battelle, 1978), which is used more and more in all kinds of metal-working. Since the fifties, however, metal-cutting has undergone major technical advances. It has, in the eyes of the layman, been 'automated'. The development of numerical control (NC) of machine-tools, which were 'hard-wired', was followed gradually by the introduction of CNC of such machines, which became 'soft-wired', involving the use of microprocessor technology. An alleged consequence of both these developments has been the polarisation of skills, with increasing 'de-skilling' postulated for the shopfloor worker (Braverman, 1974), leading to greater management control (Noble, 1978). Has technological change, and as importantly its organisational and manpower implications, in fact taken such a dramatic path? In what ways are CNC and these implications related? Innovation may produce new dimensions in variables very gradually, but this does not reduce its importance: 'the devil is in the details' as an old German phrase puts it. We try to visualise the core-technology, organisation and labour emanating from a core of key decisions; these characterise all kinds of *ad hoc*, piecemeal experiments (Warner, 1981). Such decisions might occur at any level and could even be made by the technical manager of a company or by an operator who takes charge of the first NC machine.

The *theoretical* rationale for this view is the proposition that technology affects organisation and manpower in an interactive pattern rather than any direct, casual way (c.f. Trist, 1981). It will, moreover, interact with these variables in a *dynamic*, rather than static relationship. The degree to which skills are affected cannot be understood if this is disregarded. The elements of the national culture, with its implicit work-traditions, shaped by education and training values and institutions amongst other factors, constitute the parameters of the potential socio-technical variance. These do not necessarily inhibit technological developments and applications, but nor do they automatically promote it. They guide the potential passage of such applications and suggest a 'logical' line of developments. Each country's route will follow this, although it is not narrowly determined.

Theorists who see the effects of microelectronics as due to technical imperatives or the mechanisms of the capitalist system, are prone to neglect cross-national considerations. We would rather conjecture that the work-traditions in different societies will *not* be changed by the incidence of microelectronics, but will be expressed in new ways, particularly as far as skills are concerned.

Conjectures

The development and application of microelectronics and CNC, will follow a different path in Britain and Germany given their respective backgrounds (see Fores 1981; Lay and Rempp, 1981) and thus, the integration of CNC into enterprises *grosso modo* follows quite different 'socio-technical logics' in the two countries; by this we mean that the conception and practice of technical work and training, organisation and industrial relations as interrelated will follow quite distinct paths. British companies will in turn train and use noticeably less skilled workers than German ones, and the difference will be particularly visible in production, as opposed to maintenance jobs. We expect to find these trends exemplified in the application of CNC. Such is the main theoretical thrust of the study.

It may be further hypothesised that the reverse of de-skilling, may result if 'changing technology (automation) has induced a tightening up of selection criteria because more skilled labour is required on the shop floor. This argument implies rationalisation, will not induce a constant degradation of working conditions, but is more likely to transform the division of labour into a professionalised structure' (Windolf, 1981). The demand for explicitly certified skills may thus screen out unreliable workers; and relatively more unskilled workers may be increasingly excluded (1981).

While our study did not examine trends over time quantitatively, such assessments were implicit in the interview data. The trend to using more skilled labour may be anticipated in the future, and stronger in Germany because of the relatively greater supply of trained manpower there, at all levels (Prais, 1981). In Germany, over half the primary workforce has gone through a formalised apprenticeship (Windolf, 1981).

We were, however, aware that industrial relations differences between Britain and Germany did not appear to be central to greater or lesser success of NC adoption (Swords-Isherwood and Senker, 1977), and in Britain itself, NC use did not typically lead to demarcation disputes for example (Jones, 1982). Typical industrial relations differences, as described in detail by Marsh *et al.*, (1981), are in reality closely linked with variations in manpower training and organisation (Sorge and Warner, 1980; Streeck *et al.*, 1981), but they cannot be conjectured as having a strong independent influence on differences in NC utilisation. Instead, we expect to see that this will be more influenced by wider socio-technical considerations as already hinted. It is with these broad hypotheses in mind, building on our earlier work, and anticipating a cumulative contribution to knowledge in the field, that we now turn to the *modus operandi* of the empirical study carried out.

313

Paired comparisons

Rather than attempting to measure the degree of technological complexity, workflow integration or automaticity (see Hickson and McMillan, 1981), we have adopted another approach which stresses the *qualitative* variation in the application of CNC rather than a straightforward quantitative scaling. We will then try to show how this leads to distinct patterns of variance in skill-utilisation. The aim of the study is rather to describe and then try to explain the impact of CNC technology on work in two countries. This has consequences for the research method to be employed. The theme implies both a comparison of such effects *between* the two countries and an analysis of the effects of CNC *within* the two countries. For the most part, organisation studies do not differentiate in their research method between organisational-comparison within a country and between countries. There is a tendency to consider the study of organisation as comparative in principle, and not to distinguish sectoral, technical or national lines of comparison. Our work was throughout influenced by the methods of, in particular, the Franco-German comparison of organisation and labour, developed by Maurice, Sellier and Silvestre (1979), and the partial replication for Britain, France and West Germany (Maurice, Sorge and Warner, 1980). These employed size, product technology of production, and dependence as criteria for matching. Because of detailed concern with the division of labour on the shop floor, the matching was carefully done regarding product and production techniques. This was repeated in the present study.

Some deviations from absolute matching standards were tolerated when we were convinced beyond reasonable doubt, from exploratory interviews, expert evidence, and initial visits to sites, that any deviation was not liable to influence organisation and labour differences. On the other hand, if there was such a suspicion, a unit was not included. This led to a rather lengthy search for matching units in the two countries, but it ultimately proved helpful in gaining greater familiarity with the terrain, and for generating hypotheses. In turn, knowledge about increasing diversification of CNC techniques, the increasing range of innovation across the batch size and components spectrum, and the widening range of use, was used to define more or less separable cases of application which could be compared *within* a country as well as between countries. Component average batch size or batch running time, as well as plant size, were hypothesised as influencing organisation and manpower variables. Both were used as criteria for the selection of units, and both were dichotomised as Table 17.1 shows.

Table 17.1
Criteria for selecting units

Selection criteria		Plant size (no. of employees)	
		small (less than 100)	large (over 100, up to 2000)
batch size	small (less than 100)		
	large (several hundreds at least)		

We defined each cell of Table 17.1 as a *case of application*. To make the study pertinent for the larger part of cutting operations, we included turning and milling as the most frequently used cutting types and kinds of machinery, and so we looked at these separately.

Concern with different cutting techniques (milling and turning) and shop floor details which socio-technical analysis makes necessary led us to conclude that the site level was possibly too removed to allow rigorous selection, matching, comparison and statement of results. For instance, in smaller units, milling and turning were not necessarily both represented. Larger sites were, on the other hand, often too differentiated into production departments with their own characteristics, so that reference to site-level aggregate data was meaningless. A sharper focus on departmental characteristics was therefore called for.

We had to distinguish, for this reason between *two levels of analysis*. The first, more aggregate, unit of analysis used was the reasonably self-contained production site. The second, more disaggregated unit of analysis used was the workshop or production department within the larger site. A factory may, for instance, have a milling and turning department, or NC-milling and NC-turning departments, or workshops differentiated according to batch size as well as size of machined parts, requiring promptness of delivery, precision or complexity of machines.

Production technology is not however autonomously given and taken for granted, but continuously developed. Technical differences themselves need to be explained, rather than being used merely as explanatory variables or criteria for matching. We therefore characterised and matched units of analysis following more general socio-technical

315

'challenges'. These consisted of production unit and component batch sizes, and within cases of application defined in this way, differences in technical detail are explained as arising from an interaction of technology, organisation and labour.

Since cases of application were defined as specific to milling or turning respectively, it followed that the same company could cover two cases of application when it had both CNC milling and turning sections. If it had only one, another company had to be selected to represent the other.

Difficulties of selection, matching and access precluded finding workshops for absolutely all the cases of application. Most could, however, be found, and in the cases of smaller batches in larger units, we included two organisations in each country (see Table 17.2).

Table 17.2

Pairing of units

| | | production unit size | |
		smaller	larger
batch size	smaller	D (34) GB (34) D (70) GB (70)	D (1100) GB (1450) D (1300) GB (800;2500)
	larger	D (70) GB (14)	D (2000) GB (800)

Generally, we counted as organisation size the number of employees of the company *on the local site* which was studied, including production, development, administrative and commercial staff. We, further, investigated companies or parts of companies where parts in production were of intermediate size, roughly between 'a sherry glass and a bucket', as one owner put it. Our comparison was thus not distorted by differences in produced components' size or machining times per peice; these varied more within companies than between them.

Common factors and national differences

All our data lead us to stress the extreme malleability of CNC technology, and we would argue that there was no effect of the use of CNC as such. But this is not to say that technology is unimportant; its significance unfolds through a continuous series of 'piecemeal' modification. This is part of a complex pattern of socio-technical design and improvement where technical developments interact with organisational and manpower developments (see Sorge *et al.*, 1983).

Thus, in the company context, the detailed technical specifications of the CNC system adopted may be seen to reflect the influence of corporate and departmental strategies, and the existing production, engineering and organisational procedures and the current manpower policies, all of which vary *within* a country and *between* countries and societies.

In the study, we found that solutions to CNC applications were alternatively organisationally simple or complex; some stressed functional differentiation while others emphasised functional integration within positions or departments; in some cases there was a strong element of skill polarisation, but with skill enrichment at the shop floor level. None of these contrasting policies can be said to be more 'advanced' from the technical point of view, yet at the same time it cannot be said that the application of CNC was haphazard or the subject of accidental initiatives.

There is, thus, a series of very clear 'logics' of CNC application. These different concepts are analytically distinct, but they interact, and sometimes conflict, with each other. To distinguish between the available alternatives, we need to look at:

1) National institutions and accepted practices of management and in the nature of technical work, training, status differentials, etc.;
2) Socio-economic conditions of the present situation, regarding shortage of natural resources, limitation of mass markets, slow growth, market competition, etc.;
3) Company or plant size;
4) Batch size, or conversely, the time needed to machine a batch;
5) Complexity of component, metal removal technology and machine type.

If CNC exercises different effects according to plant and batch size and type of cutting technology and machine type, it also adapts to different 'societal' environments, namely to *national institutions and cultural practices*. Our study further confirmed the existence of a series of predetermined Anglo-German differences noted in the earlier studies referred to.

The German companies, for example, distinguished less than those in Britain between specialised functions and departments for production management, production engineering, work planning and work execution functions. Similarly, there was a consistently greater use of shop floor and operator programming in Germany: programming is seen as the nucleus around which the various company personnel, the managers, engineers, planners, foremen and operators, are integrated. The differences are reinforced by the CNC dimension.

Furthermore, the greater separation of programming and operating in Britain ties in with the increasing differentiation of technician and worker apprenticeships, whereas technician training in Germany invariably comes after craft worker training and experience (see Gleeson, 1980). In addition, whilst in Britain the planning and programming function confers white-collar status, it is much less so in Germany, where blue-collar workers are more extensively used for programming, both on the machine and in the planning department. Rotation between the two groups was quite frequently observed.

National differences, in turn, interact with company and batch size differences: in Germany, the similarity between organisation, labour and technical practices of small and larger companies was greater than in Britain, where there appeared to be a split between pragmatically flexible small plants and organisationally more segmented larger plants. Formal engineering qualifications at various levels were relatively more common in Britain in larger plants, whereas often they were not represented in small British plants. In Germany, by contrast, formal qualifications were common to small and larger plants alike (c.f. Prais, 1981).

In both countries, CNC operation was generally seen as exacting less 'informatics' skills than advanced machining talents (c.f. Lee, 1980; Francis et al., 1981). Programming aids on the machine or in the planning departments are seen to be tools of increasing facility to control a process which has become ever more demanding from the point of view of precision, machining speeds, tools, fixtures and materials.

As can be seen then, there is a series of 'logics' that were moulded by distinct historical, cultural and social developments: but there was also a further thrust of CNC application which was *common to Britain and Germany*. This stemmed from the relevant existing macroeconomic factors, including competitive and marketing strategies, and which interact with socio-technical considerations. They incorporate a very broad range of factors which affect enterprises, but which they themselves attempt to influence.

Firms we studied stated that they were keen, or perhaps being forced increasingly to cater for small market 'niches' rather than for homogeneous mass markets, given that the most generally stated competitive situation was one in which there was static, or more commonly in Britain, negative economic growth. More individualised, customised products, with a greater number of product variants were seen as being required.

Complex design of components may be consistent with NC application, but the greater variability of products and components was more specifically associated with CNC application. The two most important factors which lead to increasing CNC application within manufacturing were as follows:

1) the demand for more frequent and less time consuming machine conversion from one batch to another, arising from the increased variability of products and components;

2) the inducement to minimise finished product stocks and work-in-progress which can be substantially reduced when the full potential for manufacturing 'families' of different, but similar, components is realised and/or advantage is taken of the opportunity to produce, in a single manufacturing cycle, those sub-assemblies which comprise the final product.

Thus, both market-oriented as well as financial considerations point in the direction of smaller batch sizes and more frequent conversion; this has important socio-logical implications. It is through these developments that we can see the effect on skills. The increased variability of batches is not one which can be handled bureaucratically through a conventional increase in the division of labour, and in turn mitigates or even possibly reverses the tendency to skill polarisation. It implies increased flexibility right at the level of the machine and the operator. Every CNC operator is likely to have to deal with a greater and more frequently changing range of jobs; part of this is related to the increased sophistication of the machine control system through which more flexible change-overs and improvements of programmes can be achieved. The crucial 'bottlenecks', however, may not be information-processing and calculating skills; experience indicates that the most crucial problems refer to tooling, materials, feeds, speeds, faults and breakdowns. Skills in handling these problems are most directly developed on the machine. Thus, while programming skills are required, increasing emphasis must be placed on the maintenance of 'craft' skills on the shop floor, rather than the converse (as implied by the 'pessimists' writing on the subject).

Companies, particularly in Germany, are increasingly seeing the merits of stressing craft skills. This depolarisation of skills and qualifications structures is a viable option whcih falls within the present logic of CNC development and application. This is not because it is a necessary consequence, but because CNC has been developed in a context which links economic success with depolarisation. There is a striking kinship between CNC and some of the craft trades, and the renewed interest in companies, again particularly in Germany, to train and employ skilled workers.

'High technology' by no means signifies greater bureaucratisation; the smaller plants studied combined a strikingly higher percentage of CNC machinery with personalised industrial relations, weak formal methods of organisation, and traditional entrepreneurial, paternalistic style, whereas the bigger plants were sometimes prevented from larger scale CNC use by conventional organisation and industrial relations of a more bureaucratic type. Whilst the bigger plants were starting to incorporate CNC into apprenticeships and other training schedules in a more systematic fashion, this was rarer in the smaller plants. Small companies profited from the qualifications and expertise inherent to personnel who were trained or who worked in larger plants, and although this knowledge was not developed formally, they were ingenious in pushing ahead without organisational shackles.

Whilst plant size was associated with a greater differentiation of programming functions into separate departments, increasing *batch size* was linked with the greater differentiation of programming away from machine-operating, although not necessarily into separate departments (see Göhren, 1979). Nor was it necessarily taken away from the machine; there was a strong inclination for programme input on the machine, not by the operator, but by a programmer, foreman or setter, in small companies producing large batches. This was the case of an unbureaucratic, but polarising division of labour and qualification structure. It is thus important to distinguish between bureaucratisation

Table 17.3

Skills, polarisation and bureaucratisation of programming under CNC

		Plant size: bureaucratisation of programming	
		Small	Large
Batch size: polarisation of functions and skills	small	Programming with larger involvement of operators, and small or non-existent programming department	Programming more in the hands of a programming/planning department, but skills of operators and planners overlap
	large	Programming done by setter, foreman or programmer; progr. and setting closely integrated	Programming in the hands of a progr./planning department, and differentiation between operating, setting and progr. skills.

within the organisation, and the polarisation of skills; increasing plant size is linked with the former, while increasing batch size is related to the latter. They interact, however, to bring about organisational and qualification patterns (see Table 17.3).

It can be readily, intuitively grasped that the smaller the batch size, the greater is the need for frequent conversion of machines with new tools, fixtures and component programmes, and the less is machine-setting expertise differentiated from operating. Batch size economies of scale thus involve a reduction of skills at the operator level, a factor which has no doubt coloured the 'pessimistic' literature in the field *vis-à-vis* deskilling.

Machine-setting and programme-related functions, however, overlap; the elimination of setting from machine operation also entails differentiation of programme-related functions from operating, and it is often linked with a further differentiation between setting and programming.

A technologically advanced horizontal machining centre, with automatic tool-changing facilities, was usually manned by a skilled operator because of the high costs involved in the machine itself, the necessary tooling, and frequently the nature and complexity of the components manufactured. Apart from any 'macros' or planning sub-routines, these machine types have increasingly sophisticated input systems which substantially simplify programming procedures. Thus, in this situation, the differentiation between planning and operating may not be particularly polarised. By contrast, on a simpler milling machine with less complex components, the programme is probably also less technically demanding, but the operator may only be semi-skilled. In this instance, skill polarisation may be enhanced.

The time needed to make a programme is the central factor associated with different allocations of programming related functions; the more time it takes to make a programme, the less is programming likely to occur on the shop floor. However, such a relationship presupposes that an operator cannot make a programme without the machine being idle. But this is only true to a limited extent. We have see, for example, cases of operators drafting programmes after working hours at home. It is also possible, on some machines, to compile the programme for the next job while the present one is being processed.

The allocation of programming to groups of personnel, therefore, is not a simple objective choice: this holds, above all, in turning. With this seems to be emerging an increasing tendency for operators to perform programming-related functions ranging from simple speed and feed modifications of previously compiled programmes to complete programme preparation on the shop floor. Thus, the advance of CNC technology is depolarising by comparison with previous NC methods.

Conclusions

Increased programming or programme-changing in the workshop may thus blur status boundaries for blue as well as white collar workers. It would, however, be misleading to interpret this as another step towards the 'post-industrial' society, as 'information-processing' work, or as a 'service' function, as so often happens. Whilst it is true that workers are dealing with increasingly sophisticated information technology, this may only concern the *tools of their trade* rather than their *working goals*.

The previous logic of socio-technical design, it must be noted, has to date mostly been geared to specialised, homogeneous mass markets, inflexible automation, an erosion of craft skills and an increased emphasis on separate planning and programming activities. There has been a drift, in the labour market, towards white collar occupations, information-processing, administration and different kinds of clerical work, particularly visible in the British experience. The socio-economic context of CNC application, however, may reverse this trend; there is now increasingly a focus on craft skills and the levelling-out of the growth of indirectly-productive employees, very clearly seen in the German firms studied.

This, however, basically follows the socio-technical tradition of the respective national work cultures. It is misleading to examine technological change outside this 'societal' context; rather, we see it interacting with it. In so far as the study has implications for organisation theory, it must be seen as offering support for the view that technological change needs to be seen as having much more open social implications and leaving organisation designers more options than hitherto assumed.

References

Battelle-Institut, *Der Arbeitsmarkt in Baden-Wurttemberg. Technologische Entwicklungen und ihre Auswirkungen auf Arbeitsplatze in den Bereichen Maschinenbau und Feinmechanik/Optik*, Awischenbericht: Frankfurt, Battelle, 1978.

Braverman, H., *Labour and Monopoly Capital: The Degradation of Work in the Twentieth Century*, Monthly Review Press: New York, 1974.

Fores, M., 'The Myth of a British Industrial Revolution', *History*, 66, 1981, pp.181–98.

Francis, A. and Willman, P., 'Microprocessors: Impact and Response', *Personnel Review*, 9, 1980, pp.9—16.

Francis, A., Snell, M., Willman, P. and Winch, G., *The Impact of Information Technology at Work: The case of CAD/CAM and MIS in Manufacturing*, Discussion Paper for CEDEFOP/IIM Conference, Berlin West, 9-11 December 1981.

Gerwin, D., 'Relationships between Structure and Technology', in Nystrom, P.C. and Starbuck, W.H. (eds), *Handbook of Organizational Design*, vol.2, Remodelling organisation and their environments, Oxford University Press: Oxford, 1981, pp.3—38.

Gleeson, D., 'Streaming at Work and College: On the Social Differentiation of Craft and Technician Apprentices in Technical Education', *Sociological Review*, 28, 1980, pp.745—61.

Göhren, H., 'Konstruktive und Steuerungstechnische Entwicklungen bei Maschinen fur die Mittelserienfertigung', *VDI-Z*, 121, 1979, pp.403—9.

Jones, B., Destruction or re-distribution of engineering skills? *The Case of Numerical Control*, in Wood, S. (ed.) *The Degradation of Work?*, Hutchinson: London, 1982.

Lay, G. and Rempp, H., 'CNC-Technik verandert NC-Organisation', *VDI-Nachrichten*, no.11, 13 March 1981, pp.8—9.

Lee, D.J., 'Skill, Craft and Class: A theoretical critique and a critical case', *Sociology*, 15, 1980, pp.56—78.

Marsh, A., Hackmann, M. and Miller, D., *Workplace Relations in the Engineering Industry in the UK and the Federal Republic of Germany*, Anglo-German Foundation for the Study of Industrial Society: London, 1981.

Maurice, M., Sellier, F. and Silvestre, J-J., 'La production de la hierarchie dans l'enterprise: recherche d'un effet societal', *Revue Française de Sociologie*, 20, 1979, pp.331—65.

Maurice, M., Sorge. A. and Warner, M., 'Societal Differences in Organising Manufacturing Units: A Comparison of France, West Germany and Great Britain', *Organization Studies*, 1, 1980, pp.59—86.

Noble, D.F., 'Social Choice in Machine Design: The Case of Automatically Controlled Machine Tools', in Zimbalist, A. (ed.), *Case Studies on the Labour Process*, 18-50, Monthly Review Press: New York, 1979.

Prais, S.J., *Vocational Qualifications of the Labour Force in Britain and Germany*, National Institute of Economic and Social Research, discussion paper 43, London, 1981.

Pugh, D.S., Hickson, D.J., Hinings, C.R. and Turner, C., 'Dimensions of Organization Structure', *Administrative Science Quarterly*, 13, 1969, pp.65—105.

Rada, J., *The Impact of Microelectronics*, International Labour Office: Geneva, 1980.

Sorge, A. and Hartmann, G., *Technology and Labour Markets*, International Institute of Management, discussion paper, Berlin, 1980.

Sorge, A. and Warner, M., 'Manpower Training, Manufacturing Organisation and Workplace Relations in Great Britain and West Germany', *British Journal of Industrial Relations*, 18, 1980, pp.318—33.

Sorge, A., Hartmann, G., Warner, M. and Nicholas, I.J., *Microelectronics and Manpower in Manufacturing Applications of Computer Numerical Control in Great Britain and W. Germany*, Gower Press: Farnborough, 1983.

Streeck, W., Seglow, P. and Wallace, P., 'Competition and Monopoly in Interest Representation: A Comparative Analysis of Trade Union Structure in the Railway Industries of Great Britain and West Germany', *Organization Studies*, 2, 1981, pp.307—29.

Swords-Isherwood, N.S. and Senker, P., *Social Implications of Automated Small Batch Production*, Department of Industry/National Engineering Laboratory (manuscript): London, 1977.

Trist, E., *The Evolution of Socio-technical Systems: A Conceptual Framework and an Action Research Program*, Occasional Paper, no.2, June 1981, Ontario QWL Centre: Ontario.

Warner, M. 'Organizational Experiments and Innovations' in Nystrom, P.C. and Starbuck, W.H. (eds), *Handbook of Organizational Design*, vol. 1. Adapting organizations to their environments. Oxford University Press: Oxford, 1981, pp.167—86.

Windolf, P., 'Strategies of Enterprises in the German Labour Market', *Cambridge Journal of Economics*, 5, 1981, pp.351—86.

Woodward, J., *Industrial Organization: Theory and Practice*, Oxford University Press: Oxford, 1965.

18 Computers, manpower and the Indian labour market: some experiences in a labour-surplus economy

C. P. Thakur

Progressive introduction of newer technologies is a familiar feature of developed economies, successful industries or efficient enterprises. Growth and development require transition from traditional to more efficient and productive processes. To overcome 'technological gap' through timely choices is not always easy though. Technological change affects factor use patterns. The available factor endowment of an economy, therefore, exerts a strong influence on policy makers. And, the macro policy at the national level sets the boundaries for a particular industry or an enterprise for its decision.

Among other things, technological change alters the quantity and quality of labour per unit of real output. Its advanced levels fall in the categories of automation. An automated technology (Dhingra, 1971) is broadly understood as 'replacement of human brains by versatile information processing machines'. The advent of microelectronics has accelerated the pace of automation. Its special feature like higher component density, faster processing and accelerated transmission speed have a profound impact. The phenomenal rate of development of microelectronics technology as well as its fast expanding range of applications are radically changing the output, the material input, as well as the role of human component.

It is proposed to discuss here the manpower and labour market aspects of microelectronics, particularly computerisation. Some recent experiences would be analysed in view of their value for subsequent phases of the spread of this technology within the Indian economy.

Computers and the Indian scene

Despite the constraints of macro-economic setting, microelectronics is finding an entry in the Indian economy (Bhusan, 1983). The first computer came to India in 1955. During the period 1955–72, another 86 were installed. Then a national debate on the costs and gains followed. Mere economic criterion and market forces could not be allowed to determine the pattern and pace of technological changes. The Indian Labour Conference, a tripartite policy-making body on labour issues, had earlier resolved that 'the Government might make arrangements to ensure that measures of rationalisation that did not serve real economic interests in the existing conditions of the country might be avoided' (Bagaram, 1971). The actual or apprehended social consequences of automation and its labour market impact in particular, generated a fresh round of public policy response. A Committee on Automation deliberated on its different aspects. In the process, the pace of automation, and particularly computerisation, faced a setback. But since the late seventies, the economic policy has been undergoing changes. The concern now is to accelerate industrialisation. The new technology policy, among other things, proposes to:

a)   attain technological competence and self-reliance to reduce vulnerability in critical areas;
b)   ensure a correct mix between mass production technologies with production by masses;
c)   identify obsolescence of technology in use and arrange for modernisation of both equipment and technology; and
d)   develop technologies which are internationally competitive.

Several concerns are evident from the above. But the competitive efficiency and additions to job and income opportunities, apart from the need for self-reliance in technological capability, seem to be critical. There is uneasiness on the fact that a large segment of Indian industries is lagging behind other countries in the quality of technological aid. Within the framework of the new policy, the pace of technological advancement is sought to be hastened. Efforts for absorption, adaptation and development of imported technology for achieving self-reliance are being promoted. The 1973 Panel on Minicomputers recommended that in the choice of minicomputers and their applications, the country 'would have to keep in view the present level of economic and industrial development, and their implication on employment generation'. But significantly, it also emphasised that in the early stages of computerisation 'India should take full advantage of the major technological developments in micro-computers and micro-processors which are occurring in the highly industrialised countries'.

Following these considerations, an indigenous minicomputer/microprocessor industry is being developed. System engineering capability is to be built on a priority basis. While the indigenous base for manufacture develops, certain preferred components, CPU and peripherals are being imported on a stock and sale basis. About 80 firms have obtained industrial licences to produce minicomputers and microcomputers. Supply of computers both from indigenous and international sources is growing. There are already about 15,000 computers in India, and its absorption is gathering momentum. Its areas of application are also expanding. It was initially confined to routine work like the preparation of payroll accounts, and the processing of statistical data. But some more sophisticated uses, too, are in progress. The Election Commission of India is gradually introducing the use of computerised polling machines. The Police departments are building the crucial data based on crimes, criminals and fingerprints. Land records covering tenancy, revenue, cropping pattern, etc. are being put on computers. Recent experiences of computerisation in the Indian banking industry provide some fresh data in this regard.

Computerisation in banking

Banking is a large and expanding industry in the tertiary sector of the economy. Since its nationalisation in 1966, it has expanded phenominally. A large part of Indian economy remains still unbanked. Therefore, the industry would continue to expand. About 40,000 branches and half a million bank employees handle total deposits and advances respectively of the order of Rs.30,000 crores and Rs.20,000 crores. New locations, new customers and expanding patterns of customer services are changing the dimension of banking operations. A decision on accelerated expansion on social and economic criteria was not preceded or even accompanied by a programme of developing corresponding managerial capability in the industry. The total volume of workload has multiplied. Customers are demanding better and new services. Competition in the industry is growing. And this is not confined among Indian banks and within India alone. Internationalisation of banking business is growing. The Indian banks are expanding offshore operations, while the foreign banks are obtaining licences for operations in India.

Expansion in the number of branches, and increases in manpower with better quality of the intake, have not helped in grappling with the magnitude and the complexity of demands made on their services. Deterioration in the quality of services followed even in the case of IBR, the bank under reference as a recent study (Ghosh, 1983) recorded:

> 'The current account of banks was rarely up-to-date, the backlog of applications to be processed in granting of licences and advances in case of small and medium scale industries was over 60,000 and the clearing house accounts rarely tallied. Even for mandatory tallying of accounts of Payments Department of banks, the employees would invariably sit late hours, often in the early hours of the morning. Customer service took a backseat, credit of local cheques drawn on another bank taking as much as a week, and never before 3 days'.

White collar and office jobs

The banking industry has dominantly white collar jobs. A large part of its work is done in offices. Its employees fall in three categories. (a) officers, (b) clerks, and (c) menial staff. However, clerks constitute the majority of employees, the officer-to-clerk ratio being 1:8. Work in bank offices is primarily done by the clerical staff, though the responsibility rests with the officers. Cheques are passed only after an officer's signature. The completed books of account have to be checked, and later approved by an officer. But the entries and their tallying are the jobs of a clerk.

The educational levels for entry to both the categories of jobs are comparable. High incidence of graduate unemployment, and relatively better emoluments in the banking industry, attract good quality candidates for even clerical positions. The career pattern allows smooth vertical mobility to clerks, though in part there are direct entries also to the officer's category. Strong union power, and growing numbers of job openings in the industry have encouraged collective agreements favouring internal promotions.

Productivity in offices

Production processes in industrial operations were structured and transferred to machines. And machine technology helped in accelerating the productivity of industrial jobs. But office jobs are still not fully structured. System analysis is in the process of acquiring capability to repeat, predict and quantify the different steps in office work. Microelectronics would then convert them into electronic phenomena for use by technological devices. The productivity problem

328

of office work and white collar jobs is hoped to be overcome with the aid of system engineering and microcomputers and mini-computers. Some progress is already evident. In this context the management of IBR decided to introduce technological aid for better performance.

Mechanisation and computerisation in IBR

According to a recent field study by the author, it was found that the new technology has been introduced in the IBR in two parts: (a) an automatic ledger-posting machine with 'dedicated' memory and pro- grammed to print predetermined heads and summation of sub-totals of all leaders was introduced in the Current Accounts department, (b) the mini-computers were installed. Initially these were introduced in the bank's head office. Later IBR offices in two other metropolitan centres also got them.

Some operational results

Performance in the IBR has substantially improved since the introduc- tion of new technology. Mechanisation has helped in:

a)   eliminating the errors of totalling, summation and wrong posting;
b)   completing the entire job faster and more neatly;
c)   dispensing with the tedious tasks of checking of postings and carrying over of figures from one ledger to another; and
d)   reducing the tension of the employees arising out of mistakes and delays.

Entry of a computer has also brought welcome improvements in certain critical areas:

a)   daily balancing of clearing house books;
b)   elimination of the routine delay of 3 to 4 hours per day in the bank clearing and receipt section;
c)   disappearance of familiar accounting mistakes;
d)   reduction in employees' workload; and
e)   improvement in customers' service, particularly the crediting to their account the amounts deposited through cheques drawn on other banks.

It would thus appear that the new technology is meeting the in- tended objectives. But such developments are always a part of a mixed package of experiences.

New technology and bank employees

Current employees of an organisation face the consequences of a new technology directly. Their concerns, therefore, are critical in the acceptability of this change, and the gains thereof.

Office automation has usually received stiffer opposition for several reasons:

    a)   it is more difficult to rehabilitate displaced office workers than the factory hands;

    b)   even the retraining of redundant office staff is difficult; and

    c)   incident of frustration due to displacement and re-assignment to other jobs is also high among this category.

The IBR employees' scepticism or reservations on mechanisation and computerisation related to the following aspects:

    a)   risk to their job due to possible redundancy;

    b)   loss of overtime earnings;

    c)   effect on working hours; and

    d)   possible increase in the nature of their job/task.

Inquiries indicate that all current jobs are protected. But net additions in the post-computerised phase would possibly be less. Financially, employees are somewhat worse off as their overtime earnings have been affected. However, they have been compensated partly in the form of a 'special allowance'.

Interesting effects are on the working hours. In the first place, there are no more extended working hours beyond normal closing time. Secondly, since the new technology has eliminated the routine first 90 minutes of their work, the hours are now staggered. Employees now report to work much later, rather than earlier. This is particularly welcome to those commuting long distances. Further, the work is cleaner, it is being performed faster, and without mistakes. These are very satisfying changes to the concerned employees. An added benefit is the availability of more time for personal work, domestic life and leisure time activity. Acceptability of the new technology among the employees appears encouraging as a result.

Volunteers for training

Indirect evidences to this effect come from other facts, too. Computerisation is creating new jobs. These require new skills. The policy of the organisation is to retrain internal hands, and assign them to new positions. Employees' attitudes to retraining and re-assignment is always a question mark when a new technology is introduced. The financial cost of retraining in IBR is being picked up by the organisation. But the real cost involved in new learning and job change could remain, however.

For about 20 positions for data entry terminal operators, 30 employees had to be trained out of a proposed panel of 50 names. Out of all those eligible, over 350 applied, and 300 of them took the aptitude test. An overwhelming number of these employees had earlier, however, opposed computerisation. Among a total of about 200 who qualified in the aptitude test, there was an undeclared competition for being included on the panel. Seniority, work experience, discipline and 'loyalty' were to be the criteria for empanelling. Informal social pressures as well as formal letters of recommendation were mobilised on behalf of interested candidates in the progress.

Are computer related jobs more welcome, then? It is perhaps premature to have a definite answer. Whether a new job is 'better' or 'worse' is dependant on (a) the job environment/context, (b) the content of the new job, (c) the cost of retraining, both real and financial, (d) the new hierarchical status of jobs, and (e) the revised financial rewards. Employees at this stage do not have data in all these areas. But the changed working conditions with controlled temperature, regulated humidity, adequate lighting, and markedly improved cleanliness of a computerised setting are already before them. Financially, too, there is no loss, at any rate not a marked one due to the 'special allowance' in lieu of overtime. Probably the social rating of the new jobs is also higher. These explain the enthusiasm of volunteers for training/retraining preparatory to being reassigned to new positions.

But this has not been without new demands and expectations. Typically, demands included (a) rotation of shift hours, (b) compensation for shift work, (c) special allowance, (d) special conveyance allowance for those working in the last shift, and (e) rotation of staff, in that order of perceived importance by a sample of respondents canvassed in this regard. The continuous nature of computer operation, and the need to operate and feed it, require work to be organised in shifts. With multiple shifts, employees have to be rotated from one to the other. Demands of rotation across shifts, shift allowance and conveyance allowance for the most inconvenient shift are not unique to computers. Nevertheless, these do add to changes in the work situation, and a new set of managerial problems in manpower utilisation comes up.

Computerisation would also change the job structure and the relative significance of jobs. The familiar hierarchies and their composition would give way to the new ones. Some jobs would be highly technical and professional, and others would become more routine, and thinner in skill content, and they may have to be performed in isolated settings. Responses to these changes would vary, and their ramifications for management would be different.

Trade union response

It is necessary to distinguish between an individual worker's reaction and the reactions of an institutionalised interest group like a trade union (Kassalow, 1972). A trade union may have an ideological approach depending upon its political persuasion. Macro considerations also influence their attitude. One union in India has demanded 'a ban on import and use of computers and equipment for offices and factories'. Another called for the scrutiny of the requests for installing computers in the case of table work which would displace clerical hands because of the dangerous risk of increasing educated unemployment. Regardless of ideology, they all apprehend loss of jobs and earnings both immediately after computerisation as well as later, due to the elimination of certain jobs altogether. Recently concerns have been expressed on issues like (a) radiation hazard, (b) monotony due to deskilling effects on certain categories of jobs as well as (c) the risks of electornic surveillance. Unionism is strong in the banking industry. Computerisation has been a target of union protests and the IBR management was apprehensive of union reactions. The earlier experience in the insurance industry formed the basis of such an apprehension (Raza, 1980).

In the IBR, the plan for computerisation has been there for a long time. Occasional limited union protests had been known. During 'pen-down strikes', 'gate demonstrations' and other forms of protests, opposition to computerisation did find some mention. It started acquiring visibility in union activity after it was realised that the management was keen on introducing computers. Therefore in 1982, protest gate-meetings, resolutions denouncing computerisation, protest relay fasts, demonstrations and token cessation of work around this issue became more frequent. But observers reported that protests and opposition lacked intensity and bitterness of the kind one would have apprehended. Invariably, lunch hours or extended lunch hours were utilised for these activities. Then, the turnouts of employees on such occasions were hardly impressive.

In the recent past the industrial relations climate in IBR has not been cordial, and the management got the better of the unions. This may have had a dampening influence on unions during computerisation.

Even mild steps by the management such as (a) transfer of selected employees, (b) recording of names of those attending gate meetings or participating in other forms of protest seemed to have a moderating effect. Union protests turned out to be token in nature, therefore.

A close observer felt that computerisation may not have contributed to creating a tense situation. But he cautions that the 'present state of placidity or thawing of antagonistic feeling' between management and employees could not be due to 'positive attitude as a result of changed working conditions after mechanisation and computerisation'. In any event, it would appear that initial fears on the likely magnitude and intensity of union protest were rather exaggerated. This is evident from the experience of IBS, another leading bank, in introducing computers (Dayal, 1972).

Management strategy

The IBR has so far succeeded in steering smoothly the course of computerisation. The experiences of the IBS in this regard did help substantially. Certain features of IBR strategy need to be noted. First, a task force for computerisation in the IBR was constituted with the help of personnel drawn from IBS, a large bank with experience in this regard. Secondly, considerable preparation was made, and competent people with experience were put on the job. Thirdly, it was decided to use internal hands for new jobs after training. Fourthly, the cost of training was to be the organisational responsibility. Fifthly, employees got full protection against loss of job, and a 'special allowance' as part compensation for financial loss due to the elimination of overtime.

The timing of the decision to introduce a computer could have also facilitated substantially. Subdued union postures to management as an outcome of recent encounter were fortuitous, but the management moved swiftly. Even the responses of individual employees possibly weakened the union position. There was scepticism and apprehension, but no hostility. These, too, were over once the initial set of experiences were gathered first hand.

Some issues relating to manpower, computerisation and labour market

Public policy on technological choice in India has been somewhat cautious. Economic efficiency requires adoption of the best available technology package. But such a package is not available indigenously. Development of indigenous capability to sustain subsequent growth is also necessary. Until such a situation develops, the national policy would have to reckon with the needs of conflicting considerations. Attitude to macro-electronics in government thinking currently reflects such a situation.

Computers and labour demand

Computers would find their place in the Indian economy extensively. But the difficulties before the government due to its labour displacement potential are obvious. Experiences in the USA and the OECD countries indicate that initially the demand for labour would go down. New jobs would be created, but with a time lag. They would, however, only partially offset the fall in labour demand due to computerisation. And the new jobs would not necessarily be filled by the displaced hands.

In the Indian context, even a short term added imbalance in the labour market due to structural unemployment would increase the already high pressure for employment promotion. Backlog of unemployment has been persisting. The net additions to jobs in the growth process have remained insufficient to offset the number of job seekers which includes (a) new entrants to the job market, and (b) the backlog of those unemployed.

Computerisation, at any rate currently in India, is affecting a particularly large cluster of jobs. White collar jobs in offices like clerks, typists, secretaries, telephone operators, bank tellers, record-keepers, statistical assistants, etc. are the familiar berths for graduates. For most unemployed graduates, the general education does not equip them for technical and professional jobs. They prefer wage-employment to self-employment. Jobs in this segment of the labour market are the easiest to create. But they are also the most vulnerable to destruction as a result of computerisation. Ambivalence of public policy as well as union hostility to computerisation need appreciation in this context.

Computers do create new jobs. But the skills required are entirely different from what a typical incumbent of a white collar office job possesses. Positions of systems analysts, programmers, software designers and researchers and data analysts become common. Such jobs require higher levels of qualification with an electrical engineering background. Even the software jobs require persons with an intimate understanding of the operation systems of a computer. Retraining would help in rehabilitating a part of the redundant hands. For others, the severity of displacement would continue.

334

Another aspect of labour market imbalance arises from the intermediate range outlook of the possible demand for such new category of skills outpacing their supply. Given the current arrangement for skill generation in this cluster, and the rate of computer installation and its applications, manpower gaps will be felt. It is estimated that during 1980–85, against the likely demand for 250 doctorates in computer science 1500 B.Techs, and about 2500 M.Techs, the corresponding turnouts, would be only 60 doctorates, 650 B.Techs and 600 M.Techs. If the rate of computerisation gets accelerated, the shortages would become more acute. Indeed, a well thought out supply management strategy is necessary to ease the labour market imbalance. Additional training efforts with a Rs.10.7 crores allocation to promote the supply of these skills has been launched. A 'special computer manpower' programme has also been formulated by the Department of Electronics (Government of India, Planning Commission, 1982).

Internal job market and microelectronics

Organisations are realising the need for and the value of increasing productivity of office work. Speed, accuracy and cleanliness are becoming inescapable for survival against competition and customer pressure. The banking industry in particular, and white collar job-intensive operations in general, are likely to lean more heavily on microelectronic aids. The alternative of improving office efficiency through superior 'skills of organisation and management' without mechanical and electronic technology is all the more difficult (Kaldor, 1972). A capital intensive technology must be utilised optimally to justify the high cost incurred. However, the outlook in this regard is not optimistic. The experience so far indicates their only marginal to limited use. Manpower gap and union resistance restrict its use.

Office job clusters will change in internal composition. The polarisation into the highly skilled 'knowledge workers' and the unskilled ones in routine, repetitive and dead-end jobs will change the pattern of interaction. Differentials in reward would also grow. New sources of tension would emerge. Jobs would be cleaner, and the office set up more elegant and physically more comfortable. At the same time, system analysis and electronic aid would bring more deskilled and fragmented jobs. The human groups around work would be more rigid. The social setting would change, as the jobs would be performed from isolated positions. At the same time, electronic monitoring and machine superivision would reduce personal freedom. To avoid resistance to the use of microelectronics, efforts would be required to humanise work as well as work organisations around new technology. A socio-technical system approach could be the answer. Introduction of microelectronics is only the first step. Overall performance would depend on other steps, too.

Management approach

Experience shows that for a smoother introduction of new technology management approach has to be well planned. The apparent need for better performance may not ensure its acceptance by all members of the organisation. Apart from a planned approach by a trained team, there are gains from timely and adequate communication. The exaggerated apprehension on redundancy, loss of earnings, speed-up, etc. would be dispelled by firm assurance. But assurances are effective only in a climate of credibility and trust. Under conditions of surplus in the labour market, the alternative of retraining and absorption within the organisation's internal job markets deserve careful examination and use.

Unions and workers may not react identically. Ideology and macro-policy concern may encourage a union to take a strong anti-new technology stand. But there is scope to distinguish between a token and a real opposition. Again, informed dialogue, and their involvement in the decision and its implication can create a receptive climate. A much more important issue relates to the sharing of gains. All unions demand it, few managements are willing to concede it, and fewer still care to comply honestly. This vitiates the climate, and obstructs the pace of diffusion of the technology. An agreement on limited use initially can also obtain union cooperation. And later a gradual extension of use can follow as the appreciation of its gains improves.

Conclusions

It would appear that the case for this new technology is being increasingly appreciated at the macro-policy-making level. Indigenous production and imports are making more electronic equipment available. Notwithstanding social and economic dislocation, organisations are acquiring them to improve operation efficiency. Added imbalance in the labour market would follow due to structural unemployment. The pressure for creating additional jobs would intensify. The incidence of unemployment and the rate of additional job creation would together determine the climate for its diffusion in the economy.

Internal job market of the concerned organisations would need re-adjustment. The structure and composition of total jobs would be more polarised into high skilled, marginally skilled or unskilled jobs.

Disparity ratios in reward would increase. Additional sources of conflict like isolation, surveillance, machine-pacing and fragmentation of such jobs would appear. A more imaginative management response would be required.

In the first place, research and development efforts towards finding such technologies that improve efficiency without adversely affecting the demand for labour must be intensified. Secondly, the productivity promotion through new technology must be blended with a strategy to humanise work and work organisations. Neglect of social and human dimensions around new technology would be self-defeating. In the meantime, public policy would remain somewhat ambivalent, and the use of microelectronics would be less optimum. Fuller communication on all aspects of a computerisation programme would dispel doubts and scepticism. Associating unions in its different phases had advantages in introducing changes. Management credibility in (a) protecting jobs and incomes, (b) in compensating for changes in job and work organisation, and (c) in fairly sharing the gains of productivity appear as critical determinants of the course of future computer application as well as the smoothness or explosion in the process.

References

Bhusan, B., 'The Computers are Coming', *Business India*: New Delhi, January 1983, pp.3–16.
Dayal, I., 'Preconditions for Effective use of Automated Technology in Inida', in *Automation in Developing Countries*, ILO: Geneva, 1972, pp.89–91.
Dhingra, O.P., 'In Company Training and Technological Change', in Thakur, C.P. and Aurora, G.S. (eds) *Technological Change in Industry*, Shri Ram Centre for Industrial Relations: New Delhi, 1971, pp.230–31. Also, see *Proceedings of the European Conference on Manpower Aspects of Automation and Technological Change*, OECD: Paris, 1966.
Ghosh, S., 'Impact of New Technology on Industrial Relations' (unpublished work), 1983.
Government of India, Planning Commission, *Sixth Five-Year Plan 1980-85*, Planning Commission, New Delhi, 1982.
Kaldor, N., 'Advanced Technology in a Strategy of Development', in *Automation in Developing Country*, ILO, 1972, pp.3–16.

Kassalow, E., 'Unionism, Technological Change and Automation in Less Developed Countries' in *Automation in Developing Countries*, ILO: Geneva, 1971, pp.101–16.

Raza, S.M., Industrial Relations in the Life Insurance Corporation of India (Ph.D. Thesis, unpublished), 1980.

Tulpule, B., 'Technological Change and Industrial Relations', in Thakur *op. cit.*, 1971.

19 Technology, women and employment: the Australian experience

Bill Ford

Introduction

In recent years there has been an increasing number of studies on the relationship between technology, women and employment. I do not propose to survey these studies or duplicate their analysis. In this chapter I propose firstly, to show the relationship between technological change and a number of other environmental changes affecting women and employment; secondly, to discuss a number of male technocratic concepts of society and work which are barriers to improving women's employment opportunities; thirdly, to set out a range of criteria that need to be considered in developing policies in relation to technology, women and employment, and finally, to suggest a number of specific policies that could improve the employment opportunities for women in a technology oriented society.

Environmental and technological change

The national and international environments affecting employment in Australia are undergoing complex multi-dimensional and multi-directional change. Technological change is only one of these dimensions (see Ford *et al.*, 1981). It is interrelated with other changes in an increasing interdependent world.

What are some examples of these changes which affect the position of women and technology and employment? There is a tendency to assume that technological change has an all-pervasive influence on employment. However, the introduction of new technology within an organisation is usually restricted to a particular function, department or plant. Many employees may not only be unaffected but they may not even be aware of the employment significance of the change. Also some groups may benefit from the change while others may lose promotion opportunities or even their job. Reaction to technological change in an organisation is therefore likely to be mixed. Some long term implications may not even be understood.

In a manufacturing or distribution unit, for example, new complex process technologies may reduce te number of process workers, increase the number of maintenance workers and require a significant upgrading of the skills of both process and maintenance workers. Given the existing segmentation of the workforce, these changes would normally redistribute employment and rewards in favour of the more skilled male employees. This type of change emphasises the need to significantly improve industry training programmes for women.

The ability of large organisations to invest in new technologies and to reduce their need for employees, is resulting in a continual decline in the proportion of national workforces employed in large organisations. This trend is well documented in Europe, North America and Japan. This long term trend has been accentuated by the current recession. Employment growth in the private sector in the future will be reliant on the growth of small to medium sized enterprises. This trend raises important questions for public social policies which are traditionally targeted at large organisations.

An important organisational change in recent years has been the rigid imposition of staff ceilings in large public and private bureaucracies. This has provided added incentive for the wider application of new technologies. These changes have reduced the number of entry level positions into large organisations and changed the employment opportunities of many people in these organisations. Young undereducated and inexperienced girls have been most affected by such change.

There has been a rapid increase in the past decade in the proportion of the workforce working part-time. The overwhelming proportion of these part-time workers are women, particularly married women. A major disadvantage of part-time work is the lack of opportunity for skilled technical training. Therefore if women employees are not to be further disadvantaged by technological change, technical training programmes need to be changed to allow for participation of part-time employees.

340

Employment in the manufacturing industry in Australia has declined from a peak of over 27% of the workforce to less than 19% of the workforce. However, expansion of employment in the service sector has not been matched by an equivalent expansion of technical skill training in that sector. Consequently the maintenance of technical systems in the service sector is still reliant on employees who initially developed their technical skills in manufacturing. Increased women's access to many of the interesting technical jobs in the service sector therefore, may require an increase in access of women to training in the manufacturing sector or an increase in technical training in the service sector.

A neglected area of workforce and technological change is the rural sector. Yet this is an area where there is an increasing proportion of women workers. Farmers not only have to maintain traditional equipment but increasingly they have to develop an understanding of microcomputers for the more efficient running of their farms. This has significant implications for womens' education and training in the rural sector.

Australia has traditionally used immigration to make up for the lack of skills in the resident workforce. Without immigration of skilled workers, there would have been greater incentive or local employers to develop technical skills among female members of the workforce. This is clearly apparent in high level computer occupations such as programming and systems analysts (see Australian Government, 1981).

In Finland women provide 48% of the workforce. Research indicates that the basic reason for this high level of female participation is the nation's restrictive immigration policies.

Male technocratic concepts of society and work: the need for feminine perspectives

The way people conceptualise society and work has important influence on the way they formulate policies and programmes. There is an urgent need therefore, to critically analyse the technocratic concepts which have been used to market contemporary technological societies. There is a wide range of these concepts, for instance:

> the age of communication;
> the information economy;
> the global village;
> the wired society;
> the post-industrial society;

the service society;
the leisure society;
the cashless society;
the knowledge society.

These male technocratic concepts gloss over or ignore many aspects of technological change which are critical for women, particularly in relation to employment. This can be illustrated by reference to just a few examples.

Information technocrats talk in terms of transmission of mega-information in micro seconds. The increasing pace and volume of transmission and manipulation of data dominates their vision of an information economy. They rarely discuss the issues of access, content, control, distribution, quality or origins of information or the differences in employment opportunity.

But what equality have women been offered in the information economy? Their employment opportunities have been concentrated in data preparation and input. Their position in the processes of production, distribution and administration rarely give them access to policy information. This is still predominantly a male preserve. The development of distributed processes has not changed the traditional gender hierarchies. Operational information is distributed and policy information is centralised. Women are still predominantly confined to operator status.

The introduction of word-processing technology has only rarely been accompanied by organisation change that allows the female keyboard operators to expand their career opportunities. More often it has increased the pressure on operators and reduced their non-keyboard variety of activities. The change in information technology is regularly carried out without changing traditional organisational and administrative structures. The subsequent problems are often left for the operators to sort out, often without recognition of their achievements.

The concept of the information economy is used to market information technology. It is about money, power and control. It is rarely about human communication or quality of working life. It ignores the multi-lingual and multi-cultural nature of Australia. It is certainly not about equal employment opportunity. More realistic concepts to understanding and communicating the nature of these changes would be 'the information technology society', 'the segmented information society', or 'the controlled information society'. The so-called information society has not provided women with appropriate information to gain greater control over their employment.

Proponents of the 'wired society' often expound on the advantages of not having to leave one's home for employment or entertainment. The reality, however, for many women is that this represents an industrialising of the home. Important issues which are glossed over are the quality of working life, occupational health and safety, workers' compensation, wage determination (in a weak bargaining position), sub-contracting, hours of work, training, low social contact, child care, promotion opportunity, operating and maintenance costs and rental of working space. Many women who have sought a wider basis for fulfilment outside the house are now being offered a technological vision which they may logically regard as regressive and repressive.

The post-industrial society

Daniel Bell (1974), a conservative Harvard sociologist, showed that in the United States some years ago employment in the service sector had exceeded that in the manufacturing sector. He proclaimed therefore that the United States had moved into the post-industrial society. This simplistic view of society ignores the fact that technocrats have been busy industrialising the service sector.

The ideas of Frederick Taylor of simpifying tasks and divorcing manual from intellectual work have dominated twentieth century industrial work in English speaking countries. These ideas are readily apparent in the way employment has developed in the computer related occupations in the service sector. The production line techniques of the industrial world are being moved into the offices. The time and motion specialists have expanded their activities into preparation and entry of data for the new information technologies.

The industrial occupational hazzard of repetitious strain injuries is increasing with the increasing application of new office technologies. These new technologies provide the possibility of monitoring the exact work perfrmance of keyboard operators in data entry or word processing. The secual segmentation of office work ensures that the burden of new office efficiencies are born mainly by women.

The desire to maximise the use of new information technologies has increased the percentage of women involved in shift work. The determination of their hours of work is based on industrial concepts of technological and organisational efficiency not on social concerns.

Another danger inherent in the concept of the post-industrial society is that the people left in the manufacturing sector will be forgotten. In Australia the priority for the application of new technologies has not been to get rid of dirty, dangerous and monotonous jobs. For example, the new chicken processing industry has been developed with dehumanising technological systems. Women in chicken-factories work in frightful conditions which remain unexposed

343

in a so-called 'communication or information society'.

More realistic concepts for understanding these changes would be 'the process oriented society' or 'the age of process control'. The priority for the development and application of new process technologies has been to extend the concepts of traditional industrial organisations into the service sector.

The introduction of point-of-sale terminals into retail stores is to improve the administration of the store, not the service to the client or the sales person. Many of these systems are designed without consultation with the experienced employees. In one large retail store in Sydney a saleswoman was busy punching in all the information required by the store controllers for each sale, while a large and increasingly irate group of clients waited in line. To add to her problems the dockets were inappropriately designed for the number of purchases each customer usually made at that counter. As she went through the process of feeding in another undersized ticket, the saleswoman proclaimed to those waiting for service 'this system is so bad it could only have been designed by a man'. Of course she was right.

More appropriate concepts to understand these changes would be 'the non-service society', 'the self-service society' (e.g. supermarkets), or 'the deserviced society'.

Technology and women are experiencing an age of transition. Unfortunately compared to Japanese society, English speaking societies tend to focus on objectives rather than the process or transition to those objectives. Consequently they tend to ignore the different burdens and rewards involved in the transition.

The previous discussion of technocratic concepts highlights the need for women to reshape the intellectual tools which influence policy formulation. The male technocrats' visions of the present and future gloss over or ignore many important concerns for women. If women are to break through these technocratic pacification programmes, they need to question concepts of technological change in terms of access, control, equity, objectives (including hidden agendas), processes, participation and power. Otherwise future technologies will continue to be developed and introduced into organisations based on time frames and values of the past. In such an environment, equal employment opportunity for women will only be available to those who accept the male technocrats values and visions.

Concepts and criteria for formulating a policy package for technology, women and employment

A basic problem facing social policy in relation to technological change is that Australia is a recipient of technology. The nature and pace of technological change is significantly influenced by organisational policies developed outside of Australia. For example, Australia is a leading world test-market for information technologies, 98% of computer hardware is imported into this country.

With the technology comes organisational philosophies, processes and practices. Many of these are not readily apparent; particularly as most studies of organisational change are carried out by people who do not understand the assumptions underlying the design and development of technologies. The imported technological and organisational philosophies have significant implications for equal employment policies. For instance, EEO programmes to move more women into middle management are occurring at a time when technology and organisational developments are reducing the need for middle managers.

A policy package appropriate for technology, women and employment needs to recognise:

1) diversity of concerns and interests of different groups.
   e.g. those entering the workforce;
   those re-entering the workforce;
   part-time employees;
   full-time employees;
   contract employees;
   redundant employees;
   immigrant employees;
   single parent employees:
2) diversity of opportunities and pressures depending on:
   age;
   education;
   training;
   experience;
   ethnicity;
   geographic location;
   occupation:
3) variety of possible policies and programmes, and
4) the need to change occupational, organisational and industry cultures.

Traditionally, womens' movements in Australia have looked to other English speaking countries for ideas and models of equal employment opportunity. However these countries have been the ones most influenced by Taylorism. Consequently technology in the United States and Britain has been used to deskill, dehumanise and destroy jobs. Unions in these countries have provided little effective opposition to these trends. More appropriate ideas and models for women concerned with technological change can be found in the Nordic countries and the Federal Republic of Germany. In the early 1970s, the Federal Republic of Germany introduced a major tripartite programme on the humanisation of work. Considerable amounts of government subsidies were made available to employing organisations as an incentive to use technological change to improve the quality of working life. The programme raised many of the classic dilemmas faced by unions whose members are faced with technological change. For example, how to balance the loss of some jobs with the improvement in others and how to share the burdens and rewards. These are dilemmas which must be faced in formulating policies on technological change and EEO.

What are some of the basic concepts that need to be developed and included in a policy package for technology, women and employment?

1)   concepts of equal opportunity for technical education, employment and experience;

2)   concepts of learning which enable women to understand and influence technological change throughout their lifetime;

3)   concepts of skill formation that reduce the imbalance of technological skills between men and women;

4)   concepts of mutli-skilling which enable women to have more choice in employment;

5)   concepts of technology that enhance skills and employment rather than deskill and dehumanise;

6)   concepts of organisational capital which recognise and reward the skills developed by women in a range of roles;

7)   concepts of learning leave and entitlements which recognise the diversity of women's life cycles and the need for updating and upgrading in areas of technological change;

8)   concepts of research and development that enables the increased participation of women in the R&D processes and for recognition of their different concerns.

Development of special policies

An important access to technological knowledge and skills in Australia is the traditional apprenticeship systems. However, if hairdressing is excluded, less than two percent of female school-leavers become apprentices in Australia. This compares to an overall level of apprenticeship for female school-leavers in the Federal Republic of Germany of over 65%. There is an urgent need to expand the opportunity for females to participate in regulated and systematic post-school skill formation programmes.

The overwhelming amount of already installed technologies will be operational for many years. It is essential therefore to continue to develop and retain the skills required for the optimum use of this technology. A comprehensive equal employment opportunity programme therefore requires significant increases in women's participation in areas of traditional male apprenticeship. The Women in Apprenticeship Programme developed in the energy rich Hunter Valley of New South Wales provides an important model for such developments.

Women have been increasingly accepted into a variety of activities in the Australian armed services. Yet the important apprenticeship programmes in the services have not been brought into line with governments expressed ideals of equal employment opportunity. The German policy of using female apprenticeships to reduce the number of male dominated occupations may provide a model worthy of transfer to Australia.

Unlike Germany, Austria and Switzerland, apprenticeship is English speaking countries is basically confined to traditional trades. There is an urgent need to develop systematic training programmes for people entering the information sector. Information processing is likely to become a basic craft of the future. Yet there is no systematic training programme which enables young people to gain the broad conceptual and manual skills which will enable them to develop career options in the office of the future. Young girls are being locked into narrow machine operating positions with limited future learning opportunity or career options. The narrowness of their choice of employment can be seen by reading the advertisements for word-processing operators. The advertisements normally state the name of the word-processing system with which the operator must be familiar.

The objectives of an information or administrative technology apprenticeship would therefore be, to provide a broad based skilling in the operation and maintenance of a range of office technologies; to break down sex stereotyping in relation to information technologies; to multi-skill people to enable them to exercise occupational, organisational and career choice; to develop a sound basis for recurrent learning; to reduce the stress of technological change and to reduce the possibility of people being locked into monotonous and dangerous jobs.

Space has permitted me to discuss only two specific policy options, one of which is an example of expanding existing opportunities and the other of creating new opportunities for female skill formation.

Conclusions

Let me conclude with a plea first made by Huxley many years ago, that there is an urgent need for 'new bottles for new wine'. The old man-made vessels are inappropriate for the potent new brew emerging with changing relationships between technology, women and employment.

References

Australian Government, *Technological Change: Impact of Information Technology*, Australian Government Publishing Service: Canberra, 1981.

Bell, D., *The Coming of the Post Industrial Society*, Heineman: London, 1974.

Ford, B., *et al., Technology and the Workforce: An Annotated Bibliography*, Technology: Sydney, 1981.

20 Microelectronics and Japanese industrial relations

Akihiro Ishikawa

Introduction

Since the end of the 1970s, microelectronic technology has amazingly prevailed in Japanese industry, and it is still expanding in the 1980s. To take the industrial robot as an example, it was reported by the American Robot Society at the international symposium in October 1981, that in terms of the number of working robots in factories, Japan was ranked first in the world (Ministry of Labour, 1982). A survey conducted by the Bank of Saitama in May 1982, which covered not only large scale firms but also small and medium scale businesses in Saitama Prefecture which neighbours on Tokyo, displayed that 44% of the observed establishments in manufacturing industry had introduced or were planning to introduce the robot (Bank of Saitama, 1982). A similar situation can be noticed in other types of micro-electronics (ME) applied machines such as computer numerical control machines, computer-aided-design, machining centres, video tape recorders, transfer machines and other automated equipment, as shown, for example, by a survey carried out in Kanagawa Prefecture which also neighbours on Tokyo (KPG, 1983).

One of the main reasons why the ME technology has been, and is being, accepted in Japanese industry on such a wide scale may be found in the nature of Japanese industrial relations.

The purpose of this chapter is, accordingly, to look into some functional relations of the Japanese industrial relations to the intro-duction of the ME using new technology in the past few years, as well as to reflect on some effects of the latter upon the industrial relations, based on empirical data provided by labour unions, economic and industrial circles, local governments and the state government, research institutes and other organisations which carried out surveys recently on the subject concerned. Since around 1980, more than a few institutions and organisations concerned with the problem of employment and the new technology have conducted research on this issue, and much empirical information concerning it has been accumulated. To have a bibliographical survey on such data will help us to grasp some general features of actual situations in the industrial relations which involve the new technology in contemporary Japan.

Workers' attitudes to ME applied machines

In understanding the reason for such a conspicuous spread of ME applied machines in Japanese industry, it is significant to remark how workers have reacted to it on the actual spot. Overviewing the survey results related to this subject, it will be realised that the majority of ordinary workers have accepted it positively. The following data shows us such subjective reactions of workers.

According to a survey by the Kyoto-fu Institute of Labour and Economy (KILE, 1982), based on the responses of management in metal and machine industry, ordinary workers in general have positively accepted the introduction of ME applied machines in more than three-quarters of the surveyed establishments, while the rate of those where workers' attitudes were negative or critical was only 5%. Similarly, a survey by the Hyogo-ken Institute of Labour and Economy (HILE, 1983) displayed that 60% of the surveyed establishments noticed the positiveness of workers' attitudes to the introduction of robots, while only 3% of the establishments reported the negative or critical attitudes of their employees.

Surveys conducted by labour unions also display the similar tendency. For instance, a survey by ZENKIN DOMEI (the Japanese Metal Industrial Workers' Union) on its local unit organisations at the enterprise level (ZENKIN DOMEI, 1982) illustrates that in more than half of the surveyed enterprises the industrial robot has been welcomed by union member workers, while passive or negative attitudes could only be seen in less than 5% of the enterprises observed.

Similarly, a survey by the Kawasaki City Government located just in one of the industrial centres in Japan, has provided us with the information (KOG, 1983) that more than a half of the surveyed establishments in manufacturing industry reported that their ordinary workers were willing to introduce the highly automated machines in their own shop, particularly in large scale establishments, and in only less than 10% of the establishments were the workers' attitudes marked as negative or critical. Besides the survey on establishments, the Kawasaki City Government delivered questionnaires to the ordinary workers themselves, according to which the result was almost the same as that obtained from the establishment survey: less than 10% of workers were negative or critical, while around half of the respondents showed positive attitudes to introduce the highly automated machines, and these attitudes prevailed not only among younger workers but also middle-aged or older workers. The same survey illustrates further that 80% of the respondents answered that the new technology had brought good effects in their workshop, while negative answers were negligible in ratio. Furthermore, according to this survey, more than 80% of the workers observed have an interest in working with the newly introduced automating machine, regarding it as helpful to their self-fulfilment at work. Such workers' attitudes can be seen commonly among both younger and older workers, too.

On the other hand, there are not a few workers who feel hardship in their work under the new technology which may bring about an increase in mental burdens and an intensification of work. The survey by the Kawasaki City Government (KCG, 1983) at the same time pointed out that by introducing highly automated machines 40% of the workers observed felt anxious about the increase in mental burdens and nearly 30% of them expected an increase in the obligatory amount of tasks as well as the intensity of work.

Such anxiety surely exists among more than a few workers. Nevertheless, it is likely to remain a latent feeling, neither activated nor organised to become a negative or hampering factor to the introduction of the new technology, but subordinated to the dominant sociopsychological tendency to accept it positively.

As a background to such positive attitudes among many workers, concerning the introduction of ME applied machines into their workplace, some significant changes in workers' consciousness in general about their work and life, which took place in the 1960s and the 1970s, have to be taken into acocunt. To look back on the results of much empirical research and surveys of workers' consciousness in post-war Japan, it can be seen that workers' attitudes to their work became activated remarkably and their aspiration for fulfilment through their job increased during the 1960s and the first half of the 1970s, when the Japanese economy still enjoyed high-rate growth (Ishikawa, 1975). This trend still continues, even after the first and second oil-crises, as illustrated in the outcome of surveys on workers' consciousness carried out by the Ministry of Labour and by the Prime Minister's

Office (Ministry of Labour, 1982). In this connection it is instructive to refer to research results provided by K. Tominaga and his project team that priority for most Japanese workers in their occupational life is placed upon the possibility of self-fulfilment rather than higher gains or job security, with the exception of unskilled workers who have decreased in ratio among Japanese employees. This may be partly due to the fact that many workers are likely to think of security in employment as a matter of course so long as their company survives.

Such an attitude of the majority of workers has seemingly helped to introduce the new technology of ME into Japanese industry so widely without serious conflictual situations. As observed above, although not a few workers feel their work more intensified by the new technology, many of them think their work is becoming more interesting and satisfactory. In this regard the new technology might promote the further development of workers' positive attitudes to their daily work.

Employment under technological change

In connection to such attitudes, it is noteworthy to see that there are only a few that are anxious about redundancy or forcible trans- ference by the introduction of the new technology of ME. Such a trait has been shaped on the basis of experiences of industrial relations concerning employment in the past two decades or so.

In terms of workers' consciousness concerning their employment, it is noticeable that the dependence upon their company has been psychologically reinforced in the unstable and critical environment of economy since the mid-1970s, and the new technology of ME has been introduced in such a subjective condition. The first oil-crisis and the following serious economic situations seemed to bring on a slight but noticeable change of psychological trends, that is, the increase of anxiety about employment security among workers, which lead to the reinforcement of depending psychology of employees on their company. Surveys conducted in those days by some labour unions organising big business workers, revealed the increase of workers who expressed the wish to stay long in their company and would contribute themselves to its survival and further development (Ishikawa, 1980). This can be remarked on as being one of the signific- ant subjective reasons for the development of the joint consultation mechanism in Japanese enterprises during the 1970s and later, which prepared more or less a non-conflictual process of introducing the new technology. Management in those days searched for a way to avoid the conflict which might occur with redundancy, utilising the joint-consultation mechanism.

In this regard, it is noteworthy to look back on the industrial relations around 1960 when a co-operative relationship between labour and management was seen to solve the employment problem within the enterprise under the drastic technological changes which radically transformed the employment structure and the workplace relations (Nihon Jimbun Kagaku Kai, 1963). Faced with this challenging change, labour unions expressed at first critical caution regarding the supposed redundancies from rationalisation of production processes. However, they soon began to look for a mechanism of pre-decision consultation with management to secure employment through the re-education and the peaceful transference of workers within the enterprise, while management, who had experienced serious conflict with labour for the first decade of post-war Japan, was likely to meet with unions, sometimes taking the initiative to organise the consultations. Then, largely due to the successive growth of the economy and the conditions of the labour market favourable for labour, the occurrence of crucial employment problems was evaded with a few exceptions such as coal-mining. The type of practice taken at that time has been inherited in Japanese industrial relations, and recalled at the time of the oil-crisis and then, again, at the introduction of the new technology of ME. In addition, Japanese management still keeps the 'life-time employment' policy as its basis of personnel and labour administration even with the introduction of the new technology.

Many surveys illustrate that the workers who have been assigned to the new type of jobs produced by the new technology are mostly recruited from those who have been engaged in former jobs in the same place. Besides, those ordinary workers on the production line participate more or less in decisions and implementations related to how to introduce the new ME applied machines and how to work them on the spot.

According to the survey in Kawasaki City (KCG, 1983), the establishments which have hired specialists or experts from the outside for the purpose of dealing with the newly introduced equipment are very exceptional. Nearly 90% of the surveyed establishments did not hire such specialists for this particular purpose. Most workers stay and work in the same workplace as before, dealing with the newly set ME applied machines. This survey also points out that more than 80% of the workers answered that their formerly acquired skills and experiences were largely relative to the newly introduced machines. A survey conducted by the Japan Productivity Centre shows us a similar situation (JPC, 1982), according to which more than 95% of the surveyed enterprises utilise the existing workforce within the enterprise for the operation and programming of new technology.

Regarding office automation, a similar picture can also be seen. The Shibazonobashi Public Employment Security Office in Tokyo reported that the workers using office automation equipment were recruited from those who had worked in that same section (SPESO, 1983).

Even the transference of workers induced by introducing ME applied machines has not taken place in as many enterprises as envisaged. With the former technological change around 1960, employment security was maintained by means of the transference of workforce from timeworn factories to newly built modernised ones within a given enterprise, through re-education and retraining (Matsushima, 1962; Kobayashi, 1966; Yamamoto, 1967). Compared to it, the technological change today illustrates different features in this respect.

The results of the survey in Kawasaki City (KCG, 1983) show that more than 70% of the surveyed establishments have retrained workers in some way to keep them in the same workplace, and 24% of the establishments have not made any changes in manning, particularly in small and medium scale establishments. In other cases workers have been transferred, but redundancy was found in only 5% of those surveyed. To take another example, the Department of Labour of the Aichi Prefecture Government (APG, 1982) reported, from its survey on about 1,300 employees into whose workplaces ME applied machines have been introduced, that 65% of them stayed in the same workplace as before, and about 35% moved to different places inside of the establishments. Even in the latter case, no-one suffered dismissal.

The results of two surveys shown above covered many cases of small and medium scale manufacturing establishments. To turn and look then at the data provided by DENKI ROREN (the Japan Federation of Electrical Machine Workers' Unions), which organises mostly big business workers in the industry concerned, gives us a slightly different outlook (DENKI ROREN, 1983). According to it, in about 60% of the surveyed establishments the workforce has decreased in number in the workplace where ME applied machines have been set, and the transfer of workers has taken place within the enterprises. The survey by the Japan Productivity Centre (JPC, 1982) on big businesses of general machinery, transportation machinery and electrical machinery displayed that the transfer took place in 64% of the surveyed enterprises. In these cases the surplus workforce created by the new technology has been absorbed in other shops within the given establishment. To see, as an example, a specific case of a machine producing enterprise of 460 employees, the robot created a surplus of 45 workers, among whom 25 workers have moved to the experiment and development section, 7 workers to the newly organised marketing section, and the remaining to other differentsections. Thus the robotisation did not lead to redundancy.

354

From the facts observed above, the following proposition which ZENKIN DOMEI has drawn from its survey results would be generally confirmed (ZENKIN DOMEI, 1982). The measure that management takes most frequently in the case of the occurrence of surplus work-force due to automation in the factory or the office is to transfer such a workforce to other sections within the establishment to avoid redundancy, solving the shortage of operators and programmers of the newly introduced technology, by the re-education of the existing workforce within the enterprise by means of on the job training or off the job training. This is being done by management, instead of adopting newcomers out of high school or university. Management then nurtures the employees towards the company-coloured person-ality, using the virtue of life-time employment practice. In such a situation, the new technology would not undermine the dominant practice of 'life-time employment' which is generally regarded as the basis of Japanese style of industrial relations. The new technology may more or less modify it, but on the contrary it seems to reinforce it.

The function of joint consultation mechanisms

As mentioned before, the practice of pre-decision joint consultation, to solve the problem of manpower and employment due to drastic technological changes, developed around 1960, and is built up to become a basic part of the later Japanese industrial relations. As a series of surveys by the Japan Productivity Centre on joint consultation mechanism since 1964 reveals, this practice often takes the place of collective bargaining in Japanese industry (Ishikawa, 1981).

The first oil-crisis and the following severe situation in the Japanese economy have reinforced the function of the joint consultation mechanism, and many labour unions have become involved not only in the issues of wage and working conditions but also in managerial issues such as productivity increase and cost-down measures on account of the survival of the enterprise, meaning security in employment. The typical case can be seen in the labour-management relations at the Nissan Motor Company, where the labour-management agreement was settled at the beginning of 1983 in relation to robotisation. In this case, the president of this company, Mr Ishihara, appealed to 'establish the system for introducing and developing new technology in the inseparable and co-operative relationship between management and the union', while the president of the Federation of Japan Auto-mobile Workers' Unions, originally from the All Nissan Motor Workers' Unions, emphasised 'the inevitability for car makers to increase pro-ductivity' (*Nihon Keizai Shimbun*, 2 March 1983).

On the other hand, there are also many enterprises and establishments where ME applied machines have been set without any special meeting or consultation between both parties on this issue. According to surveys by several local governments or their research institutes located in industrial districts, the joint consultation on this specific issue was held in only 26% of the surveyed establishments in Kawasaki City (KCG, 1983), 28% in the south part of Tokyo (SLAO, 1983), 30% in Aichi Prefecture (APG, 1982), 31% in Kanagawa Prefecture (KPG, 1983), and 35% in Hyogo Prefecture (HILE, 1983). In those surveys was found only a negligible difference in the percentage between the group of unionised establishments and that of non-unionised ones. The surveys above cover many small and medium scale enterprises, but a survey by the Japan Productivity Centre on big businesses illustrates almost the same outline. Acccording to it, the enterprises which held the joint consultation meeting on the introduction of new technology include only 21% of all the responding enterprises (JPC, 1982).

Several reasons can be proposed in relation to the comparatively small rate in the establishments or the enterprises where the specific joint consultation has not been held. Among others, as pointed out in the survey in Aichi Prefecture (APG, 1982), it would be necessary to take into account that in many cases ME applied machines have been introduced gradually one after another over several years so that workers, as well as management, have not perceived drastic changes such as those felt around 1960. To their general perception, there has been almost nothing new, only the usual renewing of machines. In such a situation, the transfer, if it would happen, would be naturally perceived by both workers, management and the unions as a normal, ordinary 'reshuffle' measure. Further, the Department of Labour at the Kanagawa Prefecture Government, based on case studies of 200 establishments, reported as follows: 'In nearly all of the establishments observed, management takes the basic policy not to dismiss at the introduction of highly automated machines, and on the other hand the unions or the employees take such a standpoint that the transfer of manpower is more or less inevitable if the introduction of new machines is necessary. Hence, no rejecting situation has taken place against their introduction. Further, among the establishments where the joint consultation meeting has not been held, there are many cases in which both management and the unions or employees have regarded it unnecessary because the introduction of such machines would not bring about significant effects upon working-conditions' (KPG, 1983). This statement shows us a typical dimension of Japanese industrial relations in the introduction of new technology today.

The effect of new technology on labour unions

Finally, let us reflect on how the new technology will affect the Japanese labour unions. From the above observed, the following conclusions can be drawn.

For the time being, Japanese management attempts in general to maintain the continous employment-practices. If such behaviour by management was to be kept up, and the union was to regard the survival of the enterprise as the key point for employment-security, it would be understandable that the union would agree to the managerial measure of introducing new technology for the purpose of the development of the enterprise under increasingly severe competitive circumstances. Besides, as seen before, ordinary workers themselves are inclined to approve the introduction of new technology with positive attitudes. Concurrently, the majority of union leaders do not reject the new technology. A survey by the Japan Institute of Labour indicates that the unions opposed to the introduction of ME applied machines were only 1.5% of those surveyed, whereas those positively approving it were 37% and those regarding it as inevitable were also 37% (JIL, 1982). This survey exemplifies a typical view of union leaders such as 'the enterprise which does not introduce the industrial robot, or the enterprise which does not have any interest in technological innovation, cannot survive in the severe competitive society, which will result in unemployment' (JIL, 1982).

In such situations, the new technology would encourage the union to participate in managerial affairs much further, and the union would be involved within the enterprise management more deeply, not only to secure employment but to enhance productivity and business achievement. In this sense workers' participation in management seems to be promoted by the union as its main target. As a matter of fact, according to an opinion survey on union leaders conducted by the Japan Productivity Centre (JPC, 1983), many of the leaders think that workers' participation will become much more important in union activities. Thus, the union, as an integral part of the enterprise, might increase its influence on the decision and implementation of managerial issues in its own way, as is the case with some of the big unions today. Parallel to this, the organisational integration with the union would be intensified, which might, if it were to happen, lead to oppression of the individual opinion or action that would be regarded as critical to the policy or measures of the enterprise, as critically pictured by a recent observer (Kamata, 1982). On the other hand, the effect of new technology on the change of employment structure has to be noted. While the union would become influential within the enterprise as a partner of management, the changing structure of its membership might undermine its power. In the short run, as seen before, new types of jobs which have appeared and resulted from the new technology are mostly filled by the existing workforce through re-education and retraining, but long term tendencies of the structural change in employment can be recognised already, and are as follows.

First, the rate of non-manual employees, particularly engineers of university level, is increasing remarkably in the manufacturing industry. This is a challenge to the union whose main supporting base has been consistently manual workers (JPC, 1983). Many of the highly educated non-manual workers are also union members, but their interest and aspiration, to their views, have not been sufficiently recognised in the union organisations, so that they are apt to show critical attitudes towards union activities. An interview with engineers at an institute belonging to a big firm producing electric and electronic goods displays their views as: 'I think that colleagues in the section of research and development are rather egoistic and lack the consciousness of solidarity', 'The employees, like me, who are concerned in the high speed of technological innovation are likely to feel a gap in the union movement which is based on the collective idea of the whole workers' (Kamata, 1982). The new technology may promote the increase of such a type of worker within the union organisation, and the union is necessarily faced with the problem of how to acquire their identity in the organisation.

Secondly, accompanying the new technology are other types of new jobs to be filled by part-time workers, who are mostly outside union organisations. Their needs and interests are fairly different from those of regular employees. There appear, though still exceptional, establishments where part-time workers occupy the majority of workforce and the regular, unionised workers have become a minority group.

Third, big manufacturing industry, which has shaped the main force of the union movement, as well as being one of the cores of the 'Japanese style of industrial relations' composed of the seniority-system of wage, the practice of life-time employment and the company-unit unionism, is conspicuously decreasing its workforce. Instead, employment in the tertiary sector is growing up in a striking way, where employees are mostly non-unionised with the exceptions of public sector and large scale enterprises of commerce and finance. Reflecting this change of employment structure, the rate of unionisation has become reduced, from 35.4% in 1970 to 30.5% in 1982 (Ministry of Labour, each year). In addition, the development of new technology has created a new pattern in the labour market of computer-related workforce, whose wage is not based on the seniority system and whose employment is not expected as life-time. The traditional company-unit style of union organisation seems to be unable to unionise it effectively.

Conclusions

Summing up, it may be tentatively concluded that the spread of ME applied new technology in Japanese industry would, on the one hand, intensify the Japanese style of industrial relations *within* the enterprise, but the environmental change in employment structure might undermine its effectiveness and, if it were to happen, its existence in the long run

References

APG, *Survey Report on the Introduction of ME-applied Machines*, Nagoya: Aichi Prefecture Government, (in Japanese), 1982.

Bank of Saitama, *Survey Report on the Introduction of Industrial Robot in Saitama Prefecture*, Urawa: The Bank of Saitama, (in Japanese), 1982.

DENKI, ROREN, *Survey Report on the Effect of ME Technology upon Employment and Work*, Tokyo: The Japan Federation of Electrical Machine Workers' Union, (in Japanese), 1983.

HILE, *Survey Report on the Effect of Industrial Robot upon Employment*, Kobe: Hyogo-ken Institute of Labour and Economy, (in Japanese), 1983.

Ishikawa, A., *Social Change and Workers' Consciousness*, Tokyo: Japan Institute of Labour, (in Japanese), 1975.

Ishikawa, A., 'Recent Trends of Workers' Consciousness on Employment and Work', in *Employment and Work in the 1980's*, Tokyo: The Social and Economic Congress of Japan, (in Japanese), 1980.

Ishikawa, A., 'Workers' Participation Systems in Japan', in *Workers' Participation in Management in Four Asian Countries*, Tokyo: Asian and Oceanian Subcommittee of the Research Committee, no. 10, ISA, 1981.

JIL, *Survey Report on Labour Union Activities in the 1980s*, Tokyo: Japan Institute of Labour, (in Japanese), 1982.

JPC, *White Paper on Industrial Relations*, Tokyo: Japan Productivity Centre, (in Japanese), 1982.

JPC, *White Paper on Industrial Relations*, Tokyo: Japan Productivity Centre, (in Japanese), 1983.

Kamata, S., *The Actual Spot of Robotization*, Tokyo: San'ichi-Shobo, (in Japanese), 1982.

KCG, *Kawasaki City White Paper on Labour*, Kawasaki: Kawasaki City Government, (in Japanese), 1983.

KILE, *Survey Report on ME-controlled Industrial Machines and Employment*, Kyoto: Kyoto-fu Institute of Labour and Economy, (in Japanese), 1982.

Kobayashi, K., *Employment Structure of Contemporary Japan*, Tokyo: Iwanami-Shoten, (in Japanese), 1966.

KPG, *Survey Report on the Effect of Highly Automatizing Machinery*, Yokohama: Kanagawa Prefecture Government, (in Japanese), 1983.

Matsushima, S., *Japanese Characteristics of Personnel Management and Their Change*, Tokyo: Diamond-Sha, (in Japanese), 1962.

Ministry of Labour, *White Paper on Labour*, Tokyo: Japan Institute of Labour, (in Japanese), 1982.

Ministry of Labour, *Report of Labour Union Basic Survey*, Tokyo. Ministry of Labour, (in Japanese), yearly.

Nihon, Jimbun Kagaku Kai, *Social Effect of Technological Innovation*, Tokyo: University Press of Tokyo, (in Japanese), 1963.

Nihon, Keizai Shimbun, 'Industrial Relations in the Age of Microelectronics', in *The Nihon Keizai Shimbun* (Japan Economic Newspaper), 2 March 1983, Tokyo (in Japanese).

SLAO, *Survey Report on the Introduction of Mechatronics Machinery and its Effects*, Tokyo: Shinagawa Labour Administration Office, (in Japanese), 1983.

SPESO, *The Impact of Office Automation on Enterprises and the Attitude of Job Hunters*, Tokyo: Shibazonobashi Public Employment Security Office, (in Japanese), 1983.

Tominaga, K., (ed.), *Social Stratification in Japan*, Tokyo: University Press of Tokyo, (in Japanese), 1979.

Yamamoto, K., *Structure of Japanese Labour Market*, Tokyo: University Press of Tokyo, (in Japanese), 1967.

AENKIN, DOMEI, *Survey Report on the Effect of Mechatronics Production Machinery and Office Automation Equipment upon Employment*, Tokyo: Japanese Metal Industrial Workers' Union, (in Japanese), 1982.

Epilogue

It is now nearly thirty years since Paul Einzig's prescient work *The Economic Consequences of Automation* (1956) was published. He argued that such consequences were 'liable to affect the life of every man, woman and child' (1956: vii); that 'The Trade Unions (should) realise the imperative need for helping automation instead of hindering it' (1956: x); and that there was a need for 'mutual understanding to remove all obstacles that hold up automation' (1956: x).

In this volume, the contributors have tried to explore many aspects of the new technology bearing on the issues Einzig originally raised. It can be seen how pervasive the information revolution has been and how microprocessors now affect even more aspects of production than earlier authors anticipated. Whatever the fallacies of the 'automation' debate of the post-war period, the extent of technical change ranging from NC to CNC, CAD/CAM, FMS and the onset of robots making robots has been extraordinary.

This review has tried however to restrict its coverage to areas where empirical inter-disciplinary research has been forthcoming. It has not indulged in science fiction on the lines of say Wells, or Asimov. Nor has it tried to expand the themes of Bell's (1974) study of post-industrial society, referred to in several of the papers, beyond trying to critically examine the evidence.

The effects of new technology on work are now visible (Rada, 1980), and the prospects for further automation extensive. The possibility of 'the re-making of work' *via* telecommuting, with employees linked on-line to their companies from their household-based work has also been envisaged.

However, it is not without its problems; and many firms now have reservations about its cost-effectiveness. Nevertheless, computer makers and users insist that the 'electronic cottage' will eventually become more common. Such work offers opportunities for home-bound mothers and the disabled, and savings for companies that would have to build or rent more space to expand. Advocates of such schemes say that experiments on-line are solving their problems. 'The recession delayed the computer cottage, but it's still the wave of the future' (Johnson, 1983).

We have also tried to look at the consequences for people at work, and how the organisation of their productive activities will be affected. The social impact of the new technology can be already seen in its implications for manpower training and development. Several of the contributions in this volume show how trade-union hostility need not be engendered, and how consultation with workers' representatives can mitigate the effects of change, although no single model of consultation emerged.

The modality of technologies in organisations we have described is in turn not unrelated to their diffusion in societies. Suppose new machines were very expensive, they would have been largely concentrated in large firms; the converse would have been true of inexpensive systems. As a generalisation, the newer the technology, the less likely is it to be modal for firms, and consequently for the society. Even if modal for a few companies, it may still be developmental. Moreover, its social effects may be ambiguous given the limited number of cases. Even so, the miniaturisation of computer-circuitry, and the dramatic fall in price, has opened the door to possibly very much wider levels of diffusion, which now extend to the small firm, whether covering shop floor and/or office activity.

The chapters have also covered a wide cross-national, cross-societal range, ranging from North America, Western Europe, Australasia, India, Japan and so on. The impact of the new technology has been truly worldwide, but its effects will depend on national circumstances as the evidence suggests. In order to understand the variety of societal experiences of the new technology, we need more research at the micro-level in order to build up to theories of social change. Sound technology policies cannot evolve except from this type of concrete investigation of particular implementations of specific technologies in individual, industrial and/or national contexts.

If a better understanding of technological change can be achieved, we may have a better chance of avoiding 'a class war over the proceeds of automation', where 'as in nuclear war, there can be no victors' (Einzig, 1956). The consequences, however, may be unevenly distributed, both socially and geographically, for *structural* economic change brings costs to the periphery when the older industries die. The de-centralisation process may result as much from the inability to invest in new ways. As a key technological innovation, the 'chip has not (as yet) stirred a new business-cycle. 'Economics' in turn has yet to come to terms with the new microprocessor technology; and the 'chip' has in turn neither unambiguously pushed economic theory one way or the other.

So, can we conclude that the blind are leading each other in the current debate? The conceptual basis of discussion is relatively weaker than the empirical evidence. Current unemployment levels have deep structural, cyclical as well as technological causes. The 'chip' did not in itself destroy the older industries. Longer-term questions of secular trends (the industrialisation of the Third World notwithstanding), as well as short term questions of monetarist policy must be invoked. It is thus difficult to disentangle the various strands of the process of transformation we are experiencing: meanwhile, the quest for a deeper understanding of these changes must continue.

References

Bell, D., *The Coming of Post Industrial Society*, Heinemann: London, 1974.

Einzig, P., *The Economic Consequences of Automation*, Seeker and Warburg: London, 1956.

Johnson, R., 'Computer Cottages Link Homes to City Skyscrapers', *Wall Street Journal*, 5 July 1983, p.13.

Rada, J., *The Impact of Microelectronics*, ILO: Geneva, 1980.

Index

Sorge, Arndt 72, 140, 311
Staff Numbers 224ff
Sweden 26, 259
System X 219

Taylorism 17, 285, 289, 346
Technology Agreements
106ff, 178, 221, 256, 261
Technological Choice 150,
166, 309
Telecommunications 4, 210
Thakur, C.P. 5, 325ff
Trade unions 4, 6, 111ff,
149ff, 171ff, 189ff, 255,
273, 349

Training 3, 134ff
TUC 152, 172ff, 255ff
Turn-key systems 136

Unemployment 1–2, 28, 205,
295

Visual Display Units (VDUs)
103ff, 282ff

Walsh, Vivien 4, 210
Warner, Malcolm 1, 6, 311,
323, 261
Williams, Robin 4, 171
Willman, Paul 4, 189, 224
Winch, Graham 4, 189

367